PRAISE FOR THE FIRST EDITION

'Makes an indelible mark ... It is a book that will profoundly influence generations of scholars and practitioners. The brave and bold recommendations appended by the authors for a post-pandemic world have made this book even more significant for men and women of goodwill in an increasingly unequal world.'
—Olutayo Adesina, Professor of History, University of Ibadan

'A thoroughly researched account of the global experience of the Covid pandemic.'
—Professor Robert Dingwall, member of UK SAGE

'A thoughtful analysis of the forces and attitudes that unleashed lockdowns upon the global poor, with harrowing descriptions of the consequences.'
—Sunetra Gupta, Professor of Theoretical Epidemiology, University of Oxford

'In a grave pandemic, what is the acceptable level of mortality risk relative to the damage to society, economy and poor countries from lockdowns? This searching scrutiny and anguished analysis of this dilemma is a much-needed corrective to simplistic slogans.'
—Ramesh Thakur, former Assistant Secretary-General of the United Nations

'Picks apart the damage which has affected the world's states, both rich and poor, examining the level of catastrophe which has afflicted each one. [The book] concludes that we are not facing a normal form of crisis, but that the diagnosis is difficult owing to its complexity, and as it has occurred at a moment where the world is undergoing a major economic, political and cultural restructuring.'
—*Al-Ahram*

'Important ... a valuable world perspective ... [the] attention to worldwide effects, decentering the West, has distinct value.'

—*Choice*

'A must-read book for those who are engaged in both anti-lockdown and pro-lockdown discourse. [It] will trigger some serious questions and arguments to ponder. It deals with intricate details regarding the development of the consensus ... boldly stated with conviction.'

—LSE Review of Books

'An outstanding analysis of the regressive effects of lockdown policies, and the neocolonial dimension of their imposition on the Global South.'

—*The Popular Show*

'A refreshing and eye-opening read to the impacts of the response to the virus that have been carefully omitted from daily media coverage. Instead, it modestly critiques the policy decisions without joining the bandwagon of conspiracists and those with an opposing political agenda.'

—*Keele Law Review*

THE COVID CONSENSUS

TOBY GREEN
&
THOMAS FAZI

The Covid Consensus

The Global Assault on Democracy and
the Poor—A Critique from the Left

HURST & COMPANY, LONDON

Distributed in the United States, Canada and Latin America by
Oxford University Press, 198 Madison Avenue, New York, NY 10016,
United States of America.

A Cataloguing-in-Publication data record for this book
is available from the British Library.

ISBN: 9781787388413

www.hurstpublishers.com

CONTENTS

CONTENTS

PUBLISHER'S NOTE

The Notes for *The Covid Consensus* can be found at
https://www.hurstpublishers.com/book/the-covid-consensus/

ACKNOWLEDGEMENTS

We are grateful to everyone who has struggled to combat the harmful tyranny of the Covid Consensus. It's impossible to thank them all, but we just want to thank a few people without whom we never could have written this book.

Thomas would like to thank: my wife Cristina and my daughter Viola for keeping me sane through lockdown, and for teaching me how to stay human in inhuman times.

Toby would like to thank: my wife Emily, for being my companion in angry discussion; Bob Fowke for never liking lockdowns; the Leverhulme Trust, for the award of a Philip Leverhulme Prize in History which provided the time to write and research the first edition of this book; and everyone at *Collateral Global*, for all the support they've given over the last two years.

We both owe huge gratitude to everyone at Hurst for believing in this book, and for their amazing tolerance at the fact that it was almost 50% longer than we originally anticipated: a huge thank you to Michael Dwyer, Alice Clarke, Daisy Leitch and Raminta Uselytė. We'd all like to thank those who generously gave of their time and efforts to be interviewed for this book – Olutayo Adesina, Samuel Adu-Gyamfi, George Bob-Milliar,

ACKNOWLEDGEMENTS

Pedrito Cambrão, Carlos Cardoso, Hassoum Ceesay, Ben Cowling, Reginald Oduor, John Perry, and Elsa Rodrigues; Daniel Hadas and Ewald Engelen for commenting on drafts; and all the contributors to the conference entitled *The Politics and Governance of Covid-19*, organised by Lee Jones and Shahar Hameiri – their insights and experiences were crucial in shaping the final draft.

And we'd also like to thank each other!

INTRODUCTION

The Covid-19 pandemic has upended human life as we knew it before 2020. For years, dystopian nightmares of worlds lived without human contact were the stuff of Hollywood disaster movies. The commercial reach of Hollywood meant that most of humanity probably had some sense of what was in store when disaster struck: an imaginary world which comforted and gripped us because its apocalyptic visions were both terrifying and—most importantly—fictional. And yet once the Covid-19 pandemic began, it turned out that all those years of apocalypse on the screen had psychologically prepared us to enact a disturbing new reality: we human beings had been groomed by special effects and trained in how to respond to catastrophe, and in responding we spawned a catastrophe of our own making.

Many buzzwords flew around throughout the years of the pandemic, memes which no one had heard of beforehand but which soon were imprinted on the consciousness as indelibly as if through subliminal advertising. Lockdown, social distancing, vaccine passports, green passes, Covid safety, 'no one's safe until we're all safe'... all phrases which came to define this era, and yet which hardly anyone knew of before. These new concepts shaped the way in which people responded to the crisis, which in turn of course transformed the crisis itself and how it was embedded in the world.

As a whole, the experience was transformative. However, as with all major changes in human history, it didn't really come out of the blue. In this book, we'll explore the way in which the pandemic in fact provided a radical continuity of many trends which had been latent in global society, slumbering away for decades, until being catapulted into the foreground by the emergence of the SARS-CoV-2 coronavirus. Inequality, the power of computing, information wars, and the shift towards increasingly authoritarian forms of capitalism across the world had all been growing for many years, and the response to the Covid-19 pandemic saw a radical acceleration in each one of these processes. In this book, we ask therefore if these outcomes were produced only by the virus—as many have claimed—or rather by the aggregated influence of these existing trends. As writers trained in economics and history we are used to analysing the workings of power in human societies; to us, it seems that this approach is vital in understanding what has happened since 2020, and yet it is one which has been almost entirely ignored in mainstream discussions of Covid-19 guided by 'the science'.

Social distancing offers a good example of how the response to the pandemic entrenched existing tendencies. This seemed like a radical new idea, but in fact many people in Western tech industries, academia, and finance had been working in semi-socially distanced ways for some time, and had been enabled to do so by the computing technologies of the twenty-first century. This distancing was thus a symptom of the ever-increasing removal of people in wealthier societies from economic production. The new technologies of the twenty-first century, combined with the neoliberal framework of outsourcing, meant that production had been placed out of sight. The distancing from production of Western consumers meant that the implications of lost harvests, ruptured supply chains, and abandoned industrial plant machinery were not as real as the threat of a new virus to this group of disproportionately influential people.

Thus with this process of distancing, the politics of production which had accompanied left-wing movements of the twentieth century had largely fallen into decline. This may also offer a way into addressing one of our other main concerns in this book, which is why many—though not all—politicians and writers from the left supported policies which produced such radical harms for poor people. Given that it is a movement which seeks reductions in inequality, it's hard (for us at least) to understand this if not through the distancing from production which many on the left have undergone, alongside the economic and emotional consequences that this has had. The lockdown era was in the end an opportunity to make the empty isolation of this portion of humanity's new technical carapace morally virtuous: as one wit put it, many academics had already been living in lockdown for years.

In fact, many academics from the left had been pushing the dystopian analysis of where these forces could lead for some time. French post-structuralist Jean Baudrillard's analysis of the framework of simulated reality, in which the simulation becomes the real, and Italian philosopher Giorgio Agamben's analysis of biopower and states of exception were hardly irrelevant to the world that emerged in 2020 and 2021. And yet Baudrillard was ignored, and Agamben cancelled: it turned out that the raw emotional reality of their ideas was too painful for their former followers to accept.

One characteristic of this transformation of feeling is the erosion of the boundary between the public and the private— in corporations and government on the one hand (where the revolving door between industry and politics is well-known), and reproduced on the other in the zone between people's social media profiles and their private lives. There were important consequences of this in terms of the relationship between people and political authority. Where in previous times those with political and social authority were in a position to regulate human affairs (as in Michel Foucault's idea of the panopticon), societies had become collectively self-regulating through the public arena of the internet and its reach into people's private lives.* What this meant for the transformation of feeling was that the public performance of empathy (or of performative compliance with lockdown measures) could come to be seen as more real than actual empathy (or compliance).

The way in which these emotions were experienced of course differed widely around the world, and it's important to acknowledge this. In a brilliant analysis of rural South Africa, Leslie Bank and Nelly Sharpley described how Covid containment measures upended precious and community-led rituals of mourning, as 'the government decided to stand with the hegemonic bio-medical approach of the global North, which was supported by the suburban middle classes and political insiders in the ruling party; this decision occurred in a context where the state knew and understood that the model it adopted could only provide effective care for a small minority of the population'.[1]

In an article in the South African *Mail and Guardian* from January 2021—cited by Bank and Sharpley—Paballo Chauke described the consequences of this policy choice:

> Most black people live undignified lives and only see dignity in death. Our freedom is in the afterlife and that is why we invest so much money in planning for our funerals. Covid-19 has taken this last shred of decency from us. It has stolen our rites of passage into heaven, we can't gather in the same way

---

* We are grateful to Rik Dolphijn of Utrecht University for this insight.

or practise our traditions to properly send off our own and pay our last respects (except, of course, if you are some important government official, where the same rules do not seem to apply). My mom was bundled up like trash, bound in plastic—she wasn't allowed [back] into her own yard [to say goodbye]. We couldn't wash her or dress her to the nines for the last time, couldn't watch her body over in a night-time vigil or give her a final touch goodbye.[2]

In sum, while economic and political elements drive our analysis, we try not to lose sight of these emotional and ethical frameworks. People may disagree with some aspects of the analysis that follows, and yet everyone shares in different ways the enormous emotional pain and impact which the events of the last three years have brought about—and that these are of immense significance, everyone agrees.

On the other hand, while there are many disagreements about the political side, few people would disagree that the impacts of the pandemic and pandemic response have been immense. Once the lockdown model had been rolled out, it took on a momentum of its own. Politicians could not backtrack without ruining their careers and leaving government open to mass class action legal challenges. The scientists in charge were desperate for figures to prove that they had acted correctly, as their careers and sense of having done the right thing were on the line too in a situation of crisis and personal and collective stress which must have been almost intolerable. In this situation, people have a tendency to panic. As the panic grew, political and media pressure focused relentlessly on the numbers of infections and deaths and the 'R number', because only these could provide a justification for what was happening. But the truth was, as soon as you stepped outside the Covid obsession a different picture emerged—a picture which included the whole of society and its values, and not just one tiny part.

So many questions have arisen as a result, and we will try to address as many as we can in this book. Do we want to be ruled by Big Tech supergiants who have already more or less assumed the reins of surveillance and power that used to be the province of states? Do we consent to these policies each time a new virus emerges, whether or not it causes mass mortality? Is old age to be treasured in and of itself as a place where generations meet and the wisdom of the elderly can be passed on, or is it the right of the state to step in and hermetically seal our elders from the outside, preserving them in splendid isolation for one or two more years—and to then more or less force all people to take a new vaccine which has been developed without the trial safeguards which used to be required, and regardless of whether or not they are much at risk from the new condition?

All these questions matter deeply, and yet very few of them were asked publicly in 2020 and 2021 as the nature of the world's societies and economies changed without our express consent. To answer them we first need to work out what has happened, so that we can then make value judgements and ethical evaluations. And that's how this book is structured: first we try to work out what happened in our chronicle of the pandemic (Part 1), before examining the consequences and considering the political framework and effects (Part 2).

***

Some readers may wonder what all the fuss is about. Was this not, as the public were informed at the outset of the crisis in March 2020, a once-in-a-century episode of mass mortality?[3] Members of the World Health Organization (WHO) certainly sought to draw comparisons between the Covid-19 outbreak and the infamous Spanish influenza pandemic of 1918–19, in which an estimated 50 million people died. As Dr Michael Ryan, Executive Director of the WHO's Health Emergencies

Programme, put it at the 25 May 2020 WHO press conference when discussing the possibility of a second wave, 'it certainly happened in the pandemic of 1919 in the Spanish flu'.[4]

The sense that these were unprecedented times led to novel policy responses to Covid-19. Even those who became advocates of the strictest lockdown measures, such as Professor Devi Sridhar of Edinburgh University, acknowledged during the early phase of the crisis that the initial lockdown in Hubei province was unprecedented.[5] Of course quarantines had taken place before, but these had always hitherto been localised and aimed at specific infected towns and cities—not at entire areas in which often there were no infected people at all. Yet in spite of the fact that this form of indiscriminate lockdown was contrary to the previously accepted scientific consensus (as we'll see in Chapter 2), by 3 April 2020 more than 3.9 billion people in more than ninety countries had been placed into lockdown—roughly half of the world's population.[6] As an unprecedented public health policy was implemented, human beings found themselves subjected to an enormous scientific experiment.

We think that this makes working out what happened— and how comparable it was to previous pandemics—pretty important. Moreover, as 2020 unwound, some of those involved in the highest echelons of scientific research and containment issued a warning that Covid-19 was merely the starting point for increasingly deadly waves of new viruses which were likely to overwhelm the planet in the twenty-first century during an era of intense ecological degradation. The WHO declared in a cheery warning on 29 December 2020 that Covid might not be the big pandemic that scientists had long feared, and that the world needed to prepare for even deadlier pandemics in the future.[7]

This line of thinking was widespread among those who led the global response to Covid-19. In an article published online in August 2020, Dr Anthony Fauci—Director of the US National

Institute for Allergies and Infectious Diseases (NIAID), and the best-known figure on the US Coronavirus Task Force—and David Morens suggested that Covid-19 was just the start. 'Evidence suggests that SARS, MERS, and Covid-19 are only the latest examples of a deadly barrage of coming coronavirus and other emergencies', they wrote. 'The Covid-19 pandemic is yet another reminder, added to the rapidly growing archive of historical reminders, that in a human-dominated world, in which our human activities represent aggressive, damaging, and unbalanced interactions with nature, we will increasingly provoke new disease emergences. We remain at risk for the foreseeable future. Covid-19 is among the most vivid wake-up calls in over a century. It should force us to begin to think in earnest and collectively about living in more thoughtful and creative harmony with nature, even as we plan for nature's inevitable, and always unexpected, surprises.'[8]

As Fauci and Morens suggest, the spectres of climate change, deforestation and desertification certainly offer a sobering panorama. On their account, this makes the growth of viruses spread to humans by animal populations whose habitats are being rendered ever more marginal through human activity a likely outcome—even if that may not be how Covid-19 began, as we'll explore in Chapter 1. On another level, their conclusion forces us to be clear that Covid-19 is not some political anomaly: it offers a policy precedent for what may be our collective futures. This time around, human beings more or less consented to mass surveillance, living in isolation from parents, siblings and children, and the stripping away of the most fundamental of rights relating to the human life cycle (birth, sex, and death) in order to be protected from what governments and the media told them was a killer virus which could only be compared to the Spanish flu outbreak of 1918–19 (this was, as Fauci and Morens put it, 'among the most vivid wake-up calls in over a century').

INTRODUCTION

So how accurate is this comparison? The Spanish flu outbreak of 1918–19 is widely thought to have killed around 50 million people (this is the estimate used by the US Centers for Disease Control, and also in 2005 by Professor Neil Ferguson of Imperial College London when modelling the potential mortality of avian flu).[9] The global population at the time is estimated to have been around 1.6 billion, which means that Spanish Flu killed roughly 3 per cent of the world's population at the time—approximately the initial mortality rate which, as we will see in Chapter 2, was predicted in March 2020 by the WHO for Covid-19.[10]

The world's population is currently estimated to be around 8 billion people, of which 3 per cent would be 240 million. The two pandemic years of Covid-19 (March 2020 to March 2022) were estimated by worldometer.org to have killed a recorded 6.083 million people[11]—2.5 per cent of the relative global mortality caused by Spanish flu (though Covid death statistics are rather unreliable, as we explain in Chapter 3). Some readers would argue that medical interventions are more successful now than in the past, and—though we disagree (as outlined in Chapter 3)—that Covid mortality has been significantly underestimated. But even if we were ultra-conservative, and assumed a real death toll of 10 million and that twice as many people would have died from the virus given 1919 medical care, this would give a death toll of 20 million, which is still less than 10 per cent of the relative mortality of Spanish Flu even given all these cautious riders. So we can assert with confidence that Covid-19 was responsible for between just 2.5 and 10 per cent of the mortality of Spanish flu; moreover, whereas Spanish flu targeted overwhelmingly the youngest sectors of the population, Covid-19, as readers of this book will know by now, targets much older people and those with pre-existing health conditions or comorbidities.

How comparable does that make the two pandemics? We think it's pretty clear that this doesn't make Covid a once-in-a-century event. However, we want to emphasise that we aren't Covid sceptics. Of course we know that Covid-19 is a virus that can have devastating effects among a small proportion of those who become symptomatic. People close to us have died of Covid, and we have close family members who have been affected by 'long Covid'. Nevertheless, it is our view that the virus suppression measures did not have the impacts that were claimed: while Covid-19 is one of many diseases in the world, we hold that the risks posed by it have been overstated when they are compared with the risks of the mitigation measures which we outline in this book.

Whatever beliefs readers may have as to the virulence of Covid-19, the evidence in this book shows that the mitigation strategies and medical campaigns undertaken to combat it were catastrophic. They massively accelerated existing global inequities of class, gender, and race both within Western societies and between the West and the rest of the world, as well as giving rise to a new wave of public distrust of medicine. When collated, as we have attempted here, the impacts of such mitigation strategies raise the question of whether such policies should be implemented in the future.

In our view, the combined impacts of the virus suppression and mitigation strategies point unerringly towards the conclusion that in future cases of the emergence of a new virus, governments and global institutions should assess not only the risk factors of the virus, but also the excess harms which radical suppression policies and coercive vaccination campaigns are shown in this book to have caused. So the purpose of *The Covid Consensus* is to understand what has happened, why it has happened, and what can be done to make sure that it does not happen in the same way again.

***

INTRODUCTION

The coronavirus crisis has brought so many issues into focus that a book like this, written so close to events, cannot pretend to deal with all of them. Scientists and social scientists will spend many years poring over the results of this vast experiment with human physical, mental, and social health. The deeper implications of what has gone on may not emerge for decades.

It's worth mentioning just a few of the themes which we won't have the time to dwell on so much here. The first would be what the response to the pandemic reveals about the relationship of Western societies to death. In the United Kingdom, the United States, and some (though not all) parts of Europe, we live in a world in which death is pushed into 'safe spaces': hospices, hospitals, and morgues. There is rarely a lying-in of the dead in their coffins or ritual washing of the bodies of the dead as many religions have historically required, let alone the exposing of dead bodies on hillsides which the Zoroastrians perform. Whereas in most human societies death and the dead have been intimately connected to the living, for many decades Western societies have implemented the progressive bureaucratisation of death and a cleansing of the dead from daily life.[12]

This may well explain the panic which occurred in Europe in March 2020. As the shadow loomed of death re-entering the normal spaces of society, people sought to seal themselves away from something which terrified them, owing to Western society's unusual attitude towards death. Yet the idea that the purpose of life is to extend it as far as possible is very particular to modern Western culture. In many societies throughout history, the aim has been to die honourably, rather than to preserve life at all costs. We would rather recognise the truth in the Ghanaian pidgin saying, 'All die be die'—we cannot avoid death, and what counts is the quality and dignity of each person's life, the ability to lead a good and helpful life, and the love which we can share with others whilst alive.[13] What this means is that some risks have to be taken in society in order to preserve these values, for we cannot live in a world without risk.

Indeed, the crisis is likely to see a re-evaluation of this purging of death from daily life. During the initial lockdowns in many countries, from Britain and Spain to Cabo Verde, people were unable to visit geriatric parents in care homes because of the requirement to protect these residences from the new virus and the reality that those most at risk from the virus were the elderly. Many of these aged care home residents, often suffering from dementia or terminal illness, became ever more confused and, to the horror of their relatives, died in government-enforced isolation. The response to the pandemic meant that citizens had been stripped of their rights to comfort a parent or spouse and alleviate their death—one of the most basic rites of human existence. Thus, one of the consequences of this approach has been to show that the prolonging of the end of life at all costs comes a poor second to the qualities of compassion and love which are most essential in valuing and cherishing the lives of old people, and of ensuring that those lives are rich and lived to the full.

A further theme to have emerged during 2020 is the approach to risk in the West, for the response to the virus shows very polarised attitudes towards risk in the world. In a brilliant essay written at the outset of the crisis in March 2020, the Mozambican sociologist Elísio Macamo argued that the global response to the pandemic revealed diverging approaches to risk.[14] There is no such thing as a risk-free society, as we all tacitly acknowledge every time we step into a car. African citizens, Macamo argued, have learnt to develop a sophisticated understanding of relative levels of risk, which they need to have in order to survive on a daily basis. During 2020, as time passed and the data became clearer, the levels of risk for many in society from the new virus were shown to be vanishingly small. Indeed, as Professor Neil Ferguson of Imperial College—whose computer modelling report on 16 March 2020 persuaded the British government to move into lockdown—said as early as 25 March, between half and two-thirds of those who died of Covid-19 may have died during the next twelve months anyway.[15]

Subsequent studies later in the year suggested that a terminal case of Covid-19 could certainly reduce life-years, perhaps by an average of ten (although some said by four or five years), although some countries such as Mexico did see a median age of death which was much lower than the average.[16] However, in most parts of Africa Covid-19 tended to affect the old above all, in common with most Western countries.[17] The reality that the average age of death from Covid-19 in some Western countries (including the United Kingdom) was above the national life expectancy is illustrative that, for the vast majority of people, the societal risk that was involved was minimal.[18] The willingness to live with such levels of risk in order to make the best of life may well now emerge as a keystone of good citizenship in a democratic society, since the alternative—semi-permanent restrictions on daily life as one and then another new virus comes into view—is too terrible to contemplate.

A third theme which we won't be able to address fully, but which will be a subtext of the book, is the relationship between science and social science. This emerged in the early phase of the pandemic, when many left-leaning politicians and writers claimed to be focused on 'saving lives' rather than the economy. The idea that 'the economy' and 'health' can be so neatly separated in these ways is a curious one. It only became embedded in public discourse during the pandemic because the perspectives and ideas of the social sciences were resolutely ignored by government and the media. Social science practitioners—economists, social psychologists, political scientists, sociologists, anthropologists, historians—have long been aware of the ways in which, far from being distinct, health and the economy are intimately connected. So, too, have many politicians. Indeed, in the United Kingdom, under the left-wing leadership of Jeremy Corbyn, the Labour party claimed that over 100,000 people had died in the country following the austerity policies introduced by David Cameron's Conservative government.[19] While these figures were disputed, this was proof of a clear understanding on the left of the relationship that economic depression and higher rates of mortality can have.[20]

The lockdown policies were thus developed to save lives from Covid-19 (though how many lives they saved will be discussed fully in Chapter 6). But given that they were creating a future economic depression, they were also exponentially expanding future mortality rates because of the ways in which economic and physical health are so intimately connected (something which is beginning to become clearer towards the end of 2022). Given the demographics of Covid mortality, lockdowns were thus also enacting a policy decision of generational health inequity: they were arguably prolonging the lives of predominantly elderly people by, on lower estimates, four or five years—though even that is disputable, as we will see—and reducing the life expectancies and increasing the premature mortality of younger people soon to be affected by the coming economic depression.

Understanding the interconnection of these factors required bringing perspectives from the social sciences to the handling of the pandemic. Some called for this approach: the Croatian sociologist Sarah Czerny pointed out how vital the social sciences were to the pandemic response, in providing theoretical tools through which to model potential paths which Covid-19 might take.[21] Yet following years of the undermining of social science and humanities degrees by governments of all persuasions in the Western world in favour of STEM subjects, these perspectives were routinely ignored in the shaping of major policy decisions by both governments and the media. Governments declared that they were 'following the science', without showing any awareness of how the scientific method works: that there are disagreements as to outcomes and method which may date back decades, and that there is no such thing as 'the science' or a universal scientific consensus—as indeed the different approaches of scientists to the Covid-19 crisis has made clear.

The impact of all this on public trust in science and medicine has been vast. In September 2021, the Stanford University professor of medicine John Ioannidis wrote an excoriating commentary which was almost a requiem for the scientific method—one which, he argued, had been traduced during the previous eighteen months.[22] Not only had the public narrative of the scientific method and knowledge been a fraudulent one, but the idea that 'science' somehow existed shorn of any social context was an absurdity—as the differential impacts of lockdowns in diverse urban environments (comfortable suburbs, slums, tower blocks) showed.

The refusal to integrate the perspectives of social scientists more fully into the approaches to national lockdowns is all the more curious given the centrality of these approaches during the Ebola epidemic in West Africa in 2014–15, the most recent outbreak of a virus deemed to be potentially of a global mortality risk. As the anthropologist Paul Richards has shown, it was only when global medical professionals began to integrate the medical knowledge and practice of Sierra Leonean communities affected by Ebola into their perspectives that they changed their approach towards containing the virus and the infection rates began to subside.[23] Moreover, this should certainly have been widely known among senior public health officials: for instance, the UK's Chief Medical Officer, Chris Whitty, had a key role in studying the Ebola epidemic in West Africa.[24]

In fact, what the coronavirus crisis has revealed most starkly are the severe limitations of the scientific method when stripped of its social scientific context. Not only were the data projections used by governments to shape initial policies inaccurate, but had the perspectives of child psychologists, mental health professionals, economic historians, and political scientists been more fully integrated into the initial government responses, then we would not be in the position in which we now find ourselves. Scientists and science writers at once leapt to compare the virus to the outbreak of Spanish flu in 1918–19, drawing on the epidemiology of pandemics and on the initial alarming mortality rates that circulated. Yet viruses circulate within social contexts, and these are historically constituted: understanding the relative risks of viruses thus requires a historical and social perspective as well, one which can compare the specific social contexts in which new viruses emerge. For instance, an economic and historical perspective would have shown that the likely social and economic impacts of severe virus repression were certain to be far worse in 2020 than during Spanish flu, owing to the different nature of world economies; following globalisation, world exports as a proportion of GDP were forty times larger in 2020 (in constant values) than they were in 1913, meaning that measures to close borders and halt circulation of goods were certain to have a far more devastating socio-economic impact than the much milder measures that were implemented in 1918.[25]

All these factors—approaches to death, concepts of risk, fetishisation of science—were important in what happened. In March 2020, the momentum built by government and media choices was such that there was real fear across the world about the mortality levels that the Covid-19 virus might wreak, and once people had invested in the lockdown as a humane response, it was impossible to retreat from this view without questioning the desperate sacrifices that had been made. Many readers of this book will have known people who died from the virus or contracted Covid with severe after-effects. However, owing to the segregated worlds which we inhabit both on- and offline, it is less likely that they know so many victims of the collateral damage inflicted by the response to Covid: supermarket and warehouse operatives in the West who were unable to do their jobs remotely and were forced to carry on working in cramped conditions and take risks regardless; single parents in poor accommodation suddenly unable to cope with rents as debts spiralled; women and children living in abusive situations compounded by the new layers of stress; children with hyper-anxious parents who prevented them from socialising or exercising outdoors; Mozambican parents whose children were starving; Chilean, Colombian, and Peruvian children whose futures were taken away from them as schooling ceased for a year (and in some cases two).

The importance of emotional bonds inevitably meant that people responded to the impacts of which they were most aware. This was a natural human response. Nevertheless, it is almost certainly true that had global governments been led by single parents with autistic children, taxi drivers, travel agents, working families reliant on low wages, or migrant workers in the Global South, a different set of policies would have been chosen.

***

This book looks at how the Covid consensus took shape so quickly, and who the winners and losers of that process have been. It also looks at what the consequences of this scientific experiment have been and may yet be for democratic societies, as the ideological frameworks of previous political approaches have collapsed into a mire of contradictions, frayed almost to nothing, and citizens have acquiesced to the growth of the surveillance state to help them to 'stay safe'.

The list of winners is certainly far outstripped by that of losers. Now that the dust has begun to settle on the extraordinary global policy decisions of 2020 and 2021, it is important to step back and ask with the benefit of hindsight who has gained and who has lost from the imposition of a new consensus for the organisation of human societies that emerged—literally—in the space of less than three months. The winners of the rise of the Covid consensus have been few—and that is the main point of this book, that the consensus over an unprecedented policy choice has rampantly increased poverty and inequality across the world.

Although traditional businesses suffered throughout 2020 and 2021, stockholders with a stake in technology companies have been doing fine. Of course, there are some positive aspects to the developments in the technology sector, which promise opportunities in terms of reducing international travel and meeting global climate accords. Yet it would be foolish to think that technology industry leaders were not keen to take advantage of the new opportunities that were offered by the crisis. Microsoft's profits soared in 2020 and even far outstripped Wall Street's already bullish post-March predictions for the company.[26] Meanwhile, in early June 2020 the US-based virtual conferencing platform Zoom (already a verb and noun in many languages, where most people had never heard of it at the start of 2020) projected an increase in revenue of between 200 and 300 per cent in 2020.[27] Its founder's wealth had already grown by US$2.5 billion, while Elon Musk's wealth had expanded by US$17.2 billion.[28]

Pharmaceutical companies, some of which had former employees working in the highest levels of government in the United Kingdom, France, and the United States, have also been quietly raking in record profits—mostly subsidised by public money, as we show in Chapter 4. The companies behind the two most successful Western Covid-19 vaccines—Pfizer, BioNTech, and Moderna—made combined profits of US$45 billion in 2021 (more than US$1,000 every second). Overall, amidst the global pandemic, a handful of mega-corporations in the technology and pharmaceutical sectors made a killing, raking in hundreds of billions more in 'pandemic super-profits' than over the previous four-year average.[29]

The economic transformations were also financially lucrative for a number of doctors, scientists, and healthcare entrepreneurs, fifty of whom worldwide became billionaires as a result of profits deriving from their work on the Covid-19 virus.[30] They profited from the intensity of the quest for the vaccine and tests, and from the skilled, unremitting, and exhausting work of lab researchers conducting the requisite trials and experiments.[31] They weren't the only ones to benefit, however: overall, billionaires around the world saw their wealth increase by US$3.9 trillion just in 2020[32] (the steepest increase in global billionaires' share of wealth on record),[33] more or less what workers around the world lost that same year,[34] leading even the World Bank to speak of 'the inequality pandemic'.[35]

Thus two enormous commercial sectors won hands down during 2020–21: 'Big Tech' and 'Big Pharma'. Many left-wing liberals dismissed anti-lockdown views as the domain of a libertarian press espousing corporate interests.[36] They had become so immersed in the algorithms driving internet giants that they failed to grasp that these enormous corporate interests were just as invested in the lockdown policy. Apparently, the mainstream liberal left no longer recognised this as a corporate agenda, as it had become so intimately intertwined with their lives and identities. What was at stake was therefore something much more profound than a straightforward conflict between left and right. It was a struggle at the heart of capitalism, between the traditional press and the business interests it has always represented (hotels, restaurants, high street shops) and the new corporate giants who did not require such promotion, as they had created a much vaster propaganda of their own online.

Beyond these corporate interests, there have been other individual beneficiaries of the rise of remote working which has accompanied the lockdown approach to handling Covid-19. Stressed and 'squeezed' middle classes, struggling with long commutes and jobs which often required extensive periods of travel, were released from their spinning hamster wheels (the remorseless acceleration of demands in twenty-first-century capitalism surely explains why many of them initially supported the restrictions). The response to the pandemic became above all a class issue linked to computing technology, where those able to work remotely now had a clear economic advantage over those who could not. This has represented a transformation in the interface of technology and capital, where tech-preparedness overcomes the economic (and political) claims of those previously seen as the bedrock of entrepreneurial conservatism, small business owners involved in face-to-face transactions which now seem virtually archaic.

In other words, the winners of the lockdown approach to Covid-19 in the Global North have been those in growing sectors (tech, pharma, and the financial sector) or those in jobs that can be done remotely. These beneficiaries were thus in the main those who were already enormously privileged by the direction being taken by society and the economy in the North. They were those who had already won through the growing power of computing, and who thus also held a disproportionate influence in the running of society which enabled them to promote the purportedly consensual view of the lockdown strategy to Covid-19, an approach which on such a massive scale was entirely new.

The list of losers, the discussion of which takes up much of Part 2 of the book, is much longer. Almost all the winners of the Covid consensus have been in the Global North, and yet these were Pyrrhic victories achieved at the cost of the young, the low-paid, many of the self-employed, and those involved in the arts in the West—to say nothing of the huge bulk of people who inhabit the world's poor countries.

While a small sector of the economy grew massively, those who worked in many other sectors faced a bleak future. In the arts sector, as theatres and opera houses closed, alongside other music venues such as bars and clubs, musicians from Senegal to Spain found themselves in penury.[37] In the United Kingdom, by September 2020 nearly half of musicians had been forced to leave the industry, while actors and theatre technicians found themselves working as courier drivers delivering growing piles of products to the home-working class.[38] Meanwhile, Britain's Chancellor of the Exchequer, Rishi Sunak, suggested to those in the arts that they might retrain in 'a more viable career'.[39] In other words, the response to Covid in this context was another form of continuity, accelerating the runaway train of governmental focus on STEM subjects at the expense of the arts which had been gathering steam for many years. The dystopia of a brave new world of existence within a technical prosthetic of our own making, in which we can only meet our family and friends remotely, had already been imagined by the science fiction writer J. G. Ballard in his short story *The Intensive Care Unit*, as the British writer Will Self noted at the outset of the pandemic.[40]

Meanwhile, those who worked in sectors such as hospitality, conferences, hairdressing, weddings, travel, and tourism, faced a sudden collapse in their trade to a degree that never could have been imagined. The banning of gatherings made it impossible for such industries to function. As people who had striven to establish their enterprises saw their income base collapse, they laid off their operatives and found themselves having to dig deep into the savings and pension pots they had accrued over years of hard work. Politicians, opinion-formers able to work remotely, and university scientists in secure employment announced that this was a price that had to be paid for a collective good, although none of them personally had to pay it—and, indeed, many of them saw their disposable incomes rising.

One category of people accounting for over half of the world's population that lost massively—as a group—were women. The gendered dimensions of the Covid response are so vast that many books would be required to address it, and we won't be able to tackle it in this one as deeply as we would like to—but it is vital to acknowledge the immensity of this question nonetheless. As schools and childcare provision closed, caring duties multiplied, with women as ever taking on the lion's share of the work. With stress and poverty increasing, domestic abuse soared, alongside prostitution and teenage pregnancy across the world, from the United Kingdom to Angola and Cabo Verde.[41] Meanwhile the financial burden on women in the Global South, most of whom work in the informal sector, was severe. In September 2020 the UN reported that the response to Covid-19 would widen the poverty gap between men and women: 'By 2021, for every 100 men aged 25 to 34 living in extreme poverty (living on USD 1.90 a day or less), there will be 118 women, a gap that is expected to increase to 121 women per 100 men by 2030'.[42] This was happening because, worldwide, women's employment was 18 per cent more at risk than men's; and although the impacts were worse in the Global South, the gendered imbalances were also clear in Western nations such as Spain.[43] As the UN noted, this reversed decades of work that had seen this gap narrowing.[44] So in spite of the increasing emphasis placed on gender equality in the West, when it came to Covid-19, none of this was seen as important.[45]

Worldwide, the young were losers on an immense scale, as they were taken out of socialising frameworks, their schools closed—for up to a year in many countries in the Americas, from Brazil, Chile and Colombia to Panama and Peru, and for two years in Honduras, India and Uganda—and directed towards intensive use of virtual platforms which exacerbated their screen time and intensified the harmful impact such devices were already having on their mental health.[46] By 19 March 2020, UNESCO reported that half of the world's schoolchildren were not attending school, and moved to develop a global response coalition.[47] Yet as the move into virtual learning developed, what was discussed—only then to be ignored—was the exacerbating impact which this had on social inequalities because of lack of quiet study space, good internet access, and adequate nutrition for those from poorer socio-economic backgrounds. Closing schools may have been intended to help 'keep societies safe', but it did not keep poor children safe at all.

Poverty was a clear intensifying factor when it came to the negative impacts of lockdowns. In the Global North, beyond the impact on young people and those working in the sectors discussed above, the poor were those who suffered far and away the most. By the end of October 2020, a report from Oxford University's Department of Social Policy and Intervention estimated that already poor workers across Europe had lost as much as 16 per cent of their salaries during the pandemic. The report's authors stated that: 'Our analysis reveals a sizeable potential increase in poverty across Europe. [...] [T]he burden of the pandemic will be disproportionately borne by low-wage earners'.[48] Inequality increased dramatically both within European countries and between them. The authors noted that, 'Between-country inequality increased by as much as 4% in the team's economic simulations, while within-country inequality increased by as much as 12.1%'.[49]

However, while the impact on the young, poor, and disadvantaged in the Global North was devastating, it cannot be compared to that in the Global South. Here, in many countries throughout South Asia, Africa and Latin America, the lives of hundreds of millions were upended. As early as July 2020, the UN stated that each month 10,000 children were dying from virus-linked hunger as their communities were cut off from markets and food and medical aid owing to the new restrictions, and that 550,000 new children were being struck by wasting diseases as a direct consequence of these measures taken to halt the spread of the virus.[50] Meanwhile, as countries locked down to protect against Covid-19, day-to-day medical interventions and vaccination programmes ground to a halt.

A good case study introducing the themes looked at in more depth later in the book comes from India. On 23 June 2020 UNICEF South Asia tweeted that 'decades of progress on children's health and education risks being wiped out', and that the lives of 600 million South Asian children were in the process of being upended.[51] Jean Gough, UNICEF's Regional Director, said that 'the side-effects of the pandemic across South Asia, including the lockdown and other measures, have been damaging for children in numerous ways. But the longer-term impact of the economic crisis on children will be on a different scale entirely.'[52]

Yet what is so devastating about the UNICEF report is not only its discussion of the impacts on poverty (where the report projected 120 million children might be pushed into poverty over the ensuing six months) and the schooling of the poor, but also its insights into the services provided for the wider health of the population. The report noted that there had been a 'disruption of immunization, nutrition and other vital health services, that could be potentially life-threatening for around 459,000 over the next six months'.[53] Vaccination campaigns against measles and polio had completely ceased in order to comply with social distancing guidelines.[54]

Thus the pattern in South Asia reflected that of global governments and the media more generally when it came to Covid-19. Everything stopped. But what was little reported was that this way of treating a pandemic was in fact completely new, a giant experiment. And as it turned out, the catastrophic consequences of this new approach far outweighed anything that the respiratory illness alone could bring. Many of these effects were then compounded by the rollout of highly coercive and discriminatory mass vaccination policies, as discussed in Chapters 4 and 5.

***

It's painful to recall the past two years, and perhaps for that reason there's been a notable lack of debate in the aftermath. This is only human: amnesia is certainly one approach to dealing with the experience of pain. On the other hand, the Covid crisis was quickly replaced by the war in Ukraine in the public and media imaginary. Indeed, many of the inflationary pressures which had already been building long before Putin's invasion of Ukraine were blamed on it.

How feasible is it for healthy societies to continue to live through a politics of crisis? This is a subject we come to in the book's last chapter. It's our view that the harms of the Covid-19 response and their consequences have been such that it's important to attempt to take the measure of what has happened. Beyond all the socio-economic and political upheavals, people's emotional lives have been upended. Rates of divorce and separation have soared in many places. Friendships have been sundered, and others have been born—including that between ourselves, since we'd never met before the outbreak of SARS-CoV-2.

As writers who have always understood ourselves as being on the political left, we were drawn together by our incomprehension at how the mainstream left had supported policies which so clearly and manifestly unleashed economic warfare on the poorest sections of society, as well as on women and the young. After writing several articles together which looked at these issues, we decided to collaborate on rewriting the first edition of this book, which Green had sent to press in February 2021—at a completely different point in the pandemic, before the issue of universal vaccination and vaccine passes was even on the horizon.

Our methods were qualitative (interviews, reports), and quantitative (going through the mountains of data and official reports which have been produced). In the meantime, as we were researching and writing, so much was changing as the world stumbled into a crisis of bigger proportions than anything since the Second World War.

PART 1

A CHRONICLE OF THE POLITICAL
MANAGEMENT OF THE PANDEMIC

In this first part of the book, we try to piece together a chronicle of the events of 2020 and 2021. These were so all-consuming and unprecedented in the lives of most of those reading this book that it was at the time hard to take stock of some of the things that occurred, and to make sense of the order in which they took place. With the benefit of more than two years of experience of the Covid-19 pandemic, however, it's now possible to try to chronicle what happened. We'll focus on the panic surrounding the virus when it appeared, the move to lockdowns, and the vaccine response; we'll also look at the way in which this shaped a single narrative or response to Covid-19 which, while claiming to be guided by the science, was fundamentally anti-scientific— and how this led to the bullying and trolling of any scientist who diverged from consensus opinion.

However, it's not our intention here to set out exactly why we think things happened as they did. We seek mainly to describe what happened, because for the moment that's more than enough. In an event as epochal as the Covid-19 pandemic, and in the response to it, explanations are always likely to throw up more questions than solutions. They can also be targeted and seized upon to deflect discussion from what really matters: what has happened to world societies and human beings during the Covid-19 pandemic, and what lessons can be learnt from this for the future. That's why it matters to us most of all to describe what has happened, to document it while that's still possible, so that the record of this is not lost before world societies move on to the next crisis (if that has not happened already, in fact). Of course at times the question of what happened can be quite hard to distinguish from why it happened, but we have done our best to separate the two out in what follows.

We can, though, highlight just a few of the explanations for the trajectory of the pandemic that are routinely thrown about on one side of the debate or the other. Was the cause of the Covid-19 crisis the failure of pre-existing pandemic plans, and their focus on influenza rather than coronaviruses? Was it the failure of Western political leaders to 'follow the science' and the model of virus control demonstrated in China and South-East Asia? Was it the systematic erosion of the state as a provider of goods and services, to be replaced by a regulatory state in which responsibility for outcomes is always delegated to someone else—meaning that states were incapable of enacting emergency plans when the need arose? Or was there rather a coordination of commercial interests which sought at once to profiteer from the pandemic, as only disaster capitalists know how? Had technology and pharmaceutical companies been lying in wait for years for just such an eventuality to kickstart the so-called fourth industrial revolution? Was the corruption of scientific institutions and scientific journals by major commercial interests one of the root causes of the way in which both the pandemic and the pandemic response unfolded as they did?

PART 1

Many of these views are seen as irreconcilable, but of course they don't have to be. The erosion of the state as a provider of services is one side of the coin, of which the other is the growth of private providers and their consequent influence (corrupt or not) over policy decisions. The two explanations could be entirely compatible, even if they haven't been seen to be during the last two years because of the extreme polarisation and viciousness of the debates. Indeed, the erosion of the distinction between public and private providers has been widely discussed for years, through the concept of the 'revolving door' between government and industry. Why should it be surprising—let alone conspiratorial—to suggest that this revolving door may have influenced some of the policy choices that were made?

On the other hand, some of these explanations are also known as conspiracy theories. Certainly there are many outlandish conspiracy theories regarding the Covid-19 pandemic which are rightly labelled as such (5G, vaccine microchips, global depopulation, and so on). Some who hold to these theories also see the coordination of global economic power as a conspiracy, but in our view that's a mistake: this is simply how economic power works to maintain, concentrate, and grow itself, and always has. Indeed, it's that tendency of capital to concentrate itself and produce growing inequalities that writers and activists from the left have historically sought to criticise.

At the same time, the idea that leading figures of major commercial interests meet regularly and develop visions of how they see the future unfolding, which they then seek to mould through new programmes of investment and research, should not be labelled a conspiracy. It is a simple statement of fact, as observed through the regular meetings of the World Economic Forum (WEF) at Davos. Coordination is not the same thing as conspiracy, which by definition (and unlike, for instance, the meetings at Davos) happens in secret—and that's

29

something that people on all sides of the debate could usefully keep in mind.*

In other words, the explanations for what has gone on are enormously complex. Some of them may be overlapping. We prefer to describe the what instead of the why, because this is already stark enough. What we know is that unprecedented policy decisions were enacted which saw the biggest upward transfer of wealth in history in the shortest space of time, alongside a sustained assault on poor people and democratic structures worldwide. In this first part of the book, we seek simply to describe the political and scientific frameworks through which this took place. We range as widely as we can across the world, while trying to keep the descriptive focus of what is already a difficult task.

---

* We gratefully acknowledge Alex Gourevitch of Brown University for this point.

1

THE ORIGIN-OF-THE-VIRUS DEBATE

STARTING OFF ON THE WRONG FOOT

In early January 2020, Chinese authorities investigating a mysterious outbreak of pneumonia in the city of Wuhan (more than 11 million inhabitants), in the Hubei province, announced that they had discovered a new strain of SARS-like coronavirus of probable bat origin[1]—later named SARS-CoV-2 (for severe acute respiratory syndrome coronavirus 2).[2] In early February, researchers at the Wuhan Institute of Virology (WIV) published an article in *Nature* that reached the same conclusion, noting that the genome of the new virus closely resembled that of a bat virus called RaTG13 and thus was most likely of animal origin.[3]

The Wuhan Municipal Health Commission had reported the first cases—which we now know to have been cases of Covid-19, the illness caused by SARS-CoV-2—on 31 December 2019, by releasing a briefing on its website.[4] The briefing was then picked up by the WHO Country Office in the People's Republic of China.[5] Many (but not all)[6] of these first reported early infectees were linked to Wuhan's Huanan Seafood Market,[7] leading the latter to be associated early on with the origin of the virus.

We know that the Chinese authorities initially tried to silence 'rumours' about the outbreak potentially being related to severe acute respiratory syndrome (SARS). Li Wenliang, a 33-year-old doctor who worked at the Central Hospital of Wuhan, shared his concerns that they might be dealing with a deadly SARS outbreak with his Wuhan University alumni through a WeChat group.[8] He was dubbed a whistleblower when that shared report later circulated publicly, despite his requesting confidentiality from those with whom he shared the information.

On 3 January Wuhan police were said to have summoned and admonished Li for 'making false comments on the Internet about [an] unconfirmed SARS outbreak'.[9] He returned to work and later contracted Covid, reportedly dying from the disease in early February 2020. A subsequent Chinese official inquiry exonerated him, and Wuhan police formally apologised to his family and revoked his admonishment. He was posthumously awarded the May 4th Medal, the top award for young Chinese people.[10]

Li's treatment has cast serious doubts over the official timeline of the outbreak provided by the Chinese authorities. The fact of the matter is that at the time of writing (late-2022), when, how, and even where the virus first made its appearance remains a matter of dispute.[11] Some sources claim that the Chinese authorities had already identified hundreds of individuals with similar symptoms in November 2019, at least a few weeks before they officially acknowledged the existence of the outbreak,[12] and that several of these infectees had no direct link to the Huanan Seafood Market.[13] The fact that the Chinese researchers managed to characterise the virus fully, despite its proclaimed novelty, merely seven days after officially becoming aware of the cluster,[14] and then to develop and distribute in a matter of days the first RT-PCR tests,[15] further fuelled suspicions that they knew about it beforehand.

However, even the canonically accepted timeline hypothesis—that the virus emerged in Wuhan, China, sometime between November and December 2019 and was subsequently introduced in Europe and North America in January 2020—has been the subject of debate.[16] Analysis of satellite imagery and cell phone usage has been said to suggest that the virus might have already been circulating in Wuhan in August 2019 or earlier.[17] Indeed, as early as the summer of 2019 there were 'notable, significant and abnormal' purchases of PCR equipment in Wuhan, which may suggest an even earlier outbreak.[18]

This would explain an analysis published in 2022 in the medical journal *BMJ Global Health*, which cites a growing body of studies indicating that the virus may have been spreading worldwide weeks, or even months, prior to the official timeline of the pandemic.[19] The paper notes, for example, that SARS-CoV-2 was detected in clinical samples from Lombardy, Italy—which would then go on to become the site of the first official Covid cluster outside of Asia in February 2020—dating back to September 2019, and that a higher than usual number of cases of severe pneumonia and flu were reported in Lombardy in the last quarter of 2019. This suggests that the new coronavirus might have been circulating earlier than previously thought. Traces of the virus were also found in late 2019 in the United States, the United Kingdom, Brazil, and France,[20] and in Spain even as early as March 2019 (although many researchers have deemed this an outlier which may have been misattributed).[21]

If the first appearance of SARS-CoV-2 thus remains a matter of ongoing debate, even less is certain about how the virus emerged. Almost immediately, a public narrative surrounding the origin of the virus materialised. This claimed that the virus was zoonotic in nature, meaning that it had jumped from one or more animals (probably, it was argued, bats) to one or more humans, possibly through one or more unidentified intermediate animal hosts, and most likely at the Huanan Seafood Market.[22] This transference from bats to humans had occurred either through direct contact or though the food supply chain, this public narrative held, and the mutations the virus had undergone over the course of this process had 'naturally' given rise to SARS-CoV-2.[23] That early February 2020 *Nature* article by researchers at the WIV proved crucial in setting this narrative.

Over time, however, elements of this public narrative wore thin. At the time of writing, most of these questions remain unanswered. The alleged natural reservoir of SARS-CoV-2—the animal in which the virus supposedly lives and reproduces—has not been positively identified (though SARS-CoV-2-related viruses have been found in some bats, albeit thousands of kilometres away from Wuhan),[24] and for that matter there is still no conclusive evidence that the virus is in fact natural in origin.[25] Moreover, the original source of viral transmission to humans remains unclear,[26] as does whether the virus became pathogenic (capable of causing disease) before or after the alleged 'spillover' event.[27] It also remains unclear whether the Huanan Seafood Market was the site of the alleged spillover event or if it was just the location of a massive amplifying event, in which an infected person spread the virus to many other people.[28]

According to a study by the Chinese Center for Disease Control And Prevention (China CDC), of the 457 swabs taken from eighteen species of animals in the market, none contained any evidence of the virus; however, the virus was found in seventy-three swabs taken from around the market's environment, all linked to human infections, supporting the 'amplification' theory.[29] In December 2020, even the Chinese CDC Director Gao Fu admitted leaning towards that hypothesis: 'At first, we assumed the seafood market might have the virus, but now the market is more like a victim. The novel coronavirus had existed long before'.[30] Finally, as noted already, questions have also been raised as to whether the market was really the site of the first cluster after all: the fact that the earliest cases reported by the Chinese authorities were located here does not of course mean that this was the site of origin of the transfer event.[31]

***

Early in the pandemic, an alternative theory emerged, suggesting that the Wuhan Institute of Virology—known, of all things, for its research into SARS-related coronaviruses[32] (as noted, they were among the first to report on SARS-CoV-2), and only eight miles from the Huanan Seafood Market—might have had something to do with the outbreak, through the accidental release of the virus into the environment.[33] As early as February 2020, researchers from the South China University of Technology looked into the possible origins of the new coronavirus and concluded that it 'probably originated from a laboratory in Wuhan'.[34] The paper was subsequently taken down. From a purely circumstantial standpoint, and considering the long history of safety breaches (including several SARS leaks) previously recorded at various facilities in China[35] and throughout the world,[36] one could have been justified in considering it, at the very least, a lead worth pursuing.

As Sir Jeremy Farrar, Director of the Wellcome Trust, Europe's biggest philanthropic research funding body, notes in his bestselling book *Spike*: 'It was odd for a spillover event, from animals to humans, to take off in people so immediately and spectacularly in a city with a biolab [...] which is home to an almost unrivalled collection of bat viruses'—especially with a new virus that 'seemed almost designed to infect human cells'.[37] If this were a coincidence, he adds, it would be a 'huge' one.

Yet from the beginning the very notion that the virus might have a laboratory-based—that is, artificial—origin was stifled. The hot denials came not only from the Chinese authorities and the Wuhan

Institute of Virology itself,[38] as one might expect, but also from the World Health Organization[39] and leading Western scientists (including Farrar himself; although, as he recounts in *Spike*, so seriously did he initially take this hypothesis that he was worried for his safety and purchased multiple mobile phones), institutions, and media organisations.[40] For around a year and a half, the 'lab leak' hypothesis was ridiculed and dismissed as a fringe conspiracy theory[41] and anyone who publicly raised it deemed a crackpot—and even subject to censorship and banning on social networks such as Twitter and Facebook,[42] as these companies proceeded to include the assertion that Covid-19 may have been 'man-made or manufactured' among their list of false and debunked claims.[43]

Few scientists dared to go against the conventional wisdom[44]—or what was passed off as the consensus of the scientific community or, more simply, 'The Science'. The fact that Trump endorsed the lab leak theory, weaponizing his base by referring to it as 'the Chinese virus' amidst growing US–China tensions,[45] didn't help, as it further politicised and polarised an issue of vital scientific and public importance—a recurrent theme throughout the pandemic, as we will see.

Things changed when, beginning in mid-2021, several high-profile Western scientists, intelligence officials and politicians—including US president Joe Biden[46]—started publicly acknowledging the plausibility of a laboratory accident and called for rigorous investigation.[47] Almost overnight, the lab leak scenario went from being a 'crackpot theory' to being a credible and legitimate hypothesis, and one that deserved to be scrutinised very closely. Indeed, the very same day Biden announced that his administration would be investigating the origins of Covid-19, 'including whether it emerged from human contact with an infected animal or from a laboratory accident',[48] Facebook stated that it would 'no longer remove the claim that Covid-19 is man-made or manufactured' from its apps.[49]

At the time of writing, the debate hasn't been settled. There is simply no conclusive evidence of whether the virus is zoonotic or artificial in nature.[50] Meanwhile, the public narrative continues to be heavily skewed towards the natural origin theory. A tell-tale sign of this is the fact that, as we write, Wikipedia—the closest thing to an official account of the Covid narrative—still states unequivocally that SARS-CoV-2 'is most likely of zoonotic origins'.[51]

Now, it is beyond the scope and even the purpose of this book to go into a detailed discussion about the various theories surrounding the origin of SARS-CoV-2.[52] However, we do believe that the story about how the consensus around the natural origin of the virus initially emerged—a fundamental pillar of what we have called "the Covid consensus"—deserves to be briefly recounted. This is a story that sheds light on several key aspects of the entire pandemic management: the political use of the science; the conflicted and contradictory stances of pillars of the scientific establishment (and of some of its most respected journals); the stifling of critical opinion; the role of social media and political polarisation; and the lack of transparency by public institutions—as well as the *modus operandi* of some of the key individual and institutional players of this story.

We know enough to make this assertion thanks to a Freedom of Information Act (FOIA) request that led to the publication, in mid-2021, of thousands of emails pertaining to Anthony Fauci, one of the world's leading voices throughout the pandemic.[53] Through this email dump, we now know that, in the early days of the outbreak, several top scientists—including Fauci himself—took the lab leak theory very seriously. However, what we also know is that very rapidly they changed position, apparently without having any actual scientific evidence to go on.

On 1 February 2020, Fauci convened a 'totally confidential' conference call which would have remained secret if not for the

FOIA. Attending the call were at least a dozen high-level experts from around the world, including Francis Collins, then Director of the US National Institutes of Health (NIH, of which the NIAID is a branch); Patrick Vallance, Britain's Chief Scientific Adviser; Farrar, the aforementioned head of the Wellcome Trust; and Kristian Andersen, an immunologist at the Scripps Research Institute in California. The topic of the discussion was the origin of the recently identified new virus.

We don't know the details of what was said during the 1 February call, since many of the emails released to the public were almost entirely redacted. Nonetheless, the communications show that on that occasion, and in a series of emails exchanged between the participants before and after the call, several of the scientists involved expressed serious concern about SARS-CoV-2's peculiar genomic sequence. Kristian Andersen, for example, when sent a *Science* article looking into the possible origin of the virus at the end of January, admitted that a close look at the genetic sequences of SARS-CoV-2 showed that 'some of the features (potentially) look engineered'[54] and that he and other experts on the call, including Robert Garry, Mike Farzan, and Edward Holmes, agreed the genome was 'inconsistent with expectations from evolutionary theory'.[55]

Farrar later wrote that at the end of January Andersen noted that the receptor binding domain, which attaches to infect a host cell, 'looked too good to be true—like a perfect "key" for entering human cells'.[56] Another issue that several scientists found deeply troubling is the fact that SARS-CoV-2 presents a unique furin cleavage site—a spot in the surface protein of a virus that can boost its entry into human cells—that isn't found in any other SARS-like coronavirus. Nobel Prize-winning virologist David Baltimore would later on go on to state in an interview that he considered this to be 'the smoking gun for the origin of the virus'.[57] This is exactly what you would expect to find 'if someone had set out to adapt an animal coronavirus to humans by taking a specific suit of genetic material from elsewhere and inserting it', Andersen told Farrar.[58]

Farzan, chair of the Department of Immunology and Microbiology at Scripps Research, was also 'bothered by the furin site and [had] a hard time explain[ing] that as an event outside the lab', according to notes shared after the meeting, and said that he leaned '70:30 or 60:40' towards the laboratory origin hypothesis.[59] Garry, professor of Microbiology and Immunology at Tulane Medical School, speaking of the furin cleavage site, said: 'I really can't think of a plausible natural scenario where you get from the bat virus or one very similar to it to [SARS-CoV-2]. [...] I just can't figure out how this gets accomplished in nature.'[60]

He added that the scenario proposed by the Wuhan Institute of Virology—that the furin cleavage site was naturally generated over evolutionary time through mutations of the RaTG13 virus—was 'even more implausible'. While Holmes stated that he was '80% sure this thing had come out of a lab',[61] Farrar himself had doubts: 'On a spectrum if 0 is nature and 100 is release I am honestly at 50', he emailed Fauci. 'My guess is this will remain grey unless there is access to the Wuhan lab—and I suspect that is unlikely.'[62]

In short, on that 1 February call, several of the world's most renowned experts privately admitted that there was a very high probability that the virus had been artificially engineered and had then escaped from the Wuhan lab. However, just a few days later, those very same experts all went on vehemently to argue for the exact opposite in public, scorning the very views that they themselves had held shortly before.

On 4 February, just three days after the call, Andersen told another group of scientists that 'the data conclusively show[s]' that the virus wasn't engineered, calling suggestions of engineering 'fringe' and 'crackpot' theories.[63] That same day, four participants in the conference call—including Andersen, Holmes, and Garry, all of whom had conceded leaning towards the virus being laboratory-related—authored a letter titled 'The proximal origin of SARS-CoV-2' and sent a draft to Fauci and Collins.[64] In it, the authors stated that 'Our analyses clearly show that SARS-CoV-2 is not a laboratory construct or a purposefully manipulated virus', and concluded by saying that since notable features of the virus are observed in related coronaviruses in nature, 'we do not believe that any type of laboratory-based scenario is plausible'.

'How they arrived at such certainty within [three] days remains unclear', noted a *Vanity Fair* investigative report.[65] In his book, *Spike*, Farrar claims that the authors changed their mind 'after the addition of new information, endless analyses, intense discussions and many sleepless nights'.[66] In fact, as noted, it was three sleepless nights at most—arguably a very short time for reaching such drastically dissimilar conclusions, especially in the absence of any actual new data. The abovementioned letter drafted on 4 February was published a few weeks later in *Nature Medicine*,[67] one of the world's most prestigious scientific journals, rapidly raking in millions of accesses. The research was funded by the NIH (directed by Fauci) and the Wellcome Trust (directed by Farrar), among others.[68] The letter came on the heels of another highly influential letter, published in *The Lancet* and signed by twenty-seven global experts including Farrar, which strongly condemned 'conspiracy theories suggesting that Covid-19 does not have a natural origin'.[69]

The two letters, whose message was repeated *ad nauseam* in global mass media outlets in the subsequent weeks of late February and early March 2020, had the combined effect of effectively shutting down the debate about the origin of SARS-CoV-2: on the one hand there were Trump and his gun-carrying, China-bashing followers claiming the virus was bioengineered (if not an outright bioweapon), while on the other hand there were dozens of the world's top scientists claiming in two of the world's most renowned journals that countless studies 'overwhelmingly conclude that this coronavirus originated in wildlife', and expressing solidarity with 'the scientists, public health professionals, and medical professionals of China combatting Covid-19'.[70] 'The Science' versus 'fake news', rampant America First nationalism versus international solidarity—it's easy to see why most people, especially on the left, viewed this as an open-and-shut case.

For over a year, the consensus about the natural origin of the virus, set in stone by the two letters and subsequently enshrined in the public narrative of the pandemic, was so overwhelming that it had what has been described as a 'chilling effect' on scientific research and the scientific community by implying that scientists who 'bring up the lab-leak theory [...] are doing the work of conspiracy theorists'.[71] The social scientist Filippa Lentzos said some scientists closed ranks as a result, fearing for their careers and grants.[72] The few scientists who dared to challenge the consensus were ignored—or worse.

As open discussion and empirical research are the bedrock of the scientific method, this kind of academic bullying should have been a cause for concern in and of itself, even if the *Lancet* and *Nature Medicine* letters had truly reflected the unbiased opinion of the scientists that had penned those studies and statements. However, the inner workings of 'The Science' were about to appear a lot worse. In late 2020, emails released following a Freedom of Information request showed that the *Lancet* statement had been orchestrated by one of the twenty-seven co-authors, a little-known British scientist based in the US called Peter Daszak.[73]

Right from the start, Daszak was one of the most vocal critics of the lab leak theory. In June 2020 he wrote an essay for the

Guardian attacking the former head of MI6 for saying that the pandemic could have 'started as an accident'[74] (Farrar, who co-signed the *Lancet* letter, promoted Daszak's essay on Twitter, saying that Daszak was 'always worth reading').[75] 'We're in the midst of the social media misinformation age, and these rumours and conspiracy theories have real consequences', Daszak told *Science*.[76] Months later in *Nature*, he again criticised 'conspiracies' speculating that the virus could have come from the Wuhan Institute of Virology.[77]

Yet despite declaring no conflicts of interest at the time of the *Lancet* letter, it subsequently emerged that Daszak's organisation, the US-based non-governmental organisation EcoHealth Alliance (EHA), had direct ties to the Wuhan Institute of Virology. Not only was it revealed that he was a long-time collaborator of Shi Zhengli, the Director of the Center for Emerging Infectious Diseases at the Wuhan Institute of Virology—known as 'Batwoman' for her work with bat coronaviruses[78]—with whom he had authored eighteen scientific papers[79] (it was Shi who established that the new virus closely resembled that of the bat virus RaTG13 in the early February 2020 *Nature* paper by the WIV), but, even more worryingly, it also came to light that in 2014 EcoHealth had been awarded a multi-million-dollar grant[80] by Anthony Fauci's NIAID, part of Collins's NIH, which it had then sub-awarded to the WIV.[81] Moreover, it was subsequently revealed that all but one of the twenty-seven scientists who penned the letter in the *Lancet* dismissing the possibility that the virus could have come from the WIV were linked to the lab's Chinese researchers, their colleagues, or their funders.[82]

That is disturbing in itself, considering Daszak's, Collins's, and Fauci's role in shaping the post-outbreak debate. But even more troubling is the object of the research part-funded by the NIH—that is, the US government—via Daszak's EcoHealth outfit, in Wuhan through its 2014 grant: the sequencing of high spillover-risk SARS-related coronaviruses (SARSr-CoVs) in bats in southern China, in order to understand the risk of these virus infecting humans, and build predictive models to examine future risk.[83] This included 'testing if spike proteins from naturally occurring bat coronaviruses circulating in China were capable of binding to the human ACE2' receptor.[84] The presence of the receptor binding domain in SARS-CoV-2, it will be recalled, is precisely what Andersen described as 'too good to be true—like a perfect key for entering human cells'.

The WIV is not new to this kind of research. As Wikipedia notes: 'The institute has been an active premier research center for the study of coronaviruses.'[85] To recap, it has been established that, at the very least, the research going on at the WIV and part-funded by the US government involved the handling of very dangerous coronaviruses, and the investigation of how they spread to humans. However, the NIH later acknowledged that the research group—led by Shi Zhengli, in collaboration with American coronavirus expert Ralph Baric,[86] a consultant for Daszak's EHA[87]—went beyond the simple analysis of existing coronaviruses, and actually engineered a 'chimeric' bat coronavirus (that is, a virus that contains genetic material derived from two or more distinct viruses) that had proven potentially more infectious to humans[88]—a highly risky technique known as gain-of-function.[89] Nevertheless, the NIH firmly rejects the idea that the virus created by EHA in collaboration with the Wuhan Institute of Virology could have sparked the SARS-CoV-2 pandemic, noting that the two viruses present a sizable genetic difference.[90] Moreover, the research in question took place in a US lab, not in Wuhan.[91]

But who's to say EHA and the WIV didn't carry out other gain-of-function studies in Wuhan unbeknownst to the NIH?[92] This theory gained further traction following the leak of a 2018 grant proposal submitted by EcoHealth and the WIV (in collaboration with other institutions) to the Defense Advanced Research Projects Agency (DARPA),[93] the research agency of the United States Department of Defense responsible for the development of emerging military technologies. From the seventy-five-page proposal, a striking detail stood out: a plan to examine SARS-like bat coronaviruses for furin cleavage sites and possibly insert new ones into novel coronaviruses to increase their ability to infect cells in the laboratory and make them easier to grow.[94] It will be recalled that the presence of a furin cleavage site is precisely what sets SARS-CoV-2 apart from all known SARS-like coronaviruses—and what set the alarm bells ringing in several of the scientists that participated in the 1 February conference call.

The DARPA proposal was 'basically a road map to a SARS-CoV-2-like virus', says virologist Simon Wain-Hobson.[95] It was rejected, but this doesn't rule out the possibility that EcoHealth and the WIV carried out the research anyway, possibly using other sources of funding.[96] After all, even the NIH admits that it had no direct oversight of the research conducted in Wuhan, having to rely on annual reports by EcoHealth.[97] As Jamie Metzl, a senior fellow at the Atlantic Council who sits on the WHO's advisory committee on human genome editing, noted: 'If I applied for funding to paint Central Park purple and was denied, but then a year later we woke up to find Central Park painted purple, I'd be a prime suspect.'[98]

In light of all this, it's hardly surprising that in the early days of the pandemic, at the highest levels of the US establishment, the question of whether the virus might have been engineered at the WIV, possibly through research part-funded by the US government, was taken very seriously.[99] Dr Robert Redfield, a virologist and the Director of the Centers for Disease Control and Prevention (CDC) at the time, privately urged Fauci, Farrar, and Tedros Adhanom Ghebreyesus, the Director-General of the

World Health Organization, to 'vigorously investigate' both the lab and natural hypotheses.[100]

To Redfield, it seemed not only possible but likely that the virus had originated in a lab. 'I personally felt it wasn't biologically plausible that [SARS CoV-2] went from bats to humans through an [intermediate] animal and became one of the most infectious viruses to humans', he told *Vanity Fair*[101]—a position he maintains to this day.[102] As we know, his concerns were shared by several of the scientists who were part of the 1 February conference call. However, Redfield—who arguably had every right, as Director of the CDC, to be kept in the loop—was excluded from the ensuing discussions, learning only later that they'd even occurred.[103]

When he saw the *Lancet* letter, with Farrar's name attached to it, Redfield realised that there had been a coordinated effort to construct the appearance of a scientific consensus in favour of a natural origin. 'Their goal was to have a single narrative. [...] They made a decision, almost a PR decision, that they were going to push one point of view only', stated Redfield. 'They argued they did it in defense of science, but it was antithetical to science'.[104] Ghebreyesus seemed to adhere to the same narrative as the *Lancet* signatories. A few days after Redfield reached out to him, on 30 January, he spoke of the need to 'combat the spread of rumours and misinformation' and for countries 'to work together in a spirit of solidarity'.[105]

That said, given the nexus between the Wuhan lab, Daszak, Fauci, and NIH Director Francis Collins, it is also understandable why Fauci and Collins appear to have been so adamant about nipping the lab leak hypothesis in the bud, just like Daszak. Regarding the 1 February call, notes likely communicating Collins's position state that experts needed to be convened to support the theory of 'natural origin' or the 'voices of conspiracy will quickly dominate, doing great harm to science and international harmony'.[106]

Collins subsequently went on to say that claims that SARS CoV-2 was engineered were 'outrageous', pointing to '[a] new study [that] debunks such claims by providing scientific evidence that this novel coronavirus arose naturally'.[107] The study in question was the *Nature* letter signed by Kristian Andersen and others who had previously noted that some features of the virus 'look engineered'.[108] Then, in April 2020, Collins once again asked officials at the NIH to 'put down' the 'very destructive conspiracy' that the virus was engineered.[109] That same month, Fauci too cited the 'proximal origin' letter during a press conference, claiming that a recently published analysis from a 'group of highly qualified evolutionary virologists' had concluded that the virus was 'totally consistent with a jump of a species from an animal to a human'.[110] The next day, Daszak sent an email of profuse thanks to Fauci for 'publicly standing up and stating that the scientific evidence supports a natural origin for Covid-19 from a bat-to-human spillover, not a lab release from the Wuhan Institute of Virology'. Fauci responded, thanking him back.[111] The following month, Fauci told *National Geographic* that this virus '*could not* have been artificially or deliberately manipulated' (emphasis added), leaving no room for doubt.[112]

***

In a particularly troubling turn of events, in mid-2021 an evolutionary biologist named Jesse D. Bloom discovered that at some point after March 2020, a number of early SARS-CoV-2 genomic sequences had been deleted from the NIH's own archive at the request of researchers in Wuhan.[113] He therefore sent a pre-print of the paper detailing his findings to Fauci and Collins, in order to solicit their help in identifying the deleted sequences.[114] Collins immediately convened a conference call with several scientists, including Andersen and Garry from the infamous 1 February call.

After Bloom described his research, the Zoom meeting became 'extremely contentious', he wrote.[115] Andersen leapt in, saying that he found the pre-print 'deeply troubling', and that 'if the Chinese authors had decided to delete their data, it was unethical for [Bloom] to analyze it further'. Andersen also said that he was a screener at the pre-print server to which Bloom had uploaded his paper and that 'he could delete the pre-print or revise it in a way that would leave no trace that this had been done'. At that point the call was over. The NIH never provided Bloom with the information he requested, neither pertaining to the actual sequences nor to the possible reason for their deletion.[116]

That wasn't the first time that some genomic samples and sequences pertaining to SARS-CoV-2 had disappeared. In May 2020, the Chinese authorities confirmed that they had ordered unauthorised laboratories to destroy all coronavirus samples from early in the outbreak, reportedly for 'laboratory biological safety' reasons.[117] Moreover, in September 2019, three months before the officially recognised start of the pandemic, the Wuhan Institute of Virology took down its database of some 22,000 virus samples and sequences (later citing 'repeated hacking attempts' as the motive)[118], and it has since refused to restore it despite international requests.[119] To date, Daszak has consistently refused to release that data. 'We don't think it's fair that we should have to reveal everything we do', he told *Nature* magazine in August 2021.

A year before Daszak gave that interview, in which he defended his refusal to provide information potentially relevant to the understanding of SARS-CoV-2, *The Lancet* had launched its Covid-19 Commission, chaired by Jeffrey Sachs.[120] The Commission set up several task forces in areas ranging from vaccine development to global economic recovery. The man appointed to chair the task force tasked with establishing 'the origins of Covid-19'—and this is where truth becomes stranger than fiction—was Peter Daszak. It may not surprise readers to learn that the Commission concluded that 'the evidence to date supports the view that SARS-CoV-2 is a naturally occurring virus rather than the result of laboratory creation and release'.[121]

Daszak was dismissed from the task force in June of 2021, following the revelation that he had orchestrated the February 2020 *Lancet* letter, in which he had claimed with a neck brassier even than those of the admittedly stiff competition, that he had no relevant interests to declare. That same month *The Lancet* posted an addendum to the February 2020 statement, discussing EcoHealth Alliance's funding of researchers in China and studies involving recombinant bat viruses.[122]

Daszak's credibility took a further hit when Sachs, the chair of the *Lancet* Commission, published an essay that same month calling for an independent investigation of the pandemic's origin and charging that both China and the NIH should be transparent about its coronavirus research, including any gain-of-function studies.[123] 'It is clear that the NIH co-funded research at the WIV that deserves scrutiny under the hypothesis of a laboratory-related release of the virus', Sachs wrote. A few months later the 'origins of Covid' task force was disbanded altogether when it was revealed that even the new chairman had ties to Daszak and his EcoHealth Alliance, and that several members of the task force had collaborated with Daszak or EHA on projects in the past.[124]

The strangeness, however, doesn't end here. Because prior to these revelations, in November 2020, the WHO had announced the names of eleven international experts assigned to a fact-finding mission to China to investigate the origins of the virus, in cooperation with the Chinese authorities.[125] There had been only one US representative on the list: Peter Daszak. Unsurprisingly, the WHO-China's final report, published in March 2021, found that the virus was most likely zoonotic (that is, natural) in origin, and that transmission through a laboratory incident was 'extremely unlikely'.[126] This conclusion was largely based on 'statements from WIV senior staff' themselves.[127] The report was so 'error-riddled and unpersuasive', *Vanity Fair* writes,[128] that WHO Director-General Ghebreyesus effectively disowned it the day it was released. 'As far as [the] WHO is concerned all hypotheses remain on the table', he said.[129]

Several prominent scientists, in an open letter to the WHO, called for a new investigation into the origins of the virus, saying the previous investigation was deeply flawed.[130] The US and thirteen other governments also complained that it 'lacked access to complete, original data and samples'.[131] The WHO responded by establishing, some months later, the Scientific Advisory Group on the Origins of Novel Pathogens (SAGO), with a mandate to complete 'an independent evaluation of all available scientific and technical findings [...] on the origins of SARS-CoV-2'.[132] The group called on China to supply raw data to help any new investigation but China declined, citing patient privacy rules.[133] SAGO published its first preliminary report in June 2022.[134] The results of the new investigation were inconclusive, largely because 'key pieces of data' from China were missing, the report noted, leading the WHO to assert in its strongest terms yet that a deeper probe was required into whether a lab accident may be to blame. 'That stance marks a sharp reversal of the UN health agency's initial assessment of the pandemic's origins, and comes after many critics accused WHO of being too quick to dismiss or underplay a lab-leak theory that put Chinese officials on the defensive', the Associated Press commented.[135] Jean-Claude Manuguerra, a co-chair of the twenty-seven-member international advisory group, acknowledged that some scientists might be 'allergic' to the idea of investigating the lab leak theory, but said they needed to be 'open-minded' enough to examine it.[136] 'Tragically, the Chinese government is still refusing to share essential raw data and will not allow the necessary, full audit of the Wuhan labs', Jamie Metzl, who sits on an unrelated WHO advisory group, said. 'Gaining access to this information is critical to both understanding how this pandemic began and preventing future pandemics'.[137]

Shortly before SAGO released its report, *Lancet* Commission chair Jeffrey Sachs co-authored a paper in the *Proceedings of the National Academy of Sciences* calling for an independent inquiry into the virus's origins.[138] He said there was clear proof that the NIH and many members of the scientific community had been impeding a serious investigation into the origins of Covid-19 in order to cover up evidence that US-funded research in Wuhan may have played a role in the creation of the SARS-CoV-2 virus.[139] He pointed in particular to the NIH's systematic refusal to release important documents pertaining to the research funded in Wuhan, and to the fact that when it was finally forced by a court to release some of the relevant material, as part of an ongoing litigation by the news organisation *The Intercept*, 292 out of the 314 pages—more than 90 per cent of the release—were completely redacted.[140]

In August 2022, the NIH terminated part of its grant to EcoHealth Alliance when the latter did not immediately notify the agency after its experiments showed modified coronaviruses replicated at a faster rate in experimental mice than an unmodified virus. The agency then asked for lab notebooks and other files pertaining to the experiments, and EcoHealth reported that it would relay the request to the WIV. According to the new NIH letters, the Wuhan institute never delivered.[141] Nevertheless, in a sign of how furiously the US Health Establishment is sticking to its story, in October 2022 it was reported that Daszak's outfit had received a further US$600,000 in funding from Fauci's NIAID—in spite of the fact that by this time there had been numerous calls for him to be subpoenaed over the Wuhan connection, including by the editorial board of the *Washington Post*.[142]

In light of all of this, it's safe to say that the lab leak hypothesis is no longer considered a 'fringe' or 'crackpot' theory. In the absence of any conclusive evidence demonstrating the opposite, the theory is today acknowledged as being a very real (or even likely) possibility by several prominent scientists and politicians and by the WHO, as well as by countless intelligence reports (not least the report commissioned by the Biden administration).[143]

That said, SARS-CoV-2 may ultimately be conclusively proven to be natural in origin, as many scientists, undoubtedly in good faith, claim it is. We take no stand in the scientific debate over the origin of the virus, as we are unqualified to do so. Neither do we believe that the events recounted in the preceding pages represent proof that the virus escaped from the Wuhan lab, and even less so that the release was deliberate.

However, they do undeniably point towards a massive cover-up having been orchestrated from the earliest days of the pandemic by leading members of the scientific establishment, and the Chinese authorities. This cover-up was apparently aimed at stifling an open scientific debate over the origin of the virus, shutting down any mention of a possible lab leak and imposing 'a single narrative', as Redfield said.[144] They also show conclusively the deep connections between the scientific and political-military establishments, through the role of organisations such as DARPA in funding coronavirus research—something which may also explain how a scientific question so quickly became radically politicised, and indeed how the Covid response so rapidly became militarised.

To be clear, not even this is proof that the Wuhan lab was involved. It's just as plausible that the simple *possibility* of a lab leak, based on the rather damning circumstantial evidence, would have been sufficient to put in motion the cover-up, given that the stakes for many of the powerful individuals and institutions involved couldn't have been higher. We may conclude that some of the protagonists of this story *believed* there was a good chance the virus might have escaped from the lab (which doesn't mean it *did*)—and acted accordingly.

Nor should we impugn the motives behind this decision: tensions between the US and China were high during the Trump presidency, and the scientists may well have feared that proof of the Wuhan lab's involvement could have had disastrous geopolitical consequences. This alongside, of course, fears for personal reputations may reasonably have shaped the consensus that emerged. What is clear is that an apparent panic led to a specific and coordinated policy decision, which involved stifling dissent and trying to ridicule something that was in fact quite plausible, without any scientific evidence to justify this procedure.

'A small group of scientists, and a larger group of science journalists, established and enforced the false narrative that scientific evidence supported natural spillover, and (also) the false narrative that this was the scientific consensus', said Richard Ebright, a molecular biologist and biosafety expert at Rutgers University in New Jersey.[145] According to him, the *Lancet* and *Nature* letters 'were not scientific papers, they did not present scientific evidence, they did not analyse and support scientific data, they were presenting opinion, they did not belong in scientific journals'.[146] As for the role of the WHO, Richard Horton, editor-in-chief of *The Lancet*, wrote in early 2022 that '[t]he allegation that [it] share[s] responsibility for the pandemic by adopting a policy of appeasement towards China has proven impossible to refute'.[147] Others, however, noted the instrumental role of *The Lancet* in establishing the 'consensus on origins', and point to the fact that it has three editorial offices: in London, New York—and Beijing.[148]

As a final note, it should be mentioned that China has also been peddling its own lab leak theory, alleging that the virus originated in the United States at Fort Detrick, a US Army research facility in Maryland.[149] However, as noted, it is not our concern to establish the rights or wrongs of any of these theories: our interest instead lies in exploring the methods through which the scientific establishment operated in the early times of the pandemic, and the consequences this had for the approach to science and politics.

Ultimately, the story of the suppression of the origin-of-the-virus debate is possibly even more relevant than that the origin of the virus itself. It sheds light on the deeply unscientific manner in which the 'scientific consensus' about many aspects of the pandemic came about, and how some of the leading actors of the pandemic tragedy—the WHO, Fauci, the NIH, and leading scientific journals such as *Nature* and *The Lancet*—were already engaging in the publication of papers which traduced the scientific method from the very first days of the pandemic. In many ways this set the stage for the disaster that would unfold in the coming months and years—and which is the topic of this book. Following one panic-driven coordinated act of academic and anti-scientific bullying, others followed as public health took the reins of political power—with catastrophic consequences for public health itself.

2

THE LOCKDOWN NIGHTMARE BEGINS

As recalled at the beginning of the previous chapter, Chinese authorities announced the discovery of the novel coronavirus (later named SARS-CoV-2) in early January 2020. On 11 January, Chinese state media reported the first known death from an illness caused by the virus[1]—what would later be called Covid-19. A week later, the WHO Western Pacific Regional Office (WHO/WPRO) tweeted that, according to the latest information received and WHO analysis, there was evidence of limited human-to-human transmission.[2] Chinese president Xi Jinping confirmed this on 20 January.[3] In the following days, the first cases outside mainland China were confirmed—in Japan, South Korea, Thailand,[4] and the United States.[5]

Then, on 23 January, China caught the world by surprise by announcing that it had imposed a 'lockdown' on Wuhan as a quarantine measure: residents were barred from leaving, airports and rail stations were closed, and buses, subways, and ferries within the city were suspended; at this point, however, residents were still allowed to leave their homes. The following day, citizens in twelve other cities of the Hubei province were also subjected to lockdown restrictions, bringing the number of people affected by the restrictions to more than 50 million.[6] By then, at least seventeen people had officially died of the virus and more than 570 others had been infected.[7]

It has been argued that China's response was in part driven by the negative press that it had received owing to its response to the SARS outbreak in 2003.[8] At that time, China had faced widespread criticisms, due to its lack of openness and an allegedly chaotic response.[9] There can be no doubt that Xi Jinping was keen to prove that the country had changed its state of alertness and capacity to restrain the spread of a virus. Once the novel coronavirus had been detected, he ordered that the prevention and control of its spread be the top priority for all levels of government.[10] This is probably why China then implemented measures which everyone agreed to be unprecedented.

At the time, the Western media gave ample space to a series of disturbing videos purporting to have come from Wuhan, and showing multiple people suddenly collapsing in the street or in office buildings.[11] In one of the videos, a man can be seen lying on the floor inside what appears to be a bank as people wearing masks look on. Another one depicts CCTV footage of a person wearing a face mask standing on the street, before collapsing to the floor as others rush to help. Even the *Guardian* published the picture of the man lying in the street surrounded by workers in protective suits, calling it 'the image that captures the Wuhan coronavirus crisis'.[12] Of course, we now know that Covid doesn't cause people to suddenly fall dead in the street. Subsequent research revealed that a number of the videos had fraudulent origins.[13] It's therefore hard to see those videos as anything other than propaganda, whose origin remains unknown.

It worked. Within a few months, the imposition of lockdowns to combat the spread of SARS-CoV-2 would become standard procedure in most countries around the world. Those who diverged from the consensus on lockdowns would be painted as crank scientists who wanted to 'let the virus rip' with lethal consequences, and their motivations would be impugned.[14] However, at the time of the Wuhan lockdown's imposition on 23 January, the WHO representative in China, Gauden Galea, declared to the Associated Press that 'the lockdown of 11 million people is unprecedented in public health history so it is certainly not a recommendation that the WHO has made'.[15] 'To my knowledge, trying to contain a city of 11 million people is new to science. It has not been tried before as a public health measure', Mr Galea added.[16]

Galea nonetheless commended the move, saying that sealing off Wuhan was 'a very important indication of the commitment to contain the epidemic in the place where it is most concentrated'.[17] A week later on 30 January, following the visit of a WHO delegation to China led by its Director-General Tedros Adhanom Ghebreyesus, the Organization declared the outbreak a Public Health Emergency of International Concern (PHEIC).[18] On that occasion, the WHO also praised the 'leadership and the political commitment of the very highest levels of Chinese government, their commitment to transparency, and the efforts made to investigate and contain the current outbreak'.[19]

It was not only Mr Galea who realised that this approach to controlling Covid-19 represented an unprecedented move in medical history. In an article in the *Washington Post* on 25 January, Howard Markel, a Professor of the History of Medicine at the University of Michigan, was quoted as saying: 'This is just mind-boggling: this is the mother of all quarantines. I could never have imagined it.'[20] Lawrence O. Gostin, a Professor of Public Health at Georgetown University in Washington, DC, added: 'The truth is that these kinds of lockdowns are very rare and never effective.'[21] As Baltimore's former Health Commissioner Leana Wen put it: 'We worked on numerous contingency plans to respond to outbreaks and public health crises. To my knowledge, our health department had not considered a citywide quarantine.'[22]

She was right: in all the pre-2020 influenza pandemic preparedness plans drawn up by the WHO or by national governments, the notion of city-wide, and certainly of nation-wide, quarantines wasn't even conceived of. Indeed, the WHO's 2019 report on 'Non-pharmaceutical public health measures for mitigating the risk and impact of epidemic and pandemic influenza', published in November just a few months before the SARS-CoV-2 outbreak, states that the quarantine of exposed individuals—let alone of the entire population—'is not recommended because there is no obvious rationale for this measure'.[23] It also claims that 'under no circumstances', however severe the outbreak, should contact tracing be adopted, due to its limited effectiveness, but also due to 'ethical concerns', especially 'when [...] coupled with measures such as household quarantine'. Indeed, it's instructive to note that in an interview for this book, the lead author of this report, Ben Cowling of Hong Kong University, noted that it was based on the existing state of knowledge regarding non-pharmaceutical interventions (NPIs) in public health.[24] The word 'lockdown' is not mentioned once in the report, so it's safe to say that there simply was no evidence or research suggesting that lockdowns were an appropriate model for public health prior to 2020 (something we come back to in more detail in Chapter 6). Moreover, the *Oxford English Dictionary* did not record the use of the word 'lockdown' in a public health sense prior to 2020.[25]

Instead, all pre-2020 pandemic plans were essentially based around the same philosophy: carefully balance the costs and benefits of all interventions according to the principles of proportionality and flexibility, minimise the disruptions to everyday social and economic life, and focus the resources on protecting those at risk. 'Almost all [pre-pandemic planning guides before the coronavirus] emphasized respect for civil rights, disrupting societies as little as possible, protecting the vulnerable, and not spreading panic', says Dr Jay Bhattacharya, Professor of Medicine at Stanford University. 'The lockdowns and the media narrative and the public health narrative of March 2020 violated all those principles.'[26]

This is clear in some of the plans which were initially developed to deal with SARS-CoV-2. For example, the state of Victoria in Australia (subsequently the state which had the longest lockdowns in the world), published a plan on 10 March 2020 as to how to deal with the pending pandemic. One of the four guiding principles of this report, entitled 'COVID-19: Pandemic Plan for the Victorian Health Sector', was that the response should be 'focused on protecting vulnerable Victorians, including those with underlying health conditions, compromised immune systems, the elderly, Aboriginal and Torres Strait Islanders, and those from culturally and linguistically diverse communities'.[27] While already-existing pandemic literature naturally could not make Covid-19-specific recommendations, a well-established understanding of the general ineffectiveness of universal non-pharmaceutical interventions for respiratory viruses is clear in this text. But this awareness largely went unheeded as media- and government-driven fear gripped the population in early 2020. Focused protection of the vulnerable—far from following some racist libertarian paradigm—was standard public health until then. From the March 2020 viewpoint, it certainly seemed more progressive than the focused protection of what became known as "the laptop class", which was what followed.

The fact was that these measures had never been adopted in any previous twentieth-century epidemic or pandemic: the 1918–20 Spanish flu (estimated to have killed as many as 50 million people worldwide), the 1957–58 influenza pandemic, the 1968–69 Hong Kong flu, or more recently the 2002–4 SARS outbreak and the 2009 H1N1 swine flu pandemic. On all those occasions, the norm had been to protect those most at risk, close the worst-infected areas for short periods of time, and introduce moderate elements of social distancing.[28]

The 2009 swine flu pandemic is particularly striking in terms of just how different the response was compared to Covid. At the time, the world was gripped by the fear of another new and potentially lethal disease, the H1N1 virus, or swine flu. This broke out in Mexico in the first part of 2009 before spreading around the world. At the time, there was a genuine alarm at the risks that the new virus might hold for the human population. When reflecting on the onset of Covid-19 in 2020, it's worth comparing this with the response to swine flu, so that we can better assess what has happened now.

The predictions at the time were universally grim. In mid-July 2009, the United Kingdom's Chief Medical Officer, Sir Liam Donaldson, estimated that up to 65,000 people might die in the UK, and that, in the best-case scenario, there would be a mortality of 3,100.[29] One of the leading figures in developing the initial modelling projections was Neil Ferguson, who as most readers will know would go on to play a crucial role in the Covid pandemic as well. In the US, the CDC estimated on 24 July 2009 that between 20 and 40 per cent of the American population would be stricken with the H1N1 virus over the ensuing two years. According to the WHO, two billion infections globally was 'a reasonable ballpark to be looking at'. Even though at that time there had been only 130,000 confirmed infections, Keiji Fukuda, a senior WHO official, said that the likely figure was much higher than this, with 100,000 reported infections in the UK and a million suspected in the US—and that these were the early days of the pandemic's spread. Initial estimates suggested that the number of deaths in the US could range between 90,000 and several hundred thousand.[30]

These projected levels of mortality were especially alarming since swine flu was known to be a virus which targeted children and young people (indeed, 80 per cent of those who eventually died from the pandemic were aged under sixty-five—virtually the inverse of the mortality with Covid-19).[31] This meant that although the initial projections of mortality were lower than with Covid-19, the number of life-years lost calculated through these projections was not incomparable. Unlike the case with the novel coronavirus, such projections and the age profile of the dead meant that swine flu could have had a major impact on the working population and provision of services. Yet while there was concern there was no considerable public alarm, and senior medical figures wisely cautioned against an overreaction. As the *Guardian* reported: '[UK Chief Medical Officer] Donaldson warned against panic about the projected death toll from a swine flu pandemic, noting that there had been 21,000 extra deaths over the winter of 1999–2000 due to seasonal flu and this had raised little public concern'.[32]

Meanwhile, the global medical community geared itself into action. As with Covid-19, much emphasis was placed on the development of a vaccine, the so-called Tamiflu jab.[33] In the end a vaccine was available after six months, in October 2009.[34] Where there were significant outbreaks of the virus, moderate social distancing and quarantine measures were implemented. In Mexico, schools closed between 27 April and 10 May, public events were cancelled, and public spaces closed, while commercial activity ceased, but there was no prohibition of socialising or family visits, and after this fortnight normal social life resumed.[35] In 2009, these were the measures deemed proportionate and effective to limit the spread and mortality of a virus known to target overwhelmingly the working-age population.

In the end, the dire predictions turned out to have been just that—predictions. This is discussed below in the context of Professor Neil Ferguson's modelling projections. However, several lessons could have been learnt from the swine flu pandemic of 2009. Globally, the H1N1 virus was certainly a serious disease, and in fact somewhere between 150,000 and 540,000 people died worldwide.[36] As mentioned above, 80 per cent of these fatalities were in people aged under sixty-five, and the projections had been that the death rate would be much higher. National governments such as Mexico's implemented quarantine measures but these were time-restricted to no more than a couple of weeks, and the idea of shutting down huge swathes of society for up to a year simply never occurred to policymakers and public health experts. As it turned out, society continued to function, and the initial projections of the WHO and Ferguson's team proved to have been exaggerated. As the *Guardian* had reported, the best approach was not to panic, to implement in a timely manner measured and time-restricted local restrictions which protected the vulnerable, to put everything into developing a safe vaccine as quickly as possible, and in the meantime to isolate especially severe outbreaks for as short a time as possible. This was in keeping with the response to previous pandemics. As Peter Doshi and David Robertson wrote, in all previous twentieth-century pandemics 'life either wasn't interrupted or returned to normal quickly'.[37]

On the other hand, the shutting down of entire countries and quarantining of entire populations to stop the spread of a virus had certainly never been taken into consideration, let alone implemented, prior to Wuhan. It's important to be clear as to the novelty of these measures. In the first place, the concept of the lockdown was not one which came from public health. Instead, it came from the US prison service. In the 1970s, the concept of the lockdown began to be used to refer to 'an extended state of confinement for inmates of prisons or psychiatric hospitals'.[38] This is a word which came out of the mass overcrowding and racialised abuse of the US prison system and the disturbing psychiatric hospitals of *One Flew Over the Cuckoo's Nest*—not contexts which most people would associate with a humane and socially responsible model of public healthcare. The lockdown model of disease control emerged from the context of the violent and brutal control of confined spaces; some would argue that it still bears many hallmarks of these origins.

It's no coincidence that the only instance where lockdowns had been used as a means of disease control had first occurred— as with so many new Western medical interventions in the twentieth and twenty-first centuries—on the African continent. When no one could deny the harms that the lockdowns had caused, some of the Twitterati started to point out that there was nothing novel about lockdowns, as they had been implemented in Sierra Leone and Liberia during the Ebola epidemic of 2014– 15.[39] This was indeed the case: 72-hour-long lockdowns were implemented in both Freetown and Monrovia to try to halt the spread of Ebola, a disease which has an infection fatality rate (IFR) between 25 per cent and 90 per cent.[40] But those episodes were not remotely comparable to the open-ended lockdown that had just been announced in China—and nor, of course, did they become globalised.

Moreover, they were not deemed a success by global health professionals. Prior to their implementation, Médécins Sans Frontières (MSF) warned against them.[41] Riots were caused when they were introduced in Monrovia, given the essential nature of movement to informal economies in Africa.[42] In 2021, Llanos Ortíz Montero, the recently retired Deputy-Director of MSF Spain, who had worked through the Ebola epidemic in Freetown, expressed shock that they had nevertheless been implemented again during the Covid-19 pandemic.[43]

Thus, as a basis for the universal rollout of the lockdown policy, the experiences of Liberia and Sierra Leone during the

Ebola crisis were a non-starter. Subsequent studies suggested that the West African lockdown experiment had not been effective, due to creating distrust towards public health and the government in those communities targeted by the measure:

> The president acknowledged the situation as 'difficult', although this significantly underplays the nature of the food shortages that affected some of the quarantined areas and forced people to break quarantine. Aside from the ethical concerns, many felt that mass quarantine measures were ineffective for Ebola as patients are not infectious until they become symptomatic, and they may have been counterproductive by preventing the free movement of necessary medical supplies and personnel.[44]

Even more interesting is the way Western public health experts reacted to the Ebola crisis. When it became clear that the virus had arrived in the US, killing one man in Texas and infecting two of his caregivers, a debate arose about whether temporarily to quarantine health workers returning from treating Ebola patients in Africa. Initially, New York Governor Andrew Cuomo, a Democrat, and New Jersey Governor Chris Christie, a Republican, wanted to quarantine those coming back into the NYC airports, with Christie saying: 'The government's job is to protect the safety and health of our citizens',[45] and 'I don't think when you're dealing with something as serious as this you can count on a voluntary system. This is the government's job.'[46] When Kaci Hickox, an American nurse, arrived at Newark Liberty International Airport after treating Ebola patients in Sierra Leone and became the first person placed in mandatory quarantine, the decision came under heavy fire from several quarters, including Obama administration officials and, once again, Médecins Sans Frontières, who claimed the policy was 'not grounded in science'.[47] Surprisingly, Anthony Fauci himself— who would become one of the most vehement pro-lockdown advocates in 2020—claimed at the time that quarantining people who had been in contact with Ebola was 'a little bit draconian'.[48] The same position was echoed in the liberal press as well.[49] In other words, the same people who in 2014 argued that putting a few people who had been in close contact with the deadliest virus in the world in temporary quarantine was 'draconian' and 'anti-science' would go on to promote the need to shut down entire countries to counter a significantly less deadly disease in 2020. Whatever readers might make of this particular turnabout, this makes it pretty clear on any number of levels that Ebola lockdowns can't be seen as a precedent for what happened in 2020–21.

Others may point to earlier experiences in medieval Europe of the closure of infected towns and villages during outbreaks of disease. And certainly this was a part of the historic experience of many in the era of the Black Death and other pandemics. However, notable features of these quarantines were that they targeted diseases such as smallpox and plague which had very high IFRs (close to that of Ebola), and that in these cases it was only areas with symptoms that were closed. Neither feature is approximate to that of Covid-19, where the IFR was incomparably lower.

In sum, there was no historically comparable precedent for the Covid-19 lockdowns. There was nothing unprecedented about the infectious disease discovered in Wuhan; what was utterly unprecedented was the response. It's hardly surprising that most scientists in January 2020 doubted that the Chinese lockdown would work. As the *Guardian* reported on 23 January: 'There is also no guarantee that a lockdown will work to contain the virus. If it is indeed spreading fast and widely, then more and more cases are going to pop up all over the country regardless.'[50] As readers are probably aware, and as discussed in Chapter 6, this is indeed precisely what happened—regardless of the suppression measures that were taken, once it was present, the virus spread rapidly where there was no cross-immunity from previous coronaviruses.

In general, the initial reaction of most Western commentators to the measures adopted in Wuhan ranged from scepticism to outright concern, especially as Chinese authorities proceeded, in mid-February, to introduce even tighter measures by banning all residents of the Hubei province—almost 60 million people—from leaving their homes, except to buy supplies every three days. This was even more 'brutal' and unprecedented, the *Guardian* noted.[51] Reuters reported that '[o]fficials and volunteers have sealed off buildings, erected barricades and stepped up surveillance to ensure compliance with the ban on movement, measures that are taking a toll on many in the community.'[52]

The same Reuters article noted that 'police and volunteers [are] using force to penalize residents for even gathering in groups'. 'You have to address the basic rights and well-being of people: can they get their food and water? What is their mental health status?' said Rebecca Katz, Director of the Center for Global Health Science and Security at Georgetown University.[53] Western media outlets reacted in dismay at the totalitarian scope of the containment policies employed in Wuhan, such as 'using drones to scold people in Inner Mongolia—more than 1,000 km from Wuhan—who had gone out without masks'.[54]

At the time, the consensus in the West was still that such extreme policies might be feasible in an authoritarian state such as China, but would be impossible to implement in Western democracies. Indeed, throughout most of the month of February 2020, despite rising cases, public authorities in the West downplayed the dangerousness of the virus, and the risk of it becoming a serious concern to the rest of the world. Even the WHO would later come under fire for opposing global travel restrictions against China on 4 February, just a week after labelling the outbreak a Public Health Emergency of

International Concern, on account that this would have 'the effect of increasing fear and stigma, with little public health benefit'.[55] Outside of China, the spread of the virus was garnering growing media attention but panic still hadn't set in, and the chances, or even the necessity, of Wuhan-style measures being implemented elsewhere were still viewed as extremely remote.

**

All this changed in the last week of February. Firstly, Italy, faced with the first major Covid outbreak outside of China,[56] placed eleven municipalities in the northern Lombardy region under quarantine, covering a population of around 50,000 people.[57] This was still in keeping with traditional quarantining protocols that had been used for centuries, and had also been deployed during the H1N1 swine flu pandemic of 2009: isolating places where the virus was present on a very local level.

Secondly, and even more importantly, the next day, on 24 February, the WHO published the report of its first fact-finding mission to China, co-authored by Dr Bruce Aylward of the WHO and Dr Wannian Liang from the Chinese Ministry of Health.[58] After claiming unequivocally that 'Covid-19 is a zoonotic virus'[59]—a position it would subsequently revise, adopting a more nuanced stance, as we have seen—the report proceeded to analyse China's response to the epidemic. It started out by making it clear that it was the Chinese leadership who had disregarded the recommendations of the aforementioned November 2019 WHO pandemic response report regarding contact tracing and quarantining of those who had been exposed to sick individuals. Keen to follow Xi Jinping's directives to suppress the virus, all avenues were explored, regardless of precedent or international public health policy.

The WHO report noted China's policies of virus suppression. 'China has a policy of meticulous case and contact identification for Covid-19', the report's authors said. 'For example, in Wuhan more than 1,800 teams of epidemiologists, with a minimum of 5 people/team, are tracing tens of thousands of contacts a day.'[60] Furthermore, they noted approvingly, '[t]he *cordon sanitaire* around Wuhan and neighboring municipalities imposed since 23 January 2020 has effectively prevented further exportation of infected individuals to the rest of the country.'[61] In the meantime, close contacts were isolated and placed under medical supervision—something which the November report had said should be done 'under no circumstances'. However, the unprecedented nature of this policy was not discussed in the report, and nor was the way in which all of this contravened the WHO policies on non-pharmaceutical interventions as they had just been set out a few months before—these elements and their implications were now forgotten in the rush to study, and almost extol, China's policy of virus suppression.

The authors noted that this was 'perhaps the most ambitious, agile, and aggressive disease containment effort in history'— with the positive adjectives now leading the way in assessment of the response, and the aggression all but forgotten.[62] But how had China managed to do this? The report authors found the 'uncompromising rigor of strategy application' to be 'striking', going on to assert that 'achieving China's exceptional coverage with and adherence to these containment measures has only been possible due to the deep commitment of the Chinese people to collective action in the face of this common threat'.[63]

Lost in these interpretations of the strategy and response to Covid-19 was any political context: that China was one of the most authoritarian nations on Earth, that any strategy imposed by the top levels of Chinese government would certainly be followed by 'uncompromising rigor', and that 'deep commitment' to national priorities was essential for anyone in China hoping to live a life more or less free from political interference and/

or persecution. These socio-political contexts of the health emergency were irrelevant to the concerns of 'pure science'—but they were not irrelevant to the life chances and experiences of the world and its human population.

The concluding pages of the 24 February report proposed strategies for combatting Covid-19, in which the recommendations of the November 2019 report were abandoned. It stressed that 'to reduce Covid-19 illness and death, near-term readiness planning must embrace the large-scale implementation of high-quality, non-pharmaceutical public health measures', such as case detection and isolation, contact tracing, and monitoring/quarantining. Countries with confirmed cases should also plan to deploy 'even more stringent measures to interrupt transmission chains as needed (e.g. the suspension of large-scale gatherings and the closure of schools and workplaces)'.[64]

The 'measures that have been employed to contain Covid-19 in China', the report astonishingly claimed, 'are *the only measures that are currently proven to interrupt or minimize transmission chains in humans*' (emphasis added)[65]—an assertion that ran contrary to the public health measures recommended by the WHO for mitigating epidemic and pandemic influenza up until that moment, as noted already. Finally, the report urged all countries to 'prepare to immediately activate the highest level of emergency response mechanisms to trigger the all-of-government and all-of-society approach that is essential for early containment of a Covid-19 outbreak'.[66] So much for proportionality.

Lost in this was the fact that there had been no proper scientific assessment carried out of the effectiveness of these steps, as there had been no 'control' in the experiment: the Chinese case was the very first in which it had been attempted. And although the WHO was convinced that China's 'aggressive' suppression measures were leading to the virus's decline, they failed to consider that other factors may have been at play—

including existing cross-immunity from previous coronaviruses such as SARS, later confirmed by subsequent scientific work,[67] as well as the dubious credibility of the statistics reported by the Chinese authorities.[68] Nor did this recommendation apparently consider whether the benefit of these policies would differ according to socio-economic conditions: given that one in seven people worldwide live in slums, in which often whole families share cramped conditions, the benefits of confining people together indoors for reducing virus spread were clearly extremely limited in many world contexts.[69]

Incredibly, in the space of just four weeks between the WHO leadership team's visit to Beijing at the end of January and the 24 February report, the decades-long scientific consensus on how to handle epidemics and pandemics was thrown into the dustbin of history, and the policies of one of the most repressive countries in the world became the new global scientific consensus. This was now the gold standard of pandemic management. The lack of any socio-political context in the policy recommendations led to a one-size-fits-all approach which would prove disastrous in other parts of the world with different political traditions, different economic realities, and a different approach to authority.

Indeed, the WHO acknowledged that 'much of the global community is not yet ready, in mindset and materially, to implement the measures that have been employed to contain Covid-19 in China'[70]—but also clearly implied that that needed to change. There was no question that the WHO leadership and the Chinese government were in very close alignment—and when in early March the WHO co-author of the 24 February report, Dr Bruce Aylward, was asked on Hong Kong television about Taiwan's response to the virus, he first lost his connection, and then when he returned responded, 'Well, we've already talked about China'.[71]

The pandemic had yet to be declared, but another fundamental pillar of the single-narrative Covid consensus—the unavoidability and life-saving virtues of lockdowns—had started to crystallise.

Drawing on the new WHO advice, the following day the Italian government started extending the restrictions to numerous other provinces of northern Italy.[72] Within two weeks, a quarter of Italy's population, including all of Lombardy, the country's most populous region, would find itself in quarantine. This was already a radical departure from the measures adopted by China: even though the population of the Hubei province is rather large in absolute terms—almost 60 million people—in relative terms it amounts to only around 4 per cent of the entire Chinese population of 1.4 billion people. Thus, as hard as the Hubei lockdown might have been for the province's residents, its impact on China as a whole was minimal. Quarantining one quarter of a country's population—let alone its entire population, as would soon happen—was a very different kettle of fish, a fact that was lost on many commentators at the time. As for the WHO, it praised Italy for its 'genuine sacrifices' and for 'taking, bold, courageous steps aimed at slowing the spread of the coronavirus and protecting [its] country and the world',[73] just as it had praised China—further reinforcing the lockdown framework.

The Italian government policy first showed signs of moving towards a national framework on 1 March, when ministers divided the country into three zones, or tiers: a red zone where the outbreak was at its worst and a quarantine was in place, a yellow zone where sports and cultural events were suspended and restaurants and bars could only provide table service for clients, and the rest of the country where new hygiene measures were imposed in schools, public buildings, and workplaces.[74] At the time, the government said that these measures would be in place 'at least until 8 March'[75]—but by that date, the country was on the eve of the first national lockdown in world history.

Italy's step-by-step lockdown—a classic example of the frog-in-boiling-water approach, whereby people can be made to accept even radical changes so long as these are introduced gradually—had wide-ranging international ramifications. With the benefit of hindsight, it's clear that the international response to the outbreak of Covid-19 in the country was a major push factor, gearing into place even before the publication of the WHO report on 24 February. As soon as the government had placed the eleven municipalities in quarantine, there were international ramifications. On 23 February, a train travelling from Venice to Munich was stopped at the Austrian border, and a bus heading from Milan to Lyon was intercepted at Lyon-Perrache station over concerns that passengers were exhibiting 'flu-like symptoms'.[76] On 24 February, passengers on an Alitalia flight from Rome were prevented from entering Mauritius and ordered to quarantine for two weeks or return home—forty of them decided to go straight back to Italy.[77] On 27 February, Israel barred entry for passengers from Italy, and the following day Germany implemented new entry requirements which stipulated that passengers from Italy had to declare their medical condition.[78] Numerous other countries started imposing restrictions.

***

Between the end of February and the beginning of March, Covid came to dominate headlines around the world—where it would remain for the following two years, until the Russian invasion of Ukraine. Google searches for 'Covid' and 'coronavirus', which had been scarce up to that moment, exploded.[79] Panic started setting in, as new cases and deaths were confirmed in several countries, though the focus remained on Italy—the hardest-hit country outside China at that point. All of a sudden, Covid was all the world was talking about.

The media companies' increasing reliance on click-baiting strategies for revenue purposes likely played a role in heightening the sense of panic. The increasing dependence of these companies on internet advertising driven by the volume of article clicks certainly did not encourage them to underestimate the severity of the new virus. Some important examples show how this tendency to emphasise alarm in order to attract clicks had a serious impact on the initial reporting of the pandemic. On 23 February, for example, Sky News reported in the United Kingdom that the number of cases of the virus in Italy had 'soared' to two hundred—hardly an appropriate verb to reach for where there had as yet been only seven deaths, and by contrast 634,432 people had died in Italy during 2019.[80]

Right from the start, however, there was little space for critical perspectives. On 14 February, during the Munich Security Conference, WHO Director-General Ghebreyesus declared: 'We're not just fighting an epidemic; we're fighting an infodemic. Fake news spreads faster and more easily than this virus, and is just as dangerous.'[81] 'Our greatest enemy to date is not the virus itself. It's rumours, fear and stigma', he claimed on another occasion.[82] For this reason, he said, the WHO would begin 'working with search and media companies like Facebook, Google, Pinterest, Tencent, Twitter, TikTok, YouTube and others to counter the spread of rumours and misinformation'.[83] Wikipedia was subsequently brought on board as well.[84] Much of the structure was already in place. As discussed in greater detail in Chapter 9, in mid-2019 a new global media framework called the Trusted News Initiative (TNI) had been created, led by the BBC, 'to protect audiences and users from disinformation', with partners consisting of several major news outlets as well as all Big Tech companies.[85] With the onset of the pandemic, the TNI was quick to throw its weight behind 'combatting the spread of harmful vaccine disinformation' and other 'Covid disinformation'.[86]

Over the course of the coming weeks and months, the WHO went on to establish a vast global communications strategy. An agreement was first reached with Google, 'to ensure that people seeking information about coronavirus see WHO information at the top of their search results'.[87] Then, the communications team secured the support of the main social networks and even of companies like Uber and Airbnb to spread the 'right messages'.[88] Finally, the WHO and its partners started recruiting influencers and opinion-makers to ensure control of social networks and of platforms such as YouTube, the world leader in online video (more than two billion monthly users in 2020), owned by Google. Soon thereafter, Facebook announced that it would be 'removing false claims and conspiracy theories that have been flagged by leading global health organisations'[89]—that is, the WHO.

However, at this point in time, relatively little was known about the virus or the disease—for example, about its origin, as we have seen—so it's unclear on what basis a certain claim could have been deemed 'true' or 'false'. It would soon become clear that the 'truth' was whatever the WHO said. As Susan Wojcicki, CEO of YouTube, went on to say in an interview: 'Everything that violates the recommendations of the WHO would constitute a breach against our guidelines. Therefore, deletion is another important part of our guidelines'.[90]

And this was despite the fact that in the early days of the outbreak, the WHO itself was already spreading what can only be described as misinformation—such as the claim that the virus was definitely zoonotic in origin (which wasn't backed by any scientific evidence and which was subsequently rebutted by the WHO itself, as we have seen). Indeed, the debate about the origin of the virus shows that what is deemed a 'false claim' one day can easily become a legitimate one the next—and not because new evidence has been brought to light, but simply because the politics around that claim have changed. Thus, assigning the monopoly over truth to a single organisation was bound to have devastating consequences on the quality of public debate. As we will see, it was also to have a catastrophic impact on the management of the pandemic itself, as traditional and digital media platforms and social networks proceeded relentlessly to censor any critical voice or opinion, no matter how qualified or scientifically solid.

The Covid crisis thus gave rise to an international process of editorial standardisation aimed at ensuring what the French sociologist Pierre Bourdieu called 'the monopoly of legitimate information'.[91] As the French researcher Laurent Mucchielli notes, this was 'a historically unprecedented attempt at global information control',[92] as billions of people throughout the world and across several countries were exposed, for the first time in history, to a single overarching narrative sanctioned by a single supranational organisation—the World Health Organization. In short, the WHO played a crucial role not only in coordinating the response of the various countries but also, and perhaps even more importantly, in harmonising the pandemic narrative across countries. Yet instead of harmony, panic and confusion followed.

An example of this is the claim by the WHO Director-General, on 3 March 2020, that 'globally, about 3.4% of reported Covid-19 cases have died'—a figure that was then tweeted by the WHO.[93] This statistic was then rapidly reported around the world, from the United States and Mexico to Cuba and the United Kingdom.[94] This had the equivalent effect to spraying gasoline over a spreading wildfire of hysteria, as it seemed to be saying that Covid killed, on average, 3.4 per cent of those who caught the virus—a terrifyingly high mortality rate, which was widely reported in the press as such.

Except that it didn't mean that at all. For starters, there is of course a difference between 'cases' and 'infections'. While the mass testing regime has seen anyone who has a trace of Covid-19 in their system designated as a 'case' even if they have no symptoms, traditional definitions are rather different and define cases as those who are symptomatic.[95] There is therefore a strong difference between the CFR—the case fatality rate, indicating the proportion of people diagnosed with a certain disease who end up dying of it, which the WHO was referring to—and the IFR (infection fatality rate), which considers all those who have tested positive but may not have become symptomatic.

Ultimately, however, even the IFR is a very crude estimate of the true lethality of a disease, since it depends on how much testing is carried out. In a closed, small population, determining the IFR is relatively straightforward (since everyone can be tested), but when dealing with very large populations—for example, on a national or global scale—the number of asymptomatic infectees is bound to be much higher than that of those who actually test positive (which in turn depends, of course, on how many tests are carried out, and the extent to which these are limited to people that already exhibit symptoms); thus the true IFR is bound to be much lower than the ratio found through testing. Hence different approaches have been developed to estimate the IFR in large populations,[96] but they remain just that—estimates.

This means that while the CFR of 3.4 per cent was initially being publicised as the mortality risk, the risk was in fact far lower, since many more people were being infected than were becoming actual cases. Indeed, in the initial discussion of these statistics, sources at the WHO had specifically stated that this was not a mortality rate as such (because it was not known how many people had had Covid without being tested), yet there was no correction of this misleading reporting of the statistic by the WHO or by the media outlets in question.[97] It's frankly hard to see this as anything other than misinformation—if not outright disinformation, precisely what the WHO claimed to want to fight. This is what John Ioannidis, one of the world's foremost scholars of medical and scientific methodology and leading critics of the pandemic management, wrote at the time in response to the WHO's announcement:

> Reported case fatality rates, like the official 3.4% rate from the World Health Organization, cause horror—and are meaningless. Patients who have been tested for SARS-CoV-2 are disproportionately those with severe symptoms and bad outcomes. The one situation where an entire, closed population was tested was the Diamond Princess cruise and its quarantined passengers [in February 2020]. The case fatality rate there was 1.0%, but this was a largely elderly population, in which the death rate from Covid-19 is much higher.[98]

Indeed, a study by Ioannidis published a few months later in the *Bulletin of the World Health Organization* would estimate the median IFR to be even lower than that—0.27 per cent, and 0.05 per cent for those under 70[99]—and subsequent analyses would all confirm the median IFR to be between 0.25 and 1 per cent.[100] Moreover, it was already clear by then that Covid-19 is almost exclusively a threat to the elderly and those with pre-existing illnesses, and thus that the IFR depends greatly on age—another detail glossed over by the WHO. As we've seen, Neil Ferguson of Imperial College London said as early as 25 March 2020 that between half and two-thirds of those who died of Covid-19 may have died during the next twelve months anyway.[101] Beyond this, as we will see in the following chapter, several factors combined to overemphasise the true nature of the Covid threat: questionable statistical and data acquisition methods and questions of misattribution of hospitalisation and death, not to mention the role played by government protocols in exacerbating the death toll.

Yet by this point, claiming on social media that the virus's actual lethality was most likely much lower than the one claimed by the WHO exposed one to the risk of censorship and/or banning, and to accusations of 'Covid denialism' in the public arena. Things got even worse when Trump said in a Fox News interview: 'I think the 3.4% number is really a false number. Now, this is just my hunch, but based on a lot of conversations, I'd say the number is way under 1%'.[102] As it turned out, he was right—as even the *New York Times* acknowledged at the time.[103]

However, by then, the coronavirus affair was already starting to get heavily politicised. On the one hand, Trump, who had initially brushed off warnings by his health secretary as 'alarmist',[104] was accused of downplaying the extent of the epidemic; on the other hand, Anthony Fauci, who in January had been appointed by Trump as one of the lead members of the White House Coronavirus Task Force, and who had quickly come to incarnate 'The Science' in the public debate, repeatedly disavowed the president, warning that the outbreak in the US was about to get much worse.[105] Very soon, people's preferences in terms of epidemiological strategies began to closely overlap with their political orientation. It was no longer possible for left-leaning progressives to question 'The Science', since that was what Trump had done. And yet, as we've already seen, 'The Science' had behaved in ways that demanded questioning.

Meanwhile the WHO continued, more or less explicitly, to present lockdowns as the only way to get the virus under control, stating in early March: 'Here we have a disease for which we have no vaccine, no treatment, we don't fully understand transmission, we don't fully understand case mortality, but what we have been genuinely heartened by is that unlike influenza, where countries have fought back, where they've put in place strong measures, we've remarkably seen that the virus is suppressed.'[106] All countries were therefore urged to focus on a single objective: *flattening the curve* of the contagions.[107]

At the same time as the predicted CFR of 3.4 per cent and these potential death rates were circulating, scientists were already publishing research making the case that early intervention and social distancing measures were the best way to prevent catastrophe. In an article published on 5 March, a team of scientists argued that:

> Pre-emptive, low cost, hygiene enhancement and social distancing in the context of imminent community transmission of novel coronavirus Covid-19 should be considered. Early interventions to reduce the average frequency and intensity of exposure to the virus might reduce infection risk, reduce the average viral infectious dose of those exposed, and result in less severe cases who are less infectious. A pre-emptive phase would also assist government, workplaces, schools, and businesses to prepare for a more stringent phase.[108]

The paper was cited in a press conference by Anthony Fauci on 10 March. By the time that other articles had emerged arguing that the risks posed by Covid-19 had been overstated, in a context where 2.6 million people die globally each year of respiratory illnesses and almost 10 million die from cancer,[109] the lockdown nightmares had begun.

11 March 2020 was a crucial turning point. That day the WHO officially declared Covid-19 a pandemic.[110] It's worth observing that while the term instantly conjures up images of doctors in biohazard suits and Hollywood-style doomsday scenarios, '[p]andemics mean different things to different people', as Fauci noted shortly before the WHO's declaration. 'It really is borderline semantics, to be honest with you', he added.[111] Indeed, the WHO's own definition of a pandemic has changed quite a bit over the years.[112] Prior to 2009, the WHO defined an influenza pandemic as something that 'occurs when a new influenza virus appears against which the human population has no immunity, resulting in several simultaneous epidemics worldwide with enormous numbers of deaths and illness'.[113] However, in May

2009, scarcely one month before the H1N1 swine flu pandemic was declared, the WHO web page was altered: the phrase 'enormous numbers of deaths and illness' was removed, and a pandemic was redefined as something that 'may occur when a new influenza virus appears against which the human population has no immunity'.[114] Months later, the Council of Europe would cite this alteration as evidence that the WHO changed its definition of pandemic influenza to enable it to declare a pandemic without having to demonstrate the intensity of the disease caused by the H1N1 virus,[115] causing unnecessary panic. At the time, Wolfgang Wodarg, the epidemiologist then chairing the European Union's Health Committee, criticised the influence of pharmaceutical companies on the WHO's decision-making process.[116] At a subsequent hearing, committee members questioned WHO officials 'about confusion surrounding consideration of severity in its definition of a pandemic, which was revised at about the time the novel H1N1 virus was identified', and it was noted that the declaration of a pandemic triggered lucrative vaccine contracts for powerful pharmaceutical companies.[117] Similar conflicts of interest, as we will see, would later emerge in relation to Covid vaccines as well.

Certainly, had the earlier definition been in place it would have been hard for the WHO to define Covid-19 as a pandemic as early as it did in March 2020—or perhaps ever—leading to the rollout of the lockdown measures. At that point there had been a mere 4,000 deaths worldwide.[118] Anyway, the 2009 definition is the one that stuck. Thus, today the term refers simply to the spread of a certain disease, and says nothing about the severity or preponderance of the illness it causes.[119] Nevertheless, in defining Covid-19 as a pandemic, the WHO's Director-General went out of his way to frame the virus as an enemy threatening nothing less than all of humanity, despite it being already understood at the time that the overwhelming majority of humanity—most people under sixty, around 90 per cent of the global population[120]—would develop at worst 'a mild-to-moderate but self-limiting illness—similar to seasonal flu' if they developed any illness at all,[121] a fact that events would bear out.

'This virus is presenting as an unprecedented threat', said Ghebreyesus. 'We can come together against a common enemy, an enemy against humanity.'[122] He added that the WHO was 'deeply concerned both by the alarming levels of spread and severity and by the alarming levels of inaction', and he called on countries to take action immediately to contain the virus. 'We should double down', he said. 'We should be more aggressive.'[123]

The Director-General's wording was instrumental in the crafting of the (highly misleading) narrative of the virus as a lethal threat bearing indiscriminately on all human beings, and in laying the ideological ground for its corollary: the bellicose 'global war on Covid' narrative which would soon become ubiquitous, enabling politicians around the world to reap the benefits of being 'war leaders', as we'll see below.[124] Top public health experts chimed in. Farrar, for example, welcomed the WHO's pandemic declaration: 'Infectious diseases do not respect borders. We need sustained and coordinated action by all governments and global institutions if we are to avert long-term catastrophe worldwide.'[125]

Italy, once again, moved in lockstep with the WHO. That same day, 11 March, the Italian government announced the extension of lockdown to the entire country—inaugurating the first ever national lockdown/quarantine in human history, requiring the country's entire population not to leave their homes unless for an essential reason, such as to buy food and essential goods. Moreover, 'all productive activity throughout the territory that is not strictly necessary, crucial, indispensable, to guarantee us essential goods and services' was closed down.[126] If China's lockdown had been historically unprecedented, Italy's nationwide lockdown was even more unparalleled—a policy that was literally unconceivable, and indeed unconceived, up until that moment, even in China.

Nonetheless, in late March 2020, the Vice-President of the Chinese Red Cross, during a visit to Lombardy, lamented the fact that Italy's 'policies unfortunately are still not tight enough by our standards. There are still too many people around, public transport is still active and too many people are out in restaurants and hotels.'[127] He then forcefully reminded the Italian authorities that 'it is time to close the economic activities and prohibit the movement of people. Everyone has to stay at home, in quarantine.' As Piero Stanig and Gianmarco Daniele, two professors at Bocconi University, write: 'It's worth noting that some of the slogans of the past [years] ("too many people around", "stay at home", "shut down", "prohibit travel"), absent in Western pandemic plans, make their appearance on the heels of what newspapers called an 'earful' by an envoy of the People's Republic of China.'[128] A subsequent investigation by the *New York Times* would later find evidence of a social media campaign aimed, in those very same days, at lionising China's Covid response while ridiculing the West's alleged inadequacy.[129]

That said, one cannot overemphasise the crucial role played by Italy in getting other Western countries—and especially their populations—to take such a policy into consideration. In a December 2020 interview, Neil Ferguson looked back over discussions in early 2020 as the pandemic spread.[130] Following China's decision to lock down Wuhan and then the entire Hubei province, the idea that lockdown was a genuine possibility in a modern European context initially seemed outlandish, he said. 'It's a communist one party state, we said. We couldn't get away with it in Europe, we thought... And then Italy did it. And we realised we could.'[131] Almost overnight, what was impossible became possible, even inevitable.

THE LOCKDOWN NIGHTMARE BEGINS

Most Western states—the United Kingdom, the United States, Spain, France, Ireland, Australia, New Zealand—soon undertook similar action. Quick on their heels were middle- and low-income countries in which the policy was even more catastrophic and counter-intuitive—as we'll soon see.

Meanwhile, another disturbing trend was underway, one that further intoxicated the public debate and added more fuel to the panic: the framing of what was happening as a 'global war against Covid'.[132] 'We are at war with a virus that threatens to tear us apart', the Director-General of the WHO told world leaders in a special virtual summit on the pandemic.[133] In his address to the nation, on 17 March, French President Emmanuel Macron repeated the statement 'Nous sommes en *guerre*' ('We are at war') six times,[134] while Mario Draghi, former President of the European Central Bank (ECB), declared: 'We face a *war* against coronavirus and must mobilise accordingly.'[135]

War metaphors were particularly pervasive in Italy: then-Prime Minister Giuseppe Conte remembered all the Italians who were fighting 'in the *trenches* of the hospitals'.[136] The reference to wartime was echoed on many other occasions by Domenico Arcuri (Special Commissioner for the Covid-19 Emergency until March 2021) who, on 22 March, declared: 'We are at *war*, we have to find the *weapons*',[137] and by the leader of the opposition party, Matteo Salvini, who, while commenting on the '*war* bulletin' of the death count, claimed: 'During *wartime*, *war* measures must be adopted.'[138] And (almost) everyone agreed that there was only one weapon of choice in fighting this war: lockdowns.

***

The emerging Covid consensus on lockdowns was so pervasive, so totalising, that few governments dared to go against it. One of the few countries that notably defied the consensus was Sweden—where, by law, scientific advisors were able to enact what they saw as appropriate policies without political oversight/interference.[139] During the first wave, Sweden imposed some moderate social restrictions to combat the spread of the virus—schools were closed for those aged over sixteen and together with universities transitioned to remote learning;[140] gatherings of over fifty people were banned; and bars and restaurants were only able to operate an at-table service[141]—but, unlike most Western countries, it never imposed a national lockdown, enforced general quarantine rules, or introduced a mask mandate. Hospitality and retail continued to operate throughout the pandemic,[142] and it never closed its preschools or elementary schools.[143]

Thus the country's state epidemiologist, Anders Tegnell, implemented the policy that had been the scientific consensus until March. This was the approach of a scientist who recognised that the Covid-19 virus was one which posed a dangerous risk to certain sectors of the population, but who was also aware that the complete shutdown of society brought economic, psychological, and social damage that was also extremely risky, and could in the long run engender a greater mortality than the virus itself; it was the approach of a scientific adviser who sought to balance the risks that the new virus presented with those which would arise from shutting down society and severely limiting personal freedoms. It was also an approach that privileged individual responsibility and institutional trust over top-down authoritarianism and cruel paternalism, with evidence suggesting high levels of compliance with the government's recommendation.[144]

Unlike some of his peers around Europe, Tegnell had not entered government through a revolving door following a career in the private sector. He had followed a straightforward path in public institutions conducting scientific research and epidemiology, with a deep experience of epidemics. He had worked to contain the Ebola epidemic in Zaire in 1995.[145] And perhaps of even greater relevance, as head of the Swedish Institute for Communicable Disease Control, he had had an instrumental role in the country's response to the H1N1 swine flu pandemic in 2009, preparing the rollout of vaccinations.[146] Indeed, the policy which Tegnell championed in Sweden was a clear revitalisation of the strategy that countries had adopted during the previous pandemic. Such policies had been standard until just a few months before—but no longer. They were inconvenient to the most powerful countries and health organisations in the world, which had opted for a shutdown approach.

As a result, by the time the WHO declared Covid-19 a pandemic, the Covid consensus on lockdowns was already so pervasive that Sweden's unique response became the subject of massive international controversy.[147] The country was excoriated as 'the EU's exception'[148] and a 'pariah state',[149] and its approach was derogatorily labelled 'anti-lockdown',[150] 'experimental',[151] 'light-touch',[152] and 'naïve'.[153] Tegnell in particular became the subject of hundreds of articles around the world. Yet, despite the barrage of criticism, the epidemiologist held steadfast.

Few other politicians or public health experts had Tegnell's nerves of steel, however. It's well known, for example, that President Trump initially advocated a more light-handed approach. Three times between 6 and 12 March, Trump was quoted as saying that coronavirus was something that would just 'go away'.[154] However, just a few days later, in one of his classic volte-faces, Trump began telling reporters that he had always known this was a pandemic before the WHO had called it one.[155] On 19 March Trump elaborated on his story still further, telling the journalist Bob Woodward that he had at first deliberately downplayed the virus so as not to sow panic.[156]

At that point, the United States started going into lockdown as well: by the beginning of April, most US states (all twenty-four Democratic-led states and nineteen out of twenty-six Republican-led states) had issued stay-at-home orders.[157] By then, even in the US, the power had swung decisively in favour of the 'health experts'—that is, the scientific administrators in charge of directing official policy such as Fauci and Collins. When Trump mulled over easing the restrictions by Easter, Fauci countered: 'You don't make the timeline. The virus makes the timeline.'[158]

Another country that tried to take a different approach was the UK.[159] On 12 March, at a press conference,[160] Boris Johnson revealed that the United Kingdom would no longer try to test and trace the contacts of every suspected case, and would test only people who were admitted to hospitals. In lieu of any major social-distancing measures, Johnson instead offered a suite of soft advice—people with symptoms should stay at home; schools wouldn't close but trips abroad should be avoided; people over seventy should avoid cruises. At the same time, Sir Patrick Vallance, the UK's Government Chief Scientific Adviser, introduced to the public the concept of 'herd immunity' (something which also occurred in the Netherlands, where it was initially discussed by Prime Minister Mark Rutte)—the idea that once enough of a population had been exposed to the virus, they would build up natural immunity to it.[161]

'Our aim', Vallance told BBC Radio 4's Today programme, 'is to try and reduce the peak, broaden the peak, not suppress it completely; also, because the vast majority of people get a mild illness, to build up some kind of herd immunity so more people are immune to this disease and we reduce the transmission, at the same time we protect those who are most vulnerable to it. Those are the key things we need to do'.[162] Speaking to Sky News, he added that 'probably about 60% per cent' of people would need to be infected to achieve herd immunity, which would also help reduce transmission in the event of a winter resurgence.[163]

There was nothing particularly radical about Vallance's proposal—herd immunity had been a well-established epidemiological concept for at least a century.[164] Indeed, it was in line with the WHO's own existing definition of herd immunity, as 'the indirect protection from an infectious disease that happens when a population is immune either through vaccination *or immunity developed through previous infection*' (emphasis added).[165] It was also in line with what was already known back then about the highly age-selective nature of Covid-19. As the UK government's coronavirus action plan, published on 3 March, read:

> Among those who become infected, some will exhibit no symptoms. Early data suggest that of those who develop an illness, the great majority will have a mild-to-moderate, but self-limiting illness—similar to seasonal flu. It is, however, also clear that a minority of people who get Covid-19 will develop complications severe enough to require hospital care, most often pneumonia. In a small proportion of these, the illness may be severe enough to lead to death. So far the data we have suggest that the risk of severe disease and death increases among elderly people and in people with underlying health risk conditions (in the same way as for seasonal flu). Illness is less common and usually less severe in younger adults. Children can be infected and can have a severe illness, but based on current data overall illness seems rarer in people under 20 years of age.[166]

In light of this data—which events would corroborate—the idea of letting the virus spread through those who were at low risk from it, allowing them to generate antibodies, thus blocking the network of pathways toward the high-risk group, the vulnerable and the elderly, while at the same time protecting the latter, was far from outlandish. By this stage, however, political positions around the best ways to deal with the Covid-19 outbreak had already started polarising along political lines. Ever since Trump had expressed doubts about the wisdom of a lockdown strategy, liberals and those on the left of the Western political spectrum knew which side of the containment debate they had to be on.

Once these divisions had become entrenched, it was almost impossible for advocates of either side to acknowledge any merit in their opponents' view. And this was because of the division and rancour which had characterised Western democratic politics over the preceding five years and more, aided and abetted by social media platforms (something which is beyond the scope of this book fully to address). Anything that Trump or Johnson supported was by definition problematic, objectionable, and grounded in unseemly political agendas. This polarised political sphere—further exacerbated by the single narrative being pushed by institutions such as the WHO—was exactly the wrong sort of political environment in which societies could hope to have a balanced debate about the best ways to deal with Covid.

As a result, the UK government's plan was aggressively berated by liberal and left-wing commentators.[167] On 15 March the *Observer* published a string of letters denouncing Johnson's 'Malthusian' approach as one of callous complacency.[168] Some experts condemned his refusal to implement more rigorous measures in the early weeks of March in favour of the herd immunity approach as a disastrous miscalculation: his choice to 'minimise economic disruption over saving lives' was one that would come back to haunt him.[169]

It is interesting to note how these dynamics affected the coronavirus response in other world regions as well. In Brazil, President Jair Bolsonaro, as readers will certainly be aware, opposed lockdowns right from the start. During a speech in Miami in early March, he dismissed coronavirus as a 'fantasy whipped up by the media around the world'.[170] Appearing at a mass rally in Brasília later that month without a mask, he faced criticism for interacting with his supporters, and later responded by saying that businesses were profiting from hysteria and people should fight against a coming neurosis.[171] As Brazilian state governors ignored his position and began to take their own measures, closing schools and workplaces and imposing travel restrictions, Bolsonaro took to the airwaves again on 24 March to dismiss these measures (which had been implemented on the advice of his own Health Ministry) and urged people to continue as normal.[172] At the end of March he dismissed Covid-19 as 'a little flu'[173] that was inoffensive to the majority of the young and the healthy who, like him, had an 'athletic history',[174] and urged Brazilians to abandon social distancing measures, which at this stage had already been adopted by several governors and mayors.

It is estimated that by this point 50 per cent of Brazilians were already adhering to social distancing measures.[175] When asked by a reporter how the country would protect these vulnerable groups, he answered: 'there is horizontal isolation, that they're doing here, and there's the vertical. It's the vertical [for groups at risk]'[176]—essentially arguing for some form of herd immunity strategy. Then on 16 April, to widespread disgust on all sides of the political spectrum, Bolsonaro sacked his health minister Luiz Henrique Mandetta, who had supported physical distancing measures.[177]

We are not interested in this context in discussing the pros and cons of Bolsonaro's strategy—which in any case was never explained in great detail—but rather in highlighting how the discussion in Brazil was heavily influenced by the polarisation around lockdowns that was already taking place in the UK and US. As one study notes, most Brazilian media outlets at the time,

when discussing herd immunity, made reference at some point to the United Kingdom and/or its prime minister and team. The United States and its president were also cited in six articles. Thus, we can say that the debate on social distancing, in Brazil, was closely connected to the measures and pronouncements of British and North American political authorities. Despite herd immunity having been considered and discussed in other cities/countries in Europe, the perspective that dominated the Brazilian news was that of the UK and the USA.[178]

Here we therefore have another example of a country where the debate over Covid restrictions overlapped with pre-existing political polarisation, and was further reinforced by the polarisation taking place globally around the issue. For example, left-wing Brazilians were relieved at the school closures and that there was no prospect of their reopening: this was at least one small victory that they had won over the horror of Bolsonaro.[179] This was not because these Brazilian left-wingers somehow did not care about the impacts that this would have on poorer children. It was rather because of the traumas they had endured going back five years: from the impeachment of the left-wing Dilma Rousseff by a corrupt Congress in 2016 to the election of Bolsonaro as President in December 2018. This was a president who had said that 'the Indians are evolving, more and more they are human beings like us'; who said to a female political opponent in Congress in 2014 that 'I wouldn't rape you because you don't deserve it'; that the 'dictatorship's mistake was to torture not to kill'; and that he would be 'incapable of loving a homosexual son'—it's easy to see why, for Brazilian progressives, anything in the programme of such a person automatically had to be opposed.[180]

Moreover, the polarisation around Covid in Brazil—while drawing on that in the UK and the US—was soon refracted back and exacerbated that which was developing in Western countries. In March the *Guardian* produced a video documenting Trump's responses to the crisis, which it circulated on Instagram.[181] Then, in the last week of March, the newspaper ran a series of articles on Bolsonaro. On 30 March, it reported that a group of left-wing Brazilians had published a manifesto demanding that Bolsonaro resign over his handling of the pandemic.[182] The following day, the paper published an editorial denouncing Bolsonaro as 'a danger for Brazilians'.[183]

Once political positions had been solidified around greater or lesser social restrictions, a key moment in the rollout of the policy response to the global pandemic was the presentation by Neil Ferguson, the aforementioned Imperial College epidemiologist, of his now-famous modelling report to Downing Street on 16 March 2020.[184] Ferguson's paper, part-funded by Farrar's Wellcome Trust,[185] predicted that 500,000 people would die in the United Kingdom if no steps were taken to mitigate the virus, and that 260,000 would die if the moderate measures which the government had already implemented—including recommended social distancing, working from home where possible, and limiting gatherings to thirty people, in line with the hybrid 'herd immunity' approach—were retained.

Such a massive mortality would overwhelm the National Health Service (NHS) and make it impossible to treat other diseases. It would devastate the economy owing to the numbers of people falling ill and dying. The only way to prevent it was, Ferguson's paper said, to embark on a full-scale suppression of the virus—namely lockdowns. It should be noted that the suppression strategy proposed in Ferguson's paper—a combination of social distancing of the entire population, case isolation, household quarantine, and school and university closure—represents nonetheless a 'lighter' version of the full lockdowns that were actually implemented in most countries, including the UK.[186] Interestingly, the paper concurred with Vallance that '[i]ntroducing such interventions too early risks allowing transmission to return once they are lifted (if insufficient herd immunity has developed)'. Thus, this strategy of suppression would need to be maintained 'until a vaccine becomes available'; the paper noted that a vaccine would probably take eighteen months to be rolled out in sufficient quantities. Thus Ferguson's paper was effectively advocating for what eventually took place: one-and-a-half years of lockdowns and other restrictions and then widespread vaccination—not the 'three weeks to flatten the curve' that was originally discussed. When it comes to vaccination timetables, Ferguson would certainly have known what he was talking about, since he was then (and still is at the time of writing) Acting Director of the Vaccine Impact Modelling Consortium (VIMC),[187] which is funded by the Bill and Melinda Gates Foundation[188] and by GAVI, the Vaccine Alliance.[189]

So how effective was this strategy modelled to be? The scientists in Neil Ferguson's Imperial College team themselves suggested in late March that they would consider the lockdown policy to have been a success if the number of deaths in the UK remained below 20,000 (presumably because of the high collateral damage which the policy brought with it), and predicted total deaths of 5,700 following the suppression strategy.[190] As of May 2022, after three lockdowns,[191] the UK death toll stood at 178,000, another example of the Imperial team's dubious modelling prowess.[192] Of course, they and their advocates claim that the lockdown measures were never properly implemented— but given the catastrophic consequences of the measures that were followed, and the evidence of the Zero Covid approach in China (discussed in more detail below in Chapter 6), it can only be considered that an even stronger implementation would have been ill-advised.

The Imperial College paper authors recognised that their analysis relied on 'how the coronavirus spread in China', but posited that 'even though there are differences in culture and response, most countries do match China'[193]—omitting the small detail that most are not governed by a dictatorship, and that social conditions in poor countries are vastly different; as the epidemiologists Alex Broadbent and Pieter Streicher point out, it is virtually impossible to lock down slums (in which one in seven of the world's population reside), and the health benefits of doing so in terms of the spread of disease are marginal at best.[194] Disregarding political, social, and economic differences, and sticking to Global North comparisons, even though the WHO had recommended the Chinese model for all countries, the Imperial College team likened the response to China's, but with a core difference: 'unlike in China, anything that happens in the UK will be voluntary'.[195] However, as the Imperial team were not qualitative social scientists, they had not considered the impossibility of imposing authoritarian policies without authoritarian tools with which to enforce them.

Faced with such gruesome predictions, relayed with almost mathematical certainty and coming with the seal of approval of 'The Science', Boris Johnson performed the first of a number of Covid-19 U-turns and a week later, on 23 March, placed the entire United Kingdom into lockdown. As it turned out, it was not just among the computer modellers that the Chinese approach found favour. Adopting the UK lockdown, Boris Johnson said that it would be imposed for at least three weeks, but didn't rule out extending it if necessary.[196] As it turned out, it was extended with a few breaks here and there long into 2021. Returning to the ranks of the Covid consensus, Johnson and Trump both proceeded to attempt to capitalise on the pandemic by seizing on the war metaphor and presenting themselves as *wartime* leaders, just like their 'liberal' colleagues in other countries.[197]

The influence of Ferguson's paper on promoting the pro-lockdown consensus cannot be overstated. Ferguson sent an advanced copy of his paper to the White House, in which he predicted that 2.2 million Americans might die from Covid in the first year unless the US instituted lockdowns.[198] This was almost 25 per cent higher than the Centers for Disease Control's starkest projection.[199] The study also estimated that even with 'the most effective mitigation strategy', from 1.1 to 1.2 million people would die from Covid in 2020[200] (the official tally of Covid-19 deaths in the US for 2020, after a two-month lockdown that affected most US states, was 350,831).[201] The massive death projections were widely reported in the press, contributing to a sense of impending global doom.

This was to have a major impact on the development of a new approach to the virus in the United States. 'What had the biggest impact in the model is social distancing, small groups, not going in public in large groups', said Dr Deborah Birx, one of the leaders of the White House's Coronavirus Task Force, referring to the Imperial College projection.[202] The *New York Times* reported on 16 March, shortly after the Trump administration had received Ferguson's paper: 'White House Takes New Line After Dire Report On Death Toll'.[203]

Even though it is now generally accepted that Ferguson's mortality estimates were wildly overblown,[204] under every conceivable scenario, and based on dubious modelling techniques, as several scientists had already pointed out at the time[205]—and as Ferguson himself admitted in August 2021[206]—Anthony Fauci cited Imperial College's unrealistic Covid-19 fatality projections to justify the US lockdowns.[207] Indeed, a month later the 2.2 million estimate was still being used (without revealing the source) by Trump, Fauci, and Birx to imply that up to 2 million lives had been saved by state lockdowns and business closings and/or by federal travel bans.[208] As we'll see in Chapter 6, the reality was somewhat different.

The influence of Ferguson's paper on the authorities in London and Washington soon saw these measures gaining traction worldwide. For example, reflecting on the experience of his own country, France, Laurent Mucchielli writes that from the moment it was created in March 2020, the country's Covid-19 Scientific Council immediately set out the main lines of what it called the 'scientific rationale': 'It basically consist[ed] of taking over the catastrophic statistical predictions of the mathematical epidemic modelling team of Neil Ferguson of Imperial College and Simon Cauchemez (a former student of Ferguson, member of the Covid-19 Scientific Council) of the Institut Pasteur, announcing "several hundred thousand deaths" in France'.[209]

The same thing happened in Germany. 'Regrettably, [voices of reason such as that of Ioannidis and others] remained unheard by our politicians and their advisers. Instead, the prediction ventured by Professor Neil Ferguson, Imperial College London, made the headlines [...]. Not only did this make the rounds, it struck fear into hearts and souls', wrote Professor Sucharit Bhakdi of the University of Mainz, who had been editor of the influential journal *Medical Microbiology and Immunology*— founded by Robert Koch in 1886—for twenty-two years from 1990 to 2012.[210]

In light of the wide-reaching (and ultimately devastating) impact of Ferguson's model, it is shocking that so few politicians and media organisations sought to analyse the nature of the assumptions that had led to this prediction from Ferguson and his team and his possible conflicts of interest, not to mention the epidemiologist's embarrassingly poor track record. In 2001, Ferguson was instrumental in the modelling of the British government's response to foot-and-mouth disease, which led to the slaughtering of more than 6 million animals, devastating the UK farming community.[211] Professor Michael Thrusfield of Edinburgh University claimed that Ferguson's model made incorrect assumptions about how foot-and-mouth disease was transmitted,[212] and in two subsequent reviews claimed the model was 'not fit for purpose'[213] and 'severely flawed'.[214]

Ferguson began to rise to prominence in 2002, following the outbreak of bovine spongiform encephalopathy (BSE), or mad cow disease, that had affected the United Kingdom in the 1990s. That year, he published a research article which considered the likely impact of BSE on human mortality. There were fears that BSE had entered the human food chain through transmission to sheep, and his team concluded that between 50 and 150,000 Britons were likely to die from exposure to BSE.[215] On that occasion, Ferguson and his team hit the nail on the head, since the total mortality, at 177, did fall within their range of estimates—although it was somewhat lower than their upper limit estimate of 150,000 people.[216]

Then, in 2005, during the outbreak of H5N1, or avian flu, Ferguson's team made even more alarming predictions. David Nabarro, a senior official at the WHO, had claimed that up to 150 million people could be killed by the new virus, but this was not taking the virus seriously enough, according to Ferguson and his team. As the *Guardian* put it on 30 September 2005:

> Last month Neil Ferguson, a professor of mathematical biology at Imperial College London, told *Guardian Unlimited* that up to 200 million people could be killed. 'Around 40 million people died in the 1918 Spanish flu outbreak,' said Prof Ferguson. 'There are six times more people on the planet now so you could scale it up to around 200 million people probably.'[217]

According to the WHO, the best-case scenario for that outbreak was a global mortality figure of 7.4 million people.[218] Yet in the end, five years later, the WHO reported that the total number of global deaths from H5N1 was not 200 million, nor 150 million, nor even 7.4 million, but 257 people (yes, you read that correctly).[219]

Then, in 2009, during the swine flu pandemic, the United Kingdom's Chief Medical Officer, Sir Liam Donaldson, estimated that up to 65,000 people might die, and that in the best-case scenario there would be a mortality of 3,100.[220] One of the leading figures in developing the initial modelling projections was Neil Ferguson, who predicted a CFR from swine flu in the range of 0.3 to 1.5 per cent, with 0.4 per cent the most likely outcome.[221] In the end, the dire predictions turned out to have been just that—predictions. Eventually Donaldson confirmed that the UK death toll was not 65,000, or even 3,100: it was 457, a CFR of just 0.026 per cent, while in the US the CDC estimated that it was between 0.013 and 0.027 per cent.[222] As the CDC put it, 'the impact of the (H1N1)pdm09 virus on the global population during the first year was less severe than that of previous pandemics'.[223]

This was pretty clear evidence that initial computer-modelling predictions as to the spread and severity of a virus are often inaccurate, and do not become solid until several months into a pandemic's spread when more reliable data has begun to emerge. It was also evidence that Ferguson has a tendency to predict doomsday scenarios that systematically fail to materialise. He has been wrong every time—literally. With the benefit of hindsight, it seems extraordinary that no one in senior world political circles sought to investigate the track record of Professor Ferguson and his team, or indeed the ways in which the previous outbreaks of avian flu in 2005 and swine flu in 2009 had led to predictions which turned out to be wildly inaccurate, not only from Ferguson but also from the WHO. At the very least, it should have led to his Covid mortality predictions being taken with a pinch, if not a handful, of salt.

But that didn't happen. On the contrary, senior political, journalistic, and public health authorities seized upon Ferguson's modelling to further exacerbate the global panic. Meanwhile, the acceptance of a certain set of statistics inevitably meant the marginalisation of scientists who did not go along with them and their conclusions—even though their views as to how to best handle the pandemic had until January been in step with the scientific consensus, as we have seen. The research conducted by these scientists was marginalised not for its scientific content but because it was outside the political and media consensus that had taken shape over this public health debate. In other words, data and its meanings had become politicised.

The political context of the debate also meant that people took sides quickly, and what had been accepted scientific practice until January now became anathema to many. An important example of this is the attention given in the media to Ferguson. In the UK, libertarian right-wing outlets such as the *Spectator* did report in April 2020 on the previous estimates which his team had produced, and how wrong they had been.[224] Yet this dubious track record was not reported in the mainstream liberal-left press. Moreover, when Ferguson was forced to resign ingloriously from the UK's Scientific Advisory Group on Emergencies (SAGE) in early May for breaching his own lockdown rules, the *Guardian* reported that his departure was a 'huge blow' for SAGE and for Boris Johnson, as he had '20 years of experience of studying pathogen outbreaks [...]. He modelled the spread of all those outbreaks, advising five UK prime ministers in the process.'[225] Missing in the report was how wrong those models had been, even though this had been reported several weeks earlier in right-wing outlets. A senior editorial decision had probably been taken that it would be a mistake to discuss this.

By this point, among Western and global elites, the Covid consensus in favour of lockdowns—a measure, it is worth reiterating, that had been unthinkable up until just a few months prior—had become an article of faith, supported by the overwhelming majority of self-defined progressive public opinion. This had a major impact on the globalisation of the lockdown response, as the world's most powerful governments and multilateral organisations, and their experts, turned their attention to Africa—while Western progressives looked the other way.

***

Africa had been the earliest world region outside Asia to tackle the Covid-19 outbreak with due seriousness—an indication of the way in which the response to Covid-19 has upended lazy stereotypes about governance around the world. Mass awareness campaigns on the risk of the virus and the need for handwashing and other hygiene measures were conducted in Senegal from late January 2020 onwards.[226] Bole airport in Addis Ababa, Ethiopia—one of the continent's most important air hubs— conducted temperature checks on passengers arriving on the six daily flights from China from the middle of February. President Paul Kagame closed Rwanda's borders to Chinese flights on 31 January, and by the end of February forty-two African countries had the capacity to test for Covid-19.[227]

Yet officials at the WHO, led by its Director-General Ghebreyesus (a former Ethiopian Minister of Health), worried about how countries with less well-resourced health systems would cope with the new virus.[228] On 20 March, Ghebreyesus said: 'Probably we have undetected cases or unreported cases. In other countries we have seen how the virus actually accelerates after a certain tipping point, so the best advice for Africa is to prepare for the worst and prepare today.'[229] Of course, had Covid truly had a CFR of 3.4 per cent, and had it been an illness that threatened young and old people in all countries alike, the impact on countries with weak health systems would certainly have been catastrophic. However, as mentioned already, it was known right from the start that this wasn't the case.[230] Moreover, it was well established that influenza spread is heavily influenced by climatic factors, with epidemics usually occurring in winter in temperate countries and during the rainy season in tropical countries.[231]

As a result, Africa, with its much younger population and warmer, drier climate in many regions, could reasonably have been expected to be much less vulnerable to Covid than Western and Latin American countries—as events would bear out.[232] The

UN itself had published a report in 2019 which estimated that the median age on the continent was 19.8[233]—clearly indicating that Africa would not come under great pressure from this new virus which all early data showed overwhelmingly targeted older people. Nonetheless, in March, the sense of panic grew across Africa as it did right across the world, stoked by influential foreign policy journals. As one 31 March article in *Foreign Affairs* put it: 'Were anything approximating what has hit [richer] nations to afflict poorer or conflict-ridden ones, the effect could be crushing. That moment, unfortunately, may not be too far off: India, Pakistan, Brazil, Venezuela, Argentina, Nigeria, and South Africa each have hundreds, sometimes thousands, of cases.'[234]

The consequent fear of the impact of a rapid spike in Covid cases among healthcare professionals on the continent was high. One, Ifedayo Adetifa, a clinical epidemiologist at the KEMRI-Wellcome Trust Research Programme, put it: 'Broad-based population pyramid or not, with no universal health care and no health insurance, we simply can't afford to have many Covid-19 cases because we can't manage the most severe cases.'[235] And a report by the Center for Global Development suggested that healthcare professionals would be among the major victims of the virus on the continent, as the systems in place would not be able to protect them.[236]

As such warnings multiplied, the gathering global consensus as to the dangers of the virus and the best policy approach to mitigation was effectively 'exported' to Africa. An important push factor in this sense was the nature of global power relations. For Pedrito Cambrão, a sociologist at Universidade Zambeze in Beira, Mozambique, the pressure of international organisations and especially the WHO was a significant driver for the African lockdown policy.[237]

The role of global multilateral pressure on African governments was something that lockdown advocates ignored, in some cases claiming that these were sovereign states making sovereign decisions and conveniently passing over the real pressures driving policy decisions in Africa. When multilateral donor organisations make suggestions, African leaders are constrained to respond. Key organisations on the continent depend on foreign funding, from the Foundation for Social Sciences Research in Africa (CODESRIA, five of whose seven core funders are European and American)[238] to the African Union (more than two-thirds of which was funded by development partners in China, Europe, and the US in 2020).[239] As the lockdown model came to be the global consensus, African leaders must certainly have worried about the political fallout of refusing to go along with it. In Senegal, rumours circulated that France's President Emmanuel Macron had rung the Senegalese President Macky Sall in March and ordered him to impose a lockdown (with the veiled threat of France's military base in Senegal to back him up).[240] With aid, trade, and political agreements on the line, and with the model having itself emerged in China—such a key trade partner— the 'soft power' incentives to follow the lockdown model were extremely difficult to resist.

Moreover, once the UK had moved away from the herd immunity model and followed other Western states into lockdown, the knock-on impacts globally became clear. On 24 March 2020, the day after the UK entered lockdown, India's President Narendra Modi unexpectedly announced a complete lockdown, which had devastating socio-economic effects, as discussed in Chapter 7. Lockdowns spread that week around low-income countries: Senegal entered lockdown at midnight on 23 March,[241] Angola on 27 March,[242] and Ghana on 30 March in its two major urban areas of Accra and Kumasi.[243] In short, there can be no doubt that the influence of Ferguson's model and its impact on policy responses in the UK and the US very soon had global ramifications: the new lockdown model was now a global export, without any sense of the different health parameters which might be at play, caused by different socio-economic conditions and population pyramids.

It's important, therefore, to be clear that the imposition of lockdowns in high-income countries—and the Imperial College report—were directly responsible for the rolling out of these policies in low-income countries. The development of the policy consensus around the lockdown model meant that this policy was then promoted to poor countries by organisations such as the WHO, with scant regard to their own policy recommendations and the 'ethical considerations' regarding migrant workers that they had published in their November 2019 report just a few months before. The WHO's 24 February report made it clear that the lockdown measures should be followed in all countries, and given the significant role of the WHO in funding a range of primary care facilities in low-income countries, it would have been almost impossible for African leaders to refuse to implement them. Indeed, as we'll see in Chapter 6, the WHO actively promoted them several months into the crisis, even when it was clear that their impacts were devastating.

Thus, by the end of March 2020, the policy consensus had become universal. The single narrative had shifted onto lockdowns as the universal applicable control measure—and any scientist who tried to point out that this was in breach of all previous policy directives was ruthlessly pilloried in the media. This single narrative framework did not just relate to the lockdown model, but also to the universality of its application—whether in Palo Alto, California, or Mumbai.

This sense of the global consensus as to the dangers of the virus and the best policy approach to mitigation drove countries across the African continent into lockdown. From the *confinamentos* of Angola, Cabo Verde, and Mozambique to the lockdowns of Botswana, Ghana, and South Africa and the *confinements* of

Senegal and Togo, people found themselves stranded from one day to the next as governments introduced strict curfews, social distancing measures on public transport, and school closures. This was without any discussion of the impact that attempting to impose lockdowns in poor countries heavily reliant on informal economies would have on the poorest members of society, who have no savings; on children without access to digital resources for schooling; and on the vast majority of the African population who depend on informal work and trade to survive.

African countries responded to the March 2020 crisis in very different ways. As we've seen here, many opted for some version of the lockdown model—though some, such as Tanzania, refused to (without any notable increase in mortality), while others, such as Sierra Leone, only did so for a very limited time. In terms of the ways in which they were able to try to sustain their citizens through this initial catastrophe, again the response was very different. Most governments made strong efforts to help sectors which had suddenly been devastated, drawing on emergency loans from the IMF, the World Bank, and China.[244] In Ghana, electricity and water were provided for free so that all citizens would be able to follow the hygiene advice in terms of hand washing, small business owners were able to apply for support, and tax relief was offered, while doctors and nurses saw salary increases through a new risk allowance.[245] In Gambia, rice, oil, and sugar were distributed to 85,000 compounds in June, and 90,000 households got a cash handout of 3,000 dalasi (approximately US$40) in July, relief which touched most people in the country (which has a small population, of around 2.3 million); in an interesting and imaginative response, the Gambian government also provided a 5 million-dalasi (approximately US$100,000) relief package for artists, writers, musicians, and dramatists which was administered through the National Centre for Arts and Culture.[246] In Togo, meanwhile, a new digital cash transfer system saw the government able to wire US$4.3 million to its poorest citizens to help them through the lockdown period.[247] Even some of the poorest countries on the continent, such as Guinea-Bissau, were able to offer microcredit to some small business owners and market vendors.[248] A large part of this was financed by drawing on any existing cash reserves which were held and through emergency loans.

In countries with some financial capabilities such as Nigeria, the collective community response was massive. Here people stepped in to set up food banks which were supported through online donations, as in the West, and this made up for some of the shortfall, although the impact on the already poor and dispossessed was immense.[249] However, in some countries, such as Mozambique, there was no state help at all for small businesses and market vendors whose trade had collapsed.[250] Without a large diaspora, Mozambique faced penury. It is worth pausing and trying to reflect on what this might mean in one of the poorest countries in the world, where the monthly salary for live-in domestic help in some areas may be US$10 per month (around US$0.30 per day, or a little over 1 cent per hour) plus bed and board: what it means is, as Cambrão puts it, 'the new normal is no longer a threat: the threat is to die of hunger through following the measures which go with the new normal.'[251]

In India, meanwhile, the first lockdown saw a glut of produce grown locally whose farmers could not transport it because of the restrictions; as A. R. Vasavi notes, 'the immediate beneficiaries were the privileged class who now had access to a cornucopia of a wide variety of mangoes, grapes, bananas and vegetables—all at distress sale prices', while farmers lost large sums and some burnt their crops in protest.[252] In sum, it was apparent right away in these early weeks of the crisis that lockdown policies were completely inappropriate for the world's poor—in spite of the media and political rush to implement them, and the continued hysteria which arose surrounding the 'early removal of restrictions' in countries such as India throughout 2020 and 2021, promulgated by outlets such as *Deutsche Welle*, the *Guardian*, and the *New York Times*.[253] And when the *New Left Review* did publish an early piece in March 2020 by a Mumbai-based writer on the way in which the lockdown measures might produce widespread starvation, the writer in question only felt able to write under a pseudonym (see below, Chapter 6).[254]

The devastating impact of these policies are discussed in detail in Chapter 7. However, they were amply predicted right from the start. In early 2020, the World Food Programme warned that '135 million people on earth are marching towards the brink of starvation' as a result of their economies shutting down, supposedly to inhibit the spread of Covid-19.[255] At the end of March 2020, as the world entered lockdown, the United Nations Development Programme (UNDP) warned that 'nearly half of jobs in Africa could be lost due to coronavirus' (or, rather, to the policy response to it).[256] The international community had to think further than just the immediate impacts of the virus, they said, as the response threatened to devastate the economies of the continent and increase inequality. Achim Steiner, administrator of the UNDP, said, 'the growing Covid-19 crisis threatens to disproportionately hit developing countries, not only as a health crisis in the short term but as a devastating social and economic crisis over the months and years to come'.[257]

In early April, the United Nations University World Institute for Development Economics warned that without an emergency rescue fund, over half a billion people could be pushed into poverty by the economic fallout of the response to Covid-19. That is, between 6 and 8 per cent of the world's entire population were at risk of being forced into poverty, and over half of the world's population might be living in poverty in the aftermath of the pandemic. As the report noted, 2 billion people worldwide worked informally with no access to sick pay, and in poor countries informal jobs constituted 90 per cent of the labour market as compared with just 18 per cent in rich countries.[258]

Meanwhile, the International Labor Organization (ILO) warned that almost half the global workforce were 'in immediate danger of having their livelihoods destroyed' owing to the economic fallout from the response to the Covid-19 crisis.[259] Once again, it was informal workers who were seen as most at risk, and the ILO estimated that this 2 billion-strong cohort of workers had lost 60 per cent of their wages during the first month of the crisis.[260] Guy Ryder, the Director of the ILO (a UN agency), warned that the poverty impact would be 'massive': this had translated into a fall in the earnings of informal workers of 81 per cent in Africa and the Americas, 21.6 per cent in Asia and the Pacific, and 70 per cent in Europe and Central Asia.[261]

In sum, right from the start, the economic and social policies of lockdowns in Africa and other areas of the Global South were predicted to be catastrophic. The health impacts of increased poverty and malnutrition were sure to vastly outweigh even the potential impacts of Covid-19. Global health practitioners had studied for years the impact of malnutrition on mortality and health. Yet this had no impact either on the policy recommendations of the WHO, or on the general media and political response to the virus both in the Western world and in Africa itself.

**

By April 2020, as restrictions were lifted in Wuhan, about half of the world's population was under some form of lockdown, with more than 3.9 billion people in more than ninety countries or territories having been asked or ordered to stay at home by their governments.[262] The threat was raised of health services being overrun by the new virus, and yet nowhere was there discussion of how this threat was caused not only by the virus but also by years of austerity policies visited by global policy elites on health services.

The nightmare had begun. Over the next year and a half, as predicted, lockdowns would go on to trigger death and socio-economic devastation on a global scale, in high-, middle-, and low-income countries alike, while at the same time paving the way to an increasingly authoritarian turn in global politics, as governments across the planet used the 'public health emergency' to sweep aside democratic procedures and constitutional constraints, militarise societies, crack down on civil liberties, and implement unprecedented measures of social control. All these aspects of the lockdowns are analysed in the following chapters.

3

THE RISE OF A SINGLE NARRATIVE OF 'THE SCIENCE'

AKA THE COVID CONSENSUS

We've seen many things so far in this chronicle, but one of the most important is how a 'single narrative' was promoted very early on in the Covid-19 crisis both by pillars of the scientific establishment and by the WHO. This single narrative began with the initial panic in senior scientific circles regarding the origins of the virus, but then came to encompass the question of lockdowns. Importantly, it superseded what had previously been regarded as consensual positions: that laboratory leaks were a known risk for the emergence of future pathogens, and that what would come to be known as 'focused protection' was the tried and tested response to pandemics.

Those who pushed the new consensus had no problem pivoting away from previous support for the 'old' consensus, and apparently did not care to consider what the consequence of this pivot might be, especially in poorer countries. There was seemingly no need to wait for new peer-reviewed research studies based on methodical randomised control trials (the gold standard of scientific research) to confirm their new opinions—just as we saw that 'three days of sleepless nights' was all it took for leading scientists to pivot from genuine concern that SARS-CoV-2 had leaked from the WIV to asserting that anyone who claimed this was a conspiracy theorist.

The examples of masks and asymptomatic spreading are good illustrations of this new 'single-narrative science'. On 28 January 2020, Anthony Fauci participated in a White House briefing on the new coronavirus, and was asked about asymptomatic spread, to which he responded: 'But the one thing historically people need to realise [is] that even if there is asymptomatic transmission, in all the history of respiratory-borne viruses of any type, asymptomatic transmission has never been the driver of outbreaks. The driver of outbreaks is always a symptomatic person. Even if there's a rare asymptomatic person that might transmit, an epidemic is not driven by asymptomatic carriers.'[1] Indeed, a comprehensive December 2020 study of 10 million Wuhan residents confirmed Fauci's assertion that asymptomatic transmission of Covid-19 is infinitesimally rare.[2] This fact was echoed by health experts in all major Western countries, and confirmed by a multi-authored review of 130 studies looking at the topic which was published in May 2022.[3]

Then, in a February 2020 email revealed by the Freedom of Information request mentioned before, Fauci wrote that '[t]he typical mask you buy in the drug store is not really effective in keeping out virus, which is small enough to pass through material. It might, however, provide some slight benefit in keep[ing] out gross droplets if someone coughs or sneezes on you'.[4] Even the WHO originally stated that 'the use of a mask alone is insufficient to provide an adequate level of protection' and that 'the wide use of masks by healthy people in the community setting is not supported by current evidence and carries uncertainties and critical risks'[5]—including lulling elderly and at-risk people into a false sense of security by making them mistakenly believe they will be safe while wearing them.

Subsequent studies would later find that universal masking had no statistically significant impact on the spread of SARS-CoV-2,[6] and that 'existing data do not support universal, often improper, face mask use in the general population as a protective measure against Covid-19'.[7] This was indeed the only way to make sense of the reality that had emerged by 2022, where it became clear that US states that had had mask mandates had no materially different outcomes to those which had not. This led some liberal publications such as the *New York Times* to indulge in extraordinary ideological contortions, as seen in its 31 May 2022 piece, 'Why Masks Work but Mandates Haven't'.[8]

So the recommendation to wear masks was a new one in March 2020, one which even Anthony Fauci had not gone along with just the month before. Yet, within a few months, the WHO would start advising governments to encourage the public to wear masks,[9] even though no new scientific evidence had emerged to justify the volte-face.[10] Compulsory masking (including, rather absurdly, outdoors in several countries) and the requirement for contact tracing and the quarantining of asymptomatic cases would become standard practice, with anyone who doubted this branded a 'Covid sceptic'.[11] Physical and social distancing mandates requiring people to keep a certain distance from one another (usually 1–2 metres, though this differed from country to country) also rested on an uncertain scientific footing. In September 2021, former Food and Drug Administration (FDA) Commissioner Dr Scott Gottlieb admitted that the 6-foot distancing rule recommended in the US by the Centers for Disease Control and Prevention, in line with similar recommendations adopted by other countries, was 'arbitrary' and not science-backed. The process for making that policy choice, Gottlieb continued, '[i]s a perfect example of the lack of rigor around how CDC made recommendations'.[12]

Of course, we are not taking a conclusive position here on whether asymptomatic transmission has been important in the spread of SARS-CoV-2, or on whether masks or social distancing are an effective barrier to infection. It is perfectly reasonable to assume that, for example, a certain degree of social distancing will reduce a virus's circulating viral load. Rather, we are pointing to the way in which the political and scientific establishment operated without regard for the established methods of science: to conduct controlled experiments and then draw conclusions. Instead, what had begun with a ruthless suppression of dissent surrounding the virus origins had, as we've seen, spread to the crushing of dissent around lockdowns—and would later contaminate these other aspects of the response, despite the fact that many of these measures were based on flimsy evidence, to say the least. To give an example, in mid-2021, Martin Kulldorff, Professor of Medicine at Harvard Medical School, was locked out of his Twitter account simply for stating what even the WHO had initially pointed out: 'Naively fooled to think that masks would protect [people], some older high-risk people did not socially distance properly, and some died from Covid because of it. Tragic. Public health officials/scientists must always be honest with the public.'[13]

The turnaround was incredibly quick. Academics and media analysts who had pointed to the unprecedented nature of the lockdown measures in January 2020 now backed them ruthlessly. A good example is the three authorities quoted in the *Washington Post* article of 25 January 2020 mentioned earlier, Lawrence O. Gostin, Howard Markel, and Leana Wen, all of whom had noted then how unprecedented the Wuhan lockdown was: Gostin became a trenchant advocate of vaccine and mask mandates,[14] and already by 30 March 2020 was writing in *The Atlantic* that 'a large-scale quarantine is what the country needs';[15] Wen was arguing by 19 May 2020 that Baltimore (where she had previously been health commissioner) was lifting Covid restrictions too early,[16] and became an ardent advocate of vaccine mandates;[17] while by 20 April 2020, Markel was saying that acting early was best, that Sweden had chosen the wrong policy, and that he feared SARS-CoV-2 would be far worse than the Spanish flu of 1918–19 (which, as said, is estimated to have killed around 3 per cent of the world population).[18]

We should recall that just three months earlier, Markel had said of the Wuhan lockdown: 'This is just mind-boggling: this is the mother of all quarantines. I could never have imagined it.' How to explain this extraordinary change of position? It's instructive to look away from the US and consider a similar case from the UK. On 13 March 2020, Professor John Edmunds of the London School of Hygiene and Tropical Medicine was interviewed on the UK's Channel 4 in a 1-hour coronavirus special. Edmunds rejected lockdown as an appropriate response in a debate with Tomas Pueyo, advocating herd immunity instead. When Edmunds made this case, Pueyo sank his head in his hands and accused Edmunds of wanting to kill millions of people. Within a month, when he was interviewed again on Channel 4 on 24 April, Edmunds stated that we knew lockdowns worked as they were bringing infections down. And on 6 June he said on the BBC that '[w]e should have gone into lockdown earlier'.[19]

So who was Tomas Pueyo, whose knowledge of the science was apparently so superior to that of a professor at one of the world's leading scientific institutions? Early in March 2020, Pueyo had written a lockdown-advocating piece for *Medium* which had gone viral and been viewed 30 million times in 9 days.[20] In this article, Pueyo had coined a phrase which became a byword during the first phase of the pandemic, 'the hammer and the dance'—elaborating how societies could hammer the virus with lockdowns and then try to elude its spread in between times, in a model for the way in which many countries subsequently sought to respond to the pandemic. The byline to Pueyo's piece summarised his medical qualifications: '2 MSc in Engineering. Stanford MBA. Ex Consultant.'[21]

Pueyo may have had no epidemiological or medical qualifications whatsoever, but as his *Medium* byline also noted, he was the Vice-President of an online learning platform called Course Hero, and therefore stood to make a fortune from shutting down education.[22] Indeed, Course Hero raised one of the largest Wall Street funding deals of 2020, of US$80 million,[23] which was then dwarfed by its additional funding round from Wall Street of US$380 million in December 2021.[24] This US$460-million war chest represented an increase of over 3,000 per cent on all the venture capital which Course Hero had managed to raise throughout its previous fourteen years of existence—which until Covid had been a paltry US$15 million.[25] Nice work if you can get it.

If, then, we are asking what drove these extraordinary changes of heart in world-leading scientists, apparently without any peer-reviewed or randomised controlled studies to build on, it would appear that the power of money—and the vested commercial interests that went with it—were significant in applying pressure. Of course, this is not to say that the scientists individually profited, but rather that commercial interests had enormous power to promote certain outcomes which it was hard for them to resist. Whether or not you use the word 'corruption', there is surely nothing controversial in suggesting that large sums of money can certainly have a decisive influence over the behaviour of human beings. And yet over the course of the pandemic, to question whether such factors have had any role to play in the 'single narrative' version of 'The Science' which wrought extraordinary harms around the world has been to risk being branded a conspiracy theorist. The word 'corruption' implies a moral judgement, whereas what we are describing is a statement of fact: huge financial interests and profits were certainly at stake in the choice of response to the virus, as time (and the example of Course Hero) has shown, and these factors can only have had an influence on the outcome. To dismiss this analysis is to dismiss the basis of modern economics, and more importantly to bury one's head in the sand.

Lockdowns, however, are only one part of this chronicle of the events of 2020 and 2021. One cannot understand the relentless drive towards lockdowns without taking into account the wider vaccine-centric Covid narrative, which right from the start rested on a series of undisputable, though very tenuous, assumptions: that Covid was a lethal threat bearing indiscriminately on all human beings; that no effective medical treatment for Covid existed, and hence that the pandemic would end only once a vaccine had been invented; and that it therefore followed that until then, countries had no other choice but to resort to lockdowns. This is what Laurent Mucchielli has termed 'the Covid doxa'—a self-justifying and hermetically sealed ideology which brooked no contradiction.[26] One can easily see how the 'pieces' of the narrative are mutually reinforcing, and indeed how the overall narrative would fall apart in the absence of any one of those pieces.

This 'doxa', or single narrative, was certainly promoted with a fair degree of uniformity. And again, this should not be surprising or seen as a conspiracy: this is simply how capital operates when it is without restraint, seeking to concentrate itself. As we have seen with the debate between John Edmunds and Tomas Pueyo, there were enormous vested interests at work in pushing the lockdown position. Tech and pharmaceutical companies stood to make billions from the 'single narrative', and the more it could be pushed, the more money could be made. When companies like Facebook and Twitter censored voices that deviated from the narrative, there were clear and enormous conflicts of interest. And when vaccine mandates started to be pushed, these conflicts did not go away—if anything, they became even more apparent. Yet it became almost a marker of being a nutcase to question this narrative shift—and to wonder whether universal vaccination against a condition which overwhelmingly impacts older people was the wisest use of public resources, and whether there were not vested interests that were pushing this policy and the consequent traducing of democratic and scientific norms.

In this section, we now take a closer look at some of the most salient aspects of this single narrative or doxa and how it was put together. Let's start with something that we have already touched upon, the first pillar of the narrative: the over-emphasising of the actual dangerousness of Covid through its highly misleading framing as a deadly enemy threatening nothing less than all of humanity.

As noted, it was clear from the start that the illness was highly selective. As one medical expert wrote in April 2020, just a few weeks into the pandemic:

> The overwhelming majority of people do not have any significant risk of dying from Covid-19. The recent Stanford University antibody study now estimates that the fatality rate if infected is likely 0.1 to 0.2 percent, a risk far lower than previous World Health Organization estimates that were 20 to 30 times higher and that motivated isolation policies. In New York City, an epicenter of the pandemic with more than one-third of all US deaths, the rate of death for people 18 to 45 years old is 0.01 percent, or 10 per 100,000 in the population. On the other hand, people aged 75 and over have a death rate 80 times that. For people under 18 years old, the rate of death is zero per 100,000. Of all fatal cases in New York state, two-thirds were in patients over 70 years of age; more than 95 percent were over 50 years

of age; and about 90 percent of all fatal cases had an underlying illness. Of 6,570 confirmed Covid-19 deaths fully investigated for underlying conditions to date, 6,520, or 99.2 percent, had an underlying illness. If you do not already have an underlying chronic condition, your chances of dying are small, regardless of age. And young adults and children in normal health have almost no risk of any serious illness from Covid-19. [...] Even early WHO reports noted that 80 percent of all cases were mild, and more recent studies show a far more widespread rate of infection and lower rate of serious illness. Half of all people testing positive for infection have no symptoms at all. The vast majority of younger, otherwise healthy people do not need significant medical care if they catch this infection. [...] [The virus] is so mild that half of infected people are asymptomatic, shown in early data from the Diamond Princess ship, and then in Iceland and Italy. [...] The overwhelming evidence all over the world consistently shows that a clearly defined group—older people and others with underlying conditions—is more likely to have a serious illness requiring hospitalization and more likely to die from Covid-19.[27]

The question of pre-existing medical conditions (comorbidities) is particularly relevant, since we know that health and life expectancy tend to be strictly correlated with income and socio-economic status, as well as the quality of welfare and public health systems. Other studies suggested other possible co-factors, such as air pollution (particularly acute in Northern Italy),[28] which generally plays a role in accentuating the severity of pulmonary infections. This led Richard Horton, editor-in-chief of *The Lancet*, to write polemically that 'Covid-19 is not a pandemic. It is a syndemic'[29]—that is, a situation where the dangerousness of the disease stems not so much from its intrinsic severity but rather from its synergetic interaction with an array of self-reinforcing social, economic, environmental, and health factors, and where the disease therefore tends to disproportionately affect those who are already weakened by degraded social and living conditions.

In other words, the profile of the disease—which events would subsequently confirm—was clear very early on. However, this is not the way in which the disease was framed by politicians, mainstream media outlets, and international organisations such as the WHO. On the contrary, as we saw, the official narrative was heavily skewed towards presenting Covid as an invisible killer that could strike anyone and anywhere, underemphasising or outright ignoring what the empirical evidence showed in terms of infection fatality rates or age-stratified risks, and thus leaving the public with an inflated and inaccurate impression of Covid's true lethality.

Wildly overblown mortality estimates, from the likes of Ferguson and even the WHO, and the widespread use of war metaphors further contributed to the general panic. However, arguably nothing struck the fear of the virus in people more than the daily count of new Covid cases, hospitalisations, and deaths that soon became the metric that marked the rhythm of world societies, as 'Covid dashboards' sprung up all over the internet and the media. This in itself was unprecedented. As *British Medical Journal* (*BMJ*) senior editor Peter Doshi wrote: 'People have long experienced the tragedy of sickness and unexpected death in pandemic and non-pandemic years, but the covid-19 [*sic*] pandemic is historically unique in the extent to which the interruption and resumption of social life has been so closely tied to epidemiological metrics.'[30]

In this case, however, what took place was not exactly something new, but rather a rapid acceleration in computer-driven trends towards digitisation, surveillance, and the polarisation of wealth and opinion which had already been reshaping human societies for at least three decades. During 2020, a new ethical norm was constructed in which being a 'good citizen' required compliance with the data-driven projections and computing tools that shaped the unprecedented government interventions.

It is worth noting that the scientists who spearheaded the lockdown policies were computer modellers. In the well-documented case of Ferguson, and of his professional allies such as Matthias an der Heiden and Udo Buchholz at the Robert Koch Institute in Germany, who published a paper on 22 March predicting hundreds of thousands of deaths in the country, it was computer models based on such data as was available in early March which drove everything that followed.[56] These models were attractive to governments which were already strongly drawn to data-driven models of policy development. The imposition of the initial lockdown policies thus emerged from the privileging of these computer-simulated models over the experience of medical history in the treating of new epidemics.

Allied to this initial mode of policy decision was the way in which computing power very quickly enabled the tracking and measurement of the virus impact in a manner that had never before been possible. In the US, the Johns Hopkins University Coronavirus Resource Center was launched in early March, and rapidly became world-famous in its accumulation of information on cases, deaths, and the spread of the virus, with searchable fields for individual countries and interactive maps.[57] Sites such as worldometer.org offered daily updates on the virus, with various benchmarks of mortality and spread. Meanwhile, the almost mythical 'R number'—derived from mathematical projections—made the measurement and spread of the virus the fundamental benchmark through which the new consensus was constructed.

This new focus was compromised, however, by 'fundamental flaws in data acquisition and especially on medically incorrect definitions laid down by the World Health Organization', leading to a 'distorted and misleading picture' of the actual infectiousness and lethality of the virus, wrote Professor Sucharit

Bhakdi.[31] Bhakdi was referring to statistical practices that were commonplace in virtually all Western countries throughout the first two years of the pandemic. Firstly: the designation of every positive laboratory test for the virus as a Covid-19 case, irrespective of clinical signs and symptoms, as per WHO guidelines.[32] According to Bhakdi:

> This definition represented an unforgiveable breach of a first rule in infectiology: the necessity to differentiate between 'infection' (invasion and multiplication of an agent in the host) and 'infectious disease' (infection with ensuing illness). Covid-19 is the designation for severe illness that occurs only in about 10% of infected individuals, but because of incorrect designation, the number of 'cases' surged and the virus vaulted to the top of the list of existential threats to the world.[33]

The reality of the situation was further muddled by the fact that authorities tended to present the data in a completely decontextualised manner—that is, without specifying how many tests were actually being carried out, and without clarifying that an increase in 'cases' could very well have simply reflected the fact that more people were being tested, which was often the case, even if the ratio of positives to tests had remained unchanged or possibly even decreased. Moreover, testing was generally performed on people with flu-like symptoms and a certain risk of exposure to the virus. In Italy, for example, at the height of the first wave, testing was restricted to severely ill patients upon their admission to the hospital (with all positives then counted as 'Covid hospitalisations'—see below).[34] This clearly led to massive overestimates of the positives-to-tests ratio.

Moreover, positive PCR tests were automatically counted as 'cases' even though they not only said nothing about the health or infectiousness of the person—as noted already, even totally asymptomatic infectees were considered 'cases'—but were also very poor indicators of whether the person actually had the virus at all at the moment of the test. As the Swiss immunologist Beda Stadler noted, most PCR tests are designed to detect the tiniest viral load,[35] meaning that they 'cannot tell you whether you have the virus or you just have some dead chunk of the virus which still gives you a positive result'.[36] And as the Nobel Prize-winning inventor of the test, Kary Mullis, said, it 'can find almost anything in anybody' and 'it can't tell you that you're sick'.[37]

It's important to note that these problems with the testing framework were known to key sections of the media and government. By the summer of 2020, news outlets were already reporting that

> a burgeoning line of scientific inquiry suggests that many confirmed infections of Covid-19 may actually be just residual traces of the virus itself, a contention that—if true—may suggest both that current high levels of positive viruses are clinically insignificant and that the mitigation measures used to suppress them may be excessive. [...] A growing body of research suggests that a significant number of confirmed Covid-19 infections in the US—perhaps as many as 9 out of every 10—may not be infectious at all, with much of the country's testing equipment possibly picking up mere fragments of the disease rather than full-blown infections.[38]

In short, one of the main metrics that led to widespread panic in the early months of the pandemic—the relentless rise in new 'cases'—is likely to have been overblown, but more importantly, virtually meaningless. All the same, as most readers of this book are aware, these metrics were essential in stoking the 'single narrative' surrounding both the disease and the preferred solution.

Meanwhile, the other two metrics used to gauge the risk posed by the disease—Covid hospitalisations and deaths— were framed in ways which were also liable to be misleading.

Throughout most of the pandemic, Covid hospitalisations were presented as 'the most reliable pandemic number'.[39] Yet as it turned out, this wasn't the case. It is now established that in several countries—definitely several major Western countries, as far as we have been able to ascertain—it was standard practice throughout 2020 and 2021 to classify anyone admitted to a hospital who had recently tested positive for Covid as a 'Covid patient'—regardless of the actual reason for which they were being admitted.[40] This means that someone who was admitted for reasons completely unrelated to Covid—say, for example, a car accident—but had recently tested positive would end up in the country's national statistics as a Covid patient. Considering that all hospitals, to our knowledge, required people to be tested upon admission, it's easy to see how this led to massive overestimations of Covid hospitalisations—above and beyond the equally misleading practice of not differentiating actual Covid patients based on the severity of the illness, as we've seen, not to mention the questionable reliability of the tests themselves and how they designated someone as a 'Covid patient'.

Indeed, as *The Atlantic* reported, three separate studies (on children and adults) conducted in California and published in May 2021 revealed that 'roughly half of all the hospitalized patients showing up on Covid-data dashboards in 2021 may have been admitted for another reason entirely, or had only a mild presentation of disease. [...] [This suggests] that Covid hospitalization tallies can't be taken as a simple measure of the prevalence of severe or even moderate disease, because they might inflate the true numbers by a factor of two.'[41] This was shown to be particularly true for children. As a commentary for *Hospital Pediatrics* that accompanied the studies noted, they demonstrate that reported hospitalisation rates 'greatly overestimate[d] the true burden of Covid-19 disease in children'[42]—an overestimate that would then prove instrumental in convincing millions of panic-stricken parents to vaccinate their children despite 'a very low likelihood of severe outcome',[43] as we will see in the chapters to follow. At the end of 2021, Fauci himself confirmed this, urging calm when it came to the numbers of children in hospital allegedly with Covid, and noting that 'some of the children currently being treated at medical facilities were hospitalised with Covid as opposed to 'because of Covid. [...] [They] may actually be receiving treatment for "a broken leg or appendicitis" rather than for a severe reactions [sic] to the virus'.[44]

***

Alongside the question of cause of hospitalisation, Covid death counts were plagued by comparable statistical problems. From the early days of the pandemic, there was much discussion around the fact that the overwhelming majority of 'Covid-19 deaths' were patients with pre-existing illnesses (hypertension, diabetes, heart conditions, and so on) for which a direct causality from Covid was impossible to ascertain. Death certificate guidelines published in March 2020 by the CDC, for example, stated that 'Covid-19 should be reported on the death certificate for all decedents where the disease caused or is assumed to have caused or contributed to death.'[45] As Deborah Birx, White House Coronavirus Response Coordinator under President Donald Trump from 2020 to 2021, declared: 'If someone dies with Covid-19, we are counting that as a Covid-19 death.'[46]

The same approach was adopted in most Western countries. Indeed, as early as mid-March the reliability of the Italian mortality figures had been put in serious doubt. On 17 March, Walter Ricciardi, Scientific Advisor to the Italian Minister of Health for the Coronavirus Pandemic, reported that 'on re-evaluation by the National Institute of Health, only 12% of death certificates have shown a direct causality from coronavirus, while 88% of patients who have died have at least one pre-morbidity—

many had two or three'.[47] At the same time, the Italian Gruppo Italiano per la Medicina Basata Sulle Evidenze (GIMBE)— Italian Evidence-Based Medicine Group—stated that the 'degree of severity and lethality rate are largely overestimated, while the lethality rates in Lombardy and the Emilia-Romagna region were largely due to overwhelmed hospitals'.[48] Indeed, some analysts were already noting the role that diverging causal attributions of death were playing in the mortality statistics: whereas by 20 March, Italy reported a mortality of 3,405 patients from 41,035 cases, in China the reported mortality rate was less than half of that, with 3,245 fatalities from 81,155 cases.[49]

This is what came to be known as the death 'by/with Covid' debate. Personally we aren't qualified to judge whether it was methodologically correct to classify as Covid deaths not only those that were in all likelihood caused by the virus, but also those where the end of life was simply brought forward by it. Nevertheless, we are aware that several experts criticised this practice. Sucharit Bhakdi, for example, noted that 'the true cause of a death is the disease or condition that triggers the lethal chain of events. If someone suffering from severe emphysema or end-stage cancer contacts fatal pneumonia, the cause of death is still emphysema or cancer.'[50] As non-experts, we can see why it may have been considered reasonable, especially in the early stages of the pandemic, to err on the side of caution, and consider the death of anyone who would have likely gone on living for a reasonable length of time if they hadn't contracted Covid as a 'Covid death' (though we also believe the crucial role of comorbidities should have been made clear).

Ultimately, however, this whole debate is rendered moot by a much more macroscopic problem: the fact that, just as with hospitalisations, it was standard practice in all the Western countries we looked into to classify every deceased person who had recently (or even not so recently,[51] or in some cases after death)[52] tested positive for Covid as a 'Covid death', even if the death was manifestly unrelated to Covid. Indeed, in several countries, it wasn't just fatalities with a positive Covid-19 test that entered the ranks but also those where Covid-19 was simply suspected.[53] As Ngozi Ezike, the Illinois Department of Public Health (IDPH) Director, put it in April 2020: 'Technically, even if you died of a clear alternate cause, but you had Covid at the same time, it's still listed as a Covid death. So, everyone who's listed as a Covid death doesn't mean that was the cause of death, but they had Covid at the time of death.'[54] It would later emerge that 'clear alternate causes' of death could include anything from injury and poisoning to motorcycle accidents[55] and gunshot wounds.[56]

The same was true in Germany. As openly declared by Lothar H. Wieler, President of the Robert Koch Institute (RKI), the German federal government agency and research institute for disease control, every individual with a positive test result at the time of death was entered into the statistics.[57] Indeed, the first 'Covid death' in the northernmost state of Germany, Schleswig-Holstein, occurred in a palliative ward, where a patient with terminal oesophageal cancer was seeking peace before embarking on his last journey. A swab was taken just before his demise that was returned positive—after his death.[58] Meanwhile in Kenya, Dr Reginald Oduor described how suspected Covid fatalities were buried in secret by state security personnel without family members even allowed to attend or observe the body.[59]

In the case of the UK, the retired consultant pathologist Dr John Lee wrote a searing account in late May 2020 of the way in which longstanding practices of autopsy and attribution of cause of death had been changed in the Covid-19 pandemic, and of the effects that this had had:

Normally, two doctors are needed to certify a death, one of whom has been treating the patient or who knows them and has seen them recently. That has changed. For Covid-19 only, the certification can be made by a single doctor, and there is no requirement for them to have examined, or even met, the patient. A video-link consultation in the four weeks prior to death is now felt to be sufficient for death to be attributed to Covid-19. For deaths in care homes the situation is even more extraordinary. Care home providers, most of whom are not medically trained, may make a statement to the effect that a patient has died of Covid-19. [...] From 29 March the numbers of 'Covid deaths' have included all cases where Covid-19 was simply mentioned on the death certificate—irrespective of positive testing and whether or not it may have been incidental to, or directly responsible for, death. From 29 April the numbers include the care home cases simply considered likely to be Covid-19.[60]

Following this, in June, Professor Karol Sikora, the former Director of the WHO Cancer Programme who had been in favour of the initial 23 March lockdown of the UK, stated that its Covid-19 death toll may have been half of what had been recorded.[61]

A similar state of affairs was (belatedly) brought to light in Italy when several hospital managers and directors spoke out against the pervasive practice of misattributing Covid deaths. 'Not infrequently a person who enters a hospital for, let's say, an orthopaedic problem and who then loses his life due to complications, is included in the list of deaths from Covid simply because, upon entry, they tested positive. Frankly, this doesn't make sense', said Massimo Clementi, Director of the Microbiology and Virology Laboratory at the San Raffaele Hospital in Milan.[62] Similarly, the manager of a Roman hospital, speaking anonymously to a Radiotelevisione italiana (RAI) television journalist, revealed: 'It's commonplace to classify deceased patients as Covid deaths simply because they tested positive even though their death was completely unrelated to the virus.'[63]

In sum, there's clearly a pattern at play here. So how should we explain this practice of systematic misattribution of hospitalisations/deaths, and the fact that this pattern was common to so many countries? On the part of the medics and hospital administrators, insofar as hospitalisations are concerned, it made sense to keep 'Covid-positive patients' separated from the rest, though it's less clear why a greater effort wasn't made, in terms of statistical data gathering, to distinguish Covid-positive but asymptomatic patients from symptomatic ones, which would have helped to assess the impact of the virus much more accurately. Bureaucratic overload and lack of resources may have played a role. This may also explain why, insofar as deaths are concerned, classifying 'suspect' Covid deaths as deaths from Covid was seen as an easier route than carrying out detailed diagnoses for each single case—though it doesn't explain why deaths patently unrelated to Covid were designated as such.

One possible answer is that hospitals were financially incentivised by governments to over-record Covid hospitalisations and deaths. At the start of the pandemic, several countries introduced legislation providing hefty premiums to hospitals for Covid-19 patients compared to non-Covid patients.[64] This means that hospitals were allocated much higher sums of money for a Covid-19 patient than for a patient affected by, say, a common form of pneumonia or some other respiratory infection. In the United States, for example, the coronavirus relief legislation created a 20 per cent premium, or add-on, for Covid-19 Medicare patients.[65] As the US Senator Scott Jensen stated in April 2020:

Hospital administrators might well want to see Covid-19 attached to a discharge summary or a death certificate. Why?

Because if it's a straightforward, garden-variety pneumonia that a person is admitted to the hospital for—if they're Medicare—typically, the diagnosis-related group lump sum payment would be US$5,000. But if it's Covid-19 pneumonia, then it's US$13,000, and if that Covid-19 pneumonia patient ends up on a ventilator, it goes up to US$39,000.[66]

It's easy to see how this created a perverse incentive for hospitals to misclassify hospitalisations and deaths as being due to Covid-19. Jensen clarified that he didn't think physicians were 'gaming the system' so much as other 'players', such as hospital administrators, whom he said may have pressured physicians to cite all diagnoses, including 'probable' Covid-19, on discharge papers or death certificates to get the higher Medicare allocation allowed under the Coronavirus Aid, Relief and Economic Security Act.

Similar allegations were made in other countries as well. An Italian physician working at a private hospital, speaking anonymously to RAI state television, said: 'The hospital is allocated extra money based on the number of [Covid] hospitalisations. We have received requests from above—from the general managers, the health directors—to alter medical records, to write that a patient is positive when they are not. For the hospital, out of 10 deaths, 7 are Covid: it has already been decided.'[67]

These Covid-19 premiums may also have incentivised some hospitals to go even further than simply falsifying records. In her book *Undercover Epicenter Nurse*, published in August 2020 by Simon & Schuster, the nurse Erin Olszewski detailed her experience at Elmhurst Hospital in New York, where she witnessed several patients who had tested negative multiple times for Covid-19 being labelled as Covid-confirmed and put on Covid-only floors. According to Olszewski, many of them ended up catching Covid, being placed on ventilators, and dying.[68] Thus Covid protocols did not help to reduce the number of 'Covid deaths'—it's clear from this that at least some of them weren't caused by Covid as such but rather by the protocols themselves.

This is brought into sharp focus when we consider the infamous question of ventilators. In the early stages of the pandemic, China and Italy took to using ventilators to treat virtually all severe Covid-19 cases that ended up in intensive care units (ICUs). Ventilators are machines that provide mechanical ventilation by moving breathable air into and out of the lungs via a tracheal tube to deliver oxygen to patients who have trouble breathing or exhibit very low blood oxygen levels—two common symptoms among severe Covid-19 cases. This is a technique known as invasive ventilation, which requires the patient to be sedated, as opposed to non-invasive ventilation, where ventilatory support is provided via a face mask.

One of the official reasons given for choosing invasive ventilation—up to that moment generally used as a very last resort due to its potential risks—over less invasive and generally safer ventilation methods was that, according to the WHO guidelines, non-invasive ventilation could contribute to the spread of the virus via 'aerosolisation'.[69] Invasive ventilation soon became standard protocol in most high-income countries, as governments scrambled to buy thousands of ventilators, while also offering very large premiums to hospitals for patients requiring mechanical ventilation, as noted already. The WHO reported that in the first months of the pandemic, among the 5 per cent of Covid-19 patients who required treatment in an ICU, about 90 per cent of them were placed on mechanical ventilation.[70]

It soon became clear, however, that a shockingly high number of patients put on ventilators ended up dying—between 80 and 90 per cent of them, based on early reports from China, Italy, and the United States[71]—and those who did survive tended to have permanent cognitive and respiratory damage.[72] This was compared to reported mortality rates of 17–39 per cent among critically ill Covid-19 patients,[73] in line with historical data from other respiratory illnesses and previous influenza pandemics.[74] Of course, since people placed on ventilators were already in a critical condition to begin with, a higher death rate in this cohort was to be expected. However, such statistics were also at odds with the 40–50 per cent general death rate recorded among patients with severe respiratory distress syndrome who are connected to ventilators.[75] Countries (such as South Korea) and single institutions that prioritised less invasive respiratory therapies, such as simple oxygen masks, reported much lower mortality rates.[76]

As a result, by March to April 2020, several experts were already claiming that ventilators were likely harming Covid-19 patients more than they were helping them[77]—actually killing people who could otherwise have survived. In a letter to the editor published in the American *Journal of Respiratory and Critical Care Medicine* on 30 March,[78] and in an editorial accepted for publication in *Intensive Care Medicine*,[79] Luciano Gattinoni, MD, of the Medical University of Göttingen in Germany, and colleagues made the case that protocol-driven ventilator use for patients with Covid-19 could be doing more harm than good.

A few days later, Cameron Kyle-Sidell, MD, a critical care physician working in New York City, posted a video on YouTube which soon racked up hundreds of thousands of views,[80] in which he said: 'I've talked to doctors all around the country and it is becoming increasingly clear that the pressure we're providing may be hurting their lungs. It is highly likely that the high pressures we're using are damaging the lungs of the patients we are putting the breathing tubes in. [...] I fear that this misguided treatment will lead to a tremendous amount of harm to a great number of people in a very short time.' He noted that critical Covid patients overwhelmingly did not suffer from respiratory failure but rather from oxygen failure—and that therefore the use of machines to increase pressure on the lungs to open them up was 'actually doing more harm than good', by effectively blowing up the lungs of patients. 'We are running the ventilators the wrong way', he said, calling for the protocols to be changed. 'Covid positive patients need oxygen, they do not need pressure. They will need ventilators, but they must be programmed differently.'

Erin Olszewski, the aforementioned frontline nurse at Elmhurst Hospital in New York, was even more explicit. 'It's a horror movie. Not because of the disease, but the way it is being handled', she said anonymously in April 2020 through a friend, who posted a video on YouTube that was subsequently taken down for 'violating its community standards'.[81] 'People are sick, but they don't have to stay sick [...] they are not helping them', added the friend. 'Patients are left to rot and die—her words.' Olszewski, as noted, would then go on to recount her harrowing experience in her book *Undercover Epicenter Nurse*.

Soon others started sounding the alarm elsewhere. Professor Gerhard Laier-Groeneveld from the lung clinic in Neustadt, Germany, advised that intubation should be avoided in any event.[82] In April 2020, he claimed that he hadn't intubated a single patient—and hadn't lost a single life.[83] Professor Thomas Voshaar, Chair of the Association of Pneumology Clinics in Germany, shared the same view.[84] He pointed out that the high death rates in other countries 'should be reason enough to question this strategy of early intubation'. In early April 2020, he said that he had mechanically ventilated only one of his forty patients. The patient had subsequently died—while all the others had survived.

As the weeks and months went by, and as evidence of the devastating effects of ventilators mounted, more and more doctors started moving away from using the breathing machines.[85] Yet health officials around the world continued to push to get more ventilators to treat coronavirus patients.[86] Indeed, in June 2020, the use of ventilators was still 'the mainstay of treatment for severe and critical cases of Covid-19', with almost 90 per cent of all ICU patients still being placed on ventilators, the WHO reported.[87] Over time the evidence stacked up so overwhelmingly that utilisation of ventilators decreased rapidly during the autumn period.[88] However, by then, the ventilator-based protocol had already caused immense suffering—and arguably a large number of avoidable deaths.

A back-of-the-envelope calculation can help us get a sense of the disaster. By September 2020, there had officially been a million Covid fatalities worldwide—most of them in high-income countries where the use of ventilators was commonplace. Of all Covid deaths, around 15 per cent occurred in ICUs,[89] where for several months around 90 per cent of patients were placed on ventilators. We can therefore conservatively hypothesise that, even accounting for statistical overestimations of actual Covid-19 deaths, at least tens of thousands of deaths in the early months of the pandemic weren't caused by Covid-19 itself—but rather by the biomedical response to it, including (though not limited to, as we will see) the bad practice around the use of ventilators. While many of the patients that were hooked up to mechanical breathers would have likely died shortly afterwards anyway, given their old age and pre-existing conditions, many others might have gone on to live for longer periods if they had received alternative treatments.

One might wonder why more wasn't done to investigate the cause of such unusually high mortality rates. As non-experts, it appears pretty clear to us that the easiest way to ascertain why so many patients hooked up to ventilators were dying would have been to perform autopsies on the deceased. However, in the early months of the pandemic, very few autopsies were conducted on Covid-positive fatalities. As a research paper published in the journal *Legal Medicine* noted, for quite some time there was 'a certain reluctance to perform autopsies of patients who died of Covid-19'[90]—or on any person who had died with Covid. Indeed, in some countries autopsies were explicitly discouraged or even prohibited. In Germany, the Robert Koch Institute, the country's equivalent of the CDC, advised against performing autopsies.[91] Meanwhile in Italy, on 1 April 2020, the Ministry of Health published an official document on autopsies during the SARS-CoV-2 epidemics that clearly stated that for the entire period of the emergency phase, autopsies or post-mortem diagnostic studies should not be performed in full-blown cases of Covid-19.[92]

As the author of the article wrote, '[i]t's not clear' why that was the case. To our knowledge, other large health organisations such as the WHO, the Royal College of Pathologists (UK), or the CDC didn't take a stand against autopsies, limiting themselves to outlining requirements for safe autopsies.[93] Indeed, the main reason for the great reluctance worldwide to perform autopsies seems to have been concerns about infectivity emanating from deceased persons[94]—despite the fact that a survey of 225 autopsies registered only one case of infection, in which it is considered probable that the affected person was not infected by the autopsy but by community exposure.[95]

It's regrettable that more extensive post-mortem examinations weren't carried out in the first months of the pandemic, since the few autopsies that were undertaken confirmed what some doctors had been saying since March and April 2020—many victims had lung sacs that were inflamed and deeply damaged by the virus, and therefore unable to withstand the high pressure of mechanical ventilators.[96] Yet the ventilator-centric protocol remained unchanged for several months. As Ranieri Guerra, Assistant Director-General of the WHO until September 2021, wrote in a book published that same year:

In the early phase of the pandemic, autopsies, which were discouraged and sometimes even prohibited, would have been fundamental. A subsequent study by colleagues at the San Raffaele Hospital in Milan on a hundred autopsies, for example, revealed devastating clinical evidence: lungs that practically no longer existed, as if dissolved in acid. [...] The real initial failure, on a scientific level, [...] is to have insisted on pressurised oxygen in the presence of irremediably destroyed lung tissues.[97]

***

We have thus established that a significant number of patients who ended up in hospital with severe Covid in the early months of the pandemic could most likely have been saved with less invasive treatments. But why were so many people ending up in hospital in the first place? We were told that this was due to the intrinsic severity of the illness—and, crucially, to the fact that no effective treatment existed. Indeed, virtually all Western governments adopted essentially the same protocol when it came to advising people on how to deal with the onset of mild Covid symptoms: they were told to stay at home, rest, and in the case of a high fever to take paracetamol—but *not* anti-inflammatories such as ibuprofen. If their symptoms got worse, they were told to call—but *not* to visit—their family doctor (most family doctors stopped visiting patients in person altogether;[98] in several countries they were also advised against or forbidden from doing house calls)[99] and, finally, to call emergency services if they experienced trouble breathing—at which point they would be admitted to hospital, where many of them would be placed on ventilators, as we have seen. Alternative at-home early treatments of any kind were actively and aggressively discouraged and discredited—and family doctors were strongly advised against or forbidden from administering them.[100]

In hindsight, there are several reasons for questioning the effectiveness of such a protocol. For starters, by effectively relieving general practitioners of their duty to treat their patients—and all but shutting down any form of primary care—it placed all the burden and all the pressure of managing the pandemic on hospitals, all while governments and media outlets continued to shriek about the desperate need to avoid the congestion of healthcare systems. As the French researcher Laurent Mucchielli noted:

> In this hospital-centrism lies probably the most serious (because the deadliest) fault of Western governments. [...] It is surprising (and dramatic in view of the consequences) that no one seems to have understood that such a strategy could only fail because it carried a contradiction in terms. [...] Moreover, by becoming the only place of care for patients infected with the coronavirus, hospitals also became a privileged place of contamination, causing Covid to become a dangerous nosocomial disease, which caused many infections and even a few deaths among the nursing staff.[101]

But if no effective treatment for Covid existed, one may ask, how could hospitalisations have been avoided? This brings us to one of the most controversial aspects of what is admittedly already an extremely controversial story—the early treatment debate. It is beyond the scope of this book to offer a detailed analysis of the topic; we will thus limit ourselves to a brief summary of its most salient points, as they relate to the elaboration of the single scientific narrative or doxa described above.

As noted, right from the very start, governments and media outlets went out of their way to get the message out that there was no effective early treatment for Covid—in other words, that there were no existing drugs or therapies that were proven to be effective, if taken at the onset of the illness, in reducing the risk of hospitalisation and/or death. Of course, if we take that to mean that in the early days of the pandemic no large randomised clinical trials had scientifically 'proven' the efficacy of any early treatment, that is certainly true. And it couldn't have been otherwise, since such trials usually take months. However, as frontline doctors around the world realised that the official protocol effectively meant doing nothing until the illness became life-threatening, some of them started experimenting with various therapies that had proven effective in curing similar pathologies, such as other coronaviruses, in the past. And by as early as March 2020, they were already collecting empirical evidence of the apparent effectiveness of some therapies in reducing hospitalisations and deaths.

Indeed, the Chinese published their own early treatment protocol on 3 March 2020[102]—based on prophylactic and early treatment drugs such as chloroquine, antibiotics, anti-inflammatories, and antihistamines, as well as on vitamins and other compounds known to stabilise and fortify the immune system—and some have claimed that early treatment is one of the reasons the Chinese managed to claim that they had got the pandemic under control in such a short time. Since inflammation is one of the key symptoms of Covid-19,[103] drugs with a proven track record of treating this in other illnesses were certainly worth a shot.

At this stage, doctors in the West were also getting promising results with these and other therapies. One of the most vocal advocates of early outpatient (at-home) treatment for Covid was (and still is) the American cardiologist Peter McCullough, former Vice Chief of Internal Medicine at Baylor University Medical Center, founder and current President of the Cardio Renal Society of America and Co-Editor-in-Chief of the society's journal, *Cardiorenal Medicine*, and Editor of the journal *Reviews in Cardiovascular Medicine*. 'By April and May, I noticed a disturbing trend', recalls McCullough. 'The trend was, no effort to treat patients who are infected with Covid-19 at home or in nursing homes.'[104]

McCullough thus began contacting physicians in other nations who were reporting success against the disease, including doctors in Italy, Greece, and elsewhere in Europe, in Canada, and in Bangladesh and South Africa. And he soon started developing prophylactic and early treatment protocols based on hydroxychloroquine and other repurposed drugs. By 1 July, McCullough and his team had developed the first protocol based on efficacy and safety, which they published in the prestigious *American Journal of Medicine*. That study, titled 'Pathophysiological Basis and Rationale for Early Outpatient Treatment of SARS-CoV-2 (COVID-19) Infection',[105] quickly became the world's most downloaded paper to help doctors treat Covid-19. In the study, McCullough and his colleagues acknowledged that those treatments hadn't yet undergone large randomised, placebo-controlled, parallel group clinical trials, but nonetheless, in several instances where they had been used, they had proven effective in reducing Covid hospitalisations and deaths. They therefore argued that 'in the context of present knowledge, given the severity of the outcomes and the relative availability, cost, and toxicity of the therapy, each physician and patient must make a choice: watchful waiting in self-quarantine or empiric treatment with the aim of reducing hospitalization and death'.[106]

It was a reasonable argument, that at the very least would have merited an open, rational debate—from a cost–benefit standpoint, especially insofar as elderly and at-risk people who faced a high risk of mortality were concerned, what role should have been given to therapies that hadn't undergone large clinical trials but had nonetheless proven effective in the treatment of Covid? But the public never got to hear that debate. Despite the rapidly growing literature on prophylactic and early treatment of Covid—by autumn 2020, hundreds of studies had been published alongside McCullough's—authorities refused to update their protocols. On the contrary, early therapies, and their advocates, were aggressively discredited by Western politicians, health officials, commentators, and online 'fact-checkers'. In some countries, doctors were threatened with disciplinary action and even arrest for administering therapies unsanctioned by national and international health authorities.[107]

What is to us quite disquieting—given the several studies that early in the pandemic showed a clear correlation between vitamin D deficiency and the severity of the illness, including relative increases in hospitalisations and deaths of up to 80 per cent[108]—is that even such relatively harmless treatments as the preventive and early administration of vitamin D supplements were censured, forbidden, and criminalised.[109] Even more confoundingly, government and medical authorities did little to advise citizens on how they could boost their immune system and reduce their risk of severe illness by making simple health-improving lifestyle choices—by quitting smoking (death rates among smokers were much higher);[110] getting plenty of sunlight (in order to address aforementioned vitamin D deficiencies); and dieting, exercising, and losing weight (death rates among overweight people were also particularly high).[111] In fact, when the CEO of salad chain Sweetgreen spoke in a since-deleted LinkedIn post of the link between obesity and Covid hospitalisations—a fact[112]—he faced accusations of fatphobia and body shaming.[113]

We can certainly comprehend the precautionary approach taken by authorities at the very start of the pandemic, to protect a panic-stricken public from falling prey to snake-oil sellers of various kinds. But it is hard to justify this relentless suppression of prophylactic and early therapies or treatments several months into the pandemic—including of those such as vitamin D where any associated risk was virtually nil—despite the promising results of many such therapies and, most importantly, the rapidly mounting death toll. Moreover, if the problem, as argued, was the lack of standard 'scientific' evidence of these therapies' effectiveness, why didn't the authorities promote the clinical trials whose absence they were lamenting, and mobilise public resources in order to prove or disprove the frontline clinical results? And why were they happy to perform about-turns on any number of other issues without such studies, as we've already seen in this chapter? In fact, very little public money was put into researching early treatments for Covid—only 2 per cent of NIH grants in the first year of the pandemic went to Covid research.[114] Instead, as we show in the next section, right from the start, virtually all public resources were poured into the funding of the vaccines— presented as the only possible 'cure' for Covid, in line with the 'lock down and wait for the vaccine' strategy and narrative.

Several experts noted from the start that this represented a profound and unprecedented departure from accepted public health practice. Never before had the approach to a disease been to do nothing—except take paracetamol, a simple painkiller—until people got so sick that they needed to be hospitalised, pending the arrival of a techno-medical miracle in the form of vaccines. 'That strategy kept the medical treatment on hold globally for an entire year as a readily treatable respiratory virus ravaged populations', notes the American critical care physician Pierre Kory. 'The Best Practices for defeating an infectious disease epidemic', says Yale epidemiologist Harvey Risch, 'dictate that you quarantine and treat the sick, protect the most vulnerable, and aggressively develop repurposed therapeutic drugs, and use early treatment protocols to avoid hospitalizations.'[115] McCullough concurs:

> We could have dramatically reduced Covid fatalities and hospitalizations using early treatment protocols and repurposed

drugs including ivermectin and hydroxychloroquine and many, many others. The strategy from the outset should have been implementing protocols to stop hospitalizations through early treatment of Americans who tested positive for Covid but were still asymptomatic. If we had done that, we could have pushed case fatality rates below those we see with seasonal flu, and ended the bottlenecks in our hospitals. We should have rapidly deployed off-the-shelf medications with proven safety records and subjected them to rigorous risk/benefit decision-making.[116]

McCullough believes that early treatment could have averted some 80 per cent of deaths attributed to Covid.[117] As we have pointed out on other occasions throughout the book, our aim is not to take a definitive stand on issues that are beyond our area of expertise—such as the validity of the protocols developed by McCullough—but rather to reflect on the way in which the scientific establishment operated throughout the pandemic, taking decisions which were contradictory, and which are very hard to see as motivated by a clear-eyed view of the scientific method. Here, we refer not only to the way in which political institutions made a parody of the scientific method by invoking certain data and studies, and 'cancelling' others, in order to legitimise their decisions, but also to the way in which scientific institutions themselves seem to have been suborned by political and economic interests. The early treatment debate is, in our opinion, yet another example of that. And within that debate, no story is more exemplary than that of remdesivir and hydroxychloroquine—what we could call a tale of two drugs.

From the very beginning of the Covid crisis, the pharmaceutical giant Gilead sought to peddle its antiviral medication remdesivir[118]—originally developed (with significant funding from the US government)[119] to treat Hepatitis C and subsequently investigated for Ebola, for which it proved ineffective—as a potential treatment for Covid. From the outset of the crisis, the WHO and high-profile researchers in several Western countries announced that Gilead's antiviral was the most promising solution.[120] Given the lobbying firepower of Gilead and the backing of heavyweights such as Anthony Fauci and other powerful health experts,[121] the prospects for remdesivir looked rosy indeed. Indeed, by late March and early April 2020, before the results of any clinical trial concerning the effectiveness of the drug on Covid patients had even been published, governments and institutions across the world, including the US government[122] and the European Union,[123] were already approving remdesivir for 'compassionate use'—the use of an unapproved drug by people with serious or life-threatening conditions—in Covid-19 patients. It was later revealed that Gilead had been providing remdesivir in response to compassionate use requests in the United States since 25 January.[124] And this, it will be recalled, took place while governments were invoking the precautionary principle to block any other form of preventive or early treatment, including harmless vitamin supplements—in this case, there was apparently no need to wait for randomised control trials.

At the end of April 2020 the results of the first clinical trials on remdesivir started coming in—and they didn't look good. An interim analysis from a large-scale, placebo-controlled clinical trial carried out by the NIH showed that remdesivir seemed to lower the risk of death, though that difference could have arisen by chance.[125] Fauci said that the trial showed 'quite good news' and set a new standard of care for Covid-19 patients.[126] But a second, smaller, placebo-controlled study of remdesivir on hospitalised Covid-19 patients in China, published by *The Lancet*,[127] found no statistically significant benefit from the treatment—and the antiviral had no impact on levels of coronavirus. Something which is equally if not more concerning is that this same *Lancet* trial was 'stopped early because of adverse events in 18 (12%) patients versus four (5%) patients who stopped placebo early'. Nonetheless, two days after the results from China and the United States came out, the FDA granted remdesivir an Emergency Use Authorization (EUA) for use in severe Covid-19 patients[128]—and the following week it expanded the EUA to include all hospitalised Covid-19 patients.[129]

In July, the European Medicines Agency (EMA), Europe's FDA counterpart, also granted a conditional market authorisation—similar to an EUA—to remdesivir.[130] By then, Gilead was already expecting to rake in billions from the sale of the drug—priced at a whopping US$3,120 for a standard 5-day treatment course for private insurance plans and US$2,340 per course for government purchases from developed countries.[131] Then, on 8 October, Gilead signed an agreement to supply the European Union with up to 500,000 remdesivir treatment courses over the next six months for twenty-seven European countries.[132] At the time, the price per treatment course was not disclosed, but it was later reported that the price was €2,070, thereby implying that the total value of the contract was approximately €1 billion.[133]

Just a week following this October 2020 agreement, the largest controlled study yet—undertaken by the WHO itself—delivered what some believed would be the coup de grâce for remdesivir: the WHO's Solidarity trial showed that remdesivir failed to reduce mortality, and failed to reduce the need for ventilators or the time Covid-19 patients took to recover.[134] This was surely a pretty terminal conclusion for the drug; as the *BMJ* pointed out, 'None of the randomized controlled trials published so far [...] have shown that remdesivir saves significantly more lives than standard medical care.'[135]

However, political leaders had a different view from the world's leading medical journal. Despite confirmation from a spokesperson for the European Commission that they had not been informed about the drug's failure in the Solidarity trial until the day after the new contract was signed on 8 October,[136] the Commission didn't feel the need to revise its contract with Gilead. In fact, just a week after the publication of the WHO study, the FDA officially approved remdesivir[137]—making it the first treatment for Covid-19 to be approved by the US. As *Science* wrote at the time, 'both decisions baffled scientists who have closely watched the clinical trials of remdesivir unfold over the past 6 months—and who have many questions about remdesivir's worth'.[138] 'This is a very, very bad look for the FDA, and the dealings between Gilead and EU make it another layer of badness', said Eric Topol, a cardiologist at the Scripps Research Translational Institute.[139]

A month later, in November 2020, the WHO, based on results from its Solidarity trial, officially advised against countries using remdesivir as treatment for hospitalised Covid-19 patients.[140] 'Remdesivir has no meaningful effect on mortality or on other important outcomes for patients, such as the need for mechanical ventilation or time to clinical improvement', experts from the WHO Guideline Development Group wrote in a statement.[141] However, not even that put an end to remdesivir's lucky streak. At the time of writing, remdesivir continues to be approved or authorised for emergency use to treat Covid-19 in around fifty countries and remains widely used in hospitals around the world.[142]

Remdesivir's story is baffling in itself. However, the levels of weirdness become even more astonishing when its success is juxtaposed against the story of another drug—hydroxychloroquine. Didier Raoult—one of the world's most renowned physicians and microbiologists specialising in infectious diseases; Director of IHU-Méditerranée Infection, the only French academic institution entirely devoted to the study of infectious diseases; author of more than 2,300 indexed publications;[143] and classified in 2008 by the journal *Nature* among the ten leading French scientific researchers[144]—announced in

March 2020 that a trial involving twenty-four patients from south-east France supported the claim that hydroxychloroquine, an old anti-malarial drug, in combination with an antibiotic called azithromycin was effective in treating Covid-19.[145] He published a preliminary report of his study in the *International Journal of Antimicrobial Agents.*[146] This corroborated similar findings reported by other doctors, including McCullough.[147] As noted, the Chinese had already included chloroquine, a cousin of hydroxychloroquine, in its early treatment protocol. Both hydroxychloroquine and azithromycin had long since fallen into the public domain and were out of patent, which meant they could be manufactured in generic form and at almost zero cost. In April, an Emergency Use Authorization for hydroxychloroquine was issued by the FDA.

It's easy to see why a cheap and potentially effective early treatment for Covid represented a momentous threat to Gilead's remdesivir—the latter being sold not only at a vastly more expensive price but also as a late-stage rather than an early-stage treatment. It's hardly surprising, then, to find out that right from the start the major pharmaceutical companies waged an all-out war on hydroxychloroquine in order to restrict and discredit it. They were aided by the fact that in early April Donald Trump touted hydroxychloroquine as 'one of the biggest game changers in the history of medicine'[148]—leading what should have been a scientific debate to become instantly politicised, as we have seen in other instances during the pandemic. Mainstream news outlets were quick to label hydroxychloroquine 'Trump's cure'.[149]

Then, in May 2020, a study appeared in *The Lancet*, the world's most prestigious medical journal, that seemed to strike a deadly blow to hydroxychloroquine.[150] It claimed that hydroxychloroquine not only did not reduce mortality in Covid-19 patients but actually doubled it. The study quickly made headlines around the world. 'Trump's Covid-19 "cure" increases deaths', the *Guardian* proclaimed.[151] Fauci and others saw the study as the nail in hydroxychloroquine's coffin. Another study, based on the same data, was also published in the *New England Journal of Medicine* (*NEJM*).[152] Based on these studies, the WHO and the UK immediately suspended their hydroxychloroquine clinical trials,[153] and the FDA withdrew its EUA recommendation soon thereafter.[154] Three European nations immediately banned the use of hydroxychloroquine, and others followed within weeks.[155]

This, however, wasn't to be the end of the story. Shortly after the publication of the *Lancet* article, more than 100 scientists from all over the world wrote a letter to the journal highlighting several flaws in the study and asking to access the original data on which it was based.[156] In early June, an investigative report by the *Guardian* revealed that the US-based company that had provided the data for the study—Surgisphere—was a tiny enterprise that no one had ever heard of, which employed just eleven people who had little or no scientific background. 'An employee listed as a science editor appears to be a science fiction author and fantasy artist whose professional profile suggests writing is her fulltime job. Another employee listed as a marketing executive is an adult model and events hostess, who also acts in videos for organisations.'[157]

Surgisphere had originally been a textbook marketing company which had got off the ground—according to Wikipedia—through the use of fake five-star Amazon reviews.[158] This trajectory does not seem to qualify it to emit make-or-break pronouncements over global public health, and it became apparent that the data provided by Surgisphere simply did not exist—indeed, the company itself appeared to be little more than an empty shell. As the *Guardian* summed it up: 'The World Health Organization and a number of national governments have changed their Covid-19 policies and treatments on the basis of flawed data from a little-known US healthcare analytics company, also calling into question the integrity of key studies published in some of the world's most prestigious medical journals'.

The study that was supposed to discredit hydroxychloroquine once and for all was fast turning into one of the biggest scandals in the history of medical journalism, as it became clear that the entire 'research' article had been fabricated out of thin air. After holding steadfast for 2 weeks, despite a barrage of criticisms, *The Lancet* and the *NEJM* finally retracted the original article challenging the use of hydroxychloroquine on 4 June.[159] *The Lancet's* editor himself, Richard Horton, described the paper in the *New York Times* as a 'fabrication' and 'a monumental fraud'.[160] The headline of a further piece in the *Guardian* expressed the global shock among the scientific community at the rank corruption in one of scientific publishing's most formidable pillars: '*The Lancet* has made one of the biggest retractions in modern history. How could this happen?'[161] To this day, as one commentator put it, '[i]t remains an enduring mystery just which powerful figure(s) caused the world's two most prestigious scientific journals, *The Lancet* and the *New England Journal of Medicine*, to publish overtly fraudulent studies from a nonexistent database owned by a previously unknown company'.[162] Nonetheless, the story offers a preliminary glimpse (which we'll explore in much more detail in the next chapters) of Big Pharma's breathtaking power, and the ways in which this appears to have sown corruption in the scientific world.[163]

What's worse, however, is that despite the retractions, the anti-hydroxychloroquine smear campaign had achieved its aim. As a co-investigator on a hydroxychloroquine trial that was halted following the studies told *Science*: 'The whole world thinks now that these drugs are poisonous'.[164] Indeed, the authorities' war on hydroxychloroquine continued. On 17 June 2020, the WHO called for the halt of hydroxychloroquine trials in hundreds of hospitals across the world.[165] Ghebreyesus ordered nations to stop using the drug. Portugal, France, Italy, and Belgium banned it for Covid-19 treatment. Its fate was all but sealed at that point—at least in the Western world.

Here we can add a postscript which some readers may find interesting. In Africa, hydroxychloroquine was used widely to treat Covid-19. By April 2020, countries including Senegal, Burkina Faso, Algeria, and Morocco had approved its use; it was cheap and of course, as an anti-malarial, in the African context readily available.[166] A Nigerian study from June 2020 found that it was effective,[167] and according to one observer, 'both street level analysts and some medical people encouraged the use of quinine as a remedy and treatment for Covid... it became popular and widespread'.[168] One Kenyan doctor interviewed for this book, who wished to remain anonymous, told us that '[i]n official records in Kenya you cannot find any mention of the use of quinine-based treatment, but doctors quietly used their discretion, and this included quinine-based treatment... there was even a shortage of quinine in the country, which points to the fact that it was widely used.'[169]

Beyond this informal use, research published in September 2020 showed that many African governments had approved off-the-shelf treatment of Covid with hydroxychloroquine in spite of WHO advice.[170] Indeed, we have meanwhile personally met Nigerians who described how quinine-based antimalarials (of which hydroxychloroquine is, of course, one) were often given by medical staff as a Covid treatment to patients. And the fact is—as noted in Chapter 6—that recorded Covid deaths in Africa were barely statistically significant, though they certainly were higher in South Africa and in North African countries where malaria is less common and anti-malarial drugs such as hydroxychloroquine are not in such widespread use.

Once again, our concern is to highlight the method by which the scientific establishment operated, rather than to take a position as to whether or not this is because of the use of hydroxychloroquine, and, of course, correlation does not mean causation. With no early access to vaccines or other therapeutics, African doctors took matters into their own hands—and the results were certainly no disaster, as Chapter 6 shows. This outcome may well be largely because of the lower age demographic and greater resistance to viruses in the African population, but, given this discussion, some readers may also ponder whether the African continent—sitting largely outside the framework of drug patents and their enforcers—has provided a controlled experiment in the case of hydroxychloroquine and its role in Covid treatments. Moreover, it surely isn't controversial to suggest that had this drug been introduced through the media by headlines such as 'World-leading French scientist hails new Covid cure' rather than as 'Trump's cure', the global response to this potential treatment might have been somewhat different.

Over time, some early treatments made their way into the protocols of Western countries, on the heels of a growing body of studies confirming the effectiveness of several therapies in reducing Covid hospitalisations and deaths.[171] However, one cannot help but wonder how many lives could have been saved if these treatments had been adopted sooner—and why they weren't. It certainly seems hard to deny that accepting the existence of effective early treatments in the first months of the pandemic would have jeopardised the whole vaccine-centric narrative—and, indeed, the whole Covid doxa that was central to that narrative. In the preceding pages we have seen how some of the main pillars of the doxa—such as the notion that Covid represented a deadly risk for all of humanity—were based on very shaky evidence. We have also seen how the actual dangerousness of Covid was misrepresented as a result of misplaced statistical and data-gathering techniques. Moreover, we have shown that a good number of the initial 'Covid deaths' were likely not caused by Covid itself but rather by the biomedical approach adopted by most Western governments—including, though not limited to, the suppression of early treatments.

The lack of any investigation or report into the tragic failure of ventilators, and the lack of autopsies on Covid fatalities, is symptomatic of a wider aspect of this 'single narrative'. This was its tendency to move on silently through the debris of inconvenient data, truths, and contexts which continually showed up the hollowness of its empty shell. As we've seen here, this was in complete contravention of established scientific method, which proceeds through experiments with controls and randomised control trials. Such a method can lead to results and findings which appear contradictory and then require further experiments. However, such nuanced findings couldn't work in a situation in which there was a single narrative surrounding origins and the requirement for lockdowns and then universal vaccination. The way in which the single narrative continued to ride roughshod over scientific method—while claiming to embody 'the science'—throughout the vaccination campaign is what we'll look at in the next chapter.

However, when it comes to early therapies, it might have been more than a simple question of narrative. According to both FDA and EMA regulation, new vaccines and medicines cannot qualify for an Emergency Use Authorization (in the US) or conditional marketing authorisation (in the EU) if any existing approved drug proves effective against the same malady.[172] Thus, if any drug had been proven to be effective as a prophylactic against Covid (unlike remdesivir, which was a late-stage drug), pharmaceutical companies wouldn't have been allowed to fast-track the development and rollout of the vaccines, and would instead have had to endure lengthy testing for safety and efficacy.[173] Indeed, the ultra-precautionary argument adopted by governments with regards to any form of early therapy—'no therapy can be approved, not even relatively innocuous ones such as vitamin D, until it has been unquestionably proven to be effective', despite the fact that such therapies were based on drugs that in many cases had been in use for years—rings particularly hollow when compared to the fast-track approach adopted for vaccines based on never-before-used technologies.

It is to these that we will now turn our attention in the following chapters. There we will see how the vaccine-centric narrative emerged, how several Covid vaccines were developed in record time, and how at that point, beginning in mid-2021, most countries launched campaigns of compelled—and in places mandatory—mass vaccination, often accompanied by the introduction of measures such as vaccine passports and lockdowns targeted against the unvaccinated.

4

THE DEVELOPMENT OF THE
COVID-19 VACCINES

As has already been recalled, China publicly shared the sequence of the newly discovered SARS-CoV-2 virus in the first half of January 2020.[1] Even though at that point there had been less than ten recorded deaths,[2] efforts to develop a vaccine were immediately put in motion. For all the talk of the need of a 'global response' to the novel coronavirus, it was clear from the start that the search for the vaccine would be a competitive rather than a cooperative affair, and would follow pre-existing geopolitical fault lines. Thus, major countries and geopolitical blocs such as China, India, Russia, Iran, Turkey, and Western countries, as well as smaller nations such as Cuba, all started working on their own vaccine(s),[3] in the tacit hope of beating the others to it. Just as nationalism and the polarisation around it had conditioned some of the initial responses to lockdowns, the same proved to be the case with the vaccine: with the rise of nationalist governments by 2020 in countries ranging from Czechia, Hungary, and Russia to Brazil, Turkey, the UK, and the US, any other response was in truth unlikely.

In terms of vaccine development, we'll focus our account on the West. Here, the effort was kickstarted by the US-based National Institutes of Health (NIH) and National Institute of Allergy and Infectious Diseases (NIAID)—run by Francis Collins and Anthony Fauci—and the Coalition for Epidemic Preparedness Innovations (CEPI), a global vaccine development fund created in 2015 by the Bill and Melinda Gates Foundation, Jeremy Farrar's Wellcome Trust, and the governments of India and Norway, and later joined by the European Union and the United Kingdom.[4] Many of these names will be familiar to the reader by now.

Shortly after the initialisation of the process early in 2020, the Bill and Melinda Gates Foundation launched a vast consortium comprising some of the world's major pharmaceutical companies (including Bayer, BD, bioMérieux, Boehringer Ingelheim, Bristol-Myers Squibb, Eisai, Eli Lilly, Gilead, GSK, Johnson & Johnson, Merck, Novartis, Pfizer, and Sanofi) and contributed US$125 million 'to accelerate the development, manufacture, and delivery of vaccines, diagnostics, and treatments for Covid-19'.[5] In late January 2020, NIH, NIAID, and CEPI announced that they were already at work on a vaccine through a partnership with Moderna,[6] a then-small and virtually unknown American pharmaceutical and biotechnology company founded in 2010 and focused on mRNA vaccines, a new technology that at the time had never been authorised for widespread use.[7]

The rise of Moderna is an important part of the story to be told. The CEO of Moderna, Stéphane Bancel, had appeared at a press conference at the World Economic Forum's meeting in Davos on 23 January 2020 alongside Jeremy Farrar and Richard Hatchett, the head of CEPI.[8] Although at that time Moderna was still a small company, which had launched no products on the market, an agreement had been signed the previous week between Bancel and Hatchett for it to begin work on the vaccine.[9]

This agreement had stemmed from early steps that Moderna had taken to prep a vaccine based on the genetic sequence of SARS-CoV-2, which it had picked up on 13 January 2020—and also from Bancel's plea to Hatchett for cash to support the venture.[10]

Moderna appear to have had something of a head start, although the reasons for this are not entirely clear. Curiously enough, an early 2022 study published in the journal *Frontiers in Virology* found a 100 per cent match between a portion of the SARS-CoV-2 genome, the one encompassing the aforementioned furin cleavage site, and a proprietary mRNA sequence patented in 2016 by, among others, Moderna CEO Stéphane Bancel. According to the researchers, the odds of this happening by chance are 1 in 300 billion.[11] Amazingly, or not so amazingly, just over a month after this initial agreement with CEPI, Moderna announced that it had already created the first batches of the vaccine—the first Covid vaccine in the world at that point—and would soon start testing it on humans.[12] The value of the company's shares doubled almost overnight.[13] On 18 May 2020, Moderna announced promising results from its phase one clinical trials, and Bancel was about to seek more investment when this was pre-empted by a telephone call from the CEO of Morgan Stanley, James Gorman. Gorman promised investment of US$1.3 billion—a tidy sum, which of course he must have hoped would be recouped through vaccine sales soon enough.[14]

Moderna's work on the vaccine was important for a number of reasons. In these early weeks of the outbreak, the four major vaccine players—Pfizer, Sanofi, GlaxoSmithKline (GSK), and Merck—had showed little interest in the development of a vaccine, with observers describing 'an atmosphere of extreme reluctance' among the biggest pharma groups,[15] reflecting the fact that vaccines had long been considered a high-investment, low-profit venture.[16] All this changed between/ March and April 2020, as the WHO and other global organisations started emphasising the need for a campaign of global vaccination as the only way to end the pandemic, and, perhaps most importantly, as Western governments—most notably the US government—and global financial institutions started committing billions of dollars to the development of Covid vaccines.

The relationship between lockdowns and vaccines in the pandemic response was also clear at this early point. At the 23 January press conference in which the Moderna CEO Bancel appeared at Davos, CEPI's Hatchett was asked about the Wuhan lockdown, which had been implemented the day before. According to Farrar, Hatchett said that 'when you don't have treatments and you don't have vaccines, non-pharmaceutical interventions are literally the only thing you have': on Farrar's account, Hatchett then argued that the Spanish flu pandemic of 1918–19 was a precedent for the Wuhan lockdown, and that US cities that had shielded themselves earlier had had 'much better outcomes'.[17] As head of an organisation spearheading vaccine research to respond to epidemics, Hatchett clearly had some skin in the game. His perspective on the relationship between vaccines and lockdowns stuck. Thus, right from the beginning, lockdowns and strict social distancing protocols were deemed necessary until vaccines were produced.

This framework soon enough shaped the global response to the crisis. Thus, in April, the UN secretary-general António Guterres stated that 'the world must unite' in the search for a vaccine—while also urging social media companies to do more to fight 'misinformation'.[18] That same month, the WHO, the European Commission, the French government, and the Bill and Melinda Gates Foundation launched the Access to COVID-19 Tools Accelerator (ACT-A),[19] 'a groundbreaking global collaboration to accelerate development, production, and equitable access to Covid-19 tests, treatments, and vaccines'.[20] Its main pillar, given the organisation's overwhelming focus on vaccines, was represented by COVID-19 Vaccines Global Access (COVAX)[21]—directed by the GAVI Vaccine Alliance, Hatchett's CEPI, and the WHO, alongside UNICEF—which was created with the goal of vaccinating two billion human beings 'by the end of 2021'.[22] COVAX's message was a simple but powerful one: 'Global equitable access to a Covid-19 vaccine [...] is *the only way* to mitigate the public health and economic impact of the pandemic' (emphasis added).[23]

While it may be hard to wrap one's head around all these names and acronyms, the reality is less complex than one may think, as it's a matter of record that these various institutions ultimately all lead back to Bill Gates, the second-richest man on the planet in 2022. There's nothing secret or conspiratorial about this, since Gates is quite open about the interest he has taken in promoting vaccine-driven responses to matters of global health, as he recently made clear in his book on pandemics.[24] He has coordinated the investment aims of the various foundations that he has overseen, and ensured that they coalesce around a response to epidemics that is grounded in vaccination. Whether or not this is a positive approach is a matter of debate, but no one denies that the above is a statement of fact.

How does this philanthropic interest take shape? The Bill and Melinda Gates Foundation[25]—the largest private foundation on Earth, reporting over US$51 billion in assets at the end of 2019,[26] and the self-proclaimed 'biggest funder of vaccines in the world'[27]— is among the main funders of both GAVI, an international vaccine advocacy organisation that facilitates bulk sales of vaccines to poor countries, of which Gates is also a co-founder,[28] and CEPI, as mentioned already. Thus the Gates Foundation is the major financer of COVAX itself, and has a leading role in the management of its mother organisation, ACT-A. As one civil society group stated, the WHO effectively outsourced the management of the global Covid vaccine rollout to Gates.[29]

There are other aspects of this keen interest in vaccination. The Gates Foundation was also the second-largest contributor to the World Health Organization in 2018–19,[30] after the United States—if not effectively its largest contributor, when we consider that the fourth and eighth largest contributors to the Organization during that same period were GAVI, the second-largest non-state funder after the Gates Foundation itself, and Rotary International,[31] and that the Gates Foundation is also one of the main funders of both of these organisations. Moreover, the current Director-General of the WHO, Tedros Adhanom Ghebreyesus, previously served on the boards of two organisations that Gates founded and continues to fund to this day: GAVI and the Global Fund, where Ghebreyesus was chair of the board.

At the outset of the pandemic, Bill Gates, through his foundation, had thus been at the helm of an incredibly powerful and far-reaching public-corporate global vaccination programme for several years already, and exercised an influence that exceeded that of most states on the planet over the World Health Organization. Again, this is not news or indeed a controversial view, since it has been widely reported over the past decade. Indeed, in 2012, the WHO's then Director-General Margaret Chan complained that because the WHO's budget is highly earmarked, it is 'driven by what [she calls] donor interests'.[32] As we saw above, in the aftermath of the 2009 swine flu outbreak, there were widespread criticisms of the influence of private companies over WHO policy.

These concerns have been eloquently articulated by Linsey McGoey, a professor of sociology at the University of Essex, who notes: 'According to its charter, the WHO is meant to be accountable to member governments. The Gates Foundation, on the other hand, is accountable to no one other than its three trustees: Bill, Melinda, and Berkshire Hathaway CEO Warren Buffett. Many civil society organizations fear the WHO's independence is compromised when a significant portion of its budget comes from a private philanthropic organization with the power to stipulate exactly where and how the UN institution spends its money.'[33] McGoey suggests that '[v]irtually every significant decision at WHO is first vetted by the Gates Foundation'.[34] Indeed, it has been said that 'the sheer magnitude of the foundation's financial contributions have made Bill Gates an unofficial—albeit unelected—leader at the organization'.[35]

Of course, this may be an exaggeration. Yet Gates has certainly aimed to make vaccination a major focus of WHO policy. This is a matter of record. In 2011, Gates spoke at the WHO, and declared: 'All 193 member states [must] make vaccines a central focus of their health systems.'[36] The following year, the World Health Assembly, the decision-making body of the WHO, adopted a 'Global Vaccine Plan' that the Gates Foundation co-authored,[37] and over half of the WHO's total budget now goes to vaccines. Others fear that this new central focus on vaccines has diverted the WHO's policies away 'from poverty alleviation, nutrition, and clean water'.[38] This single-minded focus on techno-centric vaccine-based solutions, in place of a more 'holistic' approach to health whereby the latter is seen as the outcome of a wide range of economic, social, and political factors,[39] has been seen by some to have seriously weakened health systems in low income countries.[40]

Some would claim that these criticisms of the Gates Foundation stem from a conspiracy-theory view of the world. But, as we say, these are not conspiracies: Gates's commitment to vaccines is well-documented, and it's something that he's very proud of. It's just a statement of fact to record this and the way that this commitment is embedded through networks of organisations committed to this end. Moreover, acknowledging the relationship between those scientists and companies developing vaccines and the running of the Gates Foundation does not come from a conspiratorial worldview: it's simply an analysis which builds on the long-standing concept of the 'revolving door' linking business and industry, given that—as we have outlined here—the Gates Foundation is now effectively an arm of global governance.

It's worth looking in some detail at the nature of this revolving door, because of course some people don't see this relationship as positively as Gates. It's been argued that 'the Gates Foundation functions as a trojan horse for Western corporations, which of course have no goal greater than an increased bottom line'.[41] Several of the former and current executives of the Gates Foundation hail from the pharmaceutical industry,[42] and the foundation invests in several of these corporations directly. Ever since its creation,[43] the foundation has owned stakes in several drug companies, and it currently holds stocks and bonds in drug companies such as Merck, GSK, Eli Lilly, Pfizer, Novartis, and Sanofi.[44] The foundation's website even candidly declares a mission to pursue 'mutually beneficial opportunities' with vaccine manufacturers.[45] This is the essence of what has been called philanthrocapitalism—'a capitalist, market-based, for-profit approach to solving the world's biggest and most pressing issues'.[46] This is an approach that many see as tailored to suit the needs and interests of the world's ultra-wealthy and corporate elites, but again it's no conspiracy to observe that the interests of capital organise themselves to embed its power—that's a framework which has been in operation for very many centuries.

So what has the outcome been of this vaccine-centred focus at the Gates Foundation and the organisations it has co-sponsored? Some activists in the Global South have especially negative views of the consequences for public health. One of India's leading human rights activists, Vandana Shiva, said:

Western nations originally conceived the World Health Organization and the United Nations to embody liberal ideologies implemented via a democratic structure of one nation, one vote. Gates has single-handedly destroyed all that. He has hijacked the WHO and transformed it into an instrument of personal power that he wields for the cynical purpose of increasing pharmaceutical profits. He has single-handedly destroyed the infrastructure of public health globally. He has privatized our health systems and our food systems to serve his own purposes. [...] The World Bank and the IMF look like midgets in front of the Gates Foundation, in terms of power and influence.[47]

Whether or not one agrees with Shiva, there can be no question that the Gates Foundation and its leadership have been pivotal in directing the public health outcomes of the SARS-CoV-2 pandemic. Given the focus of Gates and his foundation on vaccines, this hardly comes as a surprise, and is demonstrated with even more clarity by the fact that in the years leading up to the pandemic, Gates's activities had been focused on one topic in particular: pandemic prevention.[48] Indeed, in October 2019, just two months before the official start of the outbreak in Wuhan, the Gates Foundation, in collaboration with the Johns Hopkins Center for Health Security and the World Economic Forum, hosted an exercise called Event 201,[49] which simulated 'an outbreak of a novel zoonotic coronavirus transmitted from bats to pigs to people that eventually becomes efficiently transmissible from person to person, leading to a severe pandemic. The pathogen and the disease it causes are modeled largely on SARS, but it is more transmissible in the community setting by people with mild symptoms.'[50] The hypothesised virus war-gamed in Event 201 was imagined to have initially spread from China.

These kind of war games had been played for decades, and were part and parcel of the defence industry's attempts to mimic biological and chemical attack simulations. Their common currency reveals again how and why the Covid response quickly became militarised. This time, participants included the Vice-President of the American pharmaceutical giant Johnson & Johnson; a former Australian Health Minister who is also a leader of the WHO and a collaborator of the Gates Foundation; a former Senior Director of the World Bank; the President of Edelman (the world's leading corporate PR firm); a former CIA executive and security policy adviser; a CDC executive; and the Director-General of the Chinese Center for Disease Control.[51] Now, this of course doesn't mean that Gates or anyone else had prior knowledge of the pandemic, as some have claimed.[52] It simply shows that Gates and other members of the global public health establishment had been preparing for an event such as the Covid-19 pandemic for quite some time, and that this is likely to have influenced the policy responses that emerged.

Given that the Johns Hopkins Center for Health Security and the World Economic Forum both took important roles in the pandemic response—the former through the coronavirus tracker tool, and the latter through its regular meetings and briefings—this is a reasonable inference. Indeed, the similarities between Event 201's official recommendations and the policies implemented just a few months later are clear.[53] In the event of a pandemic, the organisers noted, national governments, international organisations, and the private sector should not only provide ample resources for the manufacturing and distribution of large quantities of vaccines '[i]n coordination with WHO, CEPI, GAVI' and promote 'robust forms of public-private cooperation', but should also

> assign a greater priority to developing methods to combat mis- and disinformation prior to the next pandemic response. Governments will need to partner with traditional and social media companies to research and develop nimble approaches to countering misinformation. This will require developing

the ability to flood media with fast, accurate, and consistent information. Public health authorities should work with private employers and trusted community leaders such as faith leaders, to promulgate factual information to employees and citizens. Trusted, influential private-sector employers should create the capacity to readily and reliably augment public messaging, manage rumors and misinformation, and amplify credible information to support emergency public communications. National public health agencies should work in close collaboration with WHO to create the capability to rapidly develop and release consistent health messages. For their part, media companies should commit to ensuring that authoritative messages are prioritized and that false messages are suppressed including though the use of technology.[54]

There was, however, one exception in the synergy between Event 201's recommendations and the Covid-19 response. There was no mention of lockdowns as a strategic response. This again demonstrates how new the lockdown model was for global public health, given that neither the coordinators of Event 201 nor the WHO report discussed in Chapter 2 and issued the same month saw fit to mention it. Gates had not been scheming about lockdowns for years, but he certainly had been thinking about pandemics. That's just a logical conclusion when reflecting on the significance of Event 201 and other events that occurred at around the same time, including the release of an American documentary series called *Pandemic: How to Prevent an Outbreak*, starring Bill Gates among others, which came out on Netflix on 22 January 2020—the very day before Wuhan entered lockdown.

In light of all this, it's hardly surprising that right from the outset Gates emerged as one of the leading movers and shakers in the pandemic response. He very quickly also became one of the main advocates of the pro-lockdown and vaccine-centric narratives (two sides of the same coin, as mentioned), both directly through his foundation and his ubiquitous media presence and indirectly through the global public health establishment. 'He had enough money and enough presence in the area for a long enough period of time to be positioned as the first mover and the most influential mover', says James Love, director of the NGO Knowledge Ecology International.[55]

How did this influence play out? Throughout March and April 2020, after stepping down from his position on the board of directors at Microsoft to spend 'the predominant amount of his time on the pandemic',[56] Gates penned several editorials in leading newspapers and was hosted on pretty much every major media channel and programme[57] (including CNN,[58] CNBC,[59] Fox,[60] PBS,[61] BBC,[62] CBS,[63] MSNBC,[64] The Daily Show,[65] and The Ellen Show).[66] On every occasion he repeated the same message: we are dealing with a 'once-in-a-century pandemic';[67] the new coronavirus does not only threaten very old or already sick people but 'can kill healthy adults';[68] there is no effective treatment for Covid;[69] thus, 'if we're going to return to normal, we need to develop a safe, effective vaccine' (for which mRNA and DNA vaccines are 'one of the most promising options');[70] however, for that to happen, governments will have to provide public funding to the tune of billions of dollars in order to 'minimize risk for pharmaceutical companies';[71] once a vaccine is available, '[i]n order to stop the pandemic, we need to make the vaccine available *to almost every person on the planet*';[72] 'we need all of this to happen as quickly as possible', hence 'governments will need to expedite their usual drug approval processes';[73] until then, there is no solution but to follow the example of China (which 'did a lot of things right at the beginning')[74] and 'shut down completely'.[75] There was 'no alternative' to this agenda.[76] Interestingly, in May 2022, in a conversation with Fareed Zakaria, Gates would say that in the early days of the pandemic 'we didn't understand that it's a fairly low fatality rate and that it's a disease mainly of the elderly, kind of like the flu, although a bit different than that'. In fact, as we have seen, those things were apparent from the data right from the start—and yet if anyone had dared to make such a statement at the time, they would have been treated as fringe conspiracy theorists.[77]

Western governments were quick to heed Gates's call. In the following months, they announced a series of 'unprecedented'[78] public investment programmes to support the search for a vaccine,[79] to the tune of tens of billions of dollars.[80] The vast majority of these funds came through advance market commitments like Operation Warp Speed in the US or bilateral deals concluded by the European Union and other wealthy nations such as the UK. Most of these deals were negotiated in secrecy, with even national parliaments left largely in the dark as to the contents of the vaccine contracts.[81] At that point, the larger pharmaceutical companies (known for convenience as 'Big Pharma') entered the race for the vaccine, mostly through partnerships with smaller biotech companies. It's easy to see why; as the Swiss NGO Public Eye writes: 'Public funding has covered large parts of the research and development (R&D) costs, increased manufacturing capacity and enabled advance market commitments. [...] [T]he colossal amount of public funds [the pharmaceutical companies] have benefitted from [...] has significantly, if not completely, de-risked their whole endeavour'[82]—just as Gates had requested.

'Hundreds of millions [of US dollars] were thrown at several of these companies in a way that took their breath away', according to Peter Hale, executive director of the Foundation for Vaccine Research in Washington.[83] David Mitchell, founder of Patients for Affordable Drugs, a US campaign group, said that for some companies, such as Moderna, the government seemed to be paying for everything,[84] and as we've seen, they were joined by giant banking interests such as Morgan Stanley.

It's worth looking at these relationships in some detail. In Moderna's case, the then-small Boston-based biotech company benefitted from more than US$4 billion from the US government,[85] which covered 100 per cent of its R&D costs[86] and most of its manufacturing costs resulting from its partnership with the Swiss company Lonza.[87] Pfizer-BioNtech's BNT162b2 vaccine was also massively subsidised by public money: a US$1.95 billion supply contract with the US government,[88] a non-refundable down payment from the EU of €700 million,[89] a €375 million grant from the German government, and a €100 million loan from the European Investment Bank to accelerate its development.[90] Meanwhile, the British-Swedish AstraZeneca signed a deal worth more than US$1 billion with the US government,[91] one worth more than £65.5 million with the UK government,[92] and one worth more than US$750 million with CEPI and the GAVI Vaccine Alliance (COVAX).[93] Some sources estimate the amount of public funding for the AstraZeneca vaccine to be as high as US$2.4 billion.[94] And this was on top of the fact that the vaccine had already been developed in collaboration with the University of Oxford using public funds.[95] The Gates Foundation itself donated more than US$300 million to vaccine trials which were run by several companies, including AstraZeneca and Moderna.[96]

But governments and other institutions didn't limit themselves to socialising the risks for the pharmaceutical companies. They also 'attached no strings to these billions in order to guarantee public benefit: there were no conditionalities on affordability and access, no requirement to share the know-how and intellectual property of the subsidised technologies, no duty of transparency— nothing'.[97] This is better understood if we consider that some of these public funding operations were run directly by ex-employees of the giant pharmaceutical corporations themselves, through the revolving door framework. For instance, the man called to lead Operation Warp Speed in the US and charged with allocating billions of public subsidies to vaccine makers was Moncef Slaoui, former GlaxoSmithKline executive (he formerly ran GSK's vaccines programme) and board member of Moderna, Lonza, and the International AIDS Vaccine Initiative (IAVI), a 'public-private partnership' organisation that has received more than US$359 million from the Gates Foundation.[98] Following his nomination, Slaoui was required to resign from a number of biotech boards funded by Operation Warp Speed, and agreed to sell his 155,000 shares in Moderna (whose value had grown by US$2 billion in the days following his appointment),[99] but was allowed to keep his stock in GSK (reported to be worth about US$10 million).[100]

There are many who would call this corruption, although it's also clearly an outcome that's to be expected where capital and its private interests are stripped of meaningful regulation in the model of the neoliberal state. In any case, in light of this it's hardly surprising that pharma companies were given a blank cheque with the vaccination programme. Most, if not all, of the clinical trials for the Covid-19 vaccines were fast-tracked— another one of Gates's requests. As Trump boasted while announcing Operation Warp Speed, his administration would 'cut through every piece of red tape to achieve the fastest-ever, by far, launch of a vaccine trial'.[101] This meant that the data was sent to the regulatory authorities on a rolling basis throughout the process, instead of being presented in one bulk with the request for market approval.[102] Trial phases were mostly run in parallel, 'designed to deliver the quickest possible read-out rather than addressing more relevant questions'[103] and using 'strategies that are easy to implement but unlikely to yield unbiased effect estimates'.[104] All of this was unprecedented in the development of new vaccines—in keeping with Gates's repeated statements on all kinds of media that this was an unprecedented situation.

The outcome of these strategies was record speed in trial procedures, something that many readers will doubtless see as a positive thing because of the impact this had on the speed of vaccine rollout. The other side of this accelerated procedure, however, was that serious questions of transparency as well as doubts concerning the reliability of the results being reported were raised—doubts which would subsequently be confirmed, as when the initially reported 95 per cent effectiveness of the Pfizer vaccine turned out to be less accurate than it first appeared to be. The new vaccine development procedures meant that results of treatment and vaccine clinical trials were made public through press releases or so-called pre-print publications before being peer-reviewed: essentially, companies were 'outsourcing peer review to practicing physicians and journalists',[105] and 'health professionals and the public [were] left second-guessing the reported results'.[106]

These mechanisms for the reporting of scientific results were new, alongside many of the epidemic innovations that were rolled out in 2020 and 2021. Of course, we're not opposed to innovation *per se*, and many would hold that extraordinary times call for exceptional measures. Yet it's important to grasp that this was in contravention of any previous framework for the scientific method, notwithstanding Anthony Fauci's claim that anyone who opposed his approach was 'attacking science'.[107] According to the *Financial Times*, about half of all available research on Covid-19 published by May 2020 had not been pre-approved by other academics. By September, the percentage of pre-print publications was still about five times higher for Covid-19 (17 per cent) than for the overall biomedical research published in 2020 (3.6 per cent).[108] In July 2020, the European Ombudsman urged the EMA to rapidly publish the clinical data related to its Covid-19-related activities,[109] and only after intense public pressure did some companies release trial protocols: Moderna and Pfizer in September,[110] followed by AstraZeneca and Johnson & Johnson.[111] While this was a positive step, academics and health policy experts argued that much more should have been disclosed.[112]

Essentially, pharmaceutical companies had refused to submit to serious scientific and public scrutiny the clinical trials of vaccines which they had developed with the assistance of enormous sums of public funding. The optics were made to look even worse by the fact that the companies were meanwhile already raking in billions in shareholder value—well before any vaccine had even been approved by regulators. In this new environment of unverified communication by press release, and with the world anxiously waiting for the vaccine which figures such as Gates and CEPI's Richard Hatchett had stated would be the only exit from this nightmare, even the most modest and unverified positive announcement led to an immediate jump in the stocks of the companies involved.[113]

As we saw earlier in the chapter, when Moderna announced that eight healthy volunteers had developed neutralising antibodies against the virus in May 2020,[114] the company immediately raised US$1.34 billion of capital from Morgan Stanley based on nothing more than a press release, with hardly any scientific data to back it up.[115] Moderna's Chief Medical Officer and Chief Financial Officer immediately proceeded to capitalise on the company's soaring stock value, selling a whopping US$30 million of the company's stock.[116] Then, in November, when Pfizer and BioNTech, shortly followed by Moderna, announced the first interim results of their final Covid-19 vaccine trials—which, they said, proved the vaccine had an efficacy rate of 95 per cent[117]—global stock markets were 'propelled to an all-time high', with shares of these companies jumping by between 15 and 25 per cent.[118] Pfizer CEO Albert Bourla sold 62 per cent of his stock on the same day, at an average price of US$41.94 per share, or US$5.6 million, almost its highest value in the previous year.[119] But as on other occasions, the Pfizer announcement was not accompanied by any detailed data, regulatory review, or published study (not even pre-print); it was the latest instance in the pandemic of 'science by press release'.[120] Moderna, however, was the real winner: by that point (November 2020), the company's stock had shot up more than 300 per cent,[121] while the biotech company's top five executives had already made more than US$80 million in profits through sales of their own stocks[122]—and this based on research almost fully funded with public money.

There were many experts who were unhappy with this *modus operandi*—and indeed, a critical view of the nexus between public (investment) and private (profit) is nothing new, since it was also the outcome of the quantitative easing that went alongside the financial crisis of 2008. There is nothing controversial or conspiratorial about pointing to the frameworks whereby private companies are bailed out by the state and given *carte blanche* to maximise profits, since the way in which this worked was already well-established during the financial crisis. As the American health-oriented website STAT commented: 'Biopharma companies are spreading misinformation—and taking advantage of it.'[123]

Despite the lack of hard scientific data, the pharma companies were already sealing confidential agreements with the EU and countries beyond it for the supply of several hundreds of millions of doses.[124] Indeed, in early November, before any authorisation had even been granted, Pfizer and BioNTech were already expecting to produce 'up to 1.3 billion doses in 2021'.[125] The problems inherent to such a framework can certainly give readers pause for thought regarding the general motivations and empirical findings that underpinned the Covid vaccination programme.

At the same time, it emerged that pharmaceutical companies, in an attempt to maximise their high-profit-zero-cost strategy, were lobbying governments in order to be granted full immunity from any possible vaccine-related adverse effects,[126] on top of the massive public subsidies they had received for the research and manufacturing of the vaccines. This was a troubling prospect given the unprecedentedly speedy clinical trials, the companies' refusal to share raw data, and, most importantly, the stated aim of various interested parties of 'vaccinating the entire world against Covid'. As a memo circulated to EU member states by the European industry lobby Vaccines Europe stated in August 2020:

> We need to focus on getting Covid19 [sic] vaccines to the population as quickly as possible and on a worldwide scale. We must avoid being distracted and loos[ing] [sic] time with lengthy and costly litigation [...]. Instead, we are advocating for an easily accessible, transparent and comprehensive no-fault and non-adversarial compensation system, and an exemption from civil liability to ensure that all parties involved are protected against potentially highly disruptive and ruinous financial risks from litigation.[127]

Clearly, such a framework was beneficial to the companies involved. Vaccinating 'the population as quickly as possible and on a worldwide scale' would certainly be a way of maximising profits. But in our view, profit maximisation does not necessarily mean that a policy is the best one to follow. Policies require regulation in order not to concentrate capital and foster mass inequality. As we have seen so far, the revolving door between business and government meant that the regulation available was poor. And sure enough, the month after the Vaccines Europe memo, in September 2020, it was revealed that the European Commission had included indemnity clauses in (confidential) advance purchase agreements signed with vaccine makers.[128] 'The Commission or the member states would essentially indemnify the companies against the cost of legal action that followed [vaccine-related] claims', said Sue Middleton, president of the executive board of Vaccines Europe.[129]

***

At the end of November, both Pfizer-BioNTech and Moderna completed the final leg of their rolling approval processes and submitted requests for Emergency Use Authorization or conditional marketing authorisation for the company's two vaccines, Pfizer-BioNTech's Comirnaty (also known as BNT162b2)[130] and Moderna's Spikevax (also known as mRNA-1273).[131] These requests were submitted to the three most important Western agencies responsible for regulating and approving medicinal products in their respective territories—the United States' FDA, the European Union's EMA, and the United Kingdom's Medicines and Healthcare Products Regulatory Agency (MHRA)—and initiated rolling submissions across the globe, including in Australia, Canada, and Japan.[132]

On 2 December 2020, the UK's MHRA gave temporary regulatory approval for the Pfizer-BioNTech vaccine,[133] becoming the first country to approve the vaccine and the first country in the Western world to approve the use of any Covid-19 vaccine (at that point, locally manufactured vaccines had been approved for emergency use only in China and Russia). Within a few weeks, the FDA and the EMA had approved the two vaccines for emergency use.[134] The AstraZeneca-Oxford vaccine was approved shortly after in the EU and UK (but, interestingly, not in the US).[135] Overall, it had taken less than a year to develop these vaccines, while vaccines historically had taken two to five years to develop.[136]

At this point, however, there was still very little data that had been released to the public, and indeed very little was actually known about the vaccines. Such views have often been alleged to be the purview of conspiracy theorists, but this is to mischaracterise the response among scientists. As Peter Doshi, senior editor of the *BMJ*, noted, the information provided by the companies (and regulatory agencies) was scant: he wrote that this information said little about the vaccines' absolute risk reduction, about the duration of protection, about the vaccines' ability to prevent infection and therefore the transmission of the virus, and about their effect on children, adolescents, and immunocompromised individuals. Doshi therefore called upon the companies (and/or the regulatory agencies) to release the raw data in order to allow for its rigorous scrutiny by the scientific community.[137] Like previous requests of the kind, however, this one fell on deaf ears too. Even in the subsequent months, calls for greater transparency concerning the vaccines' clinical trial data and results would remain largely unanswered, as discussed below.

Nonetheless, as soon as the emergency/conditional approvals were issued, pre-agreed bilateral procurement contracts between major Western states and the vaccine manufacturers for the rapid supply of hundreds of millions of doses immediately kicked into force. However, just like everything else regarding the vaccines (and the entire management of the pandemic, for that matter), these agreements remained secret. Despite the vaccines having been largely, if not entirely, financed with public money, the contracts were all classified as confidential and shielded from public view,[138] and have largely remained so.

This lack of transparency has been pretty universal. In the United States, the first Freedom of Information Act (FOIA) requests were rejected, leading the advocacy groups Public Citizen and Knowledge Ecology International to sue the US government.[139] Contracts were eventually released due to public and political pressure, but they were all extensively redacted, with only fourteen out of fifty-three pages of the Moderna contract free of redactions.[140] Europe was even more reluctant to publicise the contracts. Several FOIA requests were simply rejected by the European Commission.[141] The correspondence between the Commission and the advocacy group Corporate Europe Observatory showed the refusal was motivated by commercial confidentiality and claimed, astonishingly, that there was 'no overriding public interest in transparency'.[142] And in the UK, when, in June 2022, a woman, whose husband and partner of twenty-one years had died of a blood clot following the AstraZeneca vaccine, requested information from the government as to why the company had indemnity from litigation, the government responded that: 'The requested information contains commercially sensitive information with regards to the contracts with vaccine suppliers, and we consider that the disclosure of that information would prejudice the commercial interests of the companies involved.'[143]

The European Ombudsman subsequently opened an inquiry into the Commission's refusal to grant public access to documents concerning the purchase of the vaccines.[144] On several occasions, Members of the European Parliament (MEPs) called for greater transparency regarding these bilateral contracts.[145] This pressure led to the European Commission finally allowing selected MEPs to consult a heavily redacted version of the sixty-page contract with the biopharmaceutical company CureVac (whose vaccine never made it past the trial phase) for 45 minutes in a reading room, under strict conditions, and after having signed a confidentiality agreement.[146] Following mounting pressure from all sides and authorisation from CureVac—states need to obtain the pharma companies' permission before publishing any contract—the Commission finally posted the same redacted version of the CureVac contract on its website.[147] This was followed by the publications of equally heavily redacted versions of the AstraZeneca,[148] Sanofi/GSK,[149] and Pfizer-BioNTech[150] contracts. As the *New York Times* commented: 'Governments have poured billions of dollars into helping drug companies develop vaccines and are spending billions more to buy doses. But the details of those deals largely remain secret, with governments and public health organizations acquiescing to drug company demands for secrecy.'[151] A fully unredacted version of the AstraZeneca contract was eventually published by Italy's RAI television.[152]

The UK government's deals with vaccine makers were just as secretive, with the *Guardian* reporting that '[m]inisters have agreed a secrecy clause in any dispute with the drugs manufacturer Pfizer over Britain's Covid vaccine supply. Large portions of the government's contracts with the company over the supply of 189m vaccine doses have been redacted and any arbitration proceedings will be kept secret.'[153] No one could claim that such a policy was in keeping with Western nations' stated aspirations to democracy and accountability. Moreover, this was all in keeping with the secrecy which surrounded the clinical trials. In the US, as we'll see in more detail below, the FDA made an initial request that the clinical data accompanying the Pfizer trials should not be released for seventy-five years until the year 2096; a federal judge overturned this request in January 2022, and enormous batches of data started being released.[154]

So what did the released trial data show? It's worth noting that a peer-reviewed August 2022 paper published in the journal *Vaccine* analysed the trial documents alongside Moderna trial data, and was led by an illustrious team of scientists including Peter Doshi and scientists at Stanford and UCLA, among others; they determined that 'the excess risk of serious adverse events of special interest surpassed the risk reduction for Covid-19 hospitalization relative to the placebo group in both Pfizer and Moderna trials (2.3 and 6.4 per 10,000 participants, respectively)'.[155] This is quite a devastating and alarming finding, and was soon challenged by various fact-finding organisations— to which the authors then responded. However, it's not our aim here to make a judgement one way or the other about what the documents show. Of course, given the age profile of risk from Covid-19, the findings of this study don't suggest that no one should take this vaccine, and in fact indicate that for older people who are at risk from SARS-CoV-2 it is probably a good idea to get vaccinated. At the same time, what these findings do show is that—invoking the well-discussed 'precautionary principle'—hesitancy about universal vaccination is in order. It certainly isn't unreasonable, or evidence of being a 'conspiracy theorist'.

Moreover, and regardless of any of this, such lack of transparency in the initial refusal to release any of this data was absolutely unprecedented, even by the historically opaque standards of public-corporate initiatives involving Big Pharma. 'While opacity in the traditionally highly secretive pharmaceutical sector is unsurprising, governments have bowed even lower to corporate power in the Covid-19 crisis', the civil society organisation Public Eye wrote. 'They have failed to uphold their commitments to transparency and good governance, leaving even their parliaments in the dark. Nor have they leveraged public funding to demand accessibility and affordability clauses or transparency conditions, despite early calls to do so from civil society organisations'.[156]

As we have noted already, secrecy is by definition an element of conspiracy, and the complete and coordinated secrecy of these contracts and of the clinical data—when they are so clearly in the public interest—can rightly be seen as one of the elements which has driven the alarming recent rise in conspiracy theories (which we will return to in more detail in Chapter 9). Those suspicious of the general government response cannot be blamed for wondering if there was anything to hide, given that the US government and the company involved in one of the most widely administered vaccines, Pfizer, pushed for the trial data to be kept secret for seventy-five years. Ironically, just as Western governments were instrumental in creating the Covid-19 vaccines, they also had a part in creating the conspiracy theories which followed.

So what do the AstraZeneca leaked contract and the other partially redacted agreements, in the EU and elsewhere, tell us? That, as feared, governments really did hand out a blank cheque to Big Pharma, essentially granting vaccine makers close-to-full immunity from liability over a whole host of issues, such as vaccine-related adverse effects and delays in the delivery of the vaccines.[157] In the US, for example, the government invoked the Public Readiness and Emergency Preparedness (PREP) Act, a law that 'provides immunity from liability (except for wilful misconduct) for claims of loss caused by, arising out of, relating to, or resulting from the administration or use of covered countermeasures to diseases, threats and conditions identified in the declaration'.[158] That means that vaccine makers 'cannot be sued for money damages in court'[159] over injuries related to the administration or use of products to treat or protect against Covid.[160]

Even more incredibly, however, despite the vaccines being almost entirely publicly funded, governments allowed vaccine manufacturers to fully own the patents of the vaccines and thus to employ a completely pro-profit business model, meaning that it would be entirely up to them to decide how and where the vaccines would get manufactured and, most importantly, how much they would cost.[161] As economist Mariana Mazzucato at University College London argued, 'there is little justice if citizens have to bear many of the financial risks in such an endeavour, but most of the profits go to a small group of companies (and possibly a few universities) once a vaccine is ready to be rolled out'.[162]

It's hard to imagine a more fitting example of socialisation of the (huge) costs and privatisation of the (even bigger) profits, following the model of the 2008 financial crisis. Since the beginning of the pandemic, concerns had been expressed about the pricing of coronavirus vaccines. In early March 2020, a group of US lawmakers tried to include price control safeguards in the federal emergency coronavirus funding package. But these initiatives, as well as other intellectual property provisions, were frozen out of the legislation.[163]

A key figure in pushing the for-profit approach to the vaccine was Bill Gates. When the WHO launched the COVID-19 Technology Access Pool (or C-TAP) in May 2020,[164] with the aim of establishing a voluntary pool to share all 'existing and future rights in patented inventions and designs, as well as rights in regulatory test data, know-how, cell lines, copyrights and blueprints for manufacturing diagnostic tests, devices, drugs, or vaccines',[165] the pharmaceutical sector immediately dismissed the idea.[166] They instead threw their weight behind an alternative global initiative sponsored by the Bill and Melinda Gates Foundation, the aforementioned Access to COVID-19 Tools Accelerator (ACT-A),[167] which 'paved the way for a "market-based solution" that did nothing to challenge the sacrosanct monopolies of the pharmaceutical industry'.[168]

Gates, as a long-time donor to the University of Oxford's Jenner Institute, which was able to develop a vaccine candidate in early 2020, was also instrumental in pushing the institute to abandon its initial intention to adopt an open-licence (non-exclusive), royalty-free licensing model for its vaccine,[169] insisting instead that it find a large corporate partner for global manufacturing and distribution.[170] The institute ultimately struck a deal with the British-Swedish pharmaceutical giant AstraZeneca, but had to agree to give the latter the sole rights to decide which producer to work with, despite its receiving more than US$1 billion in public and philanthropic funding.[171]

The University of Oxford's decision to end its open-licence policy after being urged by the Gates Foundation to find a corporate partner is, according to civil society observers, 'the most concrete example of the consequences of the Gates Foundation approach to intellectual property'.[172] Gates's insistence on a market-based, for-profit approach to the vaccine was particularly problematic given that, as an article in *The Nation* noted, he had financial stakes worth hundreds of millions of dollars in dozens of companies working on anti-Covid vaccines.[173] By mid-2020, it was being reported that Gates's net profit had already gone up a staggering US$12 billion.[174]

In light of the profit-oriented approach to vaccines adopted in the West—in stark contrast to the publicly oriented approach embraced by other countries—it's hardly surprising that the two earliest and most touted Western vaccines, Pfizer-BioNTech and Moderna, were also among the most wildly overpriced, coming in respectively at around €/US$15–20 and €/US$18–25 per dose in the EU and US[175] (these would later be hiked),[176] compared to AstraZeneca's price per dose of just €/US$2.5–4.[177] The sheer scale of the profiteering at stake was indicated by the fact that, according to an Oxfam report from July 2021, the new mRNA vaccines were estimated to cost around US$1.20 per dose to manufacture.[178] In fact, profit margins of this type are not uncommon for drugs and vaccines, and were indeed also linked to two of the main treatments for Covid-19 which were approved by regulators, molnupiravir and remdesivir.[179] Taken all together, this therefore set the stage for what would become one of the most profitable operations in the history of Big Pharma[180]—and with the investment all coming at the public coffers' expense. It's therefore hardly surprising that, as we've just seen, groups such as Vaccines Europe were promoting universal vaccination of the population at an early point. We would argue that the money-printing framework created by this system played a crucial role in shaping the universal vaccination campaign that followed—that this was the twenty-first-century equivalent of the Californian gold rush.

None of this is to say that the vaccines were not crucial in tackling Covid-19. We're not scientists, and that's not our concern here. Instead, as writers with backgrounds in history and economics, it's our approach to dive into the economic power structures at work. We're used to analysing power relations in human societies, and it's pretty clear that these relations have an important part to play in the Covid-19 story. We think it's important to recognise the reported evidence that vaccine companies, and their investors, promoted the idea that as many people as possible should be vaccinated against Covid-19, and did so at an early stage. We've come to the conclusion that this was motivated not by scientific evidence but by a profit-driven agenda. To us, at least, it doesn't seem that this is an unreasonable—let alone a conspiratorial—interpretation.

In fact, we think it would be staggering if these motives didn't play a part. To hold that the economic interests of these companies and their shareholders had nothing to do with the policies that followed is basically to dismiss the foundations of the field of economics, as well as decades of the analysis of neoliberal politics and its public–private policy nexus. As we'll see in the next chapter, understanding this confluence of interests is important in getting a broader perspective on what happened next—the vaccine rollout.

5

VACCINATING THE WORLD AGAINST COVID—
BY ANY MEANS NECESSARY

Between December 2020 and January 2021, the EU, the US, and other major Western countries began the vaccine rollout. This spread pretty quickly to other parts of the world, as vaccines were distributed in many parts of Asia and Latin America. In Africa, however, Covid vaccines were very slow to arrive, something which liberal critics labelled 'vaccine apartheid'—even though in many African countries the real issue with the Covid vaccine was not the short supplies, but instead the way in which the single-minded focus on delivering the Covid vaccine impeded vaccination programmes for existing endemic diseases.

More on that later. In Western countries, and as with lockdowns, authorities adopted a frog-in-boiling-water approach. At first, most countries focused on prioritising the vaccination of healthcare workers, residents and staff of nursing homes, people at high risk of exposure, elderly people, and those with serious health conditions. Early messaging around Covid-19 vaccination presented it as a voluntary choice aimed at protecting the most vulnerable. Indeed, citing the potential for backlash and resistance, the director of the WHO's immunisation department stated in December 2020: 'I don't think we envision any countries creating a mandate for [Covid-19] vaccination.'[1] In the UK, once the vaccine rollout began in December 2020, government ministers declared that it was '15 million jabs to freedom'—the number of vaccinations required to immunise the over-70s with two Covid jabs.[2] This seemed to make it pretty clear that there wasn't much need for younger age groups to get vaccinated, which, given the age profile of Covid risk, was a reasonable assumption to make.

Many governments originally followed with similar public statements. However, in early-to-mid-2021, the narrative started shifting towards the need for countries to secure as many doses as possible as quickly as possible—even sparking instances of 'vaccine nationalism' as countries imposed bans on the export of vaccines to third countries[3]—in order to achieve high (and constantly moving) vaccination targets and reach herd immunity, avoid future lockdowns, 'end the pandemic', and 'get back to normal', or so we were told.[4] Countries started coming up with all sorts of incentives to 'nudge' people to get vaccinated: lotteries,[5] free beers,[6] free ice cream,[7] free entry to baseball matches,[8] even free sex.[9] At the time, however, vaccination was still mostly voluntary, though there were exceptions: in April 2021, Italy, as on other occasions throughout the pandemic, set the tone for things to come by becoming the first country in Europe to make vaccination against Covid-19 mandatory for healthcare workers.[10] Over the course of the rest of the year, many other countries would follow.

Then, in the late summer of 2021, the mainstream Western narrative pivoted once again. Now it was widely said that vaccinating the older and vulnerable alone was not enough to 'end the pandemic'. Governments made a collective move towards achieving universal Covid vaccination in order to stop viral transmission—an argument that revolved heavily around the public messaging that vaccinated people could not get or spread Covid-19.[11] At that point, the push towards mass vaccination started to get increasingly aggressive, as we'll soon see.

Why did this pivot occur? Although it's not our main aim to provide causal explanations in this part of the book, we think it's fairly clear that a range of political motives must have played a part. By the middle of 2021, many high-income countries, even though their vaccination rates already surpassed 50 per cent (with much higher rates among the elderly population),[12] had purchased enough doses to vaccinate their entire populations several times over (by December 2020, more than 10 billion vaccine doses had been pre-ordered by countries,[13] 1.5 billion of them by the EU alone).[14] While, as noted, we don't know the full contents of most of the vaccine contracts, governments had been heavily criticised back in 2009 during the swine flu outbreak for over-purchasing vaccine stocks, and probably didn't want to be accused of the same failings again. So, politically something had to be done to increase vaccine uptake, regardless of the medical cost–benefit analysis. From the economic perspective, as we've seen already, the revolving door between politics and industry meant that there were also many in government with ties to the pharmaceutical sector who were keen to push in this policy direction—and, given how invested the pharmaceutical business model had become in the Covid vaccines, renewed attention to vaccination through the booster campaign soon became a priority. Indeed, in mid-2021 EU Commission President Ursula von der Leyen negotiated the EU's biggest deal yet with Pfizer—for up to 1.8 billion doses—via a series of text messages with the company's chief.[15] When the European Ombudsman requested them, von der Leyen claimed to have lost them—and the European Commission clarified that it did not need them.[16]

In July 2021, the European Union launched the EU Digital COVID Certificate (EUDCC), also known as the 'green pass', a digitally signed proof of vaccination, recent recovery, or a recent negative test for use when travelling within the Schengen area with fewer restrictions.[17] Over the following two months, however, Ireland, France, and Italy became the first European countries to radically repurpose the EUDCC as a tool not for travel between countries but *within* their respective countries—as a requirement for participating in social life—along the lines of the green pass which had already been introduced in Israel.[18]

By this point, also thanks to regulatory agencies (notably the FDA and the EMA) approving the use of the vaccines in children as well (first above sixteen, then above twelve)[19] in spite of the vanishingly small risk which children faced from Covid-19, several governments were explicitly talking about the need to vaccinate everyone by any means necessary. In July, for example, French President Macron, shortly before issuing a 'health pass' (or *passe sanitaire*) as a requirement for accessing non-essential public spaces,[20] announced that 'we must move towards the vaccination of all French people because it is the only way to return to normal life'. He then echoed the programme of the Gates Foundation and GAVI Vaccine Alliance: 'This involves an immense but essential project which is now within our reach: vaccinating the entire world.'[21]

Although some readers may feel critical of the recurrent attention to the Gates Foundation here, this approach has even been shared by some mainstream outlets, such as *Politico* with its September 2022 report entitled 'How Bill Gates and His Partners Used their Clout to Control the Global Covid Response—with Little Oversight'.[22] Moreover, it's clear that this is the policy direction advocated by the Foundation's leadership. In his book *How to Prevent the Next Pandemic*, Bill Gates himself suggests that in the event of future pandemics vaccine infrastructure and investment need to be stepped up so that the whole world can be vaccinated against any pathogen within six months. So, again, this is not some kind of outlandish 'conspiracy theory', but merely a summary of what the major actors themselves have declared to be their policy aims.

Once Macron made the above statement, the aggressiveness of the vaccination campaign increased rapidly. Once again, governments enacted this by adopting a frog-in-boiling-water approach. Italy is a great case in point. There the green pass was announced in mid-July, pretty much out of the blue, despite very few hospitalisations for Covid and a vaccination rate well above the European average.[23] When it first came into force in August, it was initially limited to indoor restaurants, museums, cinemas, and sports venues (but unlike the French version it applied not only to adults but to all citizens above the age of twelve). Given that it was the middle of the holiday season, and that most restaurants in the summer offer outdoor seating (no green pass required), the impact of the measure was initially rather limited.

But that soon changed. In September 2021, the green pass also became mandatory for using medium- and long-distance public transport, as well as for all school teachers and staff and university students.[24] Then, in October, Italy became the first country in the West to extend these regulations to all public- and private-sector workers.[25] By that point, several European countries had similar measures in place, requiring proof of Covid status to gain access to indoor restaurants, museums, theatres, and cultural events, or to work in certain sectors such as healthcare. But nothing came close to Italy's scheme in terms of range and scope.

Finally, in January 2022, the Italian government introduced the so-called 'super green pass', which could only be obtained through vaccination or proof of recovery—evidence of a negative test would no longer be valid[26]—as a requirement for accessing all but a few public spaces: public transport, gyms, swimming pools, discos, restaurants (including open-air tables), bars, hotels, cinemas, hospitals (as a visitor or carer), ski areas, and so on.[27] And this applied to everyone above the age of twelve. At the same time, the 'basic' green pass was extended to tobacco shops, banks, post offices, clothing stores, and even hairdressers.[28] Basically, the only public spaces a non-vaccinated, non-officially recovered person (including all children above twelve) could access without proof of a negative test were supermarkets and pharmacies, and even a negative test only allowed access to basic commercial activities, and no social activity whatsoever. Meanwhile, that same month, Italy also became the first Western country to make vaccination mandatory for everyone above the age of fifty.[29]

By late 2021 to early 2022, mandatory proof-of-vaccination policies had been introduced in several countries, including most liberal democracies.[30] These policies included green passes or vaccine passports that limited access to social activities and travel (for example, in some states of the United States, Israel, Australia, Canada, New Zealand, and most European countries); workplace 'no jab, no job' mandates, covering key workers or some or all public- and/or private-sector workers (in the United States, Canada, Italy, France, Australia, and New Zealand); healthcare worker mandates (in some states of the United States, the United Kingdom, Italy, France, Germany, Canada, Australia, and New Zealand); school-based mandates (some states of the United States and Canada); full-population mandates for the elderly (in the Czech Republic and Greece); and even segregated lockdowns of the unvaccinated (in Austria, Germany, and Australia).[31]

Away from the Global North, there were also extensive vaccine mandates in other parts of the world, generally concentrated in venues which were accessed by the middle classes. In Latin America, there were requirements for government workers to be vaccinated in Costa Rica, and bans of the use of public transport for those not fully vaccinated in Chile.[32] In Africa, meanwhile, vaccine passports were rolled out to access public spaces in

Kenya[33] and Morocco,[34] and were used by some employers[35] and universities[36] in South Africa, while in Angola[37] and Cabo Verde[38] it was a requirement for government employees to have been vaccinated against Covid-19. In some countries in the Global South such as Ecuador,[39] mandatory Covid vaccination was enforced.

While the national restrictions expanded, entry requirements for international travel were widespread, and some countries even introduced fines and penalties (including restricted access to social services and medical care, business capacity restrictions, and threats of imprisonment). In Rwanda, there were tales of forcible vaccination being imposed by squads moving through the country, beating and handcuffing people until they consented to be vaccinated.[40] Some Western countries—Germany and Austria—announced their intention to introduce mandatory vaccination for all adults, as was the case in Ecuador, Indonesia, Micronesia, Turkmenistan, and Tajikistan, but such plans were either voted down by parliament or abandoned.[41]

The latter point is moot, however. As all these cases make clear, the principle of informed consent had been detonated—worldwide. Even if few countries actually implemented formal vaccine mandates, and contrary to the media portrayal that 'the unvaccinated are entirely free to decline', it is glaringly obvious that many of the measures outlined above, by making one's Covid status a precondition for leading anything resembling a 'normal' life—for eating out, going to school, playing sports, travelling, even working—amounted to a *de facto* mandatory vaccination, often extended even to minors.[42] These policies raise very serious ethical and political issues, in terms of both their means (restricted and conditional access to public spaces and workplaces) and their ends (compelled or mandatory mass vaccination), which were only exacerbated by the surreptitious nature of the mandates.

This had all been impossible to imagine at the start of 2021, when a number of politicians had gone on record saying that there would be no compulsory Covid vaccination. While some drew parallels to yellow fever vaccination, obligatory for travel to some parts of the world where that disease is endemic, it was unprecedented for proof of vaccination status to be required in order to participate in normal life within national borders—and for this to be linked to other aspects of an individual's biological status which were kept on government databases. Moreover, the 1947 Nuremberg Code—which grew out of the abuses of medical power during the Nazi regime—had enshrined informed consent to medical intervention as a key aspect of the post-war order of democracy and human rights. In the space of eighteen months, the response to Covid-19 had upended seventy-five years of democratic norms.

What had occurred was the normalisation of policies that were far from normal. Never before had QR codes been used as a regulated requirement for entry into social life[43]—yet another policy that would have been inconceivable before 2020. Vaccine policies effectively stripped citizens who hadn't broken any law whatsoever (precisely because the vaccines were not legally mandated) of their basic constitutional, civil, and human rights—the right to work, education, public transport, and social life.[44] In countries such as Italy, France, and Israel, double-vaccinated citizens lost their 'status' when passports came to require a third booster dose in 2021-22.[45] In Chile, that status was extended to a fourth dose in May 2022.[46]

The surreptitious nature of the mandates also allowed governments to sidestep the democratic debates and procedures that the introduction of outright mandates would have involved. Indeed, with the exception of a few countries, many of these vaccine policies 'were imposed as regulations, decrees, orders or directions under states of emergency and implemented in ways that allowed ad hoc juridical decisions and irregular and over-permissive private sector rules, with limited accountability or legal recourse to address rights violations'.[47] In other words, vaccine policies simply exacerbated the pandemic's authoritarian and anti-democratic turn, extending the state of exception which had come into place with the lockdown policies of the year before.

The discriminatory and segregational nature of these measures was in direct violation of EU Regulation 2021/953, which introduced the EU Digital COVID Certificate as a means to regulate travel between (not within) countries, and which stated that '[t]he issuance of [Covid] certificates [...] should not lead to discrimination on the basis of the possession of a specific category of certificate', and that '[i]t is necessary to prevent direct or indirect discrimination against persons who are not vaccinated, for example because of medical reasons [...] or because they have not yet had the opportunity *or chose not to be vaccinated*' (emphasis added).[48] This was also echoed by Resolution 2361 (2021) of the Council of Europe.[49]

In most countries, these policies were met with fierce political resistance, including massive street protests.[50] Huge protests in Trieste, London, Paris, and Melbourne and the truckers' protest in Canada took place, largely ignored by the mainstream press. Political leaders and commentators, especially on the liberal left, were quick to stigmatise the vaccine-hesitant or vaccine-resistant and/or the anti-passes/mandates movements as expressions of 'ignorance',[51] 'irrationalism',[52] and 'anti-science',[53] 'right-wing', and 'libertarian'[54] ideology, refusing to acknowledge that such positions could actually be based upon legitimate concerns. Moreover, these critiques failed to engage with the many other groups concerned by these moves, beyond the libertarian right. In New York, Black Lives Matter came out strongly against vaccine mandates in September 2021, noting that they would likely fuel increasing abuse of minorities through police searches.[55] In

Europe, major left-wing intellectuals such as Giorgio Agamben and Massimo Cacciari in Italy and Laurent Mucchielli in France opposed the mandates.[56] Moreover, the liberal position on vaccines failed completely to acknowledge the framework of disaster capitalism and profiteering which, as we've already noted, cannot be separated from the political forces driving universal vaccination. Vaccination against Covid was, of course, a wise move for those at risk—yet in the face of the many other competing health priorities brought on by the lockdown response, as well as the precautionary principle which might be invoked for the use of such a rapidly developed vaccine in younger age groups, the universality of this policy seemed to be driven by factors other than science.

All this further exacerbated the political polarisation and radicalisation already fuelled by lockdowns. As the weeks went by, the public narrative grew ever more aggressive. By mid-2021, the political discourse was increasingly making the unvaccinated the target of institutionally sanctioned hate speech, 'normalis[ing] stigma against people who remain unvaccinated, often woven into the tone and framing of media articles'.[57] As Kevin Bardosh, Alex de Figueiredo, and other researchers wrote in *BMJ Global Health* in May 2022:

> Political leaders singled out the unvaccinated, blaming them for: the continuation of the pandemic; stress on hospital capacity; the emergence of new variants; driving transmission to vaccinated individuals; and the necessity of ongoing lockdowns, masks, school closures and other restrictive measures. Political rhetoric descended into moralising, scapegoating, and blaming using pejorative terms and actively promoting stigma and discrimination as tools to increase vaccination. This became socially acceptable among pro-vaccine groups, the media and the public at large, who viewed full vaccination as a moral obligation and part of the social contract.[58]

This type of discourse is exemplified by some of the statements made by prominent political leaders. Emmanuel Macron, President of France: '[It is] only a very small minority who are resisting. How do we reduce that minority? We reduce it by pissing them off even more [...]. When my freedoms threaten those of others, I become someone irresponsible. Someone irresponsible is not a citizen.'[59] Joe Biden, President of the United States: 'This is a pandemic of the unvaccinated. [...] For the unvaccinated, you're looking at a winter of severe illness and death for yourselves, your families, and the hospitals you may soon overwhelm.'[60] Mario Draghi, Prime Minister of Italy: 'The appeal not to get vaccinated is an appeal to die, basically. You don't get vaccinated, you get sick, you die. Or you kill: you don't get vaccinated, you get sick, you contaminate, someone dies.'[61]

Others went even further, accusing the unvaccinated of being 'rats',[62] 'subhumans',[63] and 'criminals',[64] who deserved to be 'excluded from public life'[65] and 'from the national health service',[66] and even to 'die like flies'.[67] This, as was to be expected, simply had the effect of further polarising society. As Bardosh and his colleagues noted, missing from the public debate was a 'a discussion of *who* and *why* people remain unvaccinated':

> Unvaccinated or partially vaccinated individuals often have concerns that are based in some form of evidence (e.g., prior Covid-19 infection, data on age-based risk, historical/current trust issues with public health and governments, including structural racism), personal experiences (e.g., direct or indirect experience of adverse drug reactions or iatrogenic injuries, unrelated trauma, issues with access to care to address adverse events, etc.) and concerns about the democratic process (e.g., belief that governments have abused their power by invoking a constant state of emergency, eschewing public consultation and over-relying on pharmaceutical company-produced data) that may prevent or delay vaccination.[68]

This last point seems particularly relevant to us, as it ultimately encompasses all the others. Given the opacity that, as we've documented here, has characterised the entire vaccine development, approval, and rollout process, and the mind-boggling profits at stake for the vaccine makers, could people really be blamed for thinking that corporate and commercial interests, rather than the public interest or scientific knowledge, were driving the vaccination campaign? Are transparency and accountability not key prerequisites for the democratic process—and in withholding it in so many ways, on such an urgent matter, were governments not trampling on democratic norms, with potential long-term risks for democracy itself? These factors may well have persuaded some people that there were other things beyond scientific matters which were relevant in their decision whether or not to be vaccinated against Covid-19.

We'll return in more detail to these political questions towards the end of the book, but as they were so inextricably connected to the 'what' of the vaccine rollout, it's important to acknowledge them here, not least because they haven't yet been satisfactorily resolved. At the time of writing, for example, the raw clinical trial data remains unavailable for independent scientific scrutiny,[69] while a whistleblower has raised important concerns about data integrity and regulatory oversight practices at a contract company helping with Pfizer's clinical trials in the United States.[70]

Moreover, as noted above, governments and regulatory agencies have repeatedly refused to release the full documentation pertaining to the regulatory approval process and purchase agreements. Following a FOIA request by a non-profit organisation for the US FDA to expedite the release of Covid-19 vaccine review documents,[71] the FDA proposed releasing around 500 pages of the documents each month[72]—a pace at which it would have taken the FDA between fifty-five and seventy-five years to release the entire documentation (yes, you read that correctly), comprising more than 300,000 pages, which of course also begs the question of how the agency was able to thoroughly assess and green-light such a massive amount of paperwork in just a few months. Similarly, the European Union's EMA has refused requests to release the raw data pertaining to the clinical trials or to the materials used to manufacture the Covid vaccines, 'relying on the need to protect the commercial interests of the manufacturer'.[73]

Further controversy was sparked when two top scientists at the FDA resigned in protest at the US government's announcement that it intended to offer BioNTech-Pfizer and Moderna booster shots to most Americans—before either company had even made an application to the FDA to authorise a third dose.[74] In an article in *The Lancet* they claimed that '[c]urrent evidence does not [...] appear to show a need for boosting in the general population, in which efficacy against severe disease remains high',[75] and accused the government and pharmaceutical companies of essentially sidestepping the FDA's own experts. That same month, it also came to light that the British government was apparently 'furious' at the refusal of its own scientific advisors (the Joint Committee on Vaccination and Immunisation, the JCVI), to green-light the extension of mass vaccination policies to all 12–15-year-old children.[76] The government decided to push ahead anyway.[77] So much for 'following the science'.

Then, in early 2022, CNBC reported that the FDA had approved a fourth and even a fifth BioNTech-Pfizer and Moderna shot for certain categories 'without calling meetings of their vaccine advisory committees, a rare move the agencies have made more frequently over the course of the pandemic to expand uses of already-approved Covid vaccines'.[78] 'We talk endlessly about how we follow the science—it doesn't seem to work out that way', said Paul Offit, a committee member.

These episodes 'have only increased the perception that regulatory agencies are "captured" by industry', researchers have noted.[79] But is it really just a perception? Both the FDA and the EMA rely heavily on fees and charges levied on the very pharmaceutical companies they are called upon to regulate (respectively for around half and three quarters of their budgets)[80]—a fact which, according to several observers, raises serious conflicts of interest and compromises the autonomy of these agencies.[81] Moreover, and as we've seen in detail here, both agencies have long been criticised for their 'revolving door' problem[82]—the fact that regulators often come from the industry they are supposed to regulate, or will go and work for that industry once they leave their post. For example, the current executive director of the EMA, Emer Cooke, previously worked for Europe's largest pharmaceutical lobbying organisation, the European Federation of Pharmaceutical Industries and Associations (EFPIA).[83]

Indeed, scientists had long denounced these agencies' lack of transparency and their tendency to publish only a small part of the clinical trial data (often with a 'selective reporting of favourable results')[84] and to take an incredible amount of time to communicate the rest when a request is entered.[85] Nevertheless, throughout the entire process of the vaccine rollout, leading politicians and commentators did nothing to quell fears that authorities were not being transparent about the efficacy and safety of these novel vaccines. In fact, they did the exact opposite—dismissing, mocking, and censoring all concerns about vaccine-related adverse effects, despite the growing body of evidence that such effects needed further investigation, including blood-clotting events,[86] myocarditis,[87] and altered menstrual periods,[88] especially in young[89] and previously infected[90] people, and the often erratic shifts in vaccination guidelines in terms of eligibility for different vaccines in some countries.[91] Just as we have seen take place with the question of the virus's origins, and the necessity of lockdowns, a 'single narrative' soon emerged which ruthlessly trolled any opposing voices.

The censorship spared no one, no matter how scientifically qualified. A good example might be the removal from YouTube of a video of a US congressional hearing on Covid-19 vaccine adverse events. This hearing took evidence from medically confirmed vaccine-injured individuals from the original clinical trials, a US military clinician, and Peter Doshi, a senior editor of the *BMJ*. In his evidence, Doshi questioned the accuracy of the reporting of the Pfizer vaccine effectiveness, and also noted that the new mRNA vaccines had required the publication of a new definition of the word 'vaccine' in the Merriam-Webster dictionary.[92] Concerns about the never-before-used mRNA technology and its potential collateral effects—which were raised even in the scientific community,[93] including by one of the inventors of the technology itself[94]—were equally dismissed.[95]

It's hardly surprising that all this fuelled distrust over decision-making around vaccine use and ensuing mandates, especially considering the long history of corporate pharmaceutical malfeasance and criminal and civil settlements, in part resulting precisely from misrepresentation of the safety and efficacy of medicines.[96] As Doshi noted in the *BMJ*, Big Pharma is the world's 'least trusted industry',[97] and with good reason: at least three of the companies involved in the production of Covid-19 vaccines have had past criminal and civil settlements costing them billions of dollars,[98] while one pleaded guilty to fraud.[99] As the *Guardian* reported, in September 2009 Pfizer was handed the biggest criminal fine in US history, US$2.3 billion, for promoting a painkilling drug for uses for which it was not authorised;[100] two years later, in 2011, Pfizer was forced to pay out large compensation payments to the families of children who died in a clinical trial in Kano, northern Nigeria:[101] this led to the pharmaceutical giant being dubbed 'the BP of drug companies'.[102] Meanwhile, as *Nature* reported, Merck—who marketed the Covid treatment molnupiravir—had to pay out the enormous sum of US$4.85 billion in civil damages in 2007, for marketing the painkiller Vioxx even though the clinical trial showed that this drug doubled the risk of heart attack and stroke, a decision which led to at least 27,000 heart attacks and strokes.[103]

In light of all this, the question is not why some citizens had doubts about the vaccine and viewed the campaigns of compelled or enforced vaccination as unacceptably coercive, but rather why so many people, especially on the liberal and radical left— which historically has denounced the capture of governments and institutions by corporate interests—uncritically accepted the information provided by the vaccine makers and embraced the mainstream discourse around vaccines and mandates. To take Pfizer, given the company's track record, raising the question of whether the '95 per cent effectiveness' tag might have been prone to exaggeration, and whether (given the enormous and unprecedented speed of the vaccine development process) there might be some side-effects to the new drug, should not have been taken as a sign of being a raging alt-right conspiracy theorist. And yet this was how the liberal left painted this, with writers such as Naomi Klein dismissing the Canadian truckers as right-wing neo-imperialists suffering from 'toxic nostalgia' in the face of 'all mitigating evidence'.[104] In fact, as we've shown here, the mitigating evidence points unerringly to the fact that scepticism and critical analysis of the vaccines should have been a prerequisite for any scientific scrutiny of the process and their effectiveness. This should certainly have been a requirement considering the growing number of studies published in top-ranking journals that suggest that some initial concerns weren't misplaced. These might include the January 2022 study published in *JAMA* and co-authored by Matthew Oster, MD, MPH of the CDC's Vaccine

Task Force, showing an increased risk of myocarditis in the US across multiple age and sex strata, but particularly in young men, after receiving mRNA-based Covid-19 vaccines;[105] a May 2022 *Nature* study showing an increase in emergency medical service calls for cardiac events in younger people following the rollout of the Covid-19 vaccines in Israel;[106] and a June 2022 pre-print by Peter Doshi and others which found that mRNA vaccines were associated with an increased risk of serious adverse events of special interest.[107]

Indeed, given Big Pharma's track record, an open procedure would surely have been the best way of quelling any outlandish conspiracy theorists. But this isn't what happened. This is even more puzzling considering that, for all the talk of the pro- and anti-vaccine/mandate dispute being one of 'science' versus 'anti-science', the scientific rationale and public health argument in favour of blanket mandatory vaccination policies were always weak. Much of the institutional framing revolved around people's 'duty' to get vaccinated. People of all ages were told to get the jab—and to jab their children—to avoid infecting others, to help reach herd immunity and 'eradicate Covid', and to stop taking up hospital beds.

However, none of these arguments hold up to scrutiny. While the current vaccines appear to have had a significant impact on decreasing Covid-19-related morbidity and mortality among the elderly and vulnerable populations, the evidence—much of which was already available in mid-2021, when the vaccine passes and mandates started being introduced[108]—also shows that the vaccines offer a very limited and temporary protection from the possibility of getting infected and infecting others,[109] which is likely lower in younger age groups targeted for vaccine mandates and passports,[110] and thus have a very limited efficacy, if any, in reducing the spread of the virus. Indeed, in late May 2022 Bill Gates himself came out against vaccine passports,[111] since the vaccines had been shown not to prevent 'breakthrough infections', as indeed the early data from the year before showed—contrary to all the initial talk in the media that the vaccines would stop people from catching Covid, and that, as GAVI reported in August 2021, 'clinical trials of the Pfizer/BioNTech and Moderna vaccines found them to be 94–95% effective against all symptomatic Covid-19 disease after the second dose'.[112]

This is an important point, since one criticism that some readers might level at the narrative we have sketched so far is that it has not credited the vaccination programme with ending the pandemic. However, we are not seeking to criticise the Covid vaccines *per se*, but rather the ethics, politics, and economics of the universal vaccination programme and the penalisation of those who chose not to get vaccinated. As noted, Covid-19 was not a serious disease for the vast majority of people aged much under 60, and herd immunity through universal vaccination was always an unlikely scenario. In these circumstances, the broader social and political frameworks which drove this policy—and the abuse of those who opposed it—are important to consider.

Regarding the (in)ability of the vaccines to produce herd immunity, the evidence on this was quite clear from early on in the rollout. Indeed, a September 2021 study showed that there was no correlation between increases in Covid-19 cases and levels of vaccination across sixty-eight countries and 2,947 counties in the United States.[113] Recent studies even suggest that the vaccines' efficacy turns *negative* after a certain period, with higher infection rates among vaccinated than unvaccinated people,[114] possibly due to waning antibody responses.[115] This means that the main rationale for vaccine passports—that of creating 'Covid-free spaces' and reducing the spread of the virus—is completely unfounded. Moreover, the writing was already on the wall for these approaches by the last months of 2021, with countries with complete triple vaccination such as

Gibraltar,[116] and extremely high vaccination rates such as Israel,[117] experiencing renewed surges of Covid cases; subsequent studies of US campuses such as Cornell which had imposed vaccine mandates for students (alongside masking mandates and rigorous contact tracing) showed that these had done little to curb the spread of Covid-19 infections.[118]

The fact that even the vaccinated can catch and transmit the virus also means that the current vaccines will never be able to deliver herd immunity,[119] despite initial claims that it would be achieved once a certain (albeit constantly shifting) vaccination threshold had been reached.[120] This brings us to another pillar of the Covid consensus: the redefinition of the concept of herd immunity. As noted above in the discussion about the British debate over herd immunity, up until the Covid pandemic it had been a well-established immunological and epidemiological concept for at least a century that natural immunisation through previous infection plays a crucial role in the weakening or even the eradication of infectious diseases.[121] However, as we saw in the context of the aforementioned debate, with the appearance of Covid-19 this concept was called into question and even demonised as a callous 'Malthusian' approach in order to promote the idea that the only possible or acceptable strategy was to lock down and wait for a vaccine.

A key role in redefining herd immunity was played by the World Health Organization. In April 2020, for example, the WHO issued a scientific brief which made headlines around the world, claiming that: 'There is currently no evidence that people who have recovered from Covid-19 and have antibodies are protected from a second infection.'[122] This was an astonishing claim, considering that it went against everything that was known about the way infectious diseases such as Covid work—many scientists would say that the evidence provided derived not from Covid-19, but from the entire history of the study of infectious diseases. Indeed, just two days later the WHO withdrew its claim and confirmed that at least to some extent the opposite was likely true, tweeting: 'We expect that most people who are infected with #COVID19 will develop an antibody response that will provide some level of protection. What we don't yet know is the level of protection or how long it will last'[123] (it would subsequently be established that previous infection from Covid, as was to be expected, provides a strong and lasting protection).[124] As is often the case, though, this retraction didn't receive a fraction of the coverage of the initial false claim.

Then, in late 2020, the WHO went a step further. Up until November 2020, the Q&A page on Covid-19 serology on the WHO website contained a section about herd immunity that read: 'Herd immunity is the indirect protection from an infectious disease that happens when a population is immune either through vaccination or immunity developed through previous infection.'[125] This, as noted above, was in line with the established scientific consensus. However, on 13 November—just as the first anti-Covid vaccines entered the final stage of the regulatory approval process—the WHO changed its definition of herd immunity, which now read: '"Herd immunity", also known as "population immunity", is a concept used for vaccination, in which a population can be protected from a certain virus if a threshold of vaccination is reached.'[126]

At the stroke of a pen (or keyboard), the World Health Organization effectively deleted the concept of natural immunity to claim that herd immunity could be achieved only through vaccination. As one commentator noted at the time: '[T]his change [...] ignores and even wipes out 100 years of medical advances in virology, immunology, and epidemiology. It is thoroughly unscientific—shilling for the vaccine industry in exactly the way the conspiracy theorists say that WHO has been doing since the beginning of this pandemic.'[127] Indeed, it's hard to comprehend why the WHO would make such an unscientific claim, on the verge of the emergency approval of the first Covid vaccines, other than to promote the mass vaccination narrative.

As we've noted, the WHO had already been accused back in 2009 of promoting a certain narrative around swine flu which suited some of its corporate backers in the pharmaceutical sector, so it shouldn't have been a surprise if some of the same forces were at work again. On the other hand, the normative narrative of vaccination and health was much older. Many would point to the histories of the mass vaccination programmes which had disposed of previous lethal diseases such as smallpox, measles, and polio to widespread acclaim during the 1950s, 1960s, and 1970s. This historical narrative indeed seems largely convincing for these diseases, and indeed vaccination mandates were of course enforced in some times and places for smallpox. However in that case the smallpox vaccine provided sterilising immunity, and had been developed over many years and undergone a wide range of tests. As mass vaccination had never before in history eradicated a respiratory virus, the evidence that this would hold for SARS-CoV-2 was always sketchy, to say the least—and certainly did not justify this wholesale attempt to redefine longstanding scientific concepts on the basis of an aspirational vaccination programme, or indeed to introduce the vaccine mandates which we have discussed in this chapter.

Having attempted to redefine herd immunity, however, once again the WHO was forced to backtrack: on 31 December, it reinstated its original definition to include 'immunity developed through previous infection' as one of the means through which to achieve herd immunity.[128] However, it added a new paragraph stating that 'WHO supports achieving "herd immunity" through vaccination, not by allowing a disease to spread through any segment of the population'. The WHO thus confirmed its support for mass vaccination as the only acceptable way of achieving herd immunity. But even this was unprecedented. The Princeton University historian of medicine David J. Robertson noted that while mass vaccination has certainly been associated with herd immunity in recent decades, it has never previously been seen as the sole means of achieving this immunity.[129]

This was all the more bizarre given that little if anything was known at the time about the vaccines' ability to prevent transmission—which we now know to be extremely low. Indeed, the clinical trials weren't even designed to study that: 'Our trial will not demonstrate prevention of transmission', Moderna's Chief Medical Officer Tal Zaks told the *BMJ* in late 2020, 'because in order to do that you have to swab people twice a week for very long periods, and that becomes operationally untenable.'[130] This was indeed later confirmed by Pfizer, in October 2022, when Pfizer's President of International Markets Janine Small told the European Parliament that no tests had been done during the Covid vaccine development regarding their impact on transmission: a social media furore followed, although fact checking organisations stated that Pfizer had never claimed that such tests had been done.[131]

However, while they had not claimed that tests for transmission had been done, this had not stopped Pfizer CEO Albert Bourla from claiming in June 2021 that 'widespread vaccination is a critical tool to stop transmission'; or in April 2021 that research from South Africa suggested that the vaccine was '100% effective' in preventing Covid cases.[132]

That's right: in spite of the media onslaught which held that everyone needed to get vaccinated against Covid, as this prevented transmission and statements of Bourla to the same effect, senior figures in both of the main companies that had developed the Covid vaccines made it plain that the vaccine trials had shown nothing about transmission. This meant that to claim the opposite was completely unscientific—and in fact when

Deborah Birx, who had been coordinator of the US government's Coronavirus Task Force, was asked in a June 2022 Congress hearing, 'When the government told us the vaccinated could not transmit [Covid] was that a lie or a guess?', she responded, 'I think it was hope.'[133]

It's not clear that hope has ever been a reasonable ground to upend medical, scientific, and democratic norms. It certainly doesn't seem that this is a scientific mode of procedure. Yet, despite all this, the political and media establishment repeated for months that mass vaccination was the key to reaching herd immunity,[134] despite all the evidence to the contrary. Even worse, many vaccine mandate and passport policies completely ignored the role of prior infection,[135] in terms of both immunity 'status'—evidence shows that it provides comparable or superior benefits to vaccination[136]—and its potential to increase the risk of post-vaccination adverse effects.[137]

As for the notion that people should get vaccinated to avoid taking up hospital beds, it's an argument that makes little sense, for obvious reasons, if aimed at those who faced little or no risk of ending up in the hospital in the first place. Respected epidemiologists have noted that the chances of an 18-year-old dying of Covid are 1 in 10,000 of those of a 75-year-old.[138] Even for people under fifty, the risk is low. While a small number of people in this category might indeed end up in hospital as a result of their choice not to get vaccinated, it's unclear why they should be held any more responsible than someone who ends up in hospital as a result of, say, unhealthy lifestyle choices—especially considering the limited impact of Covid hospitalisations of people below the age of sixty on overall hospital capacity.[139]

Moreover, the limited benefit of risk reduction obtained from the vaccine in people with very low risks of developing serious consequences from Covid in the first place has to be weighed against the known (and, most importantly, unknown) short- and potentially long-term adverse effects of repeated vaccinations, especially in children.[140] Below a certain age, it is highly questionable whether the cost–benefit ratio of vaccination can be considered to be positive.[141] This is why some countries took a precautionary and voluntary approach to vaccinating children, with Swedish authorities, for example, stating that '[because of] a low risk for serious disease for kids, we don't see any clear benefit with vaccinating them', and Danish authorities announcing in June 2022 that the Covid booster would only be offered to the over-50s and the immunocompromised.[142] For the very same reason, the decision to introduce school vaccine mandates in several countries appears particularly questionable.[143] And this is not even considering the way in which vaccine passes and mandates exacerbated the psychosocial stress and related health effects in societies already severely tested by recurring lockdowns.

Ultimately, the scientific and public health rationale for mass or universal vaccination against Covid, especially with the current mRNA-based Western vaccines (Pfizer-BioNTech and Moderna), appears very flimsy, to say the least, from both a collectivist (cost–benefit ratio for society as a whole) as well as individualistic (cost–benefit ratio for the majority of individuals) perspective, let alone when the historical record of many of the major companies involved in developing the vaccines is taken into account. This is why the decision to enforce the mass inoculation of these fast-tracked, experimental, and, ultimately, little-known 'next-generation' vaccines, including in children as young as five (and more recently as young as 6 months old),[144] through *de facto* or *de jure* vaccine mandates, should be considered particularly deplorable from an ethical standpoint, in our opinion—alongside the role of the media and political establishment in directing what may justifiably be considered hate speech in the direction of those who had chosen not to get vaccinated against Covid.

In conclusion, the point is not whether vaccine mandates should be considered either always or never justified. The point is whether, in any given context, they satisfy the conditions of necessity and proportionality: that is, whether the expected benefits, for individuals and for society as a whole, clearly outweigh the liberty restrictions and other risks and burdens associated with the mandates. As even a WHO policy brief on the ethical consideration of mandatory Covid vaccination published in May 2022 reads:

> Vaccination mandates can be ethically justified; however, their ethical justification is contingent upon a number of conditions and considerations, including the contexts within which they are implemented. [...] Mandatory vaccination should be considered only if it is necessary for, and proportionate to, the achievement of one or more important societal or institutional objectives (typically but not exclusively public health objectives, which may also be in service of social and economic objectives). Among others, such objectives may include interrupting chains of viral transmission, preventing morbidity and mortality, protecting at-risk populations and preserving the capacity of acute health care systems or other critical infrastructure.[145]

It should be noted that the World Health Organization itself never officially endorsed vaccine mandates for Covid, and in the aforementioned policy brief reiterated that the WHO 'does not presently support the direction of mandates for Covid-19 vaccination, having argued that it is better to work on information campaigns and making vaccines accessible'.[146]

Indeed, from a public health, ethical, and even life-saving perspective, a focused protection to vaccination[147]—which would have limited the vaccination to those categories for whom the cost–benefit ratio is almost certainly positive, namely people aged over sixty and those with serious comorbidities—would not only have likely yielded the same results in terms of reduction of hospitalisations and deaths, while avoiding putting the health of young people at risk and tearing societies apart through coercive, stigmatising, and discriminatory policies, but would arguably have saved even more lives, as it would have prioritised the vaccination of those most at risk from Covid.

In terms of cost–benefit frameworks, we must also consider here the enormous amount of resources being devoted to the universal Covid vaccination programme, resources which might better be directed at other elements of creaking healthcare infrastructure, when—as we see when looking at the medical effects of these policies in Chapter 6—these had already been sidelined during the Covid policy response. As the WHO's Director-General argued in late 2021, 'It makes no sense to give boosters to healthy adults, or to vaccinate children, when health workers, older people and other high-risk groups around the world are still waiting for their first dose.'[148] And this indeed was a further glaring ethical deficiency of the vaccine mandate policy being implemented in so many Western countries, and in regions such as Latin America and parts of Asia. By forcing many people at little risk from Covid-19 into being vaccinated, Western countries were hoarding vaccines and preventing their distribution to poorer countries where many older and vulnerable people had not yet been vaccinated. For all the shrill attention in the Western liberal media to 'vaccine apartheid', this segregation when it came to vaccine access was a direct consequence of the universal vaccination policy (and accompanying moral baiting) being so widely promoted by the liberal establishment.

Regrettably, it would appear that, as with lockdowns, the enforced global vaccination campaign was not driven by public health considerations but rather by economic and political motivations—and all the available evidence which we have considered here suggests that the first and foremost of these motivations was corporate profit. In this sense, we disagree with those on the left who argue that the main problem with allowing the vaccine makers to maintain a for-profit business model was their refusal to waive the patent rights in order to allow mass vaccination campaigns to be carried out even in low-income countries. We would argue that it's the exact opposite: allowing the vaccine makers to pursue a for-profit strategy offered these incredibly powerful corporations, capable of exercising a huge influence over national governments and supranational institutions, a perverse incentive to vaccinate as many people as possible in high-income, high-paying countries, by any means necessary, regardless of the consequences or actual benefits, at the expense of elderly and high-risk categories, in high-income as well as low-income countries.

The objective was reached. At the time of writing, almost 12 billion doses of Covid-19 vaccines have been administered worldwide,[149] with 64.5 per cent of the global population having received at least one dose[150]—close to the WHO's target to vaccinate 70 per cent of the world population by mid-2022.[151] Meanwhile, pharmaceutical corporations made the killing of the century, with the companies behind two of the most successful Covid-19 vaccines—Pfizer, BioNTech, and Moderna—making combined profits of US$45 billion in 2021 (compared to the US$60 million Moderna generated in sales in 2019),[152] and looking at equally mind-blowing profits in the future if the talk of annual booster injections[153] and variant-specific vaccines[154] is anything to go by, especially given the economic and political power these companies have been allowed to accrue.

For example, Moderna informed its investors that it was expecting a robust 'variant booster market' as a source of profits.[155] Similarly, Pfizer CEO Albert Bourla suggested that a fourth dose of vaccine would be necessary, without any clinical trial data or independent evaluation to indicate that the benefits of subsequent doses outweigh any risks,[156] nor any consideration of the changing clinical dynamics with the Omicron variant. It needs to be remembered that until late 2022, the booster dose that was administered was of the very same vaccine that had been developed for the initial virus strain, despite the new Omicron variant having been the dominant strain since late 2021, and that no clinical tests had been carried out to see if that vaccine was also effective against new variants. A new Pfizer-BioNTech booster designed to target the most common Omicron subvariants was only approved by the FDA and EMA in September 2022. However, several scientists were alarmed to learn that the new booster hadn't been tested on humans, but only on... eight mice. 'For the FDA to rely on mouse data is just bizarre, in my opinion', said John Moore, an immunologist at Weill Cornell Medicine in New York. 'Mouse data are not going to be predictive in any way of what you would see in humans'.[157] No wonder that some people believe Big Pharma is driving the vaccine policies, or that, as we've seen in this chronicle of the past two years, the cornerstone of the scientific method is regarded by some to have been thrown out of the window.

Another element that further calls into question the true motivations of the vaccination campaign is the selective approval of the vaccines. Despite all the talk of vaccinating as many people as quickly as possible, at the time of writing, the FDA and EMA have yet to approve any vaccine apart from the Western ones—namely Pfizer-BioNTech, Moderna, and Janssen in the United States,[158] plus AstraZeneca and Novavax in the EU[159]—despite dozens of other vaccines having been authorised or approved around the world[160] and administered to billions of people in countries such as China and India, several of which have been deemed safe and effective by independent studies, such as the Russian Sputnik vaccine,[161] used in more than twenty nations. If protecting people from Covid-19 was the only relevant aspect of the vaccination campaign, it would seem that all vaccines should be considered and approved for use, and not just those developed by Western governments' corporate partners—and yet that hasn't proved to be the case. Thus, when one considers all the available evidence, as we've tried to do here, it's hard to conclude that public health has been the overarching driver of the vaccination campaign in the West.

Finally, there's an equally significant hypothesis when it comes to vaccine policies: that vaccine passports may not have been just a means to an end—mass vaccination—but also an end in and of themselves. As Bardosh and his colleagues wrote:

> Having set these population-wide passport precedents, it is conceivable that they could be expanded in the near future to include other personal health data including genetic tests and mental health records, which would create additional rights violations and discrimination based on biological status for employers, law enforcement, insurance companies, governments and tech companies. [...] Technology companies interested in biosurveillance using artificial intelligence and facial recognition technology have obtained large contracts to implement vaccine passports and now have a financial interest in maintaining and expanding them.[162]

This issue is discussed in greater detail in the final chapter of this book. In the end, as we'll see there, the political consequences of the 'what happened' story which we've recounted here are enormous. Politics became hard to separate from science during the Covid-19 pandemic, or at least from 'The Science', and the enormity of the social, economic, and political consequences that followed form the subject of the second part of this book.

CONCLUSION

OMICRON—THE END OF THE STORY?

So many strange things happened between March 2020 and the first months of 2022. Our main concern in this part of the book has been to document this, which in itself is a challenging task. As we come to the end of that chronicle, though, it's worth bringing together some of these events, if only to highlight just how curious they were.

A short list might include the following: the about-turn by leading scientific figures on questions ranging from virus origins and lockdowns to masking and asymptomatic transmission, in all cases without any apparent new scientific evidence; the placing of an individual who funded scientific research in Wuhan's Institute of Virology in key commissions of enquiry that were set up to establish whether or not the virus leaked from the Wuhan Institute of Virology; the repeated statements that the Covid vaccines prevented transmission, when the chief medical officer of one of the main companies developing these vaccines had specifically stated that the trials had not been established to determine this; the request by medical regulators in the US not to release the clinical data of the major vaccine trials until the year 2096; the redefinition of pillars of medical practice such as 'herd immunity' and 'vaccines' by organisations including the WHO and the Merriam-Webster dictionary, and the removal from the internet of footage of the senior editor of the world's leading medical journal pointing this out; and the staging of a 'table-top' simulation of how to combat the emergence of a new coronavirus in China, two months before a new coronavirus was reported to have emerged in China.

It's not our purpose here to establish why all these things happened. But in view of the fact that they did all happen, it's certainly important to make them a matter of record— even though these events have been almost entirely ignored by major news media outlets. None of this means that there was a conspiracy to push a pandemic response which impoverished hundreds of millions of people while the world's richest people made trillions of dollars—though this immense increase in inequality also happened. It does, however, in our view, mean that it is perfectly reasonable to ask searching and critical questions of the 'single scientific narrative' which emerged, and to examine whether non-scientific motivations connected to profit and the human will to power may have had a part to play in what happened. In fact, it's our view that when this history is taken into account, alongside the devastating social, economic, and political effects which we'll consider shortly, it's impossible to consider any aspect of the pandemic response of lockdowns and vaccine mandates as progressive. Such an analysis can also have important implications when it comes to trying to regulate in the future those medical and economic frameworks which may have produced these outcomes.

At all events, many of these frameworks came together for what we (at least) hope was one final time during the emergence of the Omicron variant at the end of 2021. Readers may recall that Omicron was initially identified in South Africa, and that news of the new variant began to spread quickly. This led to another round of measures which were hitherto unprecedented in Western democracies: in the UK there was a push to vaccinate the entire population over the age of eighteen by the end of December with a booster dose, which was said to provide strong protection against the new variant. This assertion was made even though no clinical trials had been undertaken to verify if it was true, and the vaccines themselves had not been updated to target Omicron—unlike the process with seasonal flu vaccines.[1] In fact, subsequent Freedom of Information requests showed that heavy pressure had been put on the FDA's Office for Vaccines Research and Review to approve the boosters without clinical trials—from both the pharmaceutical companies and within government itself.[2]

Modellers in the UK predicted that there could be 2 million daily cases by the end of December,[3] though in reality the peak came at around 160,000 in early January 2022.[4] By 18 December, Professor Neil Ferguson was warning that there could be 4,000–5,000 deaths per day in the UK because of Omicron.[5] Eventually, the peak day for Omicron deaths was 17 January 2022, when 276 people died instead of 5,000.[6] The alarmist predictions were used to call for further restrictions and a Christmas 'circuit-breaker' lockdown.[7] However, when the government did not move to enforce additional restrictions, the surge never came and the Omicron peak declined. The rationale for all of these measures (whether for Omicron or earlier in the pandemic) began to seem thinner than ever.

Many of the features of the previous two years were concentrated in the Omicron hysteria. Modellers over-predicted doomsday scenarios, the most extreme prediction was picked up by sections of the media to push for restrictions, and all sides then claimed that the actual outcome was entirely consistent with their predicted range. In the meantime these predictions were also used to push mass vaccination with the booster, even for people aged under forty or fifty, who were at very low risk from Covid, and even when no clinical trials had been undertaken to investigate whether the original vaccine was effective against Omicron. All this took resources away from other aspects of the medical infrastructure so that emergency care facilities were understaffed. At the same time, the entire Omicron narrative was mired in the cognitive dissonance which had been such a key feature of the entire pandemic, and which we come back to in more detail in Chapter 9: if the vaccines were as effective as claimed, why would 4,000–5,000 people be likely to die daily from the new variant?

There were, moreover, aspects of the 'single scientific narrative' and its manipulated construction which are important to identify. In February 2022, the South African doctor who first reported the variant, Dr Angelique Coetzee, protested that she had been 'pressured' by Western governments to describe the variant as more serious than it really was, and told not to call it 'mild'.[8] Meanwhile, when UK health officials were asked about initial data from South Africa suggesting that Omicron was indeed mild, they responded that the demographic was younger and so outcomes might be different[9]—a statement that flew in the face of the narrative of the previous two years, according to which all were at equal risk from the virus, and the different population pyramids of Africa had no bearing on how many people on the continent ought to be vaccinated.

As 2022 proceeded, more statements began to appear relating to the vaccination programme that flatly contradicted everything that had been said previously by public health officials. In July, Deborah Birx—who was busy promoting her book on the pandemic—went on record as saying that 'I knew these vaccines were not going to protect against infection', something that would have come as a surprise to anyone listening to the public announcements of senior officials in 2021.[10] And the following month, in August 2022, the CDC epidemiologist Greta Massetti announced that 'both prior infection and vaccination confer some protection against severe illness. And so it really makes the most sense to not differentiate with our guidance or our recommendations based on vaccination status at this time.'[11] The cognitive dissonance of stating one thing and then flatly contradicting it a few months later was part of the global assault on mental health and truth whose consequences we will consider in the second part of this book.

Meanwhile, with the arrival of Omicron we also started hearing about more and more people, adults as well as children, who were experiencing long-term consequences persisting or appearing after having had Covid—a condition that has been termed 'long Covid'. Though there is no agreement on how to define and diagnose long Covid, the World Health Organization describes it as a

> [c]ondition [that] occurs in individuals with a history of probable or confirmed SARS-CoV-2 infection, usually 3 months from the onset, with symptoms that last for at least 2 months and cannot be explained by an alternative diagnosis. Common symptoms include, but are not limited to, fatigue, shortness of breath, and cognitive dysfunction, and generally have an impact on everyday functioning.[12]

It's unclear just how many people are affected by long Covid. Some studies have suggested that it occurs in as many as 30 per cent of people infected with the virus.[13] But a November 2021 study of about 4.5 million people treated at US Department of Veterans Affairs hospitals suggests that the number is 7 per cent overall and even lower than that for those who were not hospitalised.[14] That said, we know people close to us who are suffering from long Covid, so we can testify to the fact that it's a serious issue—one that deserves to be studied much more closely than has been the case until now, as sufferers of long Covid have been demanding for some time.[15]

However, we also can't help but feel that, as so often during the pandemic, the very real suffering of people has been instrumentalised once again for political reasons—in this case to retain Covid restrictions and/or cajole people into getting vaccinated (and vaccinating their children), including in the face of Omicron's milder symptoms, by suggesting that Covid can cause very serious long-term consequences even in those who develop very mild symptoms or none at all, which happens to be the overwhelming majority of people. We find this problematic for several reasons.

For starters, as we show in the next chapter, there simply is no evidence that lockdowns and other restrictions had any enduring influence on the spread of Covid-19 or therefore on the likely prevalence of post-viral Covid conditions; moreover, a huge May 2022 study of more than 13 million people published in *Nature Medicine*[16] found that 'long Covid risk falls only slightly after vaccination'.[17] Therefore, the evidence would not appear to significantly strengthen the case for vaccinating people who are at very little risk from developing mild or no symptoms from Covid in the first place, especially children and young people.

More generally, we simply don't know enough about long Covid to base any public health response around it. Indeed, we know very little about the nature of the condition, or its mechanism. One of the most in-depth studies yet, published in May 2022 in the *Annals of Internal Medicine*, which compared 189 patients diagnosed with Covid-19 to 120 similar patients who did not get sick, was unable to find any biological explanation for long Covid symptoms.[18] 'We were not able to find evidence of the virus persisting or hiding out in the body. We also did not find evidence that the immune system was overactive or malfunctioning in a way that would produce injury to major organs in the body', Dr Michael Sneller, the infectious disease specialist who led the study, told NPR.[19] The researchers, however, stressed that their findings don't mean that patients' problems are psychological. 'I clearly don't want to send the message that this is all not real. And in people's heads. And just go home and stop worrying about it. That's not the message', Sneller said. On the contrary, the researchers noted that their study called for stepping and speeding up research into long Covid in order to gain a better understanding of it—just as sufferers of long Covid have been demanding.

The *Annals of Internal Medicine* study does, however, suggest that long Covid might be a much more complex phenomenon than we imagine, with different and at times age-related symptomatic expression. This becomes rather apparent when we look at long Covid in children. Among scientists, the existence of long Covid in children and adolescents has been the subject of much debate, mainly due to the difficulty in ascertaining whether the most common symptoms usually associated with long Covid in children—sadness, tension, anger, depression, anxiety, fatigue, sleep disorders, and so on—are due to Covid itself or to other (co-)factors. As one of the earliest cohort studies on long Covid, published in August 2021, concluded:

> [I]t is possible the symptoms associated with Long Covid are in fact a mixture of factors relating to the pandemic and lockdown as a whole rather than the viral infection itself. For example, factors such as social isolation, anxiety, depression or educational concerns may be the root cause of these symptoms in children and young people both with and without SARS-CoV-2 infection. The effects on the developing brain and behaviour of adolescents could be far reaching.[20]

Another study was conducted by the Italian Society of Pediatrics (SIP) on the initiative of the Pediatric Infectious Diseases Technical Committee and the Italian Society of Infantile Respiratory Diseases (SIMRI), in collaboration with other Italian paediatric societies, in order to establish the 'Italian intersociety consensus on management of long Covid in children'. The results were published in March 2022 in the *Italian Journal of Pediatrics*, and largely concurred with the previous study.[21] The researchers' conclusions are worth quoting at length:

> Although a strict distinction between physical and mental health symptoms is debatable as mental stress can be associated with physical symptoms and long-term physical symptoms can cause mental health disorders, these findings indicate that, with time, physical symptoms due to SARS-CoV-2, even if persisting after 4 weeks from infection, tend to regress spontaneously or under treatment in a few months, whereas mental problems can persist for a longer time. Several factors indicate that mental health problems depend on the stress conditions children underwent during the pandemic. The association between infectious epidemics and the development of mental health problems in children does not surprise. Several studies carried out during previous severe epidemics, mainly the Ebola epidemic during which several children were orphaned, have shown that, together with medical problems, children could have severe psychological repercussions, with the development of frustration, worry or sadness, and feeling of being alone and being excluded by family or community. In the Covid-19 pandemic, the impact on the mental health of children and adolescents was also greater. To the problems strictly related to the infection, such as fear of contraction of the disease and to be hospitalized, and the grief for the loss of close relatives or friends, a major role in the development of mental disturbances has been played by the measures put in place worldwide by health authorities to

reduce viral circulation and contain the number of Covid-19 cases. General lockdown was decided and maintained for a long time with very strong restrictions. This modified children's lifestyle due to school closure, absence of outdoor activities, physical distancing, quarantine, isolation. Mental health of children has been severely compromised on account of increased anxiety, changes in their diets, school dynamics and education, fear of not knowing how to deal with emerging problems. Development of mental health disfunctions during Covid-19 was found more common in older children and adolescents, in females and in those with previously diagnosed psychological problems. This is quite in agreement with what has been reported for pediatric long Covid, further suggesting that most of the clinical manifestations characterizing long Covid depend on the pandemic and not directly on the infection.

However, a more recent study conducted in Denmark and published in *The Lancet Child & Adolescent Health*, which compared 11,000 children younger than fourteen years who had tested positive for Covid-19 with 33,000 children who had no history of Covid-19, reached a different conclusion.[22] It found that the children and adolescents who presented with SARS-CoV-2 infection were at higher risk of subsequent long dyspnea, anosmia/ageusia, or fever, compared with control persons. In total, in the studies that were included, more than forty long-term clinical manifestations associated with Covid-19 in the pediatric population were identified.

Maren J. Heilskov Rytter, PhD, Associate Professor of Clinical Medicine at the University of Copenhagen, Denmark, wrote an editorial about the Danish study.[23] Until it is clarified whether SARS-CoV-2 does indeed cause persistent symptoms, she wrote, 'it seems excessive and premature to establish specific multidisciplinary clinics for children with long Covid-19'. Rytter highlighted the difficulty of interpreting the study's data, owing to recall bias, the failure to exclude other causes of symptoms in the cases analysed, and the number of symptoms in the control persons. In addition, the data analysed in Denmark are of limited clinical relevance, she said, given a greater presence of mild symptoms and, paradoxically, a higher quality of life. She concluded: 'In the majority of children with nonspecific symptoms after Covid-19, the symptoms presented are more likely to have been caused by something other than Covid-19, and if they are related to Covid-19, they are likely to go away over time.'

In sum, the debate about long Covid, at the time of writing, is far from resolved—and points to the need for more research. Based on what we do know, three conclusions seem reasonable to us: first, that everyone who develops symptomatic Covid should be given access to the best possible early treatments in order to minimise the risk of developing severe illness—something that, as we saw in Chapter 3, many people were denied throughout most of the pandemic, and are still being denied at the time of writing; second, that all future public health interventions should pay a great deal of attention to their potential psychological and mental health impact on young people in particular, which risks causing even greater long-term damage than the virus itself (as we discuss in Chapter 8); and third, that since lockdowns had little impact in halting the spread of the virus (as we will see in Chapter 6), non-pharmaceutical interventions were not a suitable measure to try to prevent long Covid.

**

Omicron was the full stop—or at least a semicolon—to a cycle which had been spinning for two years. If there is a thread which links many of these repeated waves of alarmist modelling, lockdowns, and boosters, it is probably this question of a 'single scientific narrative'. As we've seen, this was a framework which emerged quickly with the virus origins, then with lockdowns, and then with universal vaccinations. In all cases, political and media outlets quickly rushed to say that 'The Science' showed there was only one way of proceeding, in contravention of established methods of scientific procedure which have traditionally recognised the existence of competing hypotheses. Indeed, as we've seen in this first part of the book, many peer-reviewed scientific publications were produced between 2020 and 2022 which contradicted the manufactured consensus, demonstrating the divergence of scientific views on how best to tackle the pandemic—and yet this research was flatly ignored by governments and major media outlets.

Moreover, this mainstream narrative was often created by drawing on scientific experts who strayed very far from their established fields of expertise: Devi Sridhar wrote over forty op-eds for the *Guardian* in two years, having no expertise in immunology, vaccines, or infectious diseases, but rather having trained in medical anthropology, with an MPhil which focused on malnutrition in Tamil Nadu;[24] Stephen Reicher and Susan Michie were other regular contributors to the *Guardian* on the necessity of questions such as masking and lockdown, when both of them worked in experimental psychology;[25] and yet on the other hand, figures like Martin Kulldorff—who had played a significant role in developing the vaccine safety monitoring infrastructure used by the FDA in the US, and is a member of their Drug Safety and Risk Management Advisory Committee[26]—and Sunetra Gupta, who had spent all her career working in vaccines and helped to develop a universal flu vaccine,[27] were repeatedly trolled for diverging from the mainstream view. As John Ioannidis wrote, the 'we are at war' narrative led to 'a dirty war, one without dignity'—and one often directed at scientists themselves:

Consultants who made millions of dollars from corporate and government consultation were given prestigious positions, power, and public praise, while unconflicted scientists who worked pro bono but dared to question dominant narratives were smeared as being conflicted. [...] [They] were threatened, abused, and bullied by cancel culture campaigns in social media, hit stories in mainstream media, and bestsellers written by zealots. Statements were distorted, turned into straw men, and ridiculed. Wikipedia pages were vandalized. Reputations were systematically devastated and destroyed. Many brilliant scientists were abused and received threats during the pandemic, intended to make them and their families miserable. [...] Organized skepticism was seen as a threat to public health. There was a clash between two schools of thought, authoritarian public health versus science—and science lost.[28]

Why, then, did the scientific establishment respond to the crisis in this way, cohering around the opinions of scientists who often were not relevant experts, and dismissing those who often were? There are a number of potential answers, which we've outlined here, without coming down heavily one way or the other. These answers would include initial panic on the question of the virus's origins, economic profit, and the revolving door between government and industry which had been produced by several decades of neoliberal politics. To these we could add the influence of peer pressure, and the natural human desire of people not to be ostracised from their in-groups—in effect, the urge to find moral frameworks which justify the collective group response that might have been shaped by some of these aspects. As the American writer William Vollmann puts it, 'ethics is the evaluation of justifications'.[29]

It's important to recognise that all of this was seen as unprecedented. Figures on the political right wrote about the assault on bodily autonomy as a key aspect of the 'new normal'.

CONCLUSION

And yet, the assault on bodily autonomy in Western history was not as new as was assumed: it has been a key element of Western political and medical frameworks both in colonial and in more recent neocolonial history—even if this 'shadow side' of Western political and medical history is very rarely discussed. Early in the pandemic, the historian of African medicine Florence Bernault wrote a searing essay in which she noted how intertwined the histories of colonial and medical power were in the twentieth century:[30] this history includes the creation of *cordons sanitaires* in Uganda by the British to protect people from trypanosomiasis (sleeping sickness), which led to the unintended deaths of approximately 250,000 people in the Great Lakes region between 1900 and 1908, and the forced injection of a dangerous molecule, lomidine, into thousands of Cameroonian subjects in the 1950s in an ineffective campaign against trypanosomiasis.

This colonial history of medical control over the bodies of African subjects has also shaped more recent patterns of medical experimentation and control. Clinical trials of experimental drugs are often rolled out in Africa, funded by major institutions such as NIAID and the Gates Foundation. For example, in the early 2000s when NIAID was seeking clinical trial data for the experimental HIV drug nevirapine, auditors found that the NIAID researchers had lost critical records, including the logbook which monitored adverse events, that more lenient standards were applied to black Ugandan subjects than the FDA required for American subjects, and that the leader of the study had avoided reporting thousands of adverse and serious adverse events.[31] As we've seen, too, drug companies such as Pfizer have often had to pay out serious damages for experimental trials on African subjects.

In many ways, therefore, the Covid vaccination programme and coercive controls emerged from a shadow side of Western political and medical history—the ways in which this history grew out of often dangerous experiments conducted in Africa, in which colonial control over the bodies of African subjects was a key element of the political control which was exercised. In that sense, biomedical control was not an unprecedented aspect of Western history at all.

All this provides important context for the events of 2020, 2021, and the first half of 2022. Far from defending science, what we have called the Covid consensus took a sledgehammer to it—marginalising expert voices and demonising anyone who diverged from the single narrative. And yet instead of recognising and analysing the nexus of interests at play; the framework of colonial power over the bodies of others which formed historical precedents for this expansion of medical control; or the devastating impacts of many of these policies on poor people and on hard-won democratic rights, the liberal and radical left were the single narrative's most ardent champions. Rather than recognising the inherently ethnocentric assumption that what was a problem for Western nations was equally serious elsewhere, when left voices did turn to international concerns they voiced concerns about 'vaccine apartheid', and repeated the mantra that 'no one is safe until we're all safe'.

In fact, as we'll see in more detail in the next part of this book, for all the speculation that 'vaccine hoarding' by rich countries would lead to massive Covid deaths in low-income countries,[32] particularly in Africa, the reality is that African countries, despite a very low vaccine uptake[33]—and in spite of pressure from multinational donors for African countries to reach a 60 per cent vaccination target—have reported very low Covid mortality rates.[34] Indeed, the evidence all points to the fact that, in Africa, lockdowns have been far deadlier than Covid, as discussed in Chapter 7. This may explain why many critics on the continent were highly sceptical when mRNA vaccine production hubs were announced for Africa early in 2022. The

CONCLUSION

Nigerian journalist Tope Fasua, writing in *The Cable*, is worth quoting at length:

> We even heard that Nigeria has now been designated for vaccine manufacturing and a few people hailed this as an achievement. It is certainly no achievement. We can see that the whole world is moving on from the pandemic. We cannot be left holding the short end of the stick, with billions of taxpayers' monies poured into a vaccine factory to produce what no one will readily accept. Nigerians who want vaccines have taken them. [...] We did say then when this problem was at its peak, that African nations be allowed to have a say, and that we may have some antidotes that are not available in the west. The way we were shut down spoke to open racism and a desire by a few to profiteer from other people's misfortunes as they positioned to sell vaccines to the world.[35]

From this perspective, the neo-colonialism at play in the Covid pandemic did not lie in vaccine apartheid: it lay in assuming that a problem in the West would be the same problem everywhere else, and that only a Western technology could provide the solution. Indeed, for all the press given to the COVAX scheme to distribute vaccines in poor countries, and the 'donations' required to do this, an Oxfam study found that the COVAX vaccines still cost low-income countries five times more than the production cost.[36] These vaccines were not somehow 'given' to Africa, but were usually financed through World Bank loans,[37] when many Africans felt that this financing would be better directed at other healthcare priorities. The manner in which the Covid vaccination programme reproduced these age-old dynamics was described in illuminating detail by the Ghanaian medical historian Samuel Adu-Gyamfi, who recounted the way in which Ghanaians danced and performed for the plane which brought the first load of (Western) Covid vaccines.[38]

The way in which these approaches rode roughshod over African beliefs, practices, and medical ideas, constituting a form of medical colonialism, was exemplified in the analysis of rural South Africa by Leslie Bank and Nelly Sharpley, who noted how the South African state 'assumed that certain forms of social and cultural practices in these areas, based on the African philosophy of *ubuntu* ("I am because you are"), offered a special threat to containment'.[39]

As with the question of political impacts, socio-economic impacts, and the economic interests driving many aspects of policy, once again the liberal and radical left was shooting Covid blanks. This has been a subtext of this first part of the book, and as writers who have always positioned ourselves on the left it is one of our biggest concerns. In order to arrive at a sense of the enormity of these contradictions, and their devastating effects, we have to look in more detail at how these effects played out all over the world—and that's what we'll now turn to.

PART 2

THE SOCIAL, ECONOMIC, AND POLITICAL EFFECTS OF THE PANDEMIC MANAGEMENT

On 24 February 2020 the World Health Organization published its report on its fact-finding mission to Wuhan, China, to investigate the Covid-19 outbreak. In an abrupt break with previous policies, the WHO recommended countries should follow the Chinese model of lockdowns, contact tracing, and isolation which everyone agreed was unprecedented. This was advised in all circumstances, whatever the economic and political structure of a country, and without any control with which to balance and assess the experiment that had taken place in China. Less than two months later, half of the world was living in lockdown.

After two and a half years, the results of this massive scientific experiment with human societies are now in, and it's these that we turn to in the second half of this book. While in Part 1 we focused on the scientific framework that led to unprecedented policy choices—and the economic relationships in which this scientific framework was embedded—in Part 2 we examine the devastating consequences of these choices. The impacts of the suppression measures were likened in many parts of the world to a wartime situation. Political leaders sought to profit, and—as we'll now see—whether in Britain, Spain, and the United States or Peru, Mozambique, and India, this was above all a war on the poor (Chapter 7). Meanwhile, civil and political rights were torn up (Chapter 9), scientific and medical norms traduced to no discernible benefit (Chapter 6), and democracy left in tatters (Chapter 9). These cataclysmic consequences were clearly produced by the pandemic response; however, as we'll also see, they grew out of features in world societies that had been building for several decades alongside the rise of computer technologies and neoliberal political structures.

At the same time, it's also important to look here at the impact of everything that has happened on public health. Did the lockdowns save millions of lives, as was promised? What were their impacts on other medical conditions? In this part of the book, we do our best to take an overview of the full range of societal and political effects. We focus, as in Part 1, on what happened, because that is again more than enough. By the last page, many (if not all) readers may feel angry about all of this. We've written (and in one of our cases rewritten) this book so fast, and so relentlessly, because we're angry too. We've also done so because we feel that it's crucial to document as much of this as possible before it becomes an ever-harder task to accomplish. This means that this part of the book has a lot of detail. Some readers may feel this is too much, but we both felt it was vital in order to record the full enormity of what has happened.

It's hard to look at all of this without drawing the conclusion that public life in much of the world has been transformed into a nightmare (or, some would say, a steaming pile of horseshit). And yet at the same time, the fact that so many people from

PART 2

different walks of life, and from across the world, have sought to try to document at least some of what has happened, and to challenge it, is some sort of olive branch of peace and hope to take into the future. It's this which has inspired and enabled us to try to speak the truth to power that is required to ensure that nothing like this can ever happen again.

6

DID LOCKDOWNS SAVE LIVES?

The first few months of analysis and diagnosis of a new respiratory virus always throw up a raft of difficulties. As we saw in Chapter 2, recent history shows that this has tended to lead to the overestimation of the CFR of a new virus. Yet policymakers chose not to look at recent history. There were many complex issues at play. Those in Western societies with elderly populations were very concerned for their older relatives and wanted to protect them; the political and media discourse that was pushed very hard, as we have seen, was that the best way to do this was to deprive older relations of all physical contact with their loved ones.

In the health sector, of course, workers were understandably worried by the figures. They had a clear right to be protected from the additional risks under which they were put in treating the new virus. In the United Kingdom there were many heartrending stories of some of them, often from minority communities, who died prematurely (sometimes in their twenties and thirties). The extent of exposure to the virus was a high risk factor ('viral load'), and the disproportionate number of members of minority communities working in public-facing roles in healthcare and public transport clearly contributed to the higher death rate among them.

There may also have been a natural desire in human societies to come together after a period of conflict. The previous decade had been characterised by fractious divisions, and here was a crisis that could, it appeared, unite countries to defeat the new threat. This—combined with the frantic lobbying of interest groups and scaremongering by the political and media establishment—may also account for the initial consensus around the lockdowns, in the face of the alarming data that had emerged on the new respiratory virus.

In this chapter, we look at the medical impacts of these lockdowns. Did they have the beneficial effects that their advocates promised, and—if so—could these effects make the enormity of the harms that they caused a price worth paying? Did countries and states that followed the lockdown policy have materially better outcomes in questions of medical treatment, the economy, and mental health? And what were the broader impacts of the lockdown model on the treatment of other medical conditions? For, in all the frenzy of 2020–21, it often appeared to be forgotten that Covid-19 was only one element of public health: its treatment and alleviation were certainly important, but they were part of a much bigger picture. If in treating Covid-19 through severe societal control other serious medical conditions were allowed to deteriorate, the cure would turn out to have been worse than the disease.

It's important to recall what we saw in Chapter 2: that the approach that was favoured—open-ended nation-wide lockdowns—was an utterly unprecedented move in history. Not only had it never been attempted—it had never even been conceived of. And it was only possible because of the growing power of technology. People were told to stay at home and work and study remotely. Dining out would be replaced by food delivery apps. Entertainment would be provided by streaming platforms such as Netflix. In sum, the internet would be able to satisfy virtually all of people's needs—shopping, dining, working, schooling, entertainment, socialising, even sex. This clearly wouldn't have been possible just a few years earlier.

Some people fanned hope in the early months of the crisis that there might be a vaccine in the autumn, and that this would mean the end of lockdown[1]—wishful thinking on both counts. The belief that things would move quicker was built on over-promising from the pharmaceutical industry, a tendency to trust in this from high echelons of governments who had connections to this sector, and an inability to confront a situation in which any vaccine was liable to take longer to develop and offered no promise of eradicating the virus.

In this chapter, we look at the medical effects of lockdowns, and at whether they were the magic bullet that their proponents claimed. It's important to bear in mind that the evidence threshold for lockdown advocates is high here: given the enormity of the collateral effects that we will come to in the next chapter, the beneficial impacts of lockdowns in restraining virus spread would have to be comparably enormous to make them worth imposing.

As we'll see in this chapter, on no possible reading of the evidence can that be said to be the case. As we lay out in the pages that follow, it's our view that lockdowns had no measurable impact on virus spread when considered in the round, and certainly nothing like the kind of benefit that would have made them worth considering; at the same time, they had a devastating impact on the treatment of a whole range of other medical conditions around the world.

***

When talking of lockdown, it's almost common wisdom—even among lockdown critics, that is, people who recognise that lockdowns have entailed a host of negative social, economic, and psychological effects—to assume that lockdowns, at the very least, helped save lives and reduce Covid mortality. But is that really the case? As the *Guardian* reported after the lockdown had been imposed on Wuhan—and prior to its later pro-lockdown position—'large-scale quarantines are rare around the world, even in deadly epidemics, because of concerns about infringing on people's liberties, and the effectiveness of such measures is unclear'.[2] As mentioned in Chapter 2, the scientists in Neil Ferguson's Imperial College team themselves suggested in late March 2020 that they would consider the lockdown policy a success if the number of deaths in the UK remained below 20,000—far below the eventual Covid-19 death toll—and at one point predicted total deaths of 5,700 in the UK following the suppression strategy.[3]

Even though Professor Ferguson subsequently claimed that 25,000 deaths had been caused through the failure to lock down 1 week earlier in March 2020,[4] it is clear that these initial predictions of the medical benefits of the lockdown model turned out to be false; moreover, as UK excess deaths were, after two years, below the European average, it is unclear that this claim regarding the numbers of additional deaths caused by the failure to lock down early enough is entirely accurate. In any case, by mid-May 2022, over 177,000 people had died of Covid-19 in the UK according to official figures—somewhat more than the 5,700 initially predicted.[5] Lockdowns simply were not the public health miracle that had been predicted by their advocates.

However, by that point Ferguson, never one to be outdone by reality, was already trying to establish a new narrative, which we would often hear in the following months. In a remarkable study published in *Nature*, co-authored with several colleagues, he once again used his computer models to show that the global lockdown had saved many millions of lives.[6] This time, however, a string of protests by scientists of international standing rained into *Nature*'s office. They all pointed to the fundamental flaws in the analysis that had caused false conclusions to be drawn. Analysed according to a different scientific methodology to that of Ferguson, the data actually showed the opposite: the lockdown had had no discernible effect on the course of the pandemic.[7]

That said, the impacts of lockdowns remain disputed, and probably will continue to be so. There have been a vast number of scientific studies undertaken as to the efficacy (or lack thereof) of lockdowns in restraining the spread of the Covid-19 virus. On the one hand, there are a number of peer-reviewed studies which focus on the medical impacts of lockdowns in Europe and the United States on Covid-19 mortality. In early 2021, a team of Stanford University academics and research data scientists, including John Ioannidis and Jay Bhattacharya, published a paper claiming that there was no practical difference in epidemiological terms between countries that had locked down and those that hadn't.[8] '[T]here is no evidence that more restrictive nonpharmaceutical interventions ("lockdowns") contributed substantially to bending the curve of new cases in England, France, Germany, Iran, Italy, the Netherlands, Spain, or the United States in early 2020', the authors concluded. Several studies have appeared since then that confirm those initial findings. One of these—a massive meta-analysis of more than twenty other studies, published by Johns Hopkins University and authored by scholars from Denmark, Sweden, and the US—found that lockdowns had a 0.2 per cent impact on Covid mortality rates in Europe and the United States.[9]

A significant amount of research from around the world has supported these studies. One, this time by the economist Christian Bjørnskov, concluded that 'comparing weekly mortality rates from 24 European countries in the first halves of

2017–2020, and addressing policy endogeneity in two different ways, I find no clear association between lockdown policies and mortality development'.[10] A different study, authored by a team of US scientists, also came to the same conclusion: 'government actions such as border closures, full lockdowns, and a high rate of Covid-19 testing were not associated with statistically significant reductions in the number of critical cases or overall mortality'.[11] In 'Covid-19 Mortality: A Matter of Vulnerability Among Nations Facing Limited Margins of Adaptation', a team of French medical researchers concluded that the '[s]tringency of the measures settled to fight pandemia, including lockdown, did not appear to be linked with death rate'.[12] Instead, they concluded that nations with stagnating life expectancies and high rates of income and non-communicable disease—in other words, existing characteristics of a nation's demographics—faced higher mortality rates regardless of government interventions. Meanwhile, scientists at the University of Munich also found no correlation between the imposing of lockdowns and the spread of Covid-19.[13]

By the middle of 2022, the writing was on the wall when it came to the question of lockdown efficacy. Some of the countries that locked down the hardest are also those with the highest mortality figures and excess death rate. Peru is an obvious example, while Sweden's excess mortality was well below the European average for 2020,[14] as discussed in greater detail below. Of course, there remained a high degree of furious debate around many of these questions. Naturally, studies that were critical of lockdowns were dismissed as ill-founded by lockdown supporters, despite being consistent with pre-Covid pandemic literature emphasising the ineffectiveness of many now-standard non-pharmaceutical interventions, as noted in Chapter 2. At the same time, we freely admit, we might be inclined to dismiss studies that showed the beneficial impacts of lockdown measures.

Interestingly, however, moving beyond broad national comparisons, even if we look at the epidemiological trends of individual US states, we come across similar results. Already in September 2020 critics were branding lockdown a failure,[15] and yet—at the height of an election year politicised like no other—the policy continued. In the summer of 2021, a study of four US states—California, Florida, Minnesota, and Wisconsin—through the first year of the pandemic found no observable correlation between severity of restrictions and school closures and spread of the virus.[16] States which had stricter measures (California and Minnesota) did not have markedly better outcomes than those which did not (Florida and Wisconsin). Meanwhile, on the second anniversary of the declaration of the Covid pandemic by the WHO on 11 March 2020 it was instructive to compare North and South Dakota, which had followed very different pandemic paths, with North Dakota implementing serious restrictions while South Dakota did not: South Dakota's death rate of 3,219 per million was not notably higher than North Dakota's of 2,917.[17] While lockdown advocates pointed to Florida's sharp spike in Covid fatalities during the Delta wave, and the state governor Ron DeSantis was dubbed the 'angel of death' in a September 2021 *Vanity Fair* article,[18] few noted that by November the state had the lowest case rates in the United States—or that the state with by then the highest number of cases, Michigan, had had very severe restrictions.[19] Even accounting for questionable data-gathering methods, the numbers are striking.

Italy is another interesting case. Throughout the pandemic, Italy implemented some of the strictest and longest lockdowns in the world (indeed, it is the country that 'invented' the concept of national lockdown, as we saw in Chapter 2), topping every other Western country in terms of average stringency of anti-Covid measures.[20] Yet Italy is also one of the Western countries that recorded the highest Covid mortality rate per capita—well above the United Kingdom, Spain, France, Germany, Sweden, and several other countries that adopted much less restrictive measures—as well as the highest number of excess deaths after the United States.[21]

That said, we recognise that death rates are likely to be influenced by a myriad of factors—including the statistical and medical protocols adopted by individual states or countries, as we have seen—and that simply looking at the stringency of the measures adopted could lead to spurious conclusions. However, that is of course something that cuts both ways, and also makes it difficult for lockdown advocates to find conclusive data in support of their preferred non-pharmaceutical intervention.

Advocates of lockdowns point to the claimed success of China in shutting down their country, closing borders, and achieving 'Zero Covid'. And yet this success may not be all that it appears. As we saw in Chapter 1, there are a number of reasons to doubt the official timeline of the emergence of Covid-19. Peer-reviewed articles suggest that excess deaths began to surge in Wuhan in at least September 2019, and that the mortality figures indicate the true infectivity rate was six times that reported by the Chinese government;[22] *The Economist* meanwhile reported in May 2021 that initial mortality in Wuhan may have been two or three times that reported.[23] Whether or not that is true, as time has passed, many commentators have become highly suspicious of the official China death toll from Covid-19. While by mid-May 2022 it stood at 4,638 deaths, some researchers estimated that it was actually a minimum of 33,000.[24]

What was universally agreed upon by commentators was that China's refusal to release data, and the suspiciously low death count, made the real impact of the lockdown model hard to gauge. Meanwhile, the enormous human cruelty and societal control which followed a 'real lockdown' became apparent during the radical intensification of China's Zero Covid policy, commencing with the Shanghai Omicron lockdown which began in March 2022. Enormously disturbing footage of starving people begging for food and wheelchair-bound adolescents flailing hopelessly to escape their padlocked compounds, and tales of deaths from the refusal of treatment for asthma and cancer sufferers, circulated widely.[25] This followed the building of an entire bureaucracy dedicated to stamping out Covid cases, a project which soon became synonymous with the power and authority of President Xi Jinping. These developments made it all the more surprising when, on 11 May 2022, Anthony Fauci protested in a House of Representatives hearing: 'I'm not sure why you're asking me about lockdowns, because there were not complete lockdowns in this country. China is now going into a real lockdown.'[26] Moreover, the following months made the true implications of such a policy even starker: later in the year videos emerged of shoppers in a Shanghai Ikea stampeding for the exit of a supermarket after authorities sought to seal off the store and send everyone in it to quarantine following the discovery of one shopper who had been exposed to an asymptomatic 6-year-old child.[27]

In sum, what we can state relatively uncontroversially is that the benefits of the lockdown model in Western countries were not as strong as their advocates suggested. Meanwhile, the Chinese model came to seem ever less reliable as the pandemic proceeded. More generally, the Chinese case simply confirms what we have already touched upon on several occasions throughout the book: that official Covid statistics are a poor benchmark for establishing the impact of these measures, due to their questionable statistical basis. Ultimately, and as many commentators came to accept in 2022, the only scientifically meaningful metric is that of all-cause mortality—simply put, how many people died during the pandemic compared to that country's pre-pandemic average?

So were the impacts in countries which did not follow a lockdown model as bad as predicted at the outset? The most famous case was Sweden, which as we have seen refused to impose lockdown measures in March 2020. Certainly, initial predictions from lockdown media and scientists were bleak. Drawing on assumptions from the Imperial College models, scientists at Sweden's Uppsala University predicted 85,000 Covid-19 deaths in Sweden.[28] Writing in the *Observer*, meanwhile, the journalist Nick Cohen described Sweden as a 'libertarian Covid fantasy land'[29] and having followed a policy of 'deadly folly' which was a 'model for the right'[30]—somewhat ironic, as Sweden's government was in 2020 run by a coalition of Social Democrats and Greens.

What was the basis of Cohen's judgements? In the week prior to one of the articles, Sweden had the highest death rate in Europe from Covid-19. After two years, however, Sweden's total of 18,800 Covid-19 deaths in mid-May 2022 suggested that the prediction of 85,000 deaths based on the Imperial College team's projections was severely flawed—as was Cohen's short-termist and ultimately Pyrrhic triumphalism.[31] As the WHO noted, by May 2022 Sweden had one of the lowest Covid death rates in Europe, and also—more relevantly—one of the lowest excess death rates.[32] Lockdown advocates insisted that these rates were still higher than those of their Scandinavian neighbours[33]—overriding the perspectives even of epidemiologists in neighbouring Denmark, who had suggested already in September 2021 that they had things to learn from the Swedish approach.[34] Moreover, the idea that Sweden did worse than its neighbours in terms of excess deaths has been disputed by two Danish scientists: in an article published in the Danish newspaper *Berlingske Tidende* in July 2022, new data shows that excess mortality in 2020 and 2021 might be the same in both countries.[35] Finally, in November 2022 as this book went to press, one analysis suggested that over the period from March 2020 to June 2022, Sweden had had the lowest excess death rates in the entire OECD (Organisation for Economic cooperation and Development), a group of 31 of the world's most advanced economies.[36] Some of the data was of course open to dispute, but what was clear was that all the attempts to paint Sweden as a disaster in 2020 were shown up as the most extraordinarily shoddy and ill-conceived journalism and 'scientific analysis' possible.

On the other hand, no one could deny that the economic impact on the poorest sections of society has been far less severe in Sweden than in other parts of Europe. At the end of the first wave, in 2020, the IMF predicted that Sweden's economy would shrink by 7 per cent. Yet in the end, Sweden's economy shrank by just 2.8 per cent in 2020, 'significantly lower' than the EU average of 6 per cent and the UK's 9.8 per cent. Subsequently, it rebounded faster than any country in Europe, and by June 2021 it had overtaken where it was pre-pandemic.[37]

In sum, Sweden had not suffered anything like the fallout that had been predicted by lockdown advocates. At the same time, it had protected the mental and physical health of younger people by remaining open, and had safeguarded their economic futures as well (on this, see Chapter 8). This was certainly the view within the country, too, for when the Swedish Coronavirus Commission reported in late February 2022, they concluded that Sweden had fundamentally followed the right path.[38] The Swedish case suggested that lockdowns were not necessary to achieve decent public health outcomes even where there were large populations at risk—and also that a better balance could be achieved between treating new respiratory viruses and other questions of public health.

Of course, it is important not to compare dissimilar scenarios, and certainly it would be wrong to compare countries in Europe with those in the Global South. Nevertheless, the case of Sweden is supported by evidence from other countries where few restrictions were imposed. Belarus famously applied no restrictions at all. The WHO estimates for overall excess deaths in 2020 and 2021, published in May 2022, suggested that its figures, while worse than those for neighbouring countries, were not nearly as bad as lockdown advocates suggested they would be: at a mean excess death rate of 259, Belarus's rate was certainly comparable to neighbouring Ukraine (227) and Poland (209).[39]

Moving from the world's rich countries to poorer nations, the data is again clear that the lockdown model had little impact on Covid death rates.[40] In South America, advocates of lockdowns repeatedly excoriated Brazil's far-right President Jair Bolsonaro. As early as July 2020, Al Jazeera reported that Brazilian medical unions had called for the International Criminal Court to investigate whether Bolsonaro could be tried for crimes against humanity for his Covid response.[41] By October 2021, a congressional report found that Bolsonaro should be charged with crimes against humanity and jailed for his response to the Covid outbreak.[42] And yet, two years into the pandemic, Brazil's per capita Covid death rate—as far as these may be deemed reliable—of 3,041 deaths per million was not so much worse than Argentina's at 2,767 per million. It was much better than Peru's, which at 6,263 deaths per million was the worst Covid death rate in the world.[43] Excess deaths were also far worse in Peru (and also in Colombia and Ecuador, which had strong restrictions), as *The Economist*'s Covid excess deaths tracker shows, than they were in Brazil.[44] And yet Argentina and Peru had had some of the strictest lockdowns in the world. Peru's was one of the strictest during the initial 2020 breakouts,[45] while according to the researcher Maddalena Cevvese, 'Argentina not only imposed the highest number and the longest lockdowns across Latin America but its measures were among the strictest', with in total about 35 per cent of economic activity completely shut down.[46]

The important counter-example to all of this was offered by Nicaragua. Having been ruled by the leftist Sandinista government for over a decade, the country had invested heavily in healthcare prior to the pandemic, building 18 state-of-the-art hospitals and developing national healthcare brigades as part of a community-led healthcare programme. According to the journalist John Perry, in the first months of 2020 these brigades made 5 million home visits across the country—several per household, in a country with a total population of 6 million. Lockdowns were never implemented, because of the damage that this would have caused to people's livelihoods, and schools were not closed. This was in sharp contrast to neighbouring Honduras, run by a neoliberal regime, which imposed sharp lockdowns and shut schools for 2 years. At the end of that time, Nicaragua's numbers of excess deaths were among the lowest in Latin America according to the *Economist*'s excess deaths tracker, and Honduras's among the highest; moreover, Nicaragua's economy had grown by over 10% in 2021, so that Nicaraguans did not suffer the educational and socioeconomic collapse of neighbouring countries.[47]

In other words, there were alternatives to lockdowns in Latin America. But where lockdown policies were followed on the continent, the medical impacts of Covid-19 were disastrous across the board. On a continent where residential accommodation is often crowded, confining people indoors to halt the spread of a virus which spreads most virulently indoors was unlikely to yield great results. And high Covid mortality was always likely on a continent with what the United Nations described in 2019 as an 'explosive' rate of obesity[48]—so often a condition associated with poverty—when this is one of the major risk factors for Covid-19 fatalities.[49]

What did this mean in practice? One example was documented in September 2021:

A few months ago I spoke to the mother of an old friend of mine, who I have known for 30 years. I'll call her Sandra. Sandra lives in a lower-middle class district of the capital of Chile, Santiago. It's an area where people struggle to make ends meet, and there can be security problems at night. But it's also an area of very strong community spirit, and where everyone knows everyone. When lockdowns hit the world in March 2020, people in Chile scrambled to form communal kitchens or *ollas comunales*. Many people found their livelihoods suddenly destroyed, and there were more *ollas comunales* in some places than even at the height of the economic crisis of the Pinochet government in the 1980s. Sandra told me what happened to the community-spirited older man who established one in her *barrio*: as more people came to eat, he contracted Covid, it passed through his household, and three members of the family died.[50]

In other words, closing down people's avenues of work and forcing them to crowd together to access food was always likely to offer SARS-CoV-2 a breeding ground, with devastating impacts. This was also an important potential of the experience of lockdowns on the African continent, as the medical scholar Alhaji Njai argued in the *Sierra Leone Telegraph* in February 2021. In fact, as Njai argued, the lockdown measures were counterproductive in an environment like Freetown where people spend more time outdoors than indoors:

In Sierra Leone, based on observations in Freetown and other areas, people spend less time indoors even in their houses and more time outside. The 45 markets I have worked with for Freetown City Council look heavily crowded but in terms of Covid-19 transmission, the risk is far lower than if that same population was to be found indoors. This is likely so because the microdroplets that account for the lingering effects of Covid-19 infections are quickly dissipated in outdoor aerated conditions. Now, what curfews and lockdowns essentially do is to force us inside the house, which for many of us are tiny with not enough space for social distancing. The additional transportation rush to beat curfew, create crowded conditions in a more confined vehicle environment. The net effect of these actions is that you unintentionally drive the spread of the infections more than if people were allowed to stay outside more and the rush to take crowded vehicles from curfew is not there [*sic*].[51]

This points to the impossibility of neatly separating the medical and epidemiological dimension of lockdowns from the wider socio-economic dimension, which is discussed in the next chapter. This comparative data is also important because it shows that there simply is no cross-country comparative data which suggests that lockdowns had any enduring impact on the spread of the virus. As the pandemic wound on through its second year, long Covid was often invoked as a reason to retain strict Covid measures. And yet, regardless of one's opinion on the issue, there simply is no evidence that these restrictions have any enduring influence on the spread of Covid-19—in rich or in poor countries—or, therefore, on the likely prevalence of post-viral Covid conditions.

So why does the virus continue to spread in spite of the lockdowns? As the examples from Chile and Sierra Leone show, the one-size-fits-all model does not, in fact, fit all. And even in wealthier countries, where it might seem as though it should, there are other important factors. In the first place, those working in key jobs—supermarket workers, warehouse operatives, rubbish collectors, those in schools and healthcare institutions—continue to toil in challenging conditions which cannot fully safeguard their physical space; as one person put it: 'There was no lockdown: middle-class people stayed at home and working-class people brought them things.' Secondly, the virus remains live, and once the restrictions are relaxed a new upsurge inevitably begins—the second wave which, as we shall soon see, was in fact predicted by the government's own advisers if the lockdown model was followed. Thirdly, if the virus is highly contagious, it will spread once it is in the population whatever measures are taken. Fourthly, we must take into account the physical and psychological impacts for the elderly in particular of months on end of lockdown, leading often to reduced exercise and at the same time a growing terror of illness; as many studies have shown, physical and psychological well-being are important factors in a healthy immune system, cardiovascular health, and resistance to disease, and the impact on the immune system of months of lockdowns surely may have contributed to the high mortality figures among the elderly in countries where these occurred.

Finally, as the Italian social scientists Piero Stanig and Gianmarco Daniele explain in their book *Fallimento lockdown* ('Lockdown Failure'), the worst possible thing you can do when dealing with a highly infectious disease that spreads almost exclusively indoors and targets the elderly is to lock old people up inside their homes with other family members, and ban citizens from spending time in arguably the safest place of all: outdoors. This wasn't rocket science, just simple science. Indeed, in a 2009 article published in the *American Journal of Public Health* titled the 'The Open-Air Treatment of Pandemic Influenza', its authors noted that significant benefits in influenza mitigation were likely to 'be gained by introducing high levels of natural ventilation or, indeed, by encouraging the public to spend as much time outdoors as possible'.[52] Likewise, an early 2021 *Nature* article, commenting on the results of a study by physicist Mara Prentiss at Harvard University,[53] observed: 'One of the most important lessons to have emerged over the past year is that the spaces where people congregate matter when it comes to infection risk. Numerous superspreading events have occurred in crowded indoor spaces with poor ventilation.'[54] This was found to be particularly true for places where people congregate for long periods of time—that is, crossing each other at the grocery store is not the same as staying shut inside the same house for days.

This might appear commonsensical—even obvious. The reason it wasn't seen that way is that for more than a year the WHO refused to acknowledge that SARS-CoV-2 is an airborne virus. Aerosol researchers started warning that 'the world should face the reality' of airborne transmission in April 2020.[55] Then, in June, some claimed that it was 'the dominant route for the spread of Covid-19'.[56] And in July, 239 scientists signed an open letter appealing to the medical community and governing bodies to recognise the potential risk of airborne transmission. That same month, the WHO released a scientific brief on transmission of SARS-CoV-2 that stated: 'Short-range aerosol transmission, particularly in specific indoor locations, such as crowded and inadequately ventilated spaces over a prolonged period of time with infected persons cannot be ruled out.'[57] And yet, for more than a year after declaring the pandemic, the Q&A section on the WHO's website didn't acknowledge the contribution of aerosols to the transmission of the virus. Only on 30 April 2021, almost ten months after the WHO said it would review the research on airborne transmission,[58] did it finally update its Q&A page with the following statement:

> Current evidence suggests that the virus spreads mainly between people who are in close contact with each other, typically within 1 metre (short-range). A person can be infected when aerosols or droplets containing the virus are inhaled or come directly into contact with the eyes, nose, or mouth. The virus can also spread in poorly ventilated and/or crowded indoor settings, where people tend to spend longer periods of time. This is because aerosols remain suspended in the air or travel farther than 1 metre (long-range).

As Zeynep Tufekci wrote in the *New York Times*, this was perhaps one of the biggest pieces of news of the pandemic, and yet hardly anyone noticed: there was no big announcement, no press conference.[59] It's easy to see why. As several scientists and commentators noted at the time, this was too little, too late. In fact, the whole affair had been a colossal 'screwup', one journalist commented in *Wired*.[60] 'While it's obviously unfair to pin [the millions of people who have died from Covid from the start of the pandemic] on WHO, we should consider how many deaths could have been prevented if it had listened to researchers who are specialists in their field', wrote the biologist and journalist J. V. Chamary in *Forbes* at the time.[61] Speaking of Italy, though the argument could be extended to other countries as well, Stanig and Daniele wrote: 'It can legitimately be speculated (also in the light of research on the intrafamilial spread of the virus) that to some extent the lockdown, combined with the closure of schools, contributed to the development of the epidemic rather than slowing it down'.

It's unclear why it took the WHO so long to acknowledge the airborne nature of SARS-CoV-2. Several explanations have been put forward, from bureaucratic inertia[62] to a simple misunderstanding of aerosols.[63] We don't intend to provide a definitive answer to the 'why'. However, we can't help but point out that acknowledging the airborne nature of the virus would have undermined the whole lockdown narrative, which was based on forcing people to stay in the most dangerous environment of all: indoors.

This shows that even from the narrow perspective of saving lives, not only were lockdowns not in the collective interest of society—as we show below when discussing non-Covid-related deaths—but they arguably weren't even in the interest of those whose lives were actually at risk from Covid. And it's important to stress that such an outcome was easily predictable. It will be recalled that the WHO's 2019 report on pandemic preparedness stated that the quarantine of exposed individuals—let alone of the entire population—'is not recommended because there is no obvious rationale for this measure'.[64]

The grotesquery of the global responses becomes even more apparent when we take into account the fact that while governments went out of their way to keep healthy people locked in, chasing runners down solitary beaches or checking shopping trolleys to make sure people were only buying essentials, they all but abandoned those most vulnerable: nursing home residents. As one December 2021 report noted, Covid deaths in nursing homes amount on average to a staggering 40 per cent of all Covid deaths in Western countries, despite representing less than 1 per cent of the population. In some countries (Belgium, France, the Netherlands, Slovenia, Spain, Sweden, the UK, and the US), more than 5 per cent of all care home residents were killed.[65] In other words, those parts of the public health infrastructure which had been privatised to seek 'greater efficiency' had proven the least equipped to cope with the new virus. There is therefore a strong case that the Covid lockdowns did not protect those who were most at risk from the new virus—and that a strategy maximising resources for the protection of these populations would likely have been more effective, as argued early on by several world-leading epidemiologists (see below).[66]

None of this should have been a surprise to epidemiologists and those who have worked in public health for decades. Moreover, it had also long been known that an additional issue with suppressing a virus was that it had a tendency to provoke greater later waves of infection. In his 2022 book, *How to Prevent the Next Pandemic*, Bill Gates, who as we saw was one of the greatest advocates of lockdown in the early months of 2020, notes that 'countries that do the best job of suppressing the virus early on will often be susceptible to later surges'.[67] In a book called

The Year the World Went Mad, SAGE member and Edinburgh University Professor of Epidemiology Mark Woolhouse stated that 'lockdown was never going to solve the novel coronavirus problem, it just deferred it to another day'.[68] Meanwhile, in his book *Spike*, Jeremy Farrar described the response in SAGE to a modelling paper of 25 February 2020. As Farrar puts it, this paper suggested that '"aggressive NPIs [non-pharmaceutical interventions]" had the potential to slow the epidemic but there could be a rebound in infections once measures were lifted. The rebound meant the epidemic would ultimately claim the same number of casualties.'[69]

Thus it is the consensus view today that lockdowns cannot eliminate Covid-19—and that one issue that arises with them is that they can cause greater peaks of infection at later points. As noted in Chapter 2, this view was indeed in keeping with early UK government advice on this subject. It was, moreover, a view that was to be corroborated six months into the pandemic by research in October 2020 by scientists at Edinburgh University, published in the *British Medical Journal*. The paper sought to replicate and analyse the information that had been available to British policymakers when the decision to enter a national lockdown was taken in March, assuming the parameters of the Imperial College team (though as we have seen, these have been heavily criticised). The analysis concluded that 'school closures and isolation of younger people would increase the total number of deaths, albeit postponed to a second and subsequent waves'.[70] Keeping the schools open would have meant lots of younger people contracting the virus with little harm. In other words, according to this research, over the long term the benefits of severe lockdowns related to mortality became somewhat moot.

As time has gone on, this reality has become ever more apparent. Countries which did not follow the lockdown model, such as Nicaragua and Sweden, had low excess deaths. On the other hand, Germany had been widely praised in the spring of 2020 for the rigour of its test-and-trace programme and the effectiveness of its original lockdown. In the summer of 2020, this was seen to be a model for other countries, particularly in the United Kingdom. Yet the consequence in the autumn was a very severe second wave which saw deaths topping 1,000 fatalities daily by late December 2020.[71] Meanwhile, England was roundly criticised when compared to many European countries and their stricter control measures, and yet excess deaths in the UK turned out to be below the European average, in spite of the fact that many restrictions—lockdowns, masks, and vaccine passports— were far stricter in mainland Europe than in England.[72] Indeed, Scotland's excess death figures were higher than those in England, in spite of a stricter lockdown and other restrictive measures on masking and vaccine passports.[73]

Thus it turned out that Patrick Vallance, Britain's Chief Scientific Adviser, was right when he noted that allowing the virus to spread among the low-to-zero-risk population would have helped reduce transmission in the event of a second winter wave, even though soon enough he changed his mind along with the rest of the SAGE regarding the best strategy to deal with the virus (not that he was an isolated case—as we saw in Part 1, changing minds with little to go on was a key element of the scientific response). In addition to the United Kingdom, all European countries such as France, Spain, and Italy that implemented severe lockdowns in March 2020 faced deadly second waves in October and November of the same year. Meanwhile, Sweden, which as we have seen did not lock down severely initially, also faced a similar second wave. Although the mortality curves of all these countries were similar, Sweden—as we have seen—had not suffered so badly from the trashing of normal human relations and of the economy. At the same time, the impacts of the lockdowns on mental and physical health may well have contributed to a loss in overall immune strength when it came to combatting virus infection in subsequent waves.[74]

In sum, as Professor Woolhouse put it, 'lockdown was conceived by the World Health Organization and China as a means of eradicating novel coronavirus once and for all from the face of the earth. With hindsight, this plan was doomed from the outset.'[75] Never before in history had an attempt been made to eliminate a new respiratory virus. After two years, the evidence was that this was not possible. And the evidence also supported the pre-existing consensus before 2020, that radical virus suppression measures often led to worse spikes of infection at later points. By the spring of 2022, this realisation had filtered through to parts of the media, with outlets such as *The Week*,[76] *Washington Monthly*,[77] and the *Financial Times*[78] running stories about the things that Sweden had got right.

But by that time it was too late to help the tens of millions of people whose health had been shattered by the lockdown measures, including as a result of the wider socio-economic devastation wrought by such measures—which is discussed in the next chapter.

***

Indeed, if we widen our gaze beyond the simple question of the relationship between lockdowns and Covid-19 deaths, the picture is even starker. While most media coverage focused on the medical effects of Covid-19, in all the debate of the pros and cons of virus suppression policies, what was often lost was the impact that lockdown policies had on those suffering from other diseases. Sometimes it appeared as if Covid-19 was the only disease to afflict humanity, rather than one of many, and the response to it has followed this Captain Ahab-style line of thinking. The consequences have been the emergence of massive health inequality: the virus of Covid-19 has taken over, while those who suffer from heart disease, cancer, and other illnesses have been shunted aside, leading to a disturbing increase in deaths from these illnesses. We can consider this carefully by examining how the impacts unfolded in 2020, and then in 2021—beginning with the situation in Europe and the United States, and then considering the Global South.

The case of cancer is very disturbing. Quite early on in the pandemic lockdowns oncologists were sounding the alarm. In an interview for an article published on 15 May 2020, Karol Sikora suggested that only 10 per cent of new cancer cases that would normally be diagnosed had been detected since the British lockdown had begun on 23 March, meaning that 45,000 diagnoses had been missed; others put the figure lower, but even conservative estimates suggested that it was then around 15,000.[79] By late October 2020, research by Macmillan Cancer Support indicated that 50,000 people in the United Kingdom had undiagnosed cancers as a result of Covid-19-induced disruption to other parts of the healthcare system, while 33,000 cancer patients had had surgery delayed; moreover, the number of missed diagnoses was projected to double to 100,000 within a year if urgent remedial steps were not then taken.[80] When the December 2020 data on missed scans was published, Jody Moffatt, Head of Early Diagnosis for Cancer Research, said: 'There is a cohort of patients out there that have not been diagnosed yet—and who knows what state they will be in when they are.'[81]

As delays in diagnosis inevitably lead to worse health outcomes, the potential increase in mortality from delayed cancer diagnosis alone was on a par with that from Covid. Clearly the impact of Covid-19 on an already stretched British health service which had suffered from years of underinvestment played a part in this, but many oncologists—including Karol Sikora and Angus Dalgleish—felt that the balance between Covid and other conditions had quickly become needlessly skewed.[82] A 2020 study found that this meant that the proportion of cancer cases expected to lead to death within five years was projected to rise from 5 per cent to 17 per cent in the UK.[83] The requirements for social distancing, the difficulty of securing GP appointments in person leading to referrals, the quarantining of asymptomatic cases, and the isolation of staff without any actual symptoms had all interrupted the normal flow of scans and diagnoses. The scanning services were in locations which had nothing to do with Covid wards. In other words, the postponement of many non-Covid-related screenings and treatments wasn't simply a result of 'the pandemic' as such, but also and perhaps most importantly of the single-minded and (we would say) hysterical focus on Covid. And this was on top of the way in which the hospital-centric approach of Covid protocols worsened the pressure on hospitals, as noted in Chapter 3. It was really the response to Covid rather than Covid itself which led to this catastrophe.

This alarming early data for cancer treatment in the UK was compounded by the evidence for the initial impact that Covid-19 lockdowns had on heart disease. Terrified by the government and the media into thinking that the novel coronavirus was a deadly disease which would kill them if they went to hospital, or worried that they might be placing an undue burden on the health system if they sought treatment, some of those suffering symptoms of heart attacks did not seek treatment until it was too late. In mid-November 2020, a study released by the British Heart Foundation suggested that there had been 4,622 excess deaths from heart attacks since the onset of the Covid-19 crisis.[84] Admissions to British hospitals for heart attacks had fallen dramatically in April, risen slightly over the summer, and then fallen steadily from August to the end of the year.[85]

In the UK, the first year of the pandemic saw many critics from the left blame Boris Johnson's government for an inept response which made this situation unnecessarily bad. However, the evidence is clear that the initial lockdown response saw very similar outcomes throughout Europe. In France, the number of cancer diagnoses fell by 36 per cent in April 2020 compared to April 2019.[86] The National League Against Cancer (Ligue contre le cancer) estimated that by late October 2020 there had been 30,000 undiagnosed cases of cancer since March, and the Institut Gustav Roussy that cancer mortality would increase by 2–5 per cent over the next five years as a result of the ensuing backlogs.[87] One study found that 'in 2020, the number of mammograms decreased by 10% (−492,500 procedures), digestive endoscopies by 19% (−648,500), and cancer-related excision by 6% (−23,000 surgical procedures). Hospital radiotherapy activity was down 3.8% (−4,400 patients) and that in private practice was down 1.4% (−1,600 patients)'.[88]

In Spain, the picture was equally stark. There was a 43 per cent decline of cancer patients enrolled in clinical trials in a large university teaching hospital in Madrid in March and April 2020.[89] A survey of 137 cancer specialists conducted in October 2020 by the biopharma company IQVIA, and not sponsored by any interested commercial entity, produced some equally alarming statistics. The average number of patients seen weekly had fallen from seventy-eight per week prior to the Covid-19 outbreak to forty-one during the first wave, fifty-four in the summer during the period of calm, and then forty-five during the second wave—that is, only approximately 59 per cent of the usual diagnoses occurred. Meanwhile, during the first wave 61 per cent of patients experienced delays in chemotherapy and 71 per cent in surgeries; during the second wave these figures were at 65 per cent and 45 per cent.[90] A subsequent 2021 study found an overall decline of 17.2 per cent in cancer diagnoses.[91] Across the Mediterranean, Italy also registered a drastic decline in hospital care, non-urgent visits and screenings in 2020: 1.3 million fewer admissions to hospital than in 2019 (−17 per cent), including more than 500,000 fewer urgent hospitalisations, plus a drastic reduction in ER admissions. The most affected areas were oncological (–13 per cent) and cardiovascular surgery (–20 per cent).[92]

In Germany, one study between March 2020 and June 2021 found that 13 per cent of cancer patients experienced a negative change to their care plan.[93] A sample of forty-nine onco-specialists surveyed by IQVIA saw a similar spread of alarming conclusions. The average number of patients seen weekly had fallen from 125 per week prior to the Covid-19 outbreak to seventy-five during the first wave, 112 in the summer during the period of calm, and then sixty-three during the second wave—that is, only approximately 57 per cent of the usual diagnoses occurred during the first wave. Meanwhile, during the first wave 53 per cent of patients experienced delays in chemotherapy and 57 per cent in surgeries; during the second wave these figures were at 57 per cent each.[94]

Meanwhile, as in the UK, the situation was equally alarming for heart disease. Across Europe, there was a 35 per cent decline in admissions of patients presenting with heart attack symptoms in the early phase of the pandemic compared to the same period in 2019, and people generally waited significantly longer to go to hospital when experiencing these symptoms.[95] To give one example, in Germany the numbers of people seeking treatment for the symptoms of heart disease and strokes fell by 50 per cent in some areas during the first lockdown.[96]

In the United States, the picture was the same. There was a huge fall in patients attending hospital for heart attacks in the early phase of the pandemic—with doctors reporting a decline in attendance of 58 per cent in New York and people 'staying home', alongside steep increases in fatalities in states such as Michigan and New Jersey. In New York state the increase in ischemic heart disease was 139 per cent in this early 2020 phase.[97]

By May 2021, researchers were also reporting that Americans had missed almost 10 million cancer screenings during the first year of the pandemic.[98]

In other words, the coronavirus obsession of 2020 led to the sidelining of concern about the two major killers in Western societies, heart disease and cancer. This seems an especially disproportionate response if we consider that these pathologies greatly increase the risk of dying from Covid, particularly above a certain age. Given the policy choices that were made regarding virus suppression, this was not something that would have been avoided had different people been running government. The evidence shows that, regardless of who was in charge, cancer diagnoses fell off a cliff and the consequent increase in mortality will inevitably be severe. Many of those suffering from heart attacks did not seek treatment. In the short term, in the United Kingdom we know that 26,000 more people died in their private homes than is usually the case between 20 March and 11 September 2020, and of these Covid-19 was only mentioned on 2.9 per cent of the death certificates.[99] The number of deaths from Alzheimer's alone increased by 75 per cent among women, revealing, according to some specialists, the impact of enforced lockdown on the elderly and isolated in terms of confusion and distress.[100]

Moreover, these preliminary impacts became more measurable once the second year of the pandemic had ended. By 2022, the long-term impact of what—as we have seen—was a massive experiment in human health began to be perceptible, and the results were shocking on any reckoning. There was a large increase in obesity in the US across the board—a key factor in ill health—with one study finding that obesity among 5–11-year-olds increased from 36.2 per cent to 45.7 per cent,[101] something that some researchers ascribed to the ending of free school meals as educational institutions closed.[102] In the American population as a whole, obesity prevalence rates increased by 3 per cent,[103] while alcohol- and drug-related deaths in those aged fifteen to forty-four increased by over one third, from 46,147 in 2019 to 62,873 in 2020 and 66,061 in 2021.[104]

Looking at the United Kingdom as a case study, it's possible to observe in detail the differential impacts which the lockdown policy had across the board—entrenching inequalities in terms of health, society, gender, and the economy which three decades of neoliberal economic policies had not managed to achieve. While the first year of the restrictions had made it clear that this was the direction of travel, the second year knocked the door off the hinges and provided the clearest possible evidence of the regressive nature of the biopower policies that had been imposed.

The lockdown policy was supposed to protect health—that was its major rationale, at least in the beginning, that lockdowns would prevent health services from being overrun by 'flattening the curve'. However, after two years of Covid restrictions it became clear that, in fact, the lockdown policies had directly led to one of the most serious public health crises that could ever be envisaged. Whether looking at mental health, obesity, anxiety, delayed cancer diagnoses, or increased reports of cardiac arrests, alongside a sharp rise in excess deaths for the younger sections of the population, the data emerging from the UK was staggering. It can stand for the gathering understanding of the extent of the medical, social, and economic catastrophe that unfolded across the world in the two years from 2020.

We can begin with cancer diagnoses. Far from protecting the NHS from being overwhelmed, the evidence from the UK shows that the combination of asymptomatic Covid isolation on the one hand and a single-minded focus on Covid on the other flattened the health service's potential as a source of rapid treatment for serious health conditions. Following the initial alarming reports from 2020 discussed above, in July 2021 Senior Oncologist Gordon Wishart noted that there were 350,000 fewer urgent cancer referrals in the UK than in 2020, and 40,000 fewer cancer diagnoses compared to 2019. This confirmed the picture which had already emerged by the end of 2020 and was notably worse than the situation in Sweden, where Covid restrictions had of course been milder.[105] By the end of May 2021, 12,000 British women were said to be living with undiagnosed breast cancer as a result of the interruptions of routine medical care.[106] In November 2021, lung cancer experts told a committee of British MPs that the diagnosis and treatment of lung cancer had been put back by twenty-five years.[107] By the end of the year, missed cancer cases were estimated at 50,000 (almost a third of the total Covid mortality over two years),[108] and research from the Institute of Public Policy Research suggested that the cancer backlog could take a decade to clear.[109]

There had in fact been an increase across the board in the UK of medical waiting lists of all kinds, and not just those related to cancer. By February 2022, the numbers on NHS waiting lists in the UK were projected to reach 9.2 million, by far the highest level since records began.[110] In Wales, a September 2021 report suggested that the backlog of waiting lists would take years to clear, and cost an additional £300 million per year.[111] As with so many aspects of the Covid response, there was a significant gendered impact, too, as women were the worst affected, and by July 2021 there had been a 34 per cent increase in British women awaiting an appointment to see a gynaecologist.[112] The notion that the original lockdowns had helped to protect the NHS could not have been further off the mark. In fact, the evidence was crystal clear after two years: the lockdowns and restrictions on normal life had created a colossal public health crisis in the UK such as had not been seen since before the creation of the NHS in the aftermath of the Second World War.

We'll likely never know exactly how many avoidable non-Covid-related deaths were caused by lockdowns in high-income countries—especially given the statistical confusion over Covid deaths discussed in Chapter 3. The most reliable metric we have for estimating the impact of these measures, as mentioned, is that of excess deaths. The most authoritative study on global excess deaths conducted so far, published in *The Lancet* in early 2022, estimates that around 18 million more people died worldwide in 2020–21 compared to the pre-pandemic 5-year average[113]—a much higher number than the 6 million Covid deaths officially totalled during the same period. When these numbers are discussed in the press, these excess deaths tend to be automatically attributed to Covid, leading to the conclusion that the actual death toll of the virus is much higher than official estimates would seem to indicate. However, this explanation is not very convincing: as noted, the number of 'Covid deaths'—deaths directly caused by Covid—is in fact likely to be overestimated, notwithstanding the actual Covid deaths caused not so much by the virus itself but rather by the political and biomedical response to it.

The reality, as the authors of the *Lancet* study note, is that 'differentiating how much excess mortality is due to SARS-CoV-2 infection and how much is due to other societal, economic, or behavioural changes associated with the pandemic is challenging'. In high-income countries, for example, the ratio between excess deaths and reported Covid-19 deaths is close to 1—Italy being the only real exception, with a number of excess deaths double that of official Covid fatalities. This may indicate that a substantial fraction of these excess deaths is indeed due to SARS-CoV-2 infection; however, they write, it may also be due to the fact that these countries, as we have seen, adopted an 'inclusive' (that is, liberal) approach to statistical reporting of Covid deaths. Conversely, in fact, 'audited cause of death data from both Russia and Mexico indicate that a substantial proportion of excess deaths could not be attributed to SARS-CoV-2 infection in these locations'. This leads the authors to conclude that '[t]he magnitude of disease burden might have changed for many causes of death during the pandemic period due to both direct effects of lockdowns and the resulting economic turmoil'.

This is corroborated by other studies. One of these, published in the journal *Public Health*, for example, noted that 'data from different settings suggest the negative indirect effects associated with the Covid-19 lockdown and healthcare service adjustments are accounting for a substantial proportion of the reported excess mortality'.[114] Indeed, the authors estimated that as many as 'more than two-thirds of excess deaths' that occurred in Italy at the peak of the first wave 'might be due to causes other than Covid-19 [...] which could be a result of the excess burden on the health systems, in addition to reduced demand and supply of other non-Covid healthcare services'. A similar conclusion was reached by a study published in the *European Journal of Epidemiology*:

> While a considerable portion of the excess mortality is likely a direct effect of the Covid-19, indirect effects are also important. During the country-wide lock-down in Italy, access to healthcare was limited, and residents had medical procedures cancelled or delayed. The psychological effects of lock-down and coping mechanisms such as increased drug and alcohol abuse may also have a role in the excess mortality.

This research makes it clear that the attempts by many (as noted elsewhere in this book) to ascribe all excess deaths in the past two years to Covid-19 are severely flawed. What the impacts of all this will be for future health—taken in its broadest sense, as defined by the WHO in its constitution, as a 'state of complete physical, mental and social well-being'[115]—is hard to say. Without doubt, the definitions of health and healthcare were upended as the pandemic mitigation policies were enforced. It turned out that, lacking the potential for physical and emotional sympathy and empathy, virtual appointments did not offer care in the same way; this may have contributed to an 88 per cent rise in stillbirths in the UK by September 2021.[116] Society had become ill, even more so than it had already been in a condition of rising mental health crisis prior to the pandemic: there was a 29 per cent increase in referrals in the UK for cases of psychosis,[117] alcoholic liver deaths increased by 21 per cent,[118] and there was a 40 per cent increase in the number of English adults classified as 'high-risk drinkers'.[119]

The most serious indicator of this generalised social, mental, and physical ill health was the significant increase in excess deaths in the home, one that was not driven by Covid but by people dying alone and without medical care of Alzheimer's, heart disease, cancer, and dementia.[120] These excess deaths were driven by disproportionate numbers of younger people, with teenage boys seeing their mortality soar,[121] and excess deaths being high in general amongst those aged under sixty-four.[122] By September 2021, there had been 70,602 excess deaths in the home since March 2020, of which only 8,602 were attributable to Covid-19.[123] These non-Covid excess deaths were a pattern across the UK—in England and in Scotland.[124] They were caused not by Covid, but by the measures taken to control it.

Looking at the evidence overall, there is an abundance of it to show that the response to the pandemic has triggered health crises of all kinds in Western societies. After two and a half years, society is less well, more isolated, and more prone to anxiety and problems of mental health. At the same time, the burdens of this ill health are not being shared equally: they are falling on the shoulders of the young, the poor, and women, who are often already suffering from socio-economic and societal disadvantage, as discussed in the next chapter.

Of course, some of these excess home deaths were of people who would otherwise have gone to hospitals. They would also have died, but with good end-of-life care, surrounded by their loved ones. As it was, many died vulnerable, scared, and alone in their own homes. Fear and isolation caused extra stress, which may have led to the increase in heart attacks that resulted. Meanwhile, lockdown proponents declared that they were focused on protecting health services and saving lives. This is one of the many examples of the propagandised doublespeak which was enacted during 2020 and 2021: people were told that the restrictions were necessary to protect health services and prevent them from being overwhelmed, while health services were overwhelmed instead by the restrictions which the response to Covid-19 placed on them and ceased to function properly anyway.

***

If the medical impacts of the lockdown model were a disaster in rich countries, the impacts in the Global South were worse by several orders of magnitude. As time passed since the initial panic and lockdown imposition, the extent of the medical impacts became ever clearer. As in the West, routine treatment of the most severe diseases had been stalled completely because of the focus on Covid-19—where in Europe and the US these were cancer and heart disease, in Africa the impact was on the treatment of malaria, tuberculosis, and HIV/AIDS.

Some sense of the appalling catastrophe can be gauged through an April 2022 study which found that the economic collapse associated with lockdowns in poor countries 'may have contributed to the deaths of hundreds of thousands of children under the age of five in 129 of the world's low- and middle-income countries in the first year of the pandemic', with the range of estimates between 279,000 and 911,026 lives lost.[125]

As so often, it is the details which make the enormity of the whole easier to grasp. In an interview conducted two years into the pandemic, in March 2022, the Mozambican sociologist Pedrito

Cambrão described how routine vaccination programmes in Mozambique had been stalled because of the focus on Covid-19. They still had not resumed and were 'stagnant',[126] confirming a July 2022 report in *Nature* which found that the previous two years had seen the largest global drop in childhood vaccinations in thirty years.[127] Meanwhile, in a December 2021 interview, Angolan gender studies specialist Elsa Rodrigues described how Angolan hospitals had collapsed to such an extent that women attending for routine gynaecological appointments had to provide their own gloves. Both Cambrão and Rodrigues agreed that while the situations had been bad prior to March 2020, the policies that followed—and the special focus on Covid-19—had produced an unprecedented collapse in healthcare services.

The extent of these impacts on public health were clear and measurable right from the start. According to an estimate by the economist Sanjeev Sabhlok—who resigned from his role in the Australian state of Victoria in September in protest at the lockdown policy there[128]—by the end of 2020 alone, 2 million deaths had already been caused by the response to Covid-19.[129] This should not be surprising since, as we saw in the introduction, by July 2020, an estimated 550,000 new children were suffering each month from wasting diseases as a result of Covid-19-induced poverty.[130] Here we need to recall the vital connection between nutrition and public health in poor countries. The WHO factsheet on malnutrition, updated on 1 April 2020, noted that globally it is responsible for around 45 per cent of the deaths of children aged five or under.[131] Recent research on the disease burden of malnutrition in India found that 'malnutrition was the predominant risk factor for death in children younger than 5 years of age in every state of India in 2017, accounting for 68.2% (95% UI 65.8-70.7) of the total of under-5 deaths, and the leading risk factor for health loss for all ages, responsible for 17.3% (16.3–18.2) of the total disability-adjusted life years (DALYs)'.[132]

Moreover, this relationship between nutrition and health in low-income countries has long been apparent to scholars of public health. For several decades, the validity of what is known as the 'Preston Curve' has been widely accepted. This has shown the relationship between GDP and life expectancy. In already wealthy countries, increases in GDP have little impact on life expectancy. However, in low-income countries, even small increases in GDP can have a dramatic positive impact on life expectancy. The corollary of this was that the sudden economic shock and collapse in GDP in 2020 was almost certain to see many years fall from life expectancies.[133]

Thus global health professionals have emphasised repeatedly in recent years that malnutrition is the biggest killer for children worldwide, as well as the leading cause of loss of life years—and so, all in all, Sabhlok's estimates do not seem unreasonable. This was clear, if not widely discussed, from the outset. Of course, many advocates of strong Covid measures claimed that the death toll in low- and middle-income countries would have been even worse without them, and that they had been needed to protect long-term health. Yet this theory was not borne out by numerous studies which showed that the long-term impacts of the measures were worse by far than Covid.

This pattern becomes even clearer when we look at the evidence from the African continent, one which came to befuddle the 'Covid experts'. As we saw in Chapter 2 of this book, some experts did suggest that the impacts of Covid-19 might be less severe in Africa compared to elsewhere owing to the continent's young demographic and pre-existing immunities built up through exposure to multiple viruses, and the fact that most Africans spend far more time outdoors than indoors where the virus circulates. In fact, in 2019 the United Nations estimated the median age on the African continent as 19.8.[134] With Covid-19 a virus which overwhelmingly impacted older and obese populations, this alone should have been an indication that the virus would take a different path there—and that social distancing, lockdowns, restrictions on movement, and school closures might prove to exact a far greater toll. But as we saw, no one in the WHO was listening, and the lockdown model was one which they actively promoted for Africa.

So how severe was the Covid-19 pandemic in Africa? Certainly, it was worse in some countries than others. By 11 March 2022, two years after the pandemic was officially declared, Africa had experienced 251,470 deaths recorded from Covid-19.[135] Of these, a staggering 188,673 had occurred in just seven countries, meaning that only 62,797 Covid fatalities had been recorded in the entirety of the rest of the continent. These countries with higher Covid deaths were, in general, wealthier countries with older populations—as perhaps could have been predicted, given the general demographic of Covid fatalities. There had thus been 99,681 fatalities in South Africa, 16,033 in Morocco, 28,009 in Tunisia, 7,484 in Ethiopia, 6,336 in Libya, 24,269 in Egypt, and 6,861 in Algeria. Moreover, some enormous countries had tiny death figures: Nigeria, with a population of around 230 million, had had only 3,142 Covid-19 deaths, less than 1,600 per year in a country where 1.9 million people die annually. Uganda had recorded just 3,593 deaths from Covid-19, Mozambique 2,198, and Ghana 1,445.

Of course, many stated that these figures were enormous underestimates. In February 2021 the *New York Times* ran a piece called 'A Continent Where the Dead Are Not Counted',[136] and through 2021 the Bill and Melinda Gates Foundation funded long reads from countries like Sudan (in the *Daily Telegraph*)[137] and Zimbabwe (in the *Guardian*)[138] which promoted the view that there had been an enormous undercounting of Covid fatalities, and that many more had died from the disease than was truly recorded. On the other hand, a number of interviews conducted late in 2021 and early in 2022 with experts in Africa confirmed the general view that Covid-19 fatalities were low. According to Samuel Adu-Gyamfi from Kumasi in Ghana,[139] Pedrito Cambrão from Beira in Mozambique,[140] and Elsa Rodrigues from Benguela in Angola,[141] the impacts of Covid-19 were much lower than those of existing endemic diseases; Adu-Gyamfi said that 'they cannot be compared', while Cambrão described the restriction measures that had been taken as 'calamitous'. Some interviewees stated that Covid-19 was seen as almost exclusively a disease of the middle classes, and that no one in rural communities or among the urban poor knew of people who had died from it: this was the view of Olutayo Adesina from Ibadan, Nigeria, and of Cambrão.[142] Evidence also emerged from doctors on the ground that Covid simply was not a serious condition when compared to endemic diseases. In July 2021, an anonymous doctor from Mozambique wrote: 'In Mozambique, Covid-19 has not been a major health crisis when compared to other endemic diseases.'[143]

This may be the view on the ground, but some readers might still be doubtful. This was a global pandemic: was there not a more precise way of estimating the impacts of Covid on the continent than these impressionistic qualitative interviews? In an article published in July 2021, Stanford University Professor of Medicine John Ioannidis estimated that the Covid fatality estimates in poorer countries were then running at between 30 and 80 per cent of the true figures.[144] Meanwhile, the WHO declared in October 2021 that only one in seven Covid cases on the African continent were recorded (about 15 per cent).[145] Given that Covid cases alone are less likely to be recorded than Covid deaths (since they may result only in mild symptoms), these estimates of cases and fatalities are quite comparable. They would indicate that the Covid fatality rate in Africa is perhaps two or three times that recorded, in countries where diagnostics and medical facilities have not allowed for accurate recordings (that is, outside the seven countries with higher death rates noted above).

This allows us to provide a fuller comparative estimate of the impacts of Covid in Africa. We can be more conservative than the above, and assume for these purposes that the Covid fatality rates in African countries with low recorded figures are four times those stated. This would lead to the conclusion that around 250,000 people died of Covid during the two pandemic years outside the seven countries noted above, or 125,000 per year. On a continent where the UN estimated that 9.05 million people died in 2019,[146] this represents a comparatively small mortality increase. Meanwhile, the impact of the Covid restrictions in terms of access to medical care meant that one 2020 paper estimated that '[u]nder pessimistic scenarios, Covid-19-related disruption to malaria control in Africa could almost double malaria mortality in 2020, and potentially lead to even greater increases in subsequent years'.[147] A 2021 estimate revised this; the 2021 WHO malaria report suggested that there were 47,000 additional deaths from malaria in 2020, the vast majority caused in children under five in Africa—or over one third of the number of Covid-19 deaths across most of Africa as estimated above.[148] Approximately two thirds of these additional deaths were linked to disruptions in the provision of malaria prevention, diagnosis, and treatment during the pandemic. Given the age profile of both Covid-19 and malaria victims, the impact of the Covid restrictions in terms of mortality and life years lost dwarfed anything that Covid had caused on the continent—on any reading of the statistics.

Many factors had caused this tragic increase, and almost all of them can be traced back to the single-minded focus on Covid-19 to the exclusion of almost all else. Beyond the focus of hospital infrastructure, there is the question of supply chains of key diagnostic tools and medicines for malaria treatment. As early as May 2020, WHO advisers raised the alarm that companies that usually produced rapid diagnostic tests for HIV, malaria, and tuberculosis were switching away to produce rapid Covid tests.[149] Then in early July 2020, a team of authors wrote a blog for the *BMJ* and further raised the alarm that many companies that usually produced malarial rapid diagnostic tests were switching to producing Covid tests, as these were more profitable.[150] The knock-on effects in terms of diagnosis were huge, let alone the shortage of many other routine treatments that was often reported as the production framework of global health shifted decisively to Covid treatments and then vaccines, leaving many medications needed in low-income countries under-resourced.

As the pandemic entered its third year, these truths could no longer be hidden by long reads in prominent papers discussing the traumas around Covid. As early as October 2020, some reports had suggested that many Africans already had SARS-CoV-2 antibodies acquired through infection.[151] Eighteen months later, in March 2022, the *New York Times* finally ran a piece titled 'Trying to Solve a Covid Mystery: Africa's Low Death Rates'.[152] This noted that in countries like Sierra Leone, Covid had had minimal impact, and that tests from across the continent now showed that around two thirds of people had SARS-CoV-2 antibodies, overwhelmingly from infection rather than vaccination. While some epidemiologists were still assuming that there had been high numbers of Covid fatalities, this was not the perception of important figures such as Dr Thierno Baldé, head of the WHO's Covid emergency response in Africa. After two years, the evidence was in: in spite of minimal access to vaccines, Covid hadn't been a disaster in Africa. The disaster had been caused by the response.

As the 2-year anniversary of the declaration of the pandemic came around, it became clear that these longer-term impacts of the Covid restrictions in Africa were racking up. In the case of medical care, these restrictions had been brought in so as to preserve the health of populations—and yet the impact of the focus on Covid-19 to the exclusion of all other diseases was disastrous. For a start, there was the case of vaccinations. While the Western liberal media focused on 'vaccine apartheid' with regard to Covid vaccines, the impact of the single-minded focus on treating and curing a disease which is widely said to be far less serious than existing endemic diseases was catastrophic for routine medical care on the continent—including vaccination programmes against much more dangerous diseases. A report from July 2021 found that Covid restrictions in Africa had had a disastrous effect on other conditions and vaccination programmes.[153] Measles vaccination programmes were severely curtailed in Senegal, and polio vaccination campaigns were largely suspended until the second half of 2020; countries that experienced poliovirus outbreaks in Africa following curtailed vaccination programmes included Angola, Benin, Burkina Faso, Cameroon, the Central African Republic, Chad, Côte d'Ivoire, the Democratic Republic of the Congo, Ethiopia, Ghana, Mali, Niger, Nigeria, Togo, and Zambia.

Evidence from Angola and Mozambique confirmed this picture. João Blasques de Oliveira, an Angolan doctor with decades of experience, described how the lockdown restrictions meant that '[p]reventive child health services were affected, and vaccination was frequently postponed. For example, nationwide polio and measles vaccination were cancelled or delayed, and restrictions on movement presented barriers to access to the locations where routine vaccinations were provided.'[154] The anonymous Mozambican doctor mentioned above described how fuel shortages brought on by the economic crisis were having a major impact on the delivery of vaccination programmes (and this long before the Russian invasion of Ukraine).[155] Thus, while Africa suffered from low Covid mortality, as we have seen, the relentless focus on Covid treatment and funding to procure Covid vaccines—often associated with World Bank and IMF loans[156]—devastated routine medical care for endemic diseases of greater severity for the continent.

Nor were these impacts restricted to Africa. A further haunting example is that of India, where the initial onset of the lockdowns was already recognised as being accompanied by scenes of appalling tragedy. As 2021 came to an end, it was possible to begin to take stock of the consequences of the completely unprecedented upending of the daily lives of hundreds of millions of people. Across the board, the consequences had been catastrophic for societal and public health. We will look at this in more detail in the next chapter, but for now can begin with the question of the impact of these measures on India's health system.

When the 24 March 2020 lockdown was implemented, initial reports already described how regular healthcare services had been abruptly terminated.[157] The consequences of this became clearer as the next two years wore on. An Oxfam report from July 2021 described a highly unequal pattern of healthcare access across India, which had become much worse over the previous fifteen months.[158] Cities around the country began to declare health emergencies related to conditions that had previously been under control. In Gujarat, cities became prone to repeated strikes of dengue fever.[159] The first ever Zika outbreak was also reported in Kerala, which analysts related to the measures which had been taken to control Covid-19.[160] In sum, while the entire nation's medical focus had been thrust at Covid-19, other medical conditions of equal or greater severity grew worse. And this, as mentioned, is not even considering the wider economic impact of lockdowns.

How to make sense of this appalling tragedy, on so many levels? The writer Kunal Purohit summarised the starkness of the situation in a book chapter published in November 2022.[161]

Two hundred and thirty million Indians had been pushed deeper into poverty; more than half of the country's small and medium enterprises had wanted to shut down or close business by 2021, and by March 2022 6 million of them had closed (around 10 per cent of the country's total).[162] Meanwhile, only 8 per cent of rural Indian schoolkids regularly attended online classes. This could not simply be dismissed as 'collateral damage' of the pandemic: this was the main damage caused by the pandemic, and of course the response to it.

What, then, of the response of left-leaning commentators to this catalogue of tragedy? Surely, in the face of such cataclysmic evidence, progressive voices would have come down hard against these catastrophic policies. Indeed, at the outset, some critics spoke out. In its March/April 2020 issue, the *New Left Review* published an anonymous essay by a contributor from India on the situation then:

> The lockdown has transferred the burden of the coronavirus pandemic almost entirely onto the shoulders of the poor and marginalised. It is clear from the videoclips on social media of ordinary people expressing their anger and helplessness that most see the lockdown as a calamity far greater than Covid-19 itself. [...] Put brutally, workers may starve to save the primarily middle-class elderly from dying. And for anyone who doubts that the possibility of starvation is real, it's worth noting that the Chief Minister of Kerala, widely praised for his response to the pandemic, felt the need to explicitly reassure people that he would not allow anyone in the state to starve to death as a consequence of the lockdown.[163]

Moreover, it was not as if these appalling prices paid by the poor were not matched by enormous gains by India's super-rich. *Forbes* magazine described how at the end of 2021, India's richest 100 people had added US$257 billion to their wealth—a 50 per cent gain—over the previous twelve months, even throughout all the misery being visited on their compatriots.[164] So did these obscene increases in inequality brought about by pandemic policies lead to an outcry of revulsion from the progressive and liberal left at the impact of the Covid restriction policies?

Not exactly. By April and May 2021, the focus of the Western liberal media had abandoned these impacts to focus with gathering hysteria on the Delta wave in India and the numbers of dead crowding the mortuaries. A study from the Centre of Global Development from July 2021 suggested that the true Covid-19 death toll in India was far in excess of the 400,000 then said to have died, since the excess deaths in the country were probably between 3 million and 4.7 million since the onset of the pandemic.[165] And yet—as with the *Lancet* study on excess mortality mentioned above—this increase in the Covid mortality figures to millions of people was calculated on the basis of the increased death toll across India, and not post-mortem analysis.

Certainly the Covid mortality figures for India may be an underestimate. And yet they cannot account for this huge increase in excess deaths, or suggest that, as the *Guardian* reported, the Covid death toll might be ten times the official figure.[166] As we have seen here, the vast increase in India's mortality is far more likely to have been caused by the catastrophic restrictions on daily life brought on to control the Covid pandemic—restrictions which could not be made to last, and which did not in any case prevent the emergence of the Delta wave in the first months of 2021. Their impact on nutrition, and the clear connection between malnutrition and disease, was far more likely to have been the main cause of this increase in mortality. Indeed, a March 2021 UN report titled 'Direct and Indirect Effects of Covid-19 Pandemic and Response in South Asia' found that child mortality in India rose by 15.4 per cent in 2020—the highest rise in the region, followed by Bangladesh at 13 per cent—mainly due to the disruption in crucial healthcare services, ranging from treatment of malnutrition to immunisation, as a result of lockdowns.[167] Such disruptions were estimated by the UN to have led to 239,000 maternal and child deaths in South Asia—most of which were of children under five. It also estimates that there had been some 3.5 million additional unwanted pregnancies, including 400,000 among teenagers, due to poor or no access to contraception. As the BBC wrote at the time, commenting on the report: 'The full effect of the pandemic—and ensuing lockdowns—is just starting to become clear as countries take stock of their public health and education programmes.'[168] And yet, despite the growing evidence of the carnage caused by lockdowns in the Global South, after some initial criticisms, supposedly progressive voices were silent: they had drunk the corona Kool-Aid, and were unable to see the irreconcilable contradictions of their position.

***

As this book goes to press towards the end of 2022, the medical impacts of what went on in the attempt to control—and in some places, eliminate—Covid-19 can be assessed with clearer eyes. On the one hand, there is little evidence that lockdowns did much—or anything—to eliminate or even suppress to any great degree Covid-19 cases or deaths. On the other, the relentless pursuit of virus suppression caused untold harm in the treatment of pre-existing diseases.

The lockdown model was aggressively promoted in March 2020 by modelling teams who made extravagant promises as to what would happen. As we've seen, at one point Imperial College modellers predicted fewer than 6,000 Covid-19 deaths in the UK because of the implementation of lockdown measures. Yet this did not come to pass, and in the meantime the medical harms caused by the assault on daily life and people's physical, mental, and emotional health were off the charts. Moreover, in low-income countries, the assault on socio-economic livelihoods saw huge increases in malnutrition and associated mortality, as further discussed in the next chapter.

How can we be sure that the lockdown model did not work? As Mark Woolhouse put it in his book, lockdowns could buy time for new therapeutics and treatments, but they could not eliminate the virus. This had been Epidemiology 101 before 2020, and nothing that happened during Covid-19 changed that view. In an interview conducted for this book, the lead author of the WHO's November 2019 report on pandemic NPIs, Ben Cowling of Hong Kong University, noted: 'The pre-existing consensus was that a flu pandemic can't be contained—it can only be mitigated. Covid and flu spread in similar ways—there are differences but lots of similarities. So you have to look at measures that are sustainable'.[169]

Zero Covid simply was not a feasible strategy. By the end of 2021 and early 2022, and the onset of the Omicron wave, the evidence was stacking up. Hong Kong's Zero Covid policy was lauded by many as a success in 2020 and 2021, but Omicron put paid to that with huge spikes of cases, hospitalisations, and deaths which could not be entirely attributed to vaccination rates.[170] The same was true of Singapore, where lockdowns and suppression measures failed to control Omicron, which spread rapidly.[171] In Australia[172] and New Zealand,[173] the long-standing efforts to live without Covid had to be abandoned by the end of 2021: meanwhile, one in ten residents of Victoria state had seriously considered suicide during the extended lockdowns (suicide threats from teenagers alone had increased by a staggering 184 per cent),[174] while democracy came under threat as anyone attending protests faced massive fines and the army took to the streets of cities like Brisbane.[175]

Why, then, could these measures not be effective? The fundamental issue related to the interconnected nature of world societies. As we've seen in this chapter, lockdowns were utterly impractical and medically devastating in poorer countries. Moreover, in spite of all appearances to the contrary, the WHO must have known this following experiences in Sierra Leone and Liberia in 2014–15. Cowling, author of the 2019 WHO report, made this clear: 'Covid-19 lockdowns couldn't have worked in poor countries. Contact tracing was also infeasible there. You have to look at what can work and what can be sustained until vaccines are available—and these measures could not be.'[176]

Of course, the consequence was that Covid-19 could never have been eliminated. Variants were always going to appear and spread; short of total apartheid between low-income countries and the rest of the world, with enforced segregation and the complete elimination of travel, these variants were always going to spread around the world too. This also makes it clear just how politically regressive elimination and Zero Covid policies were: they could only have worked (in theory) through complete world segregation. Beyond the theory, in practice the nature of global societies and supply chains means that these measures could never have worked, which is why cases kept appearing in Australia in spite of all the restrictive measures that were taken.

The fact that lockdowns could never have eliminated Covid is one which may startle some readers, but it is not a surprise when we consider the key point: that as we saw in Part 1, all this was nothing less than a large-scale scientific experiment with human populations. Modellers and politicians did not know exactly how these lockdowns would work, and nor did they factor socio-economic variables into their calculations (rates of inequality, political structure and history, and so on), or the health impacts of the lockdowns themselves on immunity; they looked at what was said to have happened in China, assumed all societies would respond in the same way (an extraordinary assumption!), and proceeded accordingly.

In fact, Covid death rates were related to a whole host of complex factors in health and social structure which make the simplicity of the lockdown model seem unscientific and naive. On the one hand there are all the additional factors of health and immunity already noted earlier in this chapter. But beyond that we must take account of various other factors which might account for countries' Covid curves, beyond lockdowns. First, there is the case of healthcare spending. In the 2020 wave, the South American country which did best in its response to the new virus was Uruguay, in spite of pursuing limited lockdowns.[177] Uruguay has the lowest rate of inequality in South America and better public medical systems; as we've seen in this chapter, Nicaragua's medical system has similar attributes, and also did well with no lockdowns at all.[178] Meanwhile, Sweden's high levels of public spending were seen by some lockdown advocates such as Devi Sridhar as a key element of their comparatively low death figures,[179] while Britain's comparatively low level of public healthcare spending was seen by others as a cause of systemic failure.[180]

A further pertinent issue is previous exposure to relevant viruses. Indeed, this may have been a significant factor in initially low Covid-19 rates in East Asia, owing to previous exposure in 2003 to SARS, which is closely related to Covid-19. By September 2020, this possibility was already noted in the *BMJ* in spite of the fact that the policy response of the WHO was predicated on zero population immunity.[181] Sections of the media such as the *Guardian* eventually caught up with this possibility eighteen months later—but by then it was far too late to include it within a policy framework.[182]

When the influence of additional factors such as these on Covid incidence is considered, the absurdity of the lockdown model is staggering. As Omicron spread and the flaws in these assumptions became impossible to hide, alongside the harms that had been caused, Zero Covid zealots began to try to rewrite history, claiming that they had only supported elimination until vaccines became available—when there was clear evidence to the contrary.[183] Meanwhile, as the medical impacts of the lockdown measures on other conditions came into the open, some of the modellers went on record saying that the models had had too much impact—and that they had assumed that other government departments were trying to balance the risks of the policies.[184] So there was a general recognition that things had been far too extreme and that catastrophic policies had been followed—even if no one would admit this as such.

None of this could prevent the final piece in the jigsaw of the health impacts of the Covid-19 pandemic years which came to the fore in the second half of 2022. This was when it became clear that non-Covid excess deaths were soaring across many Western nations. By mid-August 2022, it was reported that over 1,000 people were dying each week in the UK above the seasonal average, most of which could not be attributed to Covid-19.[185] Indeed, the European Mortality Monitoring Agency, tracking mortality rates across the continent, reported that excess deaths in 2022 were in fact higher than in 2021 and 2020—and especially so among younger age groups.[186] This pattern was also observed in Australia and New Zealand, countries which had been celebrated by mainstream media for their Covid response: in Australia, excess deaths in by the end of May 2022 were 16.6% above the historical average, and in New Zealand between 7 and 10% above the historical average in the same period.[187]

This was the opposite of what should have been expected. The arrival of a new pandemic had targeted older vulnerable people, and with their premature passing the mortality rate ought then to have fallen—and certainly not risen to a level higher than it had been during the height of the pandemic. At the time of writing, it's too early to be certain as to what the causes of this excess mortality are, but it's important to underline the reality of this situation and that it forms a key part of the fallout of the pandemic response. The likelihood is that the reasons for this outcome are many: on the one hand, the impacts of lockdowns on various aspects of people's physical health were clearly severe, while on the other the abovementioned and noted impact of the vaccination programme on myocarditis may have had some impact on the increase in cardiovascular mortality that was noted across the board, and especially in younger age groups.

Whatever the outcome of future research, what's clear is that the increase in excess mortality after the end of the pandemic is strong evidence for the catastrophic nature of the Covid response. If the pandemic policies had been effective, such increases should never have happened. The sad and dismal increase in mortality in 2022 is evidence for the harms that have resulted from the new lockdown and coerced mass vaccination policy rolled out across the world.

The levels of medical carnage described in this chapter are so colossal that they really are hard to assimilate. Can it truly be the case that the global political establishment decided to undertake a form of virus control for which there was no precedent—and proceeded to attempt to roll it out universally? And when senior medical experts queried this, can it be that they were trashed and dismissed, rather than having their ideas engaged with? And when the medical impacts in poor and rich countries racked up so quickly, can it be the case that instead of changing tack, governments pursued the policy even more aggressively?

Incredibly, all this is true. Here we're reminded of Jonathan Swift's caustic satire, *Gulliver's Travels*—written 300 years ago in 1726. In the third book of the novel, Swift's protagonist is introduced to a number of extraordinary professors at the Academy of Balnibarbi, who have attempted to develop new technologies to reduce human excrement to its original food, replace silkworms with spiders, produce sunbeams from cucumbers, and transform labour and architecture so that they are immeasurably more productive. However, as Swift puts it:

> The only inconvenience is, that none of these projects are yet brought to perfection, and in the meantime the whole country lies miserably to waste, the houses in ruins, and the people without food or clothes. By all which, instead of being discouraged, they are fifty times more violently bent upon prosecuting their schemes.[188]

On one level, what had happened was completely unprecedented; on the other, it was just the age-old reproduction of hubris and the abuse of power. In the next chapter, we'll see exactly what the social and economic impacts of this were—and how contrary they stand to every ideal that the left purports to hold.

***

Before moving on to that, however, there's a final question that needs to be answered: what might an alternative strategy of pandemic management have looked like? As we've described already in this book, the alternative was to protect those who were most at risk from the virus—which, it soon became clear in the case of Covid-19, were the vulnerable, the elderly, and those in public-facing roles, a disproportionate number of whom were from minority communities. A 'focused protection' strategy of this kind, as an alternative to lockdown, was put forward in an open letter published on 5 October 2020 called the Great Barrington Declaration (GBD), authored by three world-leading scientists: Sunetra Gupta of the University of Oxford, Jay Bhattacharya of Stanford University and Martin Kulldorff of Harvard University.[189] It revolved around a simple but powerful idea: 'The most compassionate approach that balances the risks and benefits of reaching immunity, is to allow those who are at minimal risk of death to live their lives normally to build up immunity to the virus through natural infection, while better protecting those who are at highest risk.'

The authors would later state that their intention was simply to kickstart an open debate about potential alternatives to lockdowns—especially as their mounting social and economic costs were becoming increasingly apparent. Instead, what they got was the opposite: concerted aggression against the declaration and its authors orchestrated at the highest levels of the political, health, and media establishment, and aimed precisely at shutting down any debate about lockdowns. Interestingly, the people behind the attack were the same ones who had previously tried to shut down the debate about all the previous aspects of the pandemic—from the origin of the virus onwards. The opponents of the GBD were the proponents of what we discussed in Part 1, the 'single narrative' view of the pandemic and of its science.

In the days immediately following the GBD's publication, the declaration quickly started gathering a lot of attention in the press. Thousands of scientists from around the world rushed to sign it. The public health officials who had enforced the pro-lockdown consensus weren't happy about it. Thanks to emails obtained via a Freedom of Information Act request, we now know that Dr Collins, the then-Director of the National Institutes of Health, sent an email on 8 October—just 3 days after the publication of the GBD—to Anthony Fauci.[190] 'This proposal from the three fringe epidemiologists [...] seems to be getting a lot of attention—and even a co-signature from Nobel Prize winner Mike Leavitt at Stanford. There needs to be a quick and devastating published take down of its premises', Collins wrote. Fauci replied to Collins that the takedown was indeed underway, and a week after his initial email Collins himself spoke to the *Washington Post* about the GBD. 'This is a fringe component of epidemiology', he said. 'This is not mainstream science. It's dangerous.' His message spread and the alternative strategy was dismissed in most precincts. An article in *Wired* denied that there was any scientific divide and argued that lockdowns were a strawman and weren't coming back (the following month restrictions were reinstated).[191] As the *Wall Street Journal* wrote:

> Dr. Fauci also emailed an article from the *Nation*, a left-wing magazine, and his staff sent him several more. The emails suggest a feedback loop: The media cited Dr. Fauci as an unquestionable authority, and Dr. Fauci got his talking points from the media. Facebook censored mentions of the Great Barrington Declaration. This is how groupthink works.[192]

As on other occasions during the pandemic, the strategy was successful. As Kulldorff recalled:

> Some colleagues threw epithets at us like 'crazy', 'exorcist', 'mass murderer' or 'Trumpian'. Some accused us of taking a stand for money, though nobody paid us a penny. Why such a vicious response? The declaration was in line with the many pandemic preparedness plans produced years earlier, but that was the crux. With no good public-health arguments against focused protection, they had to resort to mischaracterisation and slander, or else admit they had made a terrible, deadly mistake in their support of lockdowns.[193]

Within a few weeks, the concerted attack on the GBD and its authors had succeeded in demonising them in the eyes of the world's public opinion. Yet another crucial debate that citizens were denied—and yet another example of the violence and authoritarianism with which the Covid consensus has been enforced over the past years. In hindsight, however, there is no doubt that the Great Barrington Declaration has been vindicated. Some heavily criticised the recommendation made by the GBD scientists of allowing normal life to continue in the main while shielding the most vulnerable, pointing to the ethical enormity of requiring a major sector of the population to isolate from the rest of society; however, the ethical dimensions of enforcing lifetimes of penury on people from a wide range of occupations and on large sections of the young, of removing all possibility of social mobility among many children from poorer backgrounds whose educations have been savaged, of policies leading to a huge increase in domestic violence, and of bringing starvation and wasting diseases to millions of children in the Global South were hardly less severe.

But looking back, the most outrageous accusation against the GBD was that it advocated a 'let it rip' strategy—that it essentially ignored the fate of the most vulnerable people in society. In fact, as Kulldorff notes, the focused protection approach is the exact opposite. 'Ironically, lockdowns are a dragged-out form of a let-it-rip strategy, in which each age group is infected in the same proportion as a let-it-rip strategy', he says.[194] Indeed, the recommendations of the GBD scientists for focused protection had clear and practical elements aimed precisely at protecting the elderly and the weakest, including free accommodation for younger members of multi-generational households and measures to reduce the spread of Covid-19 in care homes. In view of the massive number of deaths registered in care homes that we noted at the start of this chapter, there seems to be little doubt that focused protection was the right course of action. It would have avoided inflicting needless pain on workers, women, and children through repeated lockdowns, while arguably saving countless lives by focusing first and foremost on the elderly and especially on nursing homes.

At the same time, one of the key aspects of the document was, as Sunetra Gupta put it later, that it was a strategic document: 'People criticize us on the finer points; ask why didn't we lay out exactly how it was to be enacted. But a fundamental point that people fail to appreciate was that it was a strategic statement. The way that it would be implemented in different locations had to be worked out specifically within those settings.'[195] The best strategies for focused protection would not have been the same in Germany as they were in India. But certainly, had the whole of society turned its attention to developing clear and focused protection of vulnerable populations in the way in which it turned its attention to lockdowns, there can be little doubt that innovative solutions would have emerged.

In richer countries, what might these have looked like? Targeted measures could have been taken which were not so costly and did not create huge inflation of basic goods within a couple of years. Public efforts could have been directed to develop command manufacturing centres for PPE instead of handing out contracts to contacts who could source this in China. Rather than struggling to deal with the massive social fallout of the lockdown policy, the government could have focused on ensuring the efficiency of schemes to retrain and re-admit retired nurses and doctors so that they were prepared to work with Covid patients, better shielding health services and other healthcare workers for when the inevitable second wave came in the autumn of 2020 (although the British government did develop such a scheme, the doctors who tried to use it angrily described its failings by the end of the year, and only 5,000 of the 40,000 who had applied had been taken back on through it).

Meanwhile, certain times of day could have been designated exercise and shopping times for vulnerable and older members of society to ensure that they were not isolated and could at least get out a little, while allowing others to continue to circulate as normal at other times of day. Social distancing measures would have been introduced for limited time periods, especially when there was a spike of the virus in March and December during the first and second waves of Covid-19 in Europe, such as limiting the size of gatherings to around fifty, and closing schools for short periods of time as had happened in Mexico in 2009 during swine flu (see above, Chapter 2). Of course, to implement no restrictions or life changes would have been utterly wrong, but that was not the previous scientific consensus either. Rather, the previous consensus had favoured a far more measured approach than that adopted in 2020.

At the same time, a small fraction of the sum spent to support jobs on the furlough and other schemes (which by early 2022 was estimated by the UK parliament to be between £310 billion and £410 billion in the UK alone)[196] could have been spent training the retired nurses and doctors and developing the PPE manufacturing centres to expand provision for care home staff, transport workers, and doctors and nurses. This strategy would have provided existing medical staff with better protection from a high viral load, and more relief through expanding the medical workforce available. Substantial pay rises could also have been brought in for all key workers—those in supermarkets, delivery drivers, and binmen, as well as the better paid in the medical sector.

This is one view of what focused protection might have looked like in richer countries. In poorer countries with different population pyramids, the need for focused protection, and what it would have looked like, again would have been different. But one of the reasons why it was soon dismissed by popular opinion was that the GBD was labelled as taking a libertarian right-wing position and its proponents targeted as having connections with the Koch Brothers, the well-known billionaires in the US funding climate change-denying researchers.[197] In point of fact, the Koch-affiliated Mercatus Center awarded a prize to Neil Ferguson and his team at Imperial College in Spring 2020—something which GBD detractors did not seem to care about.[198] Meanwhile, although they hosted their launch meeting at the American Institute for Economic Research (AIER) office in the US in Great Barrington, the GBD received no funding whatsoever from the AIER, which had once received a £50,000 Koch Foundation donation: when this accusation was repeated in August 2021 in the *BMJ*, the journal subsequently had to retract it.[199]

The politicisation of the debate followed the political polarisation of the previous decade as discussed in Part 1—and was heightened by the fact that 2020 was a US presidential election year. Yet the irony was that the GBD authors acknowledged that they came from different political perspectives, both left and right. Sunetra Gupta, for one, was an internationalist who saw herself as 'on the left of the left'.[200] The GBD proposals were seen by their advocates as driven by science, not politics. But science had been captured by politics, and other interests. The GBD was publicly trashed in an orchestrated media blitz coordinated by figures such as Dr Anthony Fauci.[201] The consequences will be felt for years, if not decades, to come—as the next chapters make clear.

7

THE SOCIAL AND ECONOMIC EFFECTS OF THE PANDEMIC MANAGEMENT

Everyone reading this book is aware that the response to the novel coronavirus has had a bad effect on many people around them: the poor, the young, those in care homes who could not receive visits and grew confused, as well as all those whose jobs require contact with human beings (which turns out to be rather a large proportion of the working population). In general, the discourse which has emerged has been that these consequences are merely the inevitable collateral damage of the steps that had to be taken to stem the spread of Covid-19. In several countries, parallels were drawn with the Second World War.

Yet the comparison with the Second World War is tenuous. At the time, citizens were asked to make present sacrifices in order to combat a terrifying future harm—world domination by the Nazi party. In 2020 and 2021, the opposite moral judgement was made, as citizens were instructed to sacrifice future prosperity and well-being for the sake of the perceived needs of the present. It is not clear that any other moment in history has occurred in which people have been invited to sacrifice the future for the present.

2020 and 2021 came to resemble a wartime situation not because of Covid-19, but because of the response to it. The wartime comparison can certainly stand up when it comes to the harms that were caused by the response to the new virus. In brief, the world's wealthiest people accumulated vast amounts of capital, while the poorest were flattened. Meanwhile, the social fabric was shredded. All over the world the anxiety and tensions of the lockdowns saw huge increases in domestic and sexual abuse, while victims were incarcerated with their abusers. The impacts set back progress towards gender equality by decades.

As time passed and the pandemic response became ever more drawn out, the harms became impossible to hide. Poor people, everywhere, had suffered enormous losses. Rich people, everywhere, had become immeasurably richer. As the liberal Nobel Prize-winning economist Joseph Stiglitz wrote in *Scientific American* early in 2022, 'the pandemic's most significant outcome will be a worsening of inequality, both within the US and between developed and developing countries. Global trillionaire wealth grew by US$4.4 trillion between 2020 and 2021, and at the same time more than 100 million people fell below the poverty line.'[1] Yet liberals like Stiglitz were still apparently unable to compute that it was not the pandemic alone that had caused this, but rather the unprecedented policy response to it.

This flat denial of the consequences of the lockdown policy response was based on the myth that the refusal to lock down would have had even more severe economic impacts than the lockdowns themselves. Liberal publications such as *The Atlantic* and *The Conversation* published a number of essays both at the outset of and during the pandemic which proposed this idea.[2] However, this was a view that ignored the age profile of Covid-19, and also that by forcing most economic activity online lockdowns drove it into the pockets of Tech monopolists—thereby creating this aggravation of inequality. It also assumed that lockdowns had a huge impact on the spread of the virus, whereas as we saw in the previous chapter this has not proven to be the case. In fact, in the US, data one year into the pandemic showed that states which re-opened normal life earlier than others, such as Florida, Georgia, and Utah, all economically outperformed states with stricter measures, such as California and Massachusetts.[3] Moreover, as noted, countries such as Sweden that followed milder approaches underwent far fewer socio-economic impacts and recovered much quicker—while Tanzania, which was one of the few African countries to implement no lockdown measures, saw its economy grow by 4 per cent in 2020, one of only two African countries to register economic growth that year according to the African Development Bank.[4]

In the meantime, the impacts of the Covid restrictions were destructive to small and medium enterprises (SMEs), while making the already enormously wealthy tech and pharma monopolists incomparably richer. By November 2021, 26,774 businesses had been wiped from New Zealand's Companies Offices Register alone.[5] The super-rich benefitted not only from hoovering up the debris, but also from economic fillips such as the EU's exemption of private jets from carbon jet fuel duty.[6] A study by the UK's Resolution Foundation found that by July 2021, the richest 10 per cent of British households had gained £50,000 each on average.[7]

This pattern of already enormous wealth disparities becoming chasms was one that was faced around the world. Given the shuttering of SMEs and the move to the world of online monopolists as the global middle class clicked, zoomed, and fell asleep on the job, it's hardly surprising that billionaires around the world saw their wealth increase by US$3.9 trillion just in 2020.[8] In Latin America, for instance, billionaires increased their wealth by 52 per cent during the pandemic.[9] In Mexico, multimillionaires saw their wealth increase by 31.4 per cent in

2021 alone.[10] And in Africa, a January 2022 report found that Africa's eighteen billionaires had seen their wealth increase by 15 per cent, also in 2021 alone.[11]

On the other hand, countless studies through 2021 and early 2022 showed just how devastating the economic collapse had been for the world's poorest. The shutdown of hundreds of thousands of small and medium businesses triggered one of the worst job crises since the Great Depression (which was only partially cushioned by government stimulus and the relief measures put in place—and even then not in every country).[12] In 2020 alone, workers around the world cumulatively lost $3.7 trillion in earnings—an 8.3 per cent decline.[13] In Africa, a February 2022 report noted that not only had GDP fallen by as much as 7.8 per cent in some cases, but remittances from abroad had fallen by 25 per cent.[14] In a context where remittances from rich countries accounted for over half of private capital flows to Africa shortly prior to the pandemic,[15] this had a devastating effect on the daily economy, with over 40 million additional people in extreme poverty by the end of 2021.[16]

Data can present some of the real impacts of these policy decisions, which upended so many millions of lives around the world. But it is stories and the details of daily life which can give a real sense of what this has meant. In this chapter, we range widely around the world to examine the consolidated devastation which the single-minded pursuit of Covid-19 has caused. After two years, the true consequences of this policy decision became clear: the destruction of education and livelihoods and the stoking of inflation in the prices of basic goods through supply-side bottlenecks caused by the global lockdown and collapse in trade, leading to food price inflation and further spikes in global hunger which began long before the Russian invasion of Ukraine.[17]

Had Covid-19 been a disease which targeted people indiscriminately, with an IFR of over 50 per cent (as in the case of Ebola), the policy response might have made sense—even if, as we've seen, it didn't achieve what had been promised. But Covid-19 was not such a disease. Indeed, its burden was far greater in wealthier countries with older populations than it was for the world's poor. In Africa, the disease became known as one which affected only the middle class in elite areas, as Olutayo Adesina, Head of the Department of History at the University of Ibadan in Nigeria, and Pedrito Cambrão, Head of Research at the Universidade Zambezia in Beira, Mozambique, put it.[18] Many African commentators put this down to the median age of the African population (19.8 years old), the greater epidemiological resilience which the poor in Africa require, or (in one case) to the fact that poorer people spend more time outdoors and have greater exposure to Vitamin D.[19]

In any case, the facts of the relatively low Covid-19 burden in Africa became starkly clear as 2021 wore on. One study suggested that in terms of disability-adjusted life years (DALYs) lost, Covid-19 mortality in Africa comprised just 6.4 per cent, 4.8 per cent, and 6.3 per cent of the mortality caused by tuberculosis, HIV/AIDS, and malaria, respectively.[20] Essentially, the world's poor paid with their livelihoods and futures for the attempt to control a disease which for them was a minor risk in their daily lives.

In high- and middle-income countries, things were only marginally better. The poor were flattened here too, while the rich dreamt of kickstarting their globetrotting lifestyle again as soon as they could. A new socio-economic settlement had been ushered in under the guise of 'public health', while the scope for meaningful debate and critique of this framework was shut down through the creation of a wartime-style propagandist press, as we'll see in Chapter 9.

The 'shock doctrine' of 2020

The inequities of outcome stemming from the Covid restrictions are staggering. In a way they are universal, equalising the experience of people on every continent in the world. Whether in Abidjan or Chicago, London, Lima, or Hyderabad, poorer people suffered materially and in terms of future life chances. There were huge increases in gendered violence, and in Latin America women's sexual and reproductive health was said in one study to have been set backwards thirty years, alongside a huge fall worldwide in women's ability to access contraception.[21] The impacts on the young in particular were colossal, as we will see in the next chapter.

We can begin by looking at the initial impacts of lockdown measures in 2020 for the world's poorest and then for those in high- and middle-income countries. Right from the start, the disastrous nature of these policies was clear. At the end of March 2020, the United Nations Development Programme (UNDP) warned that 'nearly half of jobs in Africa could be lost due to coronavirus'.[13] The international community had to think further than just the immediate impacts of the virus, they said. Achim Steiner, administrator of the UNDP, said that 'the growing Covid-19 crisis threatens to disproportionately hit developing countries, not only as a health crisis in the short term but as a devastating social and economic crisis over the months and years to come'.[14]

Then, in April 2020, the World Food Programme (WFP) warned that the world was 'on the brink of a hunger pandemic' that could lead to 'multiple famines of biblical proportions' within a few months if immediate action wasn't taken (it wasn't).[22] WFP Executive Director David Beasley said that 135 million extra people were facing 'crisis levels of hunger or worse' and that an additional 130 million people 'could be pushed to the brink of starvation by the end of 2020'. That same month, the United Nations University World Institute for Development Economics warned that without an emergency rescue fund, over half a billion people could be pushed into poverty. That is, between 6 and 8 per cent of the world's entire population were at risk of being forced into poverty, and over half of the world's population might be living in poverty in the aftermath of the pandemic. As the report noted, worldwide 2 billion people worked informally with no access to sick pay, and in poor countries informal jobs constituted 90 per cent of the labour market as compared with just 18 per cent in rich countries.[15]

There was, moreover, a vital gendered aspect of the crisis, and one almost entirely ignored by policymakers and advocates of lockdowns alike. As the UN noted, worldwide women provided '75 percent of unpaid care, looking after children, the sick and the elderly. Women are also more likely to be employed in poorly paid precarious jobs that are most at risk. More than one million Bangladeshi garment workers—80 percent of whom are women— have already been laid off or sent home without pay after orders from western clothing brands were cancelled or suspended.'[16]

The reports kept coming. Towards the end of April 2020, the ILO warned that almost half the global workforce were 'in immediate danger of having their livelihoods destroyed' owing to the economic fallout from the response to the Covid-19 crisis.[17] They estimated that the 2 billion-strong cohort of informal workers had lost 60 per cent of their wages during the first month of the crisis.[18] Guy Ryder, the Director of the ILO (a UN agency), warned that the poverty impact would be 'massive': this had translated into a fall in the earnings of informal workers of 81 per cent in Africa and the Americas, 21.6 per cent in Asia and the Pacific, and 70 per cent in Europe and Central Asia.[19]

Then on 7 July 2020, the UN issued a report that made it clear that this problem was in fact generalised, and that across the world 'Covid-19 is reversing decades of work on poverty, healthcare and education'.[23] The major impacts were on women and children, with an increase in poverty (71 million more people were to be pushed into extreme poverty by the end of the year according to this report) meaning that 'as more families fall into extreme poverty, children in poor and disadvantaged communities are at much greater risk of child labour, child marriage, and child trafficking'.[24] A report issued by Oxfam 2 days later saw the situation in even starker terms. It predicted that 121 million people could be pushed into extreme poverty 'as a result of the social and economic fallout from the pandemic including through mass unemployment, disruption to food production and supplies, and declining aid'.[25] It was in step with a later (October) World Bank report which predicted that between 88 and 115 million people would be pushed into severe poverty by the end of the year, and that the total could reach 150 million people in 2021.[26]

Was there any way of forestalling such a disaster, one that could be seen coming right at the outset of the pandemic response? As the various UN reports issued in March and April 2020 made clear, the only way of combatting it would have been through a concerted relief effort requiring donations of hundreds of billions of dollars. Yet all international policymakers must have known that the prospects of such a fund being put together were tiny. For years, humanitarian agencies had pointed out that although Western donor governments often make generous-sounding pledges when a humanitarian disaster looms, more often than not they fail to follow through on them. When an earthquake struck Bam in Iran in 2003, killing 26,000 people, a year later the Iranian government claimed to have received just US$17.5 million of the US$1 billion pledged.[26] In 2015, Oxfam's Director of Aid Recovery Effectiveness conducted a study of three past crises to see how fully donors met their pledges, and found that on average they delivered 47 per cent of what had been pledged.[27] Thus, in the context of an economic crisis for the entire world, the prospect of any serious and effective fund being marshalled to mitigate the catastrophic consequences of the lockdown response for the world's low-income countries was virtually nil.

It was widely known that the impacts of all this would be devastating. And indeed, just a few months into the pandemic, the United Nations predicted that deaths from lockdown-induced starvation and malnutrition would exceed by far Covid deaths globally.[27] This also helps us to gain a better perspective on the global excess death number discussed in the previous chapter. Yet this had no impact either on the policy recommendations of the WHO or on the general media and political response to the virus both in the Western world and in Africa itself. Why, then, did African political leaders rush to implement a lockdown policy in March 2020, when this was predicted to immiserate so many millions of people?

As noted in Chapter 2, there were several reasons. On the one hand, many interviewees for this book pointed to a generalised sense of panic, fanned by the media, which claimed that the impacts of Covid-19 would be especially catastrophic in low-income countries.[28] According to Carlos Cardoso, Director of the Centro de Estudos Sociais Amílcar Cabral in Guinea-Bissau, and a former Research Director of the Council for the Development of Social Science Research in Africa (CODESRIA), there was a 'genuine willingness by African leaders to implement the lockdown policy, albeit a little ingenuous on their part'.[28] Politicians, and the public in general, had been spooked by the propaganda as to the devastation that the virus might cause on the continent.[29] Although such a huge percentage of the African economy is informal, this was seen as the only measure to contain a public health catastrophe—in spite of the fact that, as we have seen, the measures had been tried unsuccessfully in Sierra Leone and Liberia just a few years earlier.

But if on the one hand the panic was misplaced and the modelling wrong, another important push factor was the nature of global power relations. According to some African social scientists, such as Pedrito Cambrão in Mozambique and Samuel Adu-Gyamfi in Ghana, the pressure of international organisations and especially the WHO was a significant driver of the African lockdown policy.[30] And indeed, the role of WHO pressure in African governments adopting lockdown policies is clear, as we have seen. This is particularly puzzling if we consider that even some WHO officials were warning of the catastrophic impact lockdowns would have on low-income countries. In autumn of 2020, Professor David Nabarro, Senior Envoy on Covid-19, a position reporting to the Director-General, said:

> We in the World Health Organization do not advocate lockdowns as a primary means of controlling this virus. We may well have a doubling of world poverty by next year. We'll have at least a doubling of child malnutrition because children are not getting meals at school and their parents in poor families are not able to afford it. This is a terrible, ghastly, global catastrophe, actually, and so we really do appeal to all world leaders: Stop using lockdown as your primary control method. [...] Lockdowns just have one consequence that you must never ever belittle—and that is making poor people an awful lot poorer.[29]

In sum, right from the start, the economic and social outcomes of lockdowns in Africa and other areas of the Global South were clearly going to be catastrophic. What this meant in practice became clearer within six months of the lockdowns being imposed. On 10 October 2020, the BBC reported that over 1,000 migrants from West Africa had arrived by sea to the Canary Islands in the previous 48 hours. Thirty-seven different boats had arrived from Senegal and Gambia, and that week a Senegalese naval patrol had picked up two boats carrying 186 passengers. Although the sea route from West Africa had long been used, it had peaked in around 2006 and numbers like these had not been seen since then.[30]

Within a month, the situation had become even more critical. On 8 November, the BBC reported that 1,600 migrants had arrived in the Canaries over that weekend, with 1,000 arriving on the Saturday alone. At that point, the Spanish government said that over 11,000 arrivals had been recorded on the islands in 2020, compared with 2,557 in 2019; by the middle of December, Tenerife's authorities estimated that 8,000 people had gone on to arrive during November alone.[31]

This is a journey of terrible risks. In Senegal and Gambia, it's well known that those who die of thirst or hunger or illness on the crossing are cast overboard. In October 2020, 140 people had died when a boat carrying 200 had capsized near the Senegalese town of Mbour. According to local sources, 400 Senegalese died in October 2020 alone trying to make this journey, though the ILO reported a death toll of 414 for the whole year in November.[32] Beyond these official figures, well-informed Senegalese people estimated the real fatality figure to be at least twice that.[33]

Nevertheless, more and more people had felt compelled to attempt this crossing during 2020. Reports later explained that the Senegalese lockdown had devastated the business model of the informal economy:[34] small-scale entrepreneurs found they could not move goods to market on the backs of motorbikes as they once had—and very soon, as money evaporated from the economy, no one had money to buy anything. Meanwhile, the international media—if it reported on events in Senegal at all—focused on how well the country had done in fighting the virus.[35]

By December 2020, the economic crisis meant that whole towns across Senegal were virtually empty. Young people had gone—to attempt either the hazardous sea crossing to the Canaries or the route across the desert through Libya to the Mediterranean. What choice did they have? As one interviewee for this book put it, no one was eating more than once a day, and if you did have food in the evening you gave it to a child to make sure they did not starve.[36]

It's these details which begin to make sense of the data, and render the human impact of the initial lockdowns both more real and more devastating. Across Senegal's southern border lies the small country of Guinea-Bissau. Here, in the capital Bissau—a small and peaceful city—there was a longstanding and thriving market at the Subida da Caracol (Snail's Rise). This was a large market area attached to the major market of the capital, the Feira de Bandim, which is located at the entry to the city centre and port area. However, the stalls in the Subida da Caracol were very closely packed together and the alleys between them were also deemed by authorities not to offer a sufficient physical distancing space. Thus, in April 2020 the government simply decided to move the market completely to another neighbourhood, Ajuda. The market vendors—the vast majority of them women— affected by this decision protested, and some refused to move. The previous location of the market was placed near to the main transport artery into Bissau and thus offered good opportunities for trade, but the Ajuda location did not. Some tried to return to the old location, and managed to stay. But the overall impact was a collapse in livelihoods for thousands of poor female traders who hitherto had managed to scrape a living for their families by making day-to-day sales.[35]

Across the continent, in Mozambique, things were very similar.[36] Young people and women who depended on informal market trading to survive were prohibited from going out into the street, or else told to be at home by 6 pm, which is generally the most profitable time of day. As in Bissau, market areas were closed and street trading often prohibited. Some markets were relocated to areas with no trade, and incomes plummeted. This had a devastating impact on families: many Mozambican men are migrant workers in South Africa, and thus many families are sole-parent and largely economically supported by the mother and her informal trading.

Meanwhile, already a few months into 2020, it was also clear that this 'shock' was having a catastrophic impact on Africa's middle classes. The global economic contraction affected the whole world, but its impacts were most severe in Africa because of the economic structure that had grown up on the continent over the preceding 5 centuries. Over the long period of the global slave trades, the transition to plantation agriculture in the nineteenth century, and then the formation of structurally unequal colonial and postcolonial relations of trade, Africa had become dependent on external demand. Demand for resources—oil, minerals, diamonds—drives the African economy, and the allied service sector (hotels, restaurants, transport services, and so on) on which the African middle classes depend. It was the collapse in demand for these which triggered a crisis in Africa's formal employment sector.[37]

Thus, one of the features of the Covid-19 economic crisis in Africa is that it was often in richer countries where the levels of economic disruption were especially notable. Huge street protests took place in Lagos and Luanda, the largest cities in oil-rich Nigeria and Angola, in October and November 2020.[38] In Luanda, one of the demands was for better standards of living, something that is almost unheard of in African protests, as Carlos Cardoso notes.[39] In Gabon, a smaller oil-rich Central African country, an economic crisis was reported among oil workers and the owners of bakeries and fast food shops, who found their client base collapsing as oil prices plummeted and production slowed.[40]

In July 2020, the South African *Daily Times* reported the results of a survey conducted by a team of thirty social scientists from five South African universities, who had interviewed 7,000 people. The team found that 3 million South Africans had lost their jobs during the first month of lockdown. Almost half of the South African population (47 per cent) had experienced hunger at some point during the lockdown period through to July, an increase of 26 per cent on the pre-lockdown rate of 21 per cent. In those households, 58 per cent had not been able to shield children from hunger.[41] As in the West, those most affected were already the poorest members of society.

Meanwhile in the poorer countries of the continent, the situation for small business owners was no better. In Mozambique, owners of minivans and pick-up trucks providing public transport found their profits vanishing overnight as social distancing measures were imposed, while many hotels and restaurants closed and their employed staff were dismissed; bars and restaurants would not reopen fully until February 2022, almost two years later.[42] In Gambia, the tourism sector—contributing 20 per cent of national GDP, and responsible for a large part of the informal sector's activity—collapsed completely for a third of the 2020 season and much of the 2021 season, leading to the layoff of large numbers of staff for whom this was their only prospect of work; such government grants as were available went to owners and did nothing to alleviate the plight of the workless, many of whom, as we have seen, tried to leave by sea and across the desert for Europe.[43]

One country which is worth examining more closely in the context of this early phase of the pandemic response is Angola, the eighth richest country in Africa according to 2019 GDP figures.[44] The sudden fall in demand for oil caused by the collapse in international and national travel meant a precipitous decline in the value of its kwanza currency, from 482 to the dollar on

1 January 2020 to 645 by the end of the year, a fall of nearly 40 per cent.[45] As food imports accounted for 20 per cent of national food consumption, this led to price rises which the poor could ill afford; moreover, the closure of borders aggravated the situation with 'shortages of agricultural inputs' already by May and a decline in the availability of irrigated crops for sewing.[46] Meanwhile, in rural areas the lockdown meant that subsistence farmers were unable to access their fields and their harvests were lost.[47]

The impacts on food security were immediate, for the middle as well as the poorer sectors of society. Elsa Rodrigues, a social scientist specialising in gender studies in Benguela, a city in the centre of the country, described how by the end of 2020 ten or fifteen children were waiting outside every bakery and supermarket in the centre of the city begging for handouts—where there were none in evidence in October 2018.[48] Meanwhile, the slowdown in demand for oil and diamonds caused by the global economic crisis had seen many of the largest international companies operating in the country simply close down, creating a huge crisis in formal employment.[49] As Rodrigues put it soberly in December 2020, 'in the capital it is a thousand times worse [than in Benguela] [...] the country is essentially ruined'.[50]

Thus among middle-income African countries, the impact on major drivers of the local economy was also stark. This was true both in countries with autocratic governments, such as Angola, and those with democratic governments, such as Ghana. In testament to the different approaches to death between Africa and the West, one of the most important internal drivers for economic activity in Ghana is funerals—which are celebrations far more than dirges. The renting of canopies, hiring of sound systems, commissioning of elaborate new clothing, and payment for the feeding of large numbers of friends and relatives require years of forethought. Funerals provide a huge boost to a number of local industries, from catering to tailoring. The overnight prohibition of mass funerals therefore had a terrible impact on large numbers of small businesses, with knock-on effects in all aspects of economic life.[51]

So when the WHO stated in its 25 May 2020 press conference that African citizens thought these measures 'would be very tough on them in their households' and were 'challenging', we can begin to understand what this means. In Bissau, Carlos Cardoso stated in December 2020 that 'things have never been as bad as they are now';[52] in neighbouring Senegal, well-informed observers agreed that the situation for the urban poor had never been as bad as it was by early 2021 (and this in a context where that situation is never good).[53] In Mozambique, Pedrito Cambrão compared the reality to the height of the devastating and 20-year-long civil war in the country between the Frelimo government and South African-backed Renamo rebels in 1983, when 'there was nothing to buy in the shops. The shelves were virtually empty. It was a year of severe hunger. The difference is that now, there are things in the shops, but no one has any money to buy them.'[54]

These kinds of impacts were felt in all African countries, where the dependence on the informal sector is always high. In Gambia, many markets were closed with a major impact on the (again, usually female) vendors;[55] meanwhile, according to Hassoum Ceesay, Director General of the National Centre for Arts and Culture, 'the lockdown was a complete disaster for many small businesses'.[56] In Ghana, one of the richest and most dynamic economies in West Africa, impacts were little different. Here the informal sector is also one of the major drivers of economic life, and many people who work in it are rural migrants who sleep at their place of work—in a market area, a transport park, and so on. At the onset of the lockdown in March, however, the Ghanaian government prohibited open sleeping and told people to stay at home, even though, for this already severely marginalised group of people, home was where they worked. Many tried to return to their home villages, but with distancing measures imposed on public transport this became chaotic, and prohibitively expensive.[57]

Nor were these impacts of the lockdown policies limited to Africa. As we saw in the previous chapter, on 24 March 2020 the Indian government had, with just 4 hours' notice, declared a complete lockdown, thereby terminating the livelihoods of hundreds of millions of people. All public transport was closed and the combination of these measures led to a mass exodus of the working poor from the slums of India's cities. As in Africa, most young men had migrated alone and lived and ate where they worked, or in roadsides and so-called 'illegal settlements'. For these people, lockdown meant a loss of work, home, and the means to eat. The anthropologist A. R. Vasavi reported in June 2020 that the lockdown regime had led to 'a shattering meltdown of public life. [...] The most visible manifestations of this are not a health crisis—that a nation with dismal health facilities was expected to have—but the mass displacement and movement of the working poor, loss of livelihoods for hundreds of millions of people'.[58]

Hundreds of people collapsed and died by the roadside in exhaustion, and sixteen were killed by a goods train as they lay shattered on the railway tracks.[59] The Indian government did extend a food aid programme which aimed to reach 800 million people, but by the end of June 2020 only 13 per cent of the food had been distributed and by October there were reports of starvation looming.[60] As in Mozambique, the comparison that has been made is with previous experiences of wartime. Vasavi wrote that 'this was reminiscent of the 1947 mass movements of people between Pakistan and India, as newly independent but partitioned, postcolonial nations'.[61] And then, when people returned to their villages, they were often refused entry by state authorities because of the requirement to quarantine—some killed themselves when met with this final indignity.[62]

These documented human impacts of the 2020 lockdown policies across low-income countries thus very quickly show that the original predictions of the UN agencies were certainly in broad terms correct. So we come back to the question of why they were imposed in the first place—the combination of a panic regarding the virus which turned out to be misplaced on the one hand and the pressure from international and donor organizations to do 'good governance' on the other.

The WHO certainly believed that, short of a reliable 'test and trace' system, poor nations needed to be in lockdown. At the 25 May 2020 press conference, Dr Mike Ryan, Executive Director of the WHO's Emergencies Programme, put it thus:

> What we really would like is to be in a position where we can identify cases and contacts, and those cases can be isolated and their contacts can be quarantined. It is a much more effective strategy to do that. And effectively only isolate or quarantine a small proportion of the population, as opposed to having to isolate or effectively have the whole population in a stay at home mode. We all know the downsides of doing that economically and socially. However, in these kinds of circumstances, there may be no alternative because if you do not have the capacity to do the kind of tracing, the kind of detection, the testing that's needed, it's very, very demanding.[63]

Thus, countries without contact tracing had 'no alternative'. And yet, as we saw in Chapter 2, late in 2019 the WHO had published a report titled 'Non-pharmaceutical Public Health Measures for Mitigating the Risk and Impact of Epidemic and Pandemic Influenza'. In this report, a team of scientific experts had been led by the WHO Collaborating Centre for Infectious Disease Epidemiology and Control, in the School of Public Health at the University of Hong Kong. The experts had considered the range of options for mitigating a pandemic, including workplace and school closures and travel restrictions. When summarising their 'considerations of members of the guideline development group for determining the direction and strength of the recommendations', they had looked at 'Ethical considerations: The human right to freedom of movement should be considered, as should potential adverse economic impacts, particularly in vulnerable populations such as migrant workers.'[64] And two years later, the lead author of this report, Ben Cowling, reiterated that test and trace could not be implemented in poor countries.[65] But no one was listening, and the poorest people in the world were pushed into unsustainable policies with devastating consequences for their futures.

***

The initial impacts of the unprecedented virus suppression policies were certainly devastating in poor countries. However, that is not to say that the experience of 2020 in high- and middle-income countries was good. In fact, from North and South America to Spain, Italy, and the UK, the impacts of the Covid restrictions on health, education, and livelihoods were disturbing, and it was clear right from the start that this was the case. This was the antithesis of the professed aim of progressive politics, to reduce inequalities of gender, class, and race, because the impacts of these measures saw the swiftest increases in history in all kinds of inequality.

This was in fact a classic playbook for what the poster child of left political critique, Naomi Klein, had described as a 'shock doctrine' for disaster capitalism in her 2007 book of the same name.[66] Klein had initially written a piece in May 2020 for *The Intercept* in which she saw the parallels, and issued a warning of how the MegaTech sector was aiming to take advantage of the crisis.[67] However, as time went on her critical voice waned—taking the rest of the mainstream left with it.

As soon as the severe lockdowns were imposed in wealthy countries, the fact that they worst affected the poorest and most vulnerable was clear. As the journalist Emily Maitlis put it in a famous intervention on the BBC in early April 2020: 'They tell us that coronavirus is a great leveller. It's not. It's much, much harder if you're poor.'[68] For those in Europe with sufficient living and garden space the lockdown offered a respite from the daily grind and the opportunity to economise on everything from family holidays and children's clubs to travelling to work. For those living with young families in overcrowded flats with little outside space; single parents trying to cope with autistic children starved of their usual support; live-in domestic helps from Spain to Hong Kong prevented by their employers from leaving the house for six months for fear they would contract the virus; or those in areas without ready access to inexpensive and healthy food supplies, the reality was always going to be different.[69] As Martin Kulldorff summed it up: 'Ultimately, lockdowns protected young low-risk professionals working from home—journalists, lawyers, scientists, and bankers—on the backs of children, the working class and the poor.'[70]

As 2020 unwound, the impacts of the policy decisions that had been taken became impossible to hide from. Inequality within European countries increased by as much as 12.1 per cent over the course of the year.[71] By late December 2020, reports predicted that the Covid recession would drive 2 million families into poverty in Britain alone;[72] in Chile, a country with a population of less than 20 million, a World Bank report of late November said that 800,000 new poor people had been pushed into poverty.[73] There were several causes of this in high- and middle-income countries such as the UK and Chile: the fact that the lowest paid often had insecure contracts which could easily be terminated, the inability of employers to supplement the furlough wages (where these existed), and the evaporation of cash-in-hand work such as babysitting and odd jobs.

Meanwhile, a report from the Resolution Foundation found that not only had poverty dramatically increased, but the rich had actually increased their savings during the 2020 lockdown: 'over one-third of the richest fifth saw their savings increase in the early months of the crisis. By contrast, lower-income working-age families are more likely to have seen the amount they save each month fall during the lockdown.'[74] Thus, not only was this policy leading to terrible consequences but the rich were actually benefitting from it—not only the likes of Jeff Bezos and Elon Musk, but also their wealth managers working in financial services and ancillary industries.

The United Kingdom provides a good window onto the socio-economic gulf which was expanded enormously in the first months by these policies. The situation for the lowest paid in Britain was compounded because although low-paid workers were often furloughed, many of their employers could not afford to top up the amounts paid by the government through the scheme. A November report in the *Guardian* noted that around half of Britain's lowest-paid workers were furloughed on reduced pay, and that 2 million of these did not receive the employer's voluntary 20 per cent contribution, placing them on a salary well below the minimum wage.[75] The human costs of this in the short term included increased risks of domestic violence and abuse caused by the new stress on family finances—abuse directed both at children and at women, as a variety of reports have shown.

In the case of children, a distressing report in November 2020's *New Statesman* described how a social worker in London had visited one dwelling: 'A ten-year-old child in the household told how her mother had slapped her across the face, and she had knocked her head on the cooker as a result. "Good," her mother told her. "That's what you get." A couple of days later, the girl changed her story. "Oh no, I was wrong, everything's fine—I was just saying that because I was frustrated." She asked if her mother would go to prison'.[76]

Meanwhile, Britain's largest domestic abuse helpline saw an enormous increase in call volumes. In June 2020 these were up 80 per cent on normal figures, while there was a surge of women seeking places in refuges to escape abusers.[77] Stalking offences rose from 27,156 in 2019 to over 80,000 in 2020.[78] Then, in November 2020, there were estimates that there had been fifty murders of women in situations of domestic abuse during the first British national lockdown.[79] These were described in the media as 'shock new figures', but in truth there was nothing surprising about them: they had been all too predictable, right from the start, and many of the reports which were produced about the impacts of the lockdown policies reveal the sources of the strain as well as of the despair that can lead desperate people to become increasingly violent, and which can provoke those not hitherto violent, bullying, cruel, or malicious to become so.

In sum, and as was the case in the Global South, the catastrophic social and economic impacts of the virus suppression measures were abundantly clear from the start in high-income countries. A July 2020 report from the UK Child Poverty Action Group (CPAG) based on online interviews with 285 low-income households made the situation clear. As the executive summary noted: '8 in 10 respondents to our online survey reported a significant deterioration in their living standards due to a combination of falling income and rising expenditure. Families who responded in July and early August were less optimistic about their financial situation than those who responded in May or June. Even among those families whose employment had not been disrupted—including those who were not working prior to the pandemic—the majority reported a worsening in their financial situation.'[80] This was a deterioration in conditions where 'most of the families we interviewed are already living close to the poverty line'.[81]

Why was the situation so bad? Some had been made redundant; others had not had their furlough pay topped up by employers; others were unable to take on self-employed work because of additional caring duties. Moreover, as everyone was spending so much more time at home, there were significant new costs: 'Nearly 9 in 10 families who responded to our online survey said they faced additional costs as a result of coronavirus, and were spending substantially more on food, electricity, and other essentials.'[82] The consequence was that over three quarters of respondents were struggling to pay for food and utilities, and over half had difficulties in meeting housing costs.

However, inequalities were not only manifest in terms of material goods, wealth, and household bills. There was a massive gulf in psychological well-being and mental health exacerbated by the crisis. While those able to work remotely were adapting to their new and more flexible lifestyle, almost half the respondents to the CPAG survey reported new physical and mental health problems. As the report authors put it: 'Some commentators have talked about the benefits of living a simpler lifestyle under lockdown with more time to nurture relationships and enjoy nature, but for nearly all of the parents we spoke to life has been a constant struggle to make ends meet and manage the additional pressures on family life.'[83] As the *Guardian* reported, in many families 'life in lockdown held back progress of under-fives' as 'parents spent less time reading, chatting and playing with their children during the pandemic'.[84] So much for nurturing relationships.

In the United Kingdom, many on the left blamed these problems on an incompetent administration led by Boris Johnson. Yet there is no evidence that different leadership would have produced much better outcomes. The cause of this dramatic increase in poverty in 2020 was not the serial incompetency of the British government. The cause was the lockdown strategy, as global comparisons among rich and middle-income countries show. For across high- and middle-income countries in Europe and the Americas, the impacts of the lockdown policies were exactly the same. This was a war on the poor, as well as a way of newly immiserating many of those who had previously been middle class.

In Spain, governed by a leftist coalition, 1 million Spaniards lost their jobs when the lockdowns began, and the International Monetary Fund predicted that Spain's economy would fall by 12.8 per cent, the highest level among developed economies.[85] Madrid's food banks were swamped with demand, with one seeing it increasing from 400 people per month before the pandemic to 3,500 per day by September 2020.[86] Soon, so-called 'hunger queues' began to emerge at soup kitchens.[87] The ever-growing numbers of people requiring help meant that by October 2020 the amounts available to each family began to fall.[88]

One year later, by September 2021, Spain's economy was still the slowest to recover in the entire European Union. By that time it was still 8 per cent below pre-pandemic levels in terms of GDP, while France and Germany were just 3 per cent worse off.[89] It needs to be remembered that Spain had had one of the most stringent lockdowns in Europe, and the consequences were that the economic impacts were among the most severe—showing that there is a direct correlation (and, we would like to add, causation) between policy and socio-economic impact.

This was not, therefore, an outcome caused by right-wing governance, but by the policy that was chosen. In France, 800,000 jobs were projected to have disappeared by the end of 2020, and the National Secretary of Secours Populaire (SP), Houria Tareb, noted that October that more and more people were turning to them.[90] SP had helped 2 million more people than in 2019, an increase of 50 per cent, and as in the United Kingdom it was young workers who were the worst affected.[91] The government estimate was of 5 million people in need of food aid, and the impacts were not just restricted to large cities but being seen across the country. As Christian Favier, President of the County Council of Val-de-Marne, put it, 'we have never seen this before'.[92] Yet in spite of the work of charitable organisations and self-help groups, by November these, too, were struggling, facing a fall in donations and dwindling stores of supplies.[93]

In the US, the confusion and distress sown by then-President Trump's contradictory and bizarre initial response to the pandemic was compounded by the effects of the global slowdown. An October 2020 report from the Economic Policy Institute found that workers aged sixteen to twenty-four were facing high unemployment and an uncertain future. Unemployment in this group had soared 16 per cent to 24.4 per cent in spring 2020 compared to spring 2019, almost double the 8.5 per cent increase for workers aged over twenty-five.[94] The worst affected were members of minorities; the spring 2020 unemployment rates were even higher for young Black (at 29.6 per cent), Hispanic (27.5 per cent), and Asian American/Pacific Islander (29.7 per cent) people.[95]

Meanwhile, in middle-income Latin American countries the impacts of the lockdown policies were just as severe. A good example is Chile, often held up as a model of neoliberal economic policies. Yet just a couple of months into the Covid crisis, Chile was dealing with the return of poverty levels not seen since the Pinochet government in the 1980s. Communal cooking facilities had emerged up and down the country. In poor neighbourhoods of the capital Santiago, community leaders said that the state had abandoned them, forcing them to establish these 'communal pots (*ollas comunales*)' themselves.[96] By June 2020 there were said to be nineteen *ollas comunales* in Puente Alto, forty-six in Peñalolén, fifty in Renca, fifty-four in La Pintana and fifty-four also in El Bosque.[97] 'My people are desperate, because they haven't got anything to eat', said one leader, Sandra Cariz from Puente Alto.[98] By June, the municipality of this one *barrio* of Santiago estimated that it had already distributed 272,000 rations of food.[99]

As some of those involved in the Chilean food crisis said, this was also an opportunity to show solidarity. The creativity and strength needed to confront the crisis could bring social cohesion and a collective approach. Nevertheless, the impact on those already experiencing poverty was atrocious, here as elsewhere on the continent—and as in the rest of the world, it was clear that this was going to be the case right from the outset. In 2020, the unemployment rate was predicted to increase from 8.1 per cent to 13.5 per cent in Latin America, and the poverty rate by almost a quarter from 30.2 per cent to 37.2 per cent.[100] In Panama, the Centro Nacional de Competitividad produced a report in late August 2020 predicting the rapid rise of extreme poverty in the country.[101] In May, the country's index of economic activity had fallen by a historic margin of over 40 per cent, unemployment was predicted to increase by over 20 per cent, and extreme poverty by 25 per cent.[102] As the report authors emphasised, this would hugely increase inequality throughout the country, and in the wider Central American region.[103]

Some readers will say that an economic decline was inevitable whatever policy had been taken to confront the pandemic. Yet the evidence from Spain is clear that the hard lockdown had a correspondingly devastating economic impact. Indeed, research conducted in China's Hubei province (the epicentre of the initial reported outbreak, and poster child for lockdown advocates) drawing on 78,931 households during the initial lockdown confirmed this picture, revealing that 'the percentage of households at high risk of returning to poverty (falling below the poverty line) increased from 5.6% to 22% due to a 3-month lockdown'.[104] On the other hand, the evidence from Sweden and Tanzania which we considered earlier in this chapter shows that countries which took a different path had different economic outcomes. Moreover, in high-income countries a non-lockdown policy certainly would not have exacerbated inequalities in the ways that lockdowns did, since there would have been no need for furlough schemes and therefore the low-paid would have continued to receive their full salaries while not having to face the increased costs of spending more time at home.

In the case of rich and middle-income countries, some important aspects of the social and economic effects need to be emphasised. In the first place, there was the increase in poverty among those already poor, and in the second—and no less devastating—there was the creation of penury among those who were previously middle-income families. This is noted in all countries affected by the lockdown response. In the United Kingdom, IT consultants needing access to the homes of clients found their incomes collapsing.[105] In Spain, farmers working to supply meat and cheese to the large hotel and restaurant sector found orders disappearing.[106] In France, SP were being visited by people from socio-economic classes they had never seen before.[107]

The misfortune of working in what now seemed to be archaic industries, requiring contact with actual human beings, was thus plunging whole sections of the middle classes into a poverty that they had never known. This was part of the deeper economic struggle and transformation taking place in 2020, between those who had prospered under earlier iterations of capitalism but were now hitting the buffers and those who worked in technology-related industries and other fields which suited remote working. With the wealth of billionaires soaring, many who worked in industries that had benefitted under earlier economic frameworks were forced into penury. This wider struggle within capitalist structures was projected as part of the inevitable collateral damage. But the radical continuity with previous trends of growing inequality suggests that something deeper and more powerful was occurring: wealth was being concentrated as never before, and the very same interests which gained from this were pushing the 'single narrative' of the lockdown strategy and the 'collateral damage', as we saw in Part 1.

Perhaps the most disturbing inequality of all to emerge in high- and middle-income countries related to gender. This strong gendered impact of the lockdown policies is perhaps one of the most shocking things about the way in which they were rolled out so universally without any pause to consider the impacts. In terms of poverty, women were at a much higher risk than men of the aggregated impacts of the new policies. But there were perhaps even worse consequences in terms of domestic violence. This became clear throughout 2020, with soaring rates of domestic violence throughout the world in richer as well as middle-income countries. In Australia, one expert described 2020 as 'the worst year for domestic violence that any of us who are in the sector now have ever experienced'.[108] In Lebanon, there was a 51 per cent increase in reports of domestic violence.[109] In Israel, a June 2021 report said that there had been an 800 per cent increase in domestic violence complaints.[110] In Latin America, murders of women soared in Brazil and Mexico, and the numbers of women disappearing increased dramatically in Peru.[111] The increase in domestic violence in Mexico was so bad that several states banned the sale of alcohol.[112]

For all the claims that these impacts were the result of poor management by right-wing governments, left-wing governments in Spain and Portugal did not see a materially different outcome. Furlough schemes did not reach everyone nor replace whole salaries or fund additional household costs resulting from more time spent at home. The problem was not therefore the politics of the personnel in charge of the lockdown policy. It was the lockdown policy itself, something which everyone had agreed in January 2020 was completely unprecedented in human history. That policy had brought an unprecedented shock to world societies, in which there was only going to be one winner: the global rich.

2021: consolidating winners and losers

As 2021 began, the northern hemisphere entered another rolling cycle of lockdowns and virus suppression strategies while the rollout of the new Covid-19 vaccines commenced. Meanwhile, a new administration took charge of the White House, and President Biden—on a 'progressive' ticket with Vice-President Kamala Harris—sought to redress some of the appalling inequalities and harms that had been caused by the first year of Covid policies. But that was a tough one to sell, since it was progressives in the US who had been most in favour of severe lockdown policies.

All in all, Biden's efforts were going to prove to be as useful as placing a sticking plaster over a chainsaw wound. In fact, as 2021 passed and 2022 began, the evidence of the harms and inequalities catalysed by the lockdowns became so massive that longstanding advocates of the virus suppression policies began to row back their rhetoric. Some—such as Sir Jeremy Farrar of the Wellcome Trust and Kit Yates of the UK's Independent SAGE—claimed that it was 'meaningless' to claim to be a lockdown sceptic, since 'everyone' was a lockdown sceptic.[113] This was ironic, since in the autumn of 2020, a UK Conservative MP, Neil O'Brien, had put up a website on which he discussed these issues and made it clear that 'lockdown sceptics' were what he called 'Covid sceptics': 'A number of myths have persisted that suggest Covid isn't particularly dangerous, or that governments shouldn't try to contain the virus with lockdowns and other distancing measures. We call the people who promulgate these myths even after they have been disproved "Covid Sceptics".[114]

It was in 2021 and 2022 that some of the deeper consequences of the Covid policy measures became clearer: these were the vast transfer of wealth from the poor to the rich across the world, and a massive immiseration of the poor in Africa, Asia, and Latin America. A World Bank blog from October 2021 showed that, across the world, the poorest sectors of society had lost on average 7 per cent of their earnings since before the pandemic, and that this had not improved in 2021. The richest 20 per cent of earners would recover half of their 2020 losses, while the poorest 20 per cent would lose a further 5 per cent in 2021.[115] Then, in December 2021, a UNICEF report estimated that an additional 100 million children were growing up in poverty compared to the pre-Covid period.[116]

Meanwhile, in Rotterdam, in February 2022 Jeff Bezos made a request of the mayor.[117] The American Amazon founder and richest person in the world asked him to dismantle the historic Koningshaven Bridge, so that a superyacht worth US$500 million which he had had built nearby could exit to the sea. The bridge had been rebuilt between 2014 and 2017, at which point the local authorities had promised that it would not be touched again. Still, the bridge was too tall for the yacht to pass through—and Bezos, whose wealth increased by US$37 billion between March 2020 and May 2022,[118] was offering to pay for it. The mayor complied with Bezos's request (or command).

The enormity of the transfer of wealth upwards can only be made sense of through stories like this. While the world has been swimming in data as never before since the start of the pandemic, that data has also deadened the possibilities of action—but stories of these obscenities can be more moving, and the citizens of Rotterdam indeed gathered to greet Bezos's yacht as it passed out to sea, and pelted it with rotten tomatoes.[119]

Away from such neo-feudal displays of wealth, we can consider the depth of these impacts by looking first at what happened in high- and middle-income countries, before then considering the Global South. In the US, once in office, the Biden administration took steps to try to soften the regressive impacts through the stimulus package ('American Rescue Package') of US$1.8 trillion which was passed early in 2021.[120] This did alleviate unemployment and the effects of the Covid economic recession, but nevertheless these effects were enormous: having given SMEs an economic heart attack, government offered an aspirin by way of treatment. In the states of New York and New Jersey, nearly one third of small businesses closed in 2020.[121] By the middle of 2021, according to a report from *Alignable*, nearly two thirds of American small businesses were still earning less than half of their pre-pandemic monthly earnings, while only 50 per cent of Canadian SMEs were open.[122] Data showed that by the end of May 2021, there were 38.9 per cent fewer small businesses open in the US than at the outset of 2020.[123] Meanwhile, larger firms and tech giants grew their wealth exorbitantly, as we have already seen: the stake of investment giants such as BlackRock grew to 15 per cent of the US housing market, focusing on residential areas and 'depleting the inventory of the precise houses that might otherwise be obtainable for younger, working- and middle-class households'.[124]

By the end of 2021, the unequal impacts of the measures taken in the US to fight Covid-19 were hard to hide. The expiry of the expanded child tax credit measures in December 2021 had seen nearly 4 million children quickly fall into poverty, with the withdrawal of free meals compounding the situation.[125] Inflation of basic goods was rising across America, long before the Russian invasion of Ukraine. Women and mothers were particularly badly affected, the worst hit by the rising costs and lowered wages brought on by Covid measures.[126] An Associated Press report found that prices increased more in the US in 2021 than they had in any given year for the previous thirty-nine years.[127] Reports from January 2022 described the severe impacts that this inflation was having on the daily lives of poorer workers who had taken income cuts as they had been unable to work through the pandemic.[128] While attempts can be made to blame these on Vladimir Putin's military aggression, the facts are clear: the huge supply shock caused by the global lockdown policies had already produced inflationary pressures which had impacted poorer and middle-income families in America (and elsewhere) well before the dawn of 2022.

Thus the impacts of the Covid restrictions in the US had fallen disproportionately on poorer families—and a high number of them came from minority communities. It was the education of poor children that was most likely to be disrupted, with impacts on mental and physical health; some researchers predicted that the socio-economic achievement gap was likely to widen by 30 per cent, although subsequent studies suggested the actual gap was smaller.[129] It was poorer people who could not work remotely whose pay was cut, and who then had to face the impacts of rising inflation caused by the lockdowns. As the poor suffered, the rich grew richer: this was a picture found around the world, confirming the analysis that the Covid restrictions were as regressive a policy as any since the Second World War—the antithesis of the focus on lessening inequality supposed to be at the heart of progressive politics.

Across the Atlantic, in Europe, the regressive impacts were very similar to those in the US. By the second half of 2021, it was clear that the pandemic response had created an epidemic of poverty, mental health collapse, and inequalities, the legacy of which would last for a generation. A February 2022 report published by Caritas suggested that labour market inequalities had soared across Europe throughout the previous two years.[130] These inequalities had had all kinds of other regressive impacts. A Eurobarometer report from March 2022 suggested that 77 per cent of women across Europe felt that the previous two years had seen an intensification of physical and emotional violence directed at women, and that 38 per cent of women surveyed had seen their salaries fall.[131]

Looking closely at the example of Spain brings home just how severe the overall effects of the measures taken to combat Covid-19 proved to be. In Spain, a report from March 2022, two years after the onset of the pandemic, painted a devastating picture: the poorest households in Spain had lost 27 per cent of their income, while the richest had lost just 6.8 per cent.[132] The Gini coefficient, which measures inequality within countries, had increased by as much in one year as it had increased in the US in the previous three decades:[133] neoliberalism has long been seen by critics on the left as the handmaiden of growing inequality, but it was a poor substitute for the success of Covid restrictions in impoverishing those already poor.

Regional data brought home the reality of what this meant for people's daily lives. In Valencia in eastern Spain, the number of people experiencing severe social exclusion rose by almost 100,000 between 2018 and 2021, to 12.5 per cent of the population.[134] In Madrid, meanwhile, the evidence was that, well over a year after the onset of the measures, the number of families dependent on food handouts, and unable to recover even the precarious economic life that had sustained them before the pandemic, was large: many had faced loss of employment on the one hand and an increase in time spent at home with associated costs on the other.[135] Moreover, as in the US, many of these families in Madrid came from minority communities—around 50 per cent according to some estimates[136]—and there had been an increase of 5 per cent in the proportion of the Madrileño population suffering from severe social exclusion.[137] As in the US, the impact of this on mental health had been severe: in one survey, 85 per cent of Spanish children and young people said that they had experienced psychological disturbance brought on by the restrictions associated with the pandemic.[138]

In the UK, meanwhile, a similar pattern can be traced. One example came through the impact of the furlough scheme. By the middle of 2021, it had become clear that those who had predominantly been supported through this scheme, and yet were most likely to lose their employment finally when it was wound up in September 2021, were women and the young. Part-time workers, a significant majority of whom were women, were badly affected by the end of the furlough scheme and the increased costs faced by businesses trying to survive in the 'new normal'.[139] Suffering alongside them when the furlough scheme was closed were younger workers, with the Institute for Fiscal Studies showing in a report that those aged 19–24 were the most affected by the end of the scheme.[140] The other side of this evidence, of course, is that it was younger workers who were most likely to have been underemployed during the pandemic, confined inside and without sufficient labour experience to have developed paid work that could be carried out remotely; the lack of purpose and confidence associated with work was surely a factor in the increased mental health and eating disorder crisis for the young.

This socio-economic crisis among the young was apparent in all arenas. A report from June 2021 showed that it was pupils in the poorest areas of the UK who were the worst hit by the policies of school bubbles and the isolation of those bubbles when there was a positive Covid case; this was at a time of rising cases, when 385,000 children were off school in the UK through self-isolation, the vast majority of whom did not actually have Covid-19, and yet poorer children were twice as likely to be self-isolating as their wealthier peers.[141] Child poverty, neglect, and abuse had soared and there was a surge in family breakdowns and foster care referrals (up over 30 per cent),[142] with an increase of 40 per cent in referrals to social services in some areas, the *Guardian* reported in August 2021.[143] Meanwhile, senior educators and police officers warned that many children had been dragged into criminal networks—either as victims or perpetrators—through the endless cycles of school closures: there had been a 61 per cent increase in children entering 'county lines' drug gangs over the previous twelve months, and there had also been a disturbing increase in online sexual abuse.[144]

Beyond all this, and as seen in Chapter 5, in 2021 in many Western countries the social and economic effects of lockdowns were further exacerbated by the rollout of highly punitive, discriminatory, and segregational mass vaccination policies, which caused massive psychological stress and even economic deprivation, as unvaccinated people found themselves not only excluded from social life but in many cases also restricted from working. The unvaccinated came disproportionately from poorer and minority communities in Western nations, and thus once again these unprecedented measures had highly regressive consequences.

***

Turning from high-income to middle-income countries, the case of Latin America makes it clear that one thing the lockdowns certainly did achieve was impoverishment. In Guatemala and El Salvador, families took to waving white flags during the first months of the pandemic in search of assistance[145]—a symbolic representation of the lockdowns' war on the poor that then spread to Malaysia in July 2021, something which community organisers described as 'the clearest sign yet of the economic despair that hundreds of thousands of Malaysia's lower income families have experienced'.[146] As lockdown restrictions were imposed again and again in Argentina, and families found the economic impacts increasingly impossible to manage, what was revealed was 'an extensive unaffordability of lockdowns'.[147]

By the end of 2021, the scale of the impacts was becoming clear. In December 2021, Alicia Bárcena, Executive Secretary of the UN's Economic Commission for Latin America and the Caribbean (CEPAL), stated that 'the effect of the crisis on household income means that after the pandemic we find 200 million people in poverty, and 78 million people in extreme poverty [...] as the size of the middle class has fallen by 14%', while 167 million children missed out on a whole year of teaching and the percentage of the population in education fell from 66 per cent to 53 per cent.[148] As *El Peruano* reported in September 2021, 'the coronavirus pandemic wiped out in a matter of months, and in some cases weeks, 20 years of progress in the fight against poverty'.[149] The United Nations found that an additional 5 million people had fallen into extreme poverty in 2021 in Latin America, and that this had reached levels which hadn't been seen for thirty years.[150]

What were the causes of this enormous crisis? Many large businesses permanently closed down their offices, with home-working becoming an indefinite reality across Latin America—on a continent where comfortable home living and working space is far from universal, even for the middle classes.[151] This also saw the viability of tens of thousands of city centre businesses collapse almost overnight, from which the middle classes found it hard to recover. According to the ILO, 26 million people in Latin America and the Caribbean lost their employment.[152] At the same time, the large numbers of informal workers in the Latin American economy (54.4 per cent in 2021 according to the World Bank)[153] meant that the restrictions on movement and daily life crippled that major part of the economy. In Lima,

70 per cent of young people lost their employment, and in Colombia the rate of youth unemployment almost doubled from 16 to 30 per cent.[154] Naturally, the impacts on public health of this twin-pronged assault on socio-economic subsistence were massive—which may explain why countries with severe lockdowns such as Argentina and Peru fared badly when it came to levels of excess deaths.

Alongside the increases in the levels of absolute poverty, and as in high-income nations, one of the major impacts of these socio-economic transformations came for the middle classes. From Chile and Colombia to Brazil, many across the region described the collapse of the Latin American middle class. In a series of reports titled 'Scars of the Pandemic', published in October 2021 by the *Conectas* platform for Latin American journalism, the impacts of this socio-economic war on the middle class were brought home by reports that focused on informal work, gender equality, and medical care.[155]

One of the case studies of these reports was the Chilean Rodrigo Salinas, an English teacher in Santiago whose salary had fallen from US$1,800 dollars per month to nothing during 2020. Instead of providing furlough wages or equivalent support, the Chilean government's response to this crisis was to permit Chileans to withdraw funds from their pension pots—with terrible long-term impacts which were little discussed. With insurance and savings used up, and future pension payments already reduced, Salinas was working as a taxi driver, struggling to make mortgage repayments, and fearing for his family's future.[156]

In terms of gender equality, the restrictions were catastrophic, as these reports showed. On the one hand, women's employment levels in Latin America were put back by more than a decade according to the United Nations.[157] On the other, there were terrible increases in domestic violence and abuse, with increases of 170 per cent reported by women's rights movements in Colombia.[158] Femicide surged across the board, and by a staggering 53.3 per cent in Venezuela in 2020 compared with 2019.[159] Whatever the stated resolutions of world bodies and governments to eradicate gender inequalities and violence, the preferred policy methods adopted to combat Covid-19 did more in six months to destroy progress made than any policy framework of the previous 100 years.

The impacts in terms of specific countries soon became clear. In Peru, there had been a 10 per cent increase in poverty, with 3 million additional people falling into precarity.[160] In Mexico, suicides among the under-eighteens grew to record levels.[161] The Mexican Organization for the Rights of the Child published a report in January 2022 which found that there had been increases in child poverty, marginality, racism, and sexism, and severe impacts on the health of children.[162] In Paraguay there were enormous impacts in gender-based violence[163] and a collapse of many informal workers' incomes and savings.[164]

Latin America offers a sobering possibility for connecting Covid lockdowns to socio-economic impacts. On the one hand the beneficial impact of strong Covid restrictions on Covid mortality was low on a poor continent, as the comparison of the experiences of Argentina and Peru with Brazil and Nicaragua discussed in the previous chapter show. People could not 'lock down' without coming together in other ways to access food, helping the virus to circulate. Meanwhile, the sledgehammer taken to livelihoods increased anxiety, domestic violence, and the health impacts of poverty. It destroyed huge swathes of the middle class, created dramatic increases in extreme and relative poverty, drove record levels of school abandonment, and destroyed the education of a generation—as we will see in the next chapter.

As we've mentioned already, what had taken place was a gigantic real-time scientific experiment, and now the evidence is in: by any reckoning, and as had happened in high-income countries in Europe and North America, the lockdowns were a disaster.

***

If things were bad in high- and middle-income countries, they were far worse for the world's poor. We can now look at how the evidence grew through 2021 and 2022 as to how this ongoing crisis affected Africa and Asia. On the one hand, similar traits can be found to its effects in richer countries, revealing a continuity in the human experience which shows how much everyone on the planet has in common with one another. And yet on the other, while the impacts were similar in style, the substance was far more devastating for the world's poor.

In May 2021, we received an email from a labour rights activist in India. It was more than a year after Narendra Modi signed India's initial lockdown decree on 24 March 2020, and this was a missive seeking assistance which we could not give. The email described how (literally) millions of migrant labourers in the state of Tamil Nadu alone were still at that time without food or resources of any kind, abandoned by their former employers and offered nothing to help them return to their villages hundreds of miles away: the correspondent requested help in trying to unite these people with their families and remove them from the destitution in which they had been placed. We have already seen in this chapter how the initial lockdown in India had crippled the hundreds of millions of migrant workers, but in fact, as this missive showed, the socio-economic consequences of this devastation continued throughout the next two years—and will continue long into the future, setting back decades of progress on gender rights, education, and public health.

Across South and South-East Asia, the picture was steady. As so often, it was workers in the informal market who suffered the most. A report by the ILO from November 2021 found that eighteen months into the Covid restrictions, 40 per cent of domestic workers, street vendors, and waste pickers were still earning less than 75 per cent of their pre-Covid earnings.[165] This means penury: hunger, ill health, and the inability to fund basic needs for children such as clothing and education. But why was the informal economy so shattered by the restrictions? With wealthier people working from home where possible, the focus of the economy shifted to online and the work gained by rickshaw riders, street vendors, market stall holders, and owners of small restaurants and the like collapsed.

Shortly into another cycle of lockdowns in Bangladesh in July 2021, the *Dhaka Tribune* ran a piece on the impact of the restrictions on rickshaw drivers.[166] Takings had collapsed by around 500 per cent, in one case from 1,570 Tk in a day (c. US$18) to 280. During the 2020 lockdown, their income had fallen by a more modest 50 per cent. But in a situation where there were 2.2 million rickshaw pullers in Dhaka, the impact on them and their families easily affected up to 8 million people in this one demographic alone. Given these conditions, it was not surprising that by March 2022, one estimate suggested that the Covid crisis had pushed 4.7 million people in South-East Asia into extreme poverty.[167] And yet this is just the tip of the iceberg, since tens of millions of others were pushed to all kinds of extremes.

It was not just informal workers in the South-East Asian economies who suffered. Where strict lockdowns were enforced and factories closed, workers of all kinds bore the brunt of the 'war on Covid'. Vietnam was a good example of this. Hailed by the world's media as a success story in the fight against the virus, the experience on the ground was rather different. When a new wave of lockdowns was imposed in July 2021, lasting on into September, many factory workers experienced extreme penury—with no government support, and already in debt racked up during the previous fifteen months of restrictions.[168] Official statistics from Ho Chi Minh City alone suggested that between 3 and 4 million people had been plunged into economic difficulty since March 2020. Thus what was deemed a success by some epidemiologists on the one hand was often a human tragedy on the other.

This was borne out by the experience of Sri Lanka. By September 2021, it was widely acknowledged that a hunger crisis had exploded on the island nation. The BBC reported a food emergency in September 2021, directly connected to the new wave of lockdowns that had come to the island in the wake of the Delta variant.[169] The government had been unable to protect food supplies, following soaring foreign debt burdens, inflation, and a collapse in tourism, all of which were directly connected to the global Covid restrictions. By January 2022, one report described how food prices had doubled in the previous twelve months alone, causing hunger across the country.[170] The cost of living was such, one interview said, that 'we cannot even think of having a balanced meal'.

It's worth reiterating that this inflation in the basic cost of living for the global poor long predated the Russian invasion of Ukraine. As early as June 2021, one analysis for the Thomson-Reuters group described at length how 'soaring food prices squeeze family budgets around the world'.[171] Interviewees from South Africa and India to Costa Rica and Thailand described how the price of basic staples had already increased by between a quarter and a half during the previous year, causing enormous hardship. Mukesh Kharva, a door-to-door utensils salesman in Mumbai, India, described how his family could not have their staple meal of 'khichdi'—a dish of rice, lentils, tomatoes, and onions—because prices had gone up: 'These are terrible times and so many people have suffered loss of income. Shouldn't food prices be controlled even more now?'

The UN agreed that by June 2021, world food prices were already at their highest level for a decade.[172] When compounded by the employment crisis in the informal sector and through lockdowns, hunger was already a huge problem almost a year before Vladimir Putin's military aggression could be blamed for it. In this catastrophic situation, mental health spiralled out of control, with large increases in suicides across the region. A study from Nepal found a 16 per cent increase in suicide rates during the first year of the pandemic.[173] In the Philippines, the suicide rate increased by 57 per cent in the same period.[174] One NGO worker in South-East Asia, Helen Tindall, described how she had never known a single case of suicide during three years of working with local government and health agencies in one country; then in a single week of July 2021, she heard of three male suicides, two completed and one attempt.[175]

Of course, many advocates of strong Covid measures claimed that these multiple appalling tragedies would have been even worse without them, and that they were needed to protect long-term health. Yet this theory was not borne out by numerous studies which showed that the long-term impacts of the measures were worse by far than Covid. One study from Indonesia analysed the long-term health impacts of the socio-economic crisis brought on by Covid restrictions and found: 'The reduction in long-run real income due to the Covid-19 shock may reduce life expectancy by up to 1.7 years, compared with what could otherwise be expected. In contrast, even if the Covid-19 death toll to date were 40 times worse, life expectancy would fall by just two days.'[176]

Again, looking in detail at one case study can show how these factors came together in the most toxic of brews. The most haunting example is India. As 2021 came to an end, it was possible to begin to take stock of the consequences of the completely unprecedented upending of the daily lives of hundreds of millions of people. Across the board, in terms of education, economic subsistence, social welfare, and virtually every index it's possible to imagine for societal health, the consequences had been catastrophic.

The evidence on the socio-economic conditions in the country is stark. A heart-breaking report from the People's Archive of Rural India described the awful struggles faced by the rural poor.[177] One family recounted how their son had disappeared after migrating over 500 miles to seek work as a sugar-cane cutter. On the one hand, the ability to earn day labour had collapsed and yet, on the other, it was much harder to find work in cities because of the impacts of the restrictions. Another report from Lucknow from July 2021 described an enormous increase in indebtedness, hunger, and food prices. One interviewee, Asha Devi, had had to mortgage her land and was nearly out of food, having stopped buying milk, halved her use of cooking oil, and purchasing lentils only once every 10 days.[178] At the time, interviews with seventy-five households in eight villages in Uttar Pradesh (India's most populous state) showed household incomes had slumped nearly 75 per cent on average.[179]

Evidence from the urban poor described a situation that was little better. A study conducted in Lucknow and Pune in January and February 2021 described the situation:

> With lockdown restrictions being moderated in the cities, a large number of workers have returned to their employers to find that their old jobs aren't available anymore. The survey reveals that the availability of work has become staggered. Some workers are able to find work on a particular day but may struggle to get work for the next few days or even weeks. During the pre-lockdown period, the workers were able to find work for 20–25 days in a month, but in the post lockdown era, they only managed to get work for 10–15 days.[180]

This situation in terms of available labour was compounded by a widespread fall in day-rates of around 10 per cent.[181] Household income deriving from labour had fallen by an average of 50 per cent by February 2021, long after the initial lockdowns were over.[182] The desperate situation of informal urban workers was movingly described by one interviewee in this important study: 'Laxmi Rathod, a female worker in her 20s from Pune's labour market, says "We did not even get a single rupee during the lockdown. Whenever we went and begged for some money or support, we were beaten up by the police. Despite that, we desperately had to beg to find some food."'[183]

Widespread hunger followed with the further lockdown restrictions enacted for the Delta variant from May 2021. A report in *The Hindu* during the June 2021 restrictions described factories allowing only a 30 per cent workforce and near-universal food rationing among poor families, while the contributions of NGOs and other assistance had declined.[184] Researchers from India's Azim Premji University painted an even starker picture, stating in May 2021 that 230 million Indians had been pushed into poverty during the previous year, with an increase of 20 per cent in urban areas.[185] Meanwhile, the impact on the urban middle class was also huge. A report from the Pew Research Center in March 2021 found that the Indian middle class had shrunk by 32 million people during the first year of the pandemic.[186] This was having a major impact on the prospects of young Indian graduates, creating a white-collar labour crisis alongside that of the urban and rural poor.[187]

It's hard to read this material and not recognise that the people best equipped to make decisions about their healthcare are not armies of well-paid public health officials in Geneva and New York but communities who are affected themselves. Had rural and urban poor communities in India decided on their own account that shutting themselves away for months at a time was the best thing for them, then they would surely have been the best placed to make this judgement. Instead the judgement was made for them by global political masters—and the consequences, as we have seen, were such that it seems unlikely that it is a judgement that they would have made for themselves.

It's worth remembering that the WHO was founded on the principle of community-based healthcare—not top-down pandemic decision-making.[188] If one positive thing could come out of this catastrophe, a return to WHO founding principles would be near the top of the list.

***

The African continent has the largest number of low-income countries in the world—and yet, as we have seen, it has also been the continent where the effects of Covid-19 have been the lowest. By the end of 2021 and early 2022, it was clear that the impact of the combination of measures taken in the 'war on Covid' had been devastating—even though, as we saw in the previous chapter, Covid-19 itself had led to at most a 2 per cent increase in the continent's mortality.

We can begin with the economic impacts. As we have seen already in this chapter, initial predictions suggested almost half of Africa's formal jobs might be lost. In the end, the situation was not so severe, but remained devastating. A report from the Nigerian Statistics Agency in September 2021 suggested that 20 per cent of Nigerian workers had become unemployed during the previous eighteen months.[189] In Angola, the National Statistics Agency declared in December 2021 that the youth unemployment rate had almost doubled in the previous two years, from around 32 per cent to just under 60 per cent.[190] Meanwhile, in a continent where according to the ILO 85 per cent of the population works in the informal sector, the majority of whom are women, the severity of the impact on the informal sector was devastating.

As noted above, eighteen months into the pandemic, as many as 40 per cent of informal workers were earning only a quarter of what they had earnt before the pandemic began.

Some examples of these impacts make clear how far-reaching they were. Nigeria provides some important case studies. One published in July 2021 describes how Margaret Okuomo, a cleaner working on an informal employment agreement at the University of Lagos, lost her work and her US$44-per-month salary with no government benefits to replace them. She then had to use up all of her savings to feed her family until these too ran out by 2021, as she waited for the university to reopen fully.[191] This can begin to explain the awfulness of the cost-of-living crisis which, as we have seen in this chapter, had been growing ever since the lockdowns began: all the scant savings developed over many years of extremely hard work had already gone because of the 'Covid emergency'.

Tobi Akinde, a researcher at the University of Ibadan, made a film in December 2021 which highlighted the plight of informal workers in Ibadan during the pandemic: the fear of violent police enforcement, the steep decline in market earnings, and the complete lack of jobs available in Nigeria.[192] According to Olutayo Adesina, most people in Nigeria tried to find ways to avoid complying with the lockdown measures in 2020 since they were a fast-track to hunger. People in the informal market could manage for 3 days but no longer, he said, and soon took to using abandoned roads to transport food and provisions, while where the federal government sought to enforce the restrictions as in Lagos, widespread looting from the '1 million boys' gang began as a result.[193] 'This was not a situation which the federal government could maintain,' Adesina said, 'so they had to abandon it. And they will not try it again.'[194]

The fact that many people ignored or circumvented the lockdown measures where they could (although this was certainly not always possible) may explain why the impacts on formal employment in Africa—though severe—were not as bad as initially predicted. Nevertheless, the knock-on effects of global supply chain bottlenecks and the strangulation of the informal market meant that the impacts on economic activity soon became severe across the continent. Food insecurity soared, exacerbating a trend that had already grown in the previous five years. Between 2019 and 2020, Africa's share of global food-insecure populations rose from 54 to 63 per cent.[195] Restrictions on movement meant that harvests were lost in countries from Angola[196] to Ghana,[197] and though there were some government programmes to alleviate this, nothing could be done to address the fact that food had been lost—adding to the spike in food prices which began in 2021 and beginning the world's inflationary march which can only produce hunger and ill health for the African poor.

What this meant was made clear by a country like Zimbabwe, which saw an increase of over 20 per cent in the proportion of its population living in extreme poverty, from 6.6 million to 7.9 million people.[198] A report from the Mo Ibrahim Foundation in June 2021 described how Africa faced 'severe repercussions for unemployment, poverty, inequalities and food insecurity', and that already there had been serious increases in violence.[199] This was seen on the ground, with looting and street violence breaking out in July 2021 in South Africa as the impacts of the economic shocks became ever harsher.[200]

The economic shocks of the supply-side crisis and inflation were compounded in the first months of 2022 when a debt crisis took hold across much of the continent. By January 2022, the World Bank was reporting an urgent debt crisis for the world's low-income countries. Covid loans had not been the panacea to the initial lockdown shock that had been hoped for, as many countries had rejected them for fear of increased borrowing costs brought on by credit downgrades.[201] By this time the economies of wealthier African nations such as Ghana and Nigeria were in a parlous state. One Ghanaian economist warned that the country's economy was on the brink of collapse,[202] while in Nigeria, even though economic activity had begun to recover, inflation had started to accelerate, especially for food items crucial for consumption among the poor and vulnerable.[203] This was already creating fuel shortages and associated price increases in Nigeria, prior to the Russian invasion of Ukraine.[204] Thus while in the short term the impacts of the initial lockdowns on daily life and people's ability to feed and clothe their families were immense, in the longer term the impacts of the associated debt crisis threatened to be even worse.

Where had this debt crisis come from? As we have already seen earlier in this chapter, multilateral donor organisations recognised at the onset of the Covid-19 crisis that only a massive debt relief package could mitigate the effects on impoverishment and livelihoods precipitated by the response to the new virus. African nations had already had a high foreign debt burden, but the combination of the collapse in demand for goods and services with that in remittances from the African diaspora in high-income countries had had a devastating impact on the continent's debt burden. This had been recognised right from the outset, and yet the long march to lockdown had begun—and no one was allowed to question whether this had not been a catastrophic top-down policy mistake of 'global governance'.

The question of remittances offers a key example of how decisions taken to 'save lives' through lockdowns in the West had serious implications for livelihoods in the Global South. It shows the implications of the ultra-nationalist policies of countries such as Australia and New Zealand which closed their borders. In Africa, remittances from relatives in richer economies account for half of private inward investment in the continent; although relatives sent money where they could during the crisis, the sudden contraction had serious implications.[205] Elsewhere, a good example was the situation in Yemen, where the collapse of remittances by 80 per cent or US$253 million had caused food shortages and price hikes in a country which imports 90 per cent of its food.[206] And yet by October 2020, Yemen—alongside Burkina Faso, the Democratic Republic of Congo, Nigeria, and Somalia, designated one of the five worst hunger zones in the world—had received zero Covid-related nutrition assistance such as had been promised by donor countries.[207]

This failure to meet aid pledges was something that, as we saw in the first pages of this chapter, should have been surprising to no one in global policy circles. Indeed, as of mid-October 2020, donors had pledged only 28 per cent of the total Covid relief package that had been mooted in March, meeting just a fraction of pledges in every sector: gender-based violence (58 per cent), protection (27 per cent), health (26.6 per cent), water, sanitation, and hygiene (17.2 per cent), food security (10.6 per cent), and nutrition (3.2 per cent).[208] The *Guardian's* Economics Editor Larry Elliott reported in August 2020 that the IMF were predicting that the world's poorest countries faced a lost decade without urgent remedial action, yet none of this appears to have affected either major policy choices or the media discourse surrounding the politics of the pandemic.[209] Having pressured African nations to follow a disastrous lockdown route which was contrary to the WHO's own 2019 report on the need to balance economic factors in responding to a pandemic, the international community abjured itself of responsibility for the debt crisis that was produced.

The pathetic response from the international community began with a debt relief package in April 2020.[210] However, this initial package neither reduced nor eliminated debt; it merely suspended payments for six months, a pledge which was extended for a further six months at a meeting in October.[211] There was a failure to cancel future debt repayments, and moreover, as Oxfam reported after this meeting, private sector debt was not included in the package.[212] Considering that private sector debt held by enormous corporations such as BlackRock Asset Management, Goldman Sachs, HSBC, and JP Morgan constituted 47 per cent of the total debt package of poorer nations in 2018, this meant that half of the debt crisis was not resolved at all.[213] In spite of continued lobbying by powerful figures, including David Malpass, the President of the World Bank, these institutions did not budge on their schedule of debt repayments, meaning that they remain due. Even Malpass, a Trump administration appointee and someone reported by the *New York Times* as historically reluctant to disburse large sums in new loan money to poor nations, was reported as saying: 'these investors are not doing enough and I am disappointed with them'.[214]

Private institutions claimed that they were unwilling to offer debt suspensions as it was not clear whether African nations would simply use the relief to borrow further from Chinese investment arms. Moreover, they said that poor countries had not requested relief, as credit rating agencies had begun to treat debt suspension of nations such as Cameroon and Zambia as a default, leading them to downgrade their credit ratings and jeopardising their future ability to borrow.[215] And this indeed turned out to be the case, with a smaller number of countries than imagined taking on these additional loans. Debt suspension initiatives sought to postpone about US$20 billion owed by seventy-three countries to bilateral lenders between May and December 2020. Yet, in the end, just forty-two countries received relief totalling US$12.7 billion.[216]

The consequences were enormous. Desperate not to default on their debts and trigger a credit crisis, which would ruin their economies even further than the slump in demand had yet achieved, nations were forced to take further loans. In November

2020, Kenya borrowed US$690 million from the IMF; this was classed as debt relief, while adding to the already huge indebtedness of the country.[217] Bangladesh, a country with an annual budget deficit of US$17.65 billion accrued by late November, was forced to allocate US$6.2 billion to service external debt agreements. In Zimbabwe, GDP contracted by 10.1 per cent during 2020, and almost 50 per cent of the population were classed as living in extreme poverty.[218] Meanwhile, trying to look for alternatives to this mortgaging of future spending on health, education, and welfare, many countries did seek debt refinancing in China, extending the country's influence on the continent.[219]

By January 2022, in spite of reluctance to take on new loans, the fact was that low-income countries faced an additional US$10.9 billion in debt repayments.[220] And this is where the deepest impact of the Covid crisis in the Global South lies. For as these emergency credits and additional loans are extended, what is at stake is future spending to improve health and education outcomes for billions of people, as countries may be forced to cut back on vital services in health and education, either to meet their foreign debt's higher servicing costs or simply to meet lenders' requests. Indeed, an April 2022 Oxfam report noted that almost 90 per cent of loans negotiated with the IMF to deal with the fallout from the pandemic were conditional upon developing countries implementing tough austerity measures.[221]

Across Africa, the Covid restrictions, increases in indebtedness, and educational shutdowns reversed decades of progress in tackling gender inequalities—while current and future health was mortgaged to pay for a new virus which wasn't even that serious on the continent. There weren't just increases in child marriage, prostitution,[222] and school absenteeism, but also in access to basic healthcare. Studies from Kenya, Uganda, and Zambia found serious falls in women's access to antenatal care, while teenage girls who relied on schools for access to sanitary equipment were abandoned to make the best of it themselves.[223] One study confirmed that domestic violence rates had soared across Uganda, Kenya, and Senegal during the pandemic, to name just three countries.[224]

Meanwhile, what was the daily experience of this like? In Senegal, people ate once a day if they were lucky—and adults passed up their portions of meals to give some to the children.[225] In Nigeria, by May 2022, the one thing preventing food riots, according to Olutayo Adesina, was an immense collective effort in the community.[226] In Ghana, George Bob-Milliar described how even two years after the initial lockdowns, there was very little money in the informal economy where 85 per cent of people work: it had all been spent to pay the debts of the initial lockdowns, and now there was nothing left.[227] In Angola, as we've seen, almost two in three young people had no employment of any kind—twice the figure from two years before.

It's hard to make sense of so much destruction, throwing out of the window proclaimed policy priorities such as protecting the rights of women, girls, and children, reversing inequalities, and reducing poverty which had been the cornerstone of global health for several decades. Children locked up for months at a time without being allowed out in Angola. Medical facilities shredded to target a disease which isn't even a major factor for most Africans. Futures destroyed. Debts accrued, making the prospect of climbing out of this awful cavern ever harder. All in the name of 'global health'.

***

Two years after the pandemic had been declared by the WHO on 11 March 2020, there was scope for reflection. By early 2022, as we have seen in this chapter, the evidence was immense: the Covid restrictions had immiserated the poor and enriched the rich more quickly than any other policy decision taken in human history. It was impossible not to wonder whether the immensity of the approach taken to suppress the virus had been wise—and what the consequences would be.

There was some attempt by the mainstream press at a slow reversal of positions. When Carl Heneghan, Professor of Evidence-Based Medicine at Oxford University and a regular critic of lockdown policies, was banned from Twitter in March 2022, the *Guardian* columnist Zoe Williams criticised the decision and said that he had been following a 'gestalt' view of health throughout the pandemic.[228] This was ironic when her *Observer* colleague Sonia Sodha had described Heneghan and his Oxford colleague Sunetra Gupta as 'captured by anti-science' in October 2020.[229]

While media commentators tried to adjust to the reality that Zero Covid policies had failed, the scientists who had backed the restrictions began to attempt to reframe definitions. Instead of acknowledging the colossal harms to decades of progress on the rights of women, the young, and the poor, those who had been the strictest advocates for Covid restrictions instead took to trying to rewrite history as the impacts of their preferred policy became clear, while gaslighting those who had always criticised the lockdown policy. In a *Guardian* op-ed published to coincide with the second anniversary of the UK lockdown, Devi Sridhar asked, 'Why can't some scientists just admit they were wrong about Covid?'[230] In an essay which would make for rich pickings for a psychoanalyst, Sridhar attempted to paint Zero Covid as a policy that she had only supported while vaccines were being developed—in spite of huge amounts of evidence that showed that she had favoured an elimination strategy even after the vaccine rollout began.[231] Others such as the science writer Laura Spinney tried to compare Covid with measles—an inappropriate comparison where vaccines against measles and/or infection provide lifelong sterilising immunity, but this is not so with Covid.[232]

Meanwhile Kit Yates, a prominent member of Independent SAGE, wrote an op-ed for the *BMJ* in which he both attacked opponents of lockdowns as having uncaring values, and also—incredibly—claimed that 'no one is in favour of lockdowns',[233] throwing out two years of evidence to the contrary as if they counted for nothing. Unfortunately for Yates, the same day that his piece was published, Sir Chris Whitty admitted that the long-term health of children had suffered and their life expectancies had fallen as a result of lockdown,[234] showing up, for the cynical ploy that it was, Yates's claim that lockdowns had protected long-term health and that those who opposed them did not value this.

In all this furious rewriting of history by those who had supported such catastrophic policies, concern for the impacts of their policy choices on hundreds of millions of people came a poor second to concern for their reputation. What of the children whose educations and future work prospects had been ruined? The hunger, and the disease caused by it? The erosion of women's reproductive and sexual health? Let alone the impact on the elderly abandoned isolated in care homes, single parents with autistic children, and the world's huge informal workforce who had had the ground ripped from under them? None of it had mattered in the War on Covid—and now the price would have to be paid.

The bill was huge. Debt levels in poor countries at record levels according to the World Bank, with the external debt burden of the poorest countries increasing by 12 per cent in eighteen months[235]—and, even more dramatically, with the IMF now forcing countries to introduce austerity measures in exchange for the loans, with major impacts on education and healthcare.[236] By late 2021, tuberculosis deaths were at a 7-year high across the world because of a delay in notifications and outpatient visits, with a decline of 1.3 million cases detected around the world according to the WHO.[237] Measles outbreaks were on the rise because of the impacts on vaccination programmes we have described in the previous chapter.[238] Meanwhile, by July 2021 Oxfam was reporting that eleven people per minute were starving to death because of hunger exacerbated by Covid lockdowns.[239]

Not only had lockdowns in poor countries had little tangible effect in reducing the spread of the virus—as indeed had been predicted following the Ebola lockdowns in Liberia and Sierra Leone in 2014—but they had worsened the prospects for safeguarding future public health. Had Covid-19 been a virus which targeted people indiscriminately, the panic and catastrophic impacts might have been excusable. But it wasn't, and the recent history of pandemics and modelling should have made it predictable that the initially high predicted CFR would prove to be exaggerated. Lockdowns were imposed, and then in spite of the evidence already racking up as to their colossal harms, they were imposed again and again. After two years, the benefits of their work in mitigating the virus were unimpressive. At the same time, a March 2022 report from Oxford University described the generalised picture we have seen in detail in this chapter: huge increases in the numbers worried about food supplies, mental health crises, and a large increase in the gender employment gap.[240]

Some advocates of the lockdown measures that were taken will claim that things could and should have been better organised—and that the fault lies not with the measures themselves but with the lack of appropriate implementation strategies. Yet this fails to take into account the inflation which was caused long before Russia's invasion of Ukraine, with devastating consequences for the food security of the poorest—alongside the debt crisis in developing countries that has been provoked.

Meanwhile, for wealthy people and the super-rich, there was a bonanza such as could scarcely have been imagined two years before. One report showed that by the end of March 2021, employment had declined for lower-wage workers by 27.6 per cent and for middle-wage earners by 4.5 per cent, while for high-wage earners (over US$60,000) it had increased by 2.5 per cent.[241] An Oxfam report showed that between March 2020 and March 2022, the wealth of billionaires increased at ten times the rate of the previous two decades—a period which had already seen massive increases in inequality.[242] Elon Musk's wealth increased by 1,000 per cent, to over US$250 billion.[243] There were fifty-one new billionaires in India alone in 2021.[244] But 263 million people risked being pushed into poverty in 2022, while the billionaires' playground (otherwise known as the planet Earth) was put back on the road.[245]

So what does it mean to face what Oxfam predicted could be a '10-year retreat in the fight against poverty'?[246] Where is the logic in terminating vaccination and maternity programmes in the world's poorest countries because of the threat of Covid-19, risking hundreds of thousands of lives according to the UN?[247] How is it decided that it makes sense to close the children's hospital in Sierra Leone completely from 6 April to 24 May because one of the doctors has contracted Covid-19, and then to cut the number of beds back from 190 to 110 to meet WHO social distancing advice?[248] These measures imposed by the computer-projection models were illogical; they were counterproductive, and contrary to existing policy; they were symptoms of a panic brought on by the 'single-narrative' version of science and pandemic response, and of the logic of a global society which now lives in a world where the computer is always right, even if it is profoundly, humanly wrong.

8

AND THE WEAK SUFFER WHAT THEY MUST

THE OLD AND THE YOUNG

The Covid-19 restrictions, the lockdowns, and the universal vaccination drive have all been propelled by the stated desire to preserve life and preserve health services. As we saw in Chapter 6, health services were not protected, and it is very debatable that any lives were saved. At the same time, enormous collateral harms ensued, as we saw in the previous chapter. But what of the older generation: surely these measures at least protected them and secured their quality of life into old age?

In this chapter we demolish this myth, while looking at the impacts of the Covid restrictions at both ends of the demographic spectrum. As with the case of the impacts of lockdowns, we take a global approach, looking at the effects both in high-income countries and in the Global South. For old people, lockdowns made them more isolated, caused their mental health to deteriorate, and exacerbated mortality from other conditions such as Alzheimer's. For the young, the measures were an assault on their mental and physical health, and on their social and economic futures.

We have chosen to focus on these groups because the impacts are so stark, inhumane, and contrary to historical cultural norms—and because such impacts really bring into focus how lockdown was a policy designed by the middle-aged for the middle-aged, as the behavioural scientist from the London School of Economics Paul Dolan put it.[1] Given the enormity of the effects, it also forces us to ask some difficult questions: why did progressives support such regressive policies, and what will the long-term impacts of this be?

We can start with two cases which give a sense of just how extreme the restrictions and their impacts have been. The first is from the Philippines, which had what is widely acknowledged as the most extreme lockdown in the world: all in all, the under-eighteens and over-sixty-fives were not allowed out of their homes for twenty months, until November 2021.[2] It's quite hard to grasp the enormity of this policy for a country where the majority of people may not have decent access to basic amenities.

The impact for children was especially concerning. A lot of Filipino kids live in very cramped conditions. As one report noted, 'poor Filipinos typically escape the heat from their tin roofs and windowless parlours by stepping outdoors and promenading in the streets.'[3] Many neighbourhoods contain houses of apartments with no yards, narrow alleys, and homes tightly crowded next to one another.[4] Of course, in practice, enforcement of the lockdown law was impossible to achieve completely in these circumstances, and people often emerged into neighbourhoods once the police had gone—but still there were many cases where the law was complied with absolutely, and where young kids born just before or during the pandemic had never been outside.[5]

The awful tragedy was of course that the alleged protection of children from Covid-19 (from which all the age-related mortality shows they were at very low risk) exposed them to all manner of other dangers. This did not just relate to anxiety and depression, but also profound evils such as sexual exploitation; children were effectively incarcerated with their abusers with no recourse or escape. The risks of this became heightened because of the confinement and stress brought on by the restrictive measures and the pandemic, so that according to one report 'there are clear indicators that Covid-19 is creating an unprecedented surge in online abuse of vulnerable Filipino children'.[6] The major child helpline in the country, Bantay Bata, registered a 167 per cent increase in calls between March and June 2020, and the Philippine Department of Justice's Office on Cybercrime registered a 260 per cent increase in cyber-tips on online sexual abuse.[7] And when Filipino children were finally allowed to go out, public attitudes had become so toxic and entrenched that, according to one report, 'policies and popular attitudes continued to single out children, to a point where parents who let their kids go out are being shamed'.[8]

The Philippine case was extreme, but not unique: it was illegal for children in Angola to go outside for almost seven months in 2020.[9] Indeed, in March 2021 UNESCO released a report in which they stated that one in seven of the world's children— approximately 330 million kids—had lived under rules requiring or recommending that they stay at home for most of the previous year, and that 139 million of these had lived with rules obliging their lockdown at home during this time.[10] A good example of what an intermediate case looked like was Colombia, where children aged from six to seventeen were allowed out from May, but only within 1 kilometre of their homes; bicycles and rollerblades were banned, children's play parks were closed, and these measures remained in place until September.[11]

The cruelty of requiring hundreds of millions of people in poor countries—where they may have no sanitation or electricity—to stay at home for such extended periods is staggering. Nor is it at all clear what greater public good policymakers can possibly have hoped to achieve through taking this stance. However, it may be no accident that Angola, Colombia, and the Philippines were all governed by authoritarian leaders who doubtless felt they stood to gain by macho grandstanding: lockdown measures were a gift to authoritarians, and these political consequences of the measures are an important aspect which we will come on to in the next chapter. This was glimpsed when in January 2021 Filipino President Rodrigo Duterte overturned the decision of the country's coronavirus commission that 10–14-year-olds should be allowed outside in February: as a report in *The Lancet* later noted, 'President Rodrigo Duterte stated that new stay at-home orders were to protect children from infection from new Covid-19 variants. [...] He said they should just "glue their attention to the TV all day".'[12]

Meanwhile, to consider the other demographic extreme, we can reflect on the 'kind and caring' Covid policies in wealthy countries through the tragic case of Mario Finotti.[13] Finotti was a 91-year-old resident of a care home in the town of Papozze, in the Veneto region of north-eastern Italy. He died in January 2022, trying to escape what for him was a prison by tying a bedsheet around his waist and lowering himself down from an upper-floor window of the care home in which he lived, which had barred residents from leaving to protect them. The gulf in human sympathy which had emerged in the restrictive policies 'keeping people safe' in care homes was revealed by Finotti's retirement home director, Luca Avanzi, who told the *Corriere della Sera*: 'It is not known what was going through his head because, from a psychological point of view, he was peaceful. Also, last week, his niece had spoken to the psychologist via video call and a good psychological picture of the elderly man had emerged.'

The 'psychological picture' of this distraught and isolated nonagenarian, then, was 'good'—but clearly not that good. Children, we were told, were resilient—but as the evidence emerged of the crimes committed against them, it turned out that they were not that resilient either. Meanwhile, large numbers of elderly people died alone. The enormity of the restrictions imposed, and of their impacts on both young and old, is such that it is hard even to formulate the questions that must be asked: why were those child psychologists who screamed about this from the beginning, like Ellen Townsend and Michael Absoud, ignored? Why did meaningless phrases about 'preserving life' win out over the evidence: that children were at little or no risk from Covid-19, while enormous harm was being caused to them by keeping them at home; that teachers were statistically at no greater risk than any other profession (the justification for closing schools);[14] that schools were far from being 'super-spreaders',[15] as ubiquitously claimed for months; and that the life expectancy of people in care homes in wealthy countries was only two years (and one year in settings without nursing),[16] and their human dignity at the end of life required contact with their loved ones, even if their lifespan was eroded by a small amount? And what does all this mean for the future, given the traumas that an entire young generation now carries and the difficulties this may cause them later in life? To give just one indication, for the Angolan social scientist Elsa Rodrigues, the trauma of this confinement is likely a driving cause of a huge increase in reports of fights and aggression now faced in Angolan schools.[17]

For the young, we desperately need to understand how this came to pass, why it persisted for so long even though the impacts were clear right from the start, and what the evidence for the consequences really is. And for the older sectors of society, and those nearing the end of life, we have to try to understand what it says about modern society that it was deemed kind to isolate them from their loved ones and to deprive them of all their daily activities. In the end, it's hard not to agree with the Mozambican sociologist Pedrito Cambrão, who wrote in late May 2022:

> The current decay of Western democracy and morals marks the end of the Western order [...] Starved of spirituality and meaning, the secular West has essentially turned science into a religion and scientists and healthcare workers into a priestly caste that cannot be challenged.[18]

The experience of older people

We begin this chapter looking at the impacts on the elderly—those most at risk from Covid-19, and who were said to have the most to gain from these policies. But was this true? As seen in the previous chapters, it is highly questionable that the prevailing pandemic policies—lockdowns, the initial disregard for care home risk, the ignoring of the potential role of early anti-Covid therapies and then the rush to vaccinate everyone rather than prioritise those at risk—were effective even from a purely life-saving and age-enhancing perspective. Notwithstanding this, from a more nuanced quality-of-life perspective, the evidence is even more damning. Far from embracing the wisdom and potential of elderly people, and what they have to offer in interaction with younger sectors of the population, the lockdown response pushed them out of society—isolating them and shutting down the most meaningful elements of their lives whether through barring contact with their children and grandchildren or through shuttering their social activities.

Care home residents such as Mario Finotti suffered the most. On the one hand they were not protected from Covid, as the death figures showed. On the other, many aged residents, often suffering from dementia or terminal illness, became ever more unwell. People described in horror how their parents had died in care homes of terminal cancer during the first lockdowns, and how for the last few days of their lives all they could do was talk to and comfort them via Facetime.[19] Even by the end of 2021, severe restrictions on visiting rights remained the case in many of these institutions, from Argentina to the United Kingdom (often coupled, by that point, with discriminatory practices against the unvaccinated).[20]

The lockdown policies have been especially promoted as protecting the elderly and the vulnerable, but we must ask how well all of them have actually been served. Healthy elderly people who were in practice not at great risk from Covid-19 have been unable to see their loved ones without fear and to share the wisdom of their lives with those who most need it—the young who must grow on through the world. The voluntary and social activities which often give much meaning to their lives—whether in a religious institution, an outdoor conservation space, or a space for indoor recreation—have been closed for long periods. The frail and infirm in care homes, meanwhile, have been starved of contact with their loved ones as they enter the final phases of life. Many may think that to write a book that attacks lockdowns is to reveal the authors as callous and cruel Malthusian spirits, insensitive to the fate of older people, but we would argue to the contrary that lockdowns have constituted an assault on the rights of elderly people to be offered the love and care of those who love them when they most need it in life, and when they also have so much to give in return.

What was the impact on the health of elderly people of these isolation policies? Around the world, the devastation was immense. Much of the media coverage has focused on Western nations, but things were little better in low-income countries. A systematic review and meta-analysis of over 100 studies from Africa, published in October 2021, showed that the prevalence rate for depression during the pandemic was higher than in other continents.[21] One qualitative study from Ghana revealed the negative impacts on people's daily lives, with increased isolation and loneliness, insomnia, and withdrawal from key social networks and daily lives fuelling depression.[22] In Nigeria, older adults suffering non-Covid chronic conditions such as diabetes, dementia, and cancers were unable to attend treatment centres during the first wave of the pandemic;[23] meanwhile, a 2020 study from rural Nigeria found that 'the Covid-19 pandemic has led to a reduction in both material support in the forms of food and money, and intangible support in the forms of assistance, communication and care, due to limited social contact. Furthermore, the economic consequence of the pandemic may have severe implications for the health and wellbeing of older people.'[24]

In Latin America, the picture was very similar. In Ecuador, a study undertaken in 2020 showed a large increase in depression and isolation among older people. Whereas before the pandemic 60 per cent of elderly people had seen relatives daily, during the pandemic 40 per cent of respondents saw them hardly at all, and while only 18 per cent said they had felt sad before the pandemic, that figure had increased to 71 per cent.[25] In Cuba, one study showed a 47 per cent increase in anxiety levels among older people to February 2021.[26] In El Salvador, the anxiety associated with the pandemic was revealed when Ruperto Umaña, a 73-year-old living in the town of San Miguel, killed himself in his garage on receiving a Covid-19 diagnosis.[27] In sum, older people in low-income countries faced increases in human, social, economic, and public health deprivations; depression soared, and in some extreme cases—as we have seen above—they were actually barred from circulating outside their homes. Even assuming that some older people were saved from Covid by these policies, we can ask how many of them subsequently 'died of sadness' as a result of those very same policies.

In high-income countries, the consequences were equally shattering. Much focus in the United Kingdom has been on the decision to discharge untested elderly people from hospitals into care homes, which had devastating impacts on Covid mortality during the first wave in 2020,[28] as was discussed in Chapter 6. At the same time, there are many other aspects of the pandemic which have been shattering for the lives and well-being of the old: in the first year of the pandemic, this was perhaps best captured by the story of police being called in Britain when a woman tried to sneak into a care home to move out her 83-year-old husband, after being denied visits for eight months.[29]

However, away from the care homes, for older people living in their own homes the situation was also very sad. Alzheimer's deaths in the UK increased overall by a quarter during the first year of the pandemic.[30] Certainly, since the WHO's factsheet on dementia notes that 'risk factors include depression, social isolation [...] [and] cognitive inactivity', all features associated with lockdowns, it's impossible to escape the conclusion that they had a large part to play in these increases.[31] Indeed, according to some studies, loneliness increases the risk of death by 26 per cent.[32] By February 2022, Age UK reported that 33 per cent of older people felt more anxious, that 34 per cent felt less motivated to do things they enjoyed, and that '[the] harrowing results of the research reveal that many older people are experiencing anxiety, memory loss, low mood and depression. In some cases, older people report feeling suicidal.'[33]

Why, then, was it seen as a caring response for older people to isolate them? The only older people who may have benefitted from this approach were wealthier couples who could provide one another with company, and had sufficient living and amenity space comfortably to weather the storm—a small segment of the population, who would have been quite capable of isolating themselves in any case had they chosen to do so.

Meanwhile, for the rest of the population, deaths from dementia soared. Disturbingly, many more deaths from Alzheimer's took place away from medical and palliative care, with people isolated in their own homes. One report showed that by October 2020, the number of people dying from dementia in their own homes in the United Kingdom had risen by 79 per cent: as Samantha Benham-Hermetz, Director of Policy and Public Affairs at Alzheimer's Research UK, put it, 'it's likely that factors such as social isolation and people's fear of coming forward to access the medical care they need has led to such a huge increase'.[34]

This pattern of isolated deaths of older people was common across the Western world. In the early stages of the pandemic, elderly people dying in American hospitals had to have the final goodbyes of their children relayed to them via a nurse, as families were barred from visiting.[35] A June 2020 report from Chicago found that many older Americans living in subsidised housing had been dying alone in their apartments, as outreach workers began to work from home and staffing levels dropped.[36] In the UK, isolation caused by lockdowns also saw a huge rise in bodies found decomposing at home, as the numbers of people dying alone and out of sight soared.[37] Meanwhile, the fear and anxiety brought on by the economic collapse also brought many tragedies: in France, a 65-year-old brother and his 54-year-old sister were found dead in their home in Lens, having stopped eating owing to hyper-indebtedness brought on by the Covid economic crisis.[38]

Alongside the increases in the fear, trauma, and anxiety of those dying alone at home, there was a huge increase in depression among older people across the board in Western countries, as in Africa and Latin America. Studies confirmed this in the UK, and in many other countries.[39] In a report published by the Spanish paper *El País*, Ana Velasco, a 70-year-old from

Madrid, said that 'this is embittering the end of our lives'; a picture emerged of people isolated, unable to participate in their regular activities which had provided a sense of community and solidarity, and unsure how easy it would be to resume them.[40] 'The new normality', as the reporters put it, was of an 84-year-old sitting alone in his social centre which he used to visit with friends, watching a TV soap in an empty bar from behind a mask.

It's hard to consider these cases without feeling a sense of anger, shame, and disgust—anger that older people were put in this position, shame at the way in which society colluded in claiming that this was for their care, and disgust at the consequences. Some form of restrictions while health services were prepared was of course advisable—but starving older people of human and social contact, and ensuring that their lives dwindled away into anxiety, fear, and bitterness, served no one. This was all done with the stated aim of preserving life. And yet, as noted in the introduction, we must recognise that this approach to death—of stretching out a lifespan for as long as possible—is one that is very particular to modern Western culture.

In sum, during the lockdowns of 2020 and 2021 older people were abandoned and not cared for—and those who suffered the most were generally the poorest members of society, those without decent living and amenity space in which to make the isolation semi-palatable.

The impact of pandemic policies on the young

Around the world, it has become clear during 2022 that the impacts on young people of the lockdowns have been shattering. And yet in truth it was always evident that this was going to be the case—and that, moreover, these impacts were certain to be rich with inequities, and to target the poorest and most vulnerable members of society. We've seen already in this chapter how this affected children in Angola, Colombia, and the Philippines, and in fact this policy had shattering impacts on mental and physical health and on future socio-economic well-being that may last for decades.

In countries with overcrowded housing, in which electricity and running water are often lacking, the extent of what this has meant for many millions of young people is hard to fathom. But the truth was that young people everywhere suffered enormous harms. A March 2022 poll of Australians aged sixteen to twenty-four revealed that one in four had considered suicide during the lockdown era, and that 15 per cent had attempted self-harm; 82 per cent said that they had experienced mental health issues during the Covid restrictions.[41] In the US, the proportion of mental health-related emergency visits for those aged twelve to seventeen increased by 31 per cent in 2020 compared with 2019; suspected suicide visits for girls in this age group increased by more than 50 per cent.[42] One heart-breaking story from the UK was of Beth Palmer, a teenager from Manchester who dreamt of becoming a singer and took her life in the early days of the first lockdown.[43]

The enormity of the evidence related to the impacts of the Covid measures on young people is staggering. The role of closed schools in creating a nutrition crisis was significant, given the importance of schools in providing meals for poor children; as early as January 2021, UNICEF estimated that 39 billion meals had been missed.[44] Meanwhile, for the first time in two decades, the scale of child labour grew—a UNICEF report from the middle of 2021 found 8.4 million more children had entered the labour market.[45] Harrowing stories of children as young as nine forced to go panning for gold in Uganda,[46] and 14-year-olds abandoning school in Sierra Leone,[47] were many.

When we consider the enormity of the evidence, the question of how far the 'cure' for Covid-19 has been worse than the disease comes ever more clearly into focus—alongside one of the animating questions of this book, which is to ask why left-leaning progressives supported measures certain to lead to a huge increase in inequalities. Children's lives and livelihoods were ruined, when all the while the wealth of the world's richest people increased hand over fist on every continent. As with older people, difficult questions demand to be asked: why was this deemed a sacrifice that young people had to make, when they were at little risk from Covid-19, and why were older people not prepared to take risks on their behalf? Was this in fact the form of discrimination which Liz Cole and Molly Kingsley have called 'childism'?[48] Why was the high-quality evidence of the negative impacts of school closures not taken into account—and when these began to stretch towards the end of a first year and into a second, why was no concerted international pressure taken by governments and global health professionals to bring these closures to an end? And why was widespread talk of a mental health crisis for the young not a factor in policy discussions in the autumn and winter of 2020–21 in the Northern hemisphere, when the decision to close schools was taken again?

In the first place, it needs to be made clear that the devastation of the impacts for the young of the lockdown policies was clear right from the outset. While by July 2022 some publications such as *The Economist* were trying to claim that the impact of 'shutting down schools has been worse than anyone expected',[49] the inequities and mental health devastation were predicted with unerring accuracy in a report issued by UNESCO on 19 March 2020. In that publication, UNESCO reported that half of the world's schoolchildren were not attending school, and moved to develop a global response coalition.[50] Yet as the move into virtual learning developed, what was discussed—only then to be ignored—was the impact which virtual learning had on exacerbating social inequalities because of lack of quiet study space, good internet access, and adequate nutrition in those from poorer socio-economic backgrounds. Closing schools may have been intended to help 'keep societies safe', but it did not keep poor children safe at all.

In the curious paradox by which left-leaning institutions pressed for actions exacerbating socio-economic divides, teaching unions in the United Kingdom were among the most vocal, demanding that the British government 'follow the science' and keep schools closed into July 2020 (and then re-close them in November during the second wave).[51] By December 2020, education leaders and specialists were emphasising the appalling long-term effects that this was having, but it was a tough fight, and unions were among the first to call for schools not to reopen after the Christmas holiday.[52] And that was what happened, with British schools closed again through January and February, so that most children only had at most four months of normal education within the twelve months between March 2020 and March 2021.

All these debates were conducted with their protagonists apparently unconcerned that, as UNESCO made clear in its 19 March 2020 report, the longer that schools remained closed the worse the impact would be in terms of enhanced socio-economic inequalities:

> The adverse impacts of school closures are difficult to overstate and many [of] them extend beyond the education sector. UNESCO has compiled a short list of these impacts to help countries anticipate and mitigate problems. They include:
>
> • Interrupted learning: The disadvantages are disproportionate for under-privileged learners who tend to have fewer educational opportunities outside school.
> • Nutrition: Many children and youth rely on free or discounted school meals for healthy nutrition. When schools close, nutrition is compromised.

- Protection: Schools provide safety for many children and youth and when they close, young people are more vulnerable and at risk.
- Parents unprepared for distance and home schooling: When schools close, parents are often asked to facilitate the children's learning at home and can struggle to perform this task. This is especially true for parents with limited education and resources.
- Unequal access to digital learning portals: Lack of access to technology or good internet connectivity is an obstacle to continued learning, especially for students from disadvantaged families.
- Gaps in childcare: In the absence of alternative options, working parents often leave children alone when schools close and this can lead to risky behaviors, including increased peer pressure and substance abuse.[53]

Thus the warnings were clear: this was a measure filled with risks for children vulnerable to abuse, and bound drastically to increase the inequalities within society. Time and again during the initial onset of the response to the pandemic, questions regarding young people's mental health, educational impact (already discussed in the introduction), domestic abuse by stressed and newly jobless parents, and other issues were raised by experts in the relevant sectors. However, none of this was deemed to matter enough in the all-consuming war on the virus.[54] Although experts from these fields on UK's SAGE warned government ministers several times, very little was done to mitigate these impacts. As a result, these experts warned in late October 2020, the whole generation aged seven to twenty-four risked negative impacts that 'could become entrenched, with potentially enduring consequences'.[55] This collection of experts was also among the first publicly to acknowledge the long-term economic impacts of what had happened on the young.[56]

Beyond these socio-economic impacts of school closures, a range of further devastating effects for the young were predicted by specialists within weeks of the strict lockdown policies being implemented in March. An April 2020 report by Plan International stated that over a third of young Spanish people were at serious risk of social exclusion as a result of the response to Covid-19.[49] Another April report issued by the charity UK Youth was just as stark:

> Feedback from the UK Youth Movement predicts that the impact on young people will include the following, ranked by order of importance (based on number of responses).
>
> 1. Increased mental health or wellbeing concerns
> 2. Increased loneliness and isolation
> 3. Lack of safe space—including not being able to access their youth club/service and lack of safe spaces at home
> 4. Challenging family relationships
> 5. Lack of trusted relationships or someone to turn to
> 6. Increased social media or online pressure
> 7. Higher risk for engaging in gangs, substance misuse, carrying weapons or other harmful practices
> 8. Higher risk for sexual exploitation or grooming.[50]

Moreover, the report made it clear that those providing vital services for vulnerable young people expected to be forced to retrench their provision. Some 88 per cent of service providers said they were certain or very likely to reduce service provision, 31 per cent said staff redundancies were likely, and 71 per cent said that they were likely to reduce staff hours, while 64 per cent said they would probably lose sources of funding.[51] The risks of a devastating impact on the young were clear, and as one respondent put it:

> Young people are facing many worries and challenges at this
> time. Some of us are on zero hours contracts and are losing jobs
> or their work has closed so they have zero income, and no-one is
> around to tell you what's happening and help you understand it
> at all. Many people rely on jobs as an escape from my home life
> [*sic*], especially me, and I have been so eager to go to work. Me
> myself, I have zero knowledge if my work will ever open again, it
> could be back to square one in the job hunt, which will be soul
> destroying for me.[52]

Yet none of these forewarnings were enough to encourage
governments to amend their courses of action. The impacts on
the young simply had no influence at all on the 2020 policy, and
nor on the way in which it was discussed in the press. As the year
approached its end, the implication of this for future generations
became clearer. One headteacher, Dani Worthington, reported
how the gap between poor children and their peers had grown
exponentially through the year. Lack of access to Wi-Fi or
educational input for children in temporary accommodation or
poor housing had had a terrible effect, as the March UNESCO
report had shown would occur. As Ms Worthington said: 'The
educational gap between children with a secure home and
those without is growing as a result of Covid-19—and some
educators fear it may never close'.[57] Thus any opportunity for
social mobility, or for children to drag themselves out of poverty
as young people, was disappearing as a result of the lockdown
policy and the closure of schools.

But nevertheless, in spite of the enormity of the evidence
mounting up, children were forced to go through the whole
trauma again as schools closed at the start of 2021 across much of
Europe and North America. In terms of social justice, the policy
was a disaster not just in the present—it will have effects lasting
for decades. For many young people, however, the economic
impacts were immediate as well as longer-term. In France,

the many younger members of the workforce who rely on the freelance gig economy found the work in this sector drying up.[58] In Spain, a June 2020 study found that there had been an 82.4 per cent increase in the number of young people seeking work in April, in comparison to March: the numbers had risen from 862,801 to 1,350,736.[59] Meanwhile, the unemployment rate for the young had soared to 25.2 per cent, showing double the increase as compared to those aged between thirty and sixty-four.[60] In southern Italy, young people who had worked for years to obtain stable positions as chefs suddenly found themselves jobless and relying on their parents' meagre pensions, as the Mafia swept up most of the job opportunities that were left.[61]

In the United Kingdom, official data showed a dramatic fall in employment for young men aged sixteen to twenty-four: in August they accounted for 60 per cent of the increase in unemployment attributed to men.[62] A survey by the Institute of Student Employers found that the number of graduate jobs had fallen by 12 per cent, with a further decline anticipated the following year.[63] Employers similarly reported a decrease of 29 per cent in internships and 25 per cent in work placements.[64] Moreover, these effects are not necessarily short-term. Economists recognise that there is a serious risk that they might persist for years, since research shows that early phases of unemployment in a career make periods of joblessness more likely in future years.[65]

Given these age-related educational and economic inequalities so abundant in the West, and the different needs and energy levels of young people as opposed to older sectors of the population, a malignant aspect of the political and media response to the virus was therefore a tendency to blame young people for its spread into a second wave in the autumn of 2020. As noted throughout the book, existing scientific research and consensus suggested that stringent suppression of the virus tended to lead to a more severe second wave. And yet, when case numbers began to rise in late August and early September 2020 ministers and health professionals warned that this was because of the actions of young people—not because of their misplaced lockdown policy which previous research had suggested would itself lead to a second peak. This was a classic case of projection, blaming the victim for something that you have caused yourself. It also ignored the fact that across the board the young had already made significant sacrifices.

The campaign began in late July 2020. The WHO's regional director for Europe, Dr Hans Klugge, was reported as saying that younger people might be the cause of the climb in cases that was then beginning.[66] 'We're receiving reports from several health authorities of a higher proportion of new infections among young people', he said. 'So for me, the call is loud enough to rethink how to better involve young people.'[67] By early September, Canadian health officials were pointing to the spread of the virus among the young as part of a global trend.[68] In Britain, it was the Health Secretary Matt Hancock who took to the airwaves in early September to point the finger at young people. Looking at the situation in France and Spain, he noted that 'the second wave started largely amongst younger people [...]. [Y]ounger people spread the disease, even if they don't have symptoms. Don't kill your gran by catching coronavirus and then passing it on.'[69]

The young were an easy target. They were poorer, with less accrued social and political capital, had no easy means to defend themselves, and were less likely to vote at elections than their elders. They were the perfect scapegoat for the strict lockdown policy which had been implemented against the previous scientific consensus and was beginning to unravel into the inevitable second wave, which governments' own scientific advice had predicted.

It's important, too, to recognise that these initial impacts of the 2020 lockdowns were not localised. They united the young across the world in their marginalisation and impoverishment, just as was the case with older people, as we have already seen in this chapter. One report on social media described how a charity in northern Ghana had seen over 100,000 teenage pregnancies since the imposition of lockdowns in March 2020: parents were deprived of income as markets closed, and so teenage girls were forced into prostitution.[70] In India, children under eighteen dying from suicide increased from 9,613 in 2019 to 11,396 in 2020.[71] Meanwhile, in Latin America, 70 per cent of young people lost their employment in Lima, and in Colombia the rate of youth unemployment almost doubled from 16 to 30 per cent.[72] What the lockdown pivots of early 2020 had done was to unleash a socio-economic war on the young—worldwide.

However, what was to become most famous worldwide in terms of this global assault on young people was the question of education—which, as we have seen, UNICEF had summarised very effectively already on 19 March 2020, at the outset of the virus suppression policy. Across the world, it was this gulf in access to education that perhaps most defined the inequalities driven by the lockdown response to the pandemic—and was also common to both rich and poor countries. In Peru, a 16 October 2020 *Washington Post* report described how 'remote learning is deepening the gulf between rich and poor'.[73] A UNICEF report from the country demonstrated that it was the young who were most affected, and that an extra 1.2 million children and adolescents were at risk of falling into extreme poverty.[74] While the rich in neighbourhoods like Miraflores swapped private school for learning in their apartments, the poor in the *pueblos jóvenes* ('young towns', or shantytowns) that ring the city were stripped of education. In a country where the poverty rate had soared to over 30 per cent, higher than it had been for nearly twenty years, there were huge numbers of newly unemployed people—and as elsewhere, in a familiar pattern, the already poor were the worst affected.[75] Parents worried about how to feed their families, and many could not even begin to provide pencils and paper so that their children could do any studying—only one in three households owned a home computer.[76]

In Africa, things were little different. In Angola, where internet data is very expensive and most people rely on mobile phones and messaging services like WhatsApp, the requirements that children and university students should study remotely inevitably had a polarising effect. Schools closed for virtually an entire academic year; as we have seen, young people were forbidden to leave their homes for seven months, and when they did do so the physical space of Angolan schools did not permit them to operate with social distancing and most parents could not afford to send their children to school with soap to ensure regular handwashing. At the same time, social distancing requirements meant that university classes were running at a third of their usual size, and that students had to study remotely for 2 out of 3 weeks. Many simply could not do this, and fell behind their peers who were able to find access to the materials provided.[77] In Mozambique, meanwhile, online learning became the norm in 2020, which was described as a fantasy because the country did not have the infrastructure that could make this possible; certainly, internet speeds in many parts of the country are extremely slow.[78]

Throughout 2020, the harms mounted up, and they were then compounded in 2021. By the end of that year, UNICEF was reporting:

> The quantity of education lost is momentous. At its peak school closures affected 1.6 billion children in 188 countries. Education systems were on average fully closed for 121 instructional days and partially closed for 103 days. [...] Classroom closures continue to affect more than 635 million children globally, with younger and more marginalised children facing the greatest loss in learning after almost two years of Covid.[79]

The world's poor were disproportionately affected:

> The percentage of 10-year-olds in low- and middle-income countries [who] cannot read or understand a simple text will rise to 70%. In Brazil, students in São Paulo learned only 28% of what they would have in face-to-face classes and the risk of dropout increased more than threefold. In South Africa schoolchildren are between 75% and a whole school year behind where they should be, with up to 500,000 having dropped out of school altogether between March 2020 and October 2021. In Ethiopia, primary age children are estimated to have learned between 30–40% of the maths they would have in a normal school year. In Mexico the number of 10–15 year olds not able to read has risen by 25%.

By January 2022, UNICEF was describing the scale of education loss as virtually insurmountable.[80] Meanwhile, the physical and mental health of young people was shredded: the impacts on education were so severe that many doubted that a meaningful recovery was possible. And they were so severe in part because the policies of 2021 continued and exacerbated many of the harms caused in 2020. How to make sense of these appalling tragedies, touching so many people across even rich countries? How can we understand the political process which saw children traumatised, while education was uprooted completely?

One study from the Netherlands found that children being schooled remotely made 'little or no progress while learning from home', in spite of favourable conditions such as good broadband access and equitable school funding.[81] Another study, from Brazil, found that with remote schooling for an entire year the dropout risk rose by 365 per cent, while students' test scores decreased so severely that it was as if they had only learnt 27.5 per cent of the normal equivalent.[82] Meanwhile, a study from the US found 'striking evidence of declining overall cognitive functioning in children beginning in 2020 and continuing through 2021'.[83] All these studies pointed to the fact that learning losses would continue even after schools reopened. Indeed, a study in *JAMA*, based on an understanding of the associations between school disruption and decreased educational attainment and between decreased educational attainment and lower life expectancy, found that missed education during 2020 could be associated with an estimated 13.8 million years of life lost based on data from US studies and an estimated 0.8 million years of life lost based on data from European studies.[84]

So why did politicians continue to promote severe restrictions on daily life, when the outcomes for socio-economic lives, mental and physical health, and the education of the adults of the future were so clearly devastating—and in spite of the fact that, as we have just seen, the evidence for this was enormous within just a few months, and had in fact been predicted? While these experiences cut across communities in all parts of the world, the impacts were certainly more severe in poor countries than in rich ones.

Examples help to put what happened into context. By September 2021, India's schools had been closed for over 500 days, as Finnish economist Mikko Packalen pointed out;[85] this situation was not unusual in the region, since as we have seen they had also been closed for the same duration in the Philippines.[86] A devastating report published that month by a team of four researchers found that 37 per cent of children from underprivileged households in India were not studying at all, and that only 8 per cent had access to online education.[87] In a context where UNICEF had estimated that only one in four children in India had access to a digital device and the internet, the impacts of these ongoing school closures on learning and educational development and on the futures of young people could only have been catastrophic.[88] The human impact of this was brought home by a short film made by Abeer Khan and Kunal Purohit on the plight of Mumbai's sex workers after lockdown, which showed how immensely the education of their children had suffered from the societal collapse.[89] As Anjela Taneja, advocacy lead at Oxfam India put it: 'It is effectively a lost generation. It's a cliche but that probably is how it is.'[90]

In Africa, the collapse of education disturbed educators. From Nigeria and Mozambique to Angola and Gambia, people described the hopelessness of the remote learning model which was recommended. We have already seen that children in Angola were not even allowed to leave their homes for the first seven months of the pandemic, with 'remote schooling' practised in a situation of overcrowded accommodation without electricity and running water.[91] Drop-out rates soared, in a distressing partnership with the increase in child labour that we observed earlier in the chapter. By July 2021, in South Africa it was estimated that half a million additional children were out of school, while younger grades lost a whole year of learning.[92] In Nigeria, a World Bank study saw a correlation of school closures with a near 7 per cent dropout rate (9 per cent for those aged twelve to eighteen) and increased child marriage, with girls 10 per cent less likely to recommence school than boys in north-western Nigeria.[93] This confirmed a UNICEF report from March 2021 warning that school closures and poverty caused by the pandemic measures had placed 10 million additional children worldwide at risk of child marriage.[94] When schools closed, the pressure on adolescent girls became significant in poorer societies, and an October 2021 survey from the Global Schools Forum found that only three schools in Kenya (out of twenty-two surveyed) and eleven schools in Nigeria (out of forty-seven surveyed) reported that over half of their students had had access to learning during the previous eighteen months.[95]

In Uganda, when schools finally reopened in January 2022 after a closure of nearly two years, it was estimated by the National

Planning Authority that up to 30 per cent of the 15 million school-age students would not return to their school desks due to teen pregnancy, early marriage, and child labour.[96] That's 4.5 million children lost to education altogether in Uganda alone; meanwhile, data from UNICEF showed a 22.5 per cent increase in pregnancies for those aged ten to twenty-four in the country in the same period.

As so often, an individual story or perspective can speak much louder than data. In November 2021, Ugandan writer and International PEN honouree Kakwenza Rukirabashaija published a devastating portrait of the wasteland which school closures had left behind:

> Last weekend I took a trip to the Eastern part of the Uganda. I saw [...] an entire generation of our children is being plunged into the bottomless abyss of illiteracy and ignorance. I saw a docile wasted generation of young defenseless victims of Gen. Museveni's warped Covid-19 directives loitering about and dwindling in hopelessness. It is an undeniable fact that the coronavirus pandemic has heavily affected all groups of people but no group has felt the excruciating impact more than adolescent girls in Uganda. A single district like Luuka has reported nearly 1,000 teenage pregnancies ever since the lockdown was declared. Young girls are idle at home and being preyed upon by predators of all sorts. If we were to add results from all the districts of the country, we would find that more than 80% of school girls in the whole country will not be going back to school due to pregnancies. A total of 354,736 teenage pregnancies were registered in 2020, and 196,499 in the first six months of 2021. [...] These are the outcomes of Gen. Museveni's despicable decision to keep schools closed even when the country had attained low positive test rates. The youth are defenseless victims of stupid decisions of one man advised by incompetent greedy elite whose members milk the

Covid pandemic without thinking about the future of Uganda's children. Meanwhile, their own children are educated [outside] Uganda or have private tutors who come to their gated homes to offer them education.[97]

This framework of corruption in the elite as a factor related to lengthy school closures was also noted by educational experts who campaigned for schools to reopen in Turkey.[98] But in the end, when schools did finally reopen across the world more fully in the second half of 2021, the volume of lost learning was vast. In Ghana and Kenya, well-placed observers described how by 2022 attempts to catch up for the lost learning involved cramming more material and information into the already stretched school timetable—meaning that, inevitably, much of the lost material was simply lost.[99]

While these experiences cut across communities in all parts of the world, the impacts were certainly more severe in poor countries than in rich ones. However, as we have seen, none of that is to say that the experience in rich countries was good. In North America, inequalities of all kinds exploded for the young between March 2020 and the end of 2021. We can return for a moment to the question of health. While the lockdown restrictions were said to be designed to preserve public health, their impacts were skewed in terms of age distribution. People aged fifteen and under were 10,000 times less likely to die from Covid than those aged seventy-five or over,[100] and yet the Covid measures had a disproportionate impact on the health of the young. In Canada, a report from July 2021 found that during the first year of the pandemic, people aged under sixty-five were much more likely to have died from 'unintentional side effects of the pandemic' (that is, restrictions) than from Covid itself; while by April 2020 there had been only 1,380 Covid-related deaths in Canada, there had been 5,535 excess deaths, four times the figure of Covid deaths.[101]

What was causing this sharp increase in deaths for younger people at little risk from Covid-19? In the US, evidence suggested that drug overdoses precipitated by deteriorating mental health and isolation had a strong role to play in it. Figures showed that more than 100,000 Americans died of drug overdoses between April 2020 and April 2021, an increase of 28.5 per cent (or over 20,000 people) on the previous year.[102] In other words, the impacts of the Covid restrictions on social isolation, optimism for the future, and young people's employment prospects all conspired to turn vulnerable people towards self-medication through drugs which had disastrous consequences for their health.

There's certainly no question that the mental health of American children and young people deteriorated catastrophically throughout the era of Covid restrictions. In October 2021, the American Academy of Child and Adolescent Psychiatry and the Children's Hospital Association declared a national emergency in children's mental health. Their research had found that between March and October 2020, emergency department visits for mental health emergencies went up by 24 per cent for children aged five to eleven and 31 per cent for those aged twelve to seventeen. Suicide attempts for adolescent girls (aged twelve to seventeen) leading to visits to emergency departments had increased by 51 per cent when comparing early 2021 with the same period in 2019.[103]

So there was strong evidence that the collapse in the mental health of young Americans and Canadians had had negative outcomes in terms of their physical health, clearly a factor in the increased mortality faced by young North Americans in the era of the Covid restrictions. The health burden wasn't being shared equally, and people weren't 'all in this together': the mental and physical health of young people was being sacrificed to fight a disease from which school-age children were at less risk of dying than a lightning strike.[104]

Evidence from the US also showed that there were serious negative impacts of the Covid restrictions on poorer children from minority communities. A September 2021 report published by *JAMA* investigated the impact of school closures in a survey of over 2,300 families with at least one child. The findings showed that children from lower-income families and belonging to minority groups were most likely to experience school closures, and that poorer families also faced more mental health problems linked to school closures.[105] Meanwhile, as the Uvalde school shooting grabbed world headlines in May 2022, according to a report from 31 December 2021 in the *Washington Post*, the previous year (2021) had in fact seen a record number of school shootings across the US, affecting students from minorities.[106]

In other words, the increase in mental health problems in young American people, with direct consequences in terms of physical health, was disproportionately experienced by the poor and by minority communities. Their schools were more likely to be closed for longer periods, with consequent educational and employment disadvantages in the future. There was a disturbing increase in violence and shootings at schools, which can only have been connected to the mental health disturbances faced by young Americans. There was, in sum, nothing progressive about the measures taken to 'stay safe': they protected the wealthy and disadvantaged the poor in the present, and into the future.

The picture from the US was replicated across the Western world. By the end of December, psychologists in Portugal stated that they were facing a mental health 'tsunami'.[107] By early February 2022, doctors at the important Gregorio Marañón hospital in Madrid were reporting a huge increase in the number of adolescents requiring psychiatric treatment.[108] Meanwhile, turning to the UK, the catalogue of evidence for the catastrophe that had been unleashed was genuinely difficult to compute, and hard to put into words. A terse list of the impacts will do: the closure of youth clubs leading to children lost to the streets;[109] a 'tsunami' of anxiety cases in schools leading to persistent absence,[110] with 100,000 children disappearing permanently from school registers by early 2022;[111] half of teenagers reporting battling anxiety and trauma in the wake of the lockdowns;[112] a 50 per cent increase in the number of children in emergency care because of mental health issues;[113] a 50 per cent increase in the number of young people hospitalised because of eating disorders;[114] a 20 per cent increase in death and serious harm caused to children during the period of lockdowns;[115] a 15 per cent increase in referrals of children for specialist mental health help, with the Royal Society of Psychiatrists saying the situation was becoming impossible to manage;[116] a sharp rise in vulnerable children hospitalised for self-harming, with no possibility of being removed to a safe home in which they could be cared for;[117] and a record rise in obesity among children, with cases among 5-year-olds rising by 45 per cent in just one year.[118] By mid-2022, it was being reported that more than 400,000 children and young people a month were being treated for mental health problems—the highest number on record—prompting warnings of an unprecedented crisis in the well-being of under-eighteens.[119]

It's quite a catalogue—and difficult to read without feeling sick. As one doctor put it on Twitter on 3 August 2021: 'It's my last day working with an inpatient children and adolescent mental health service. All I have to say is that we have broken young people socioeconomically, mentally, biologically, and spiritually. We will see the repercussions of our actions for years to come.'[120]

Ultimately, the mental health, educational, and even, yes, spiritual consequences of lockdowns for younger people are the most pernicious aspect of this whole story. Because while a case can be made that the strictly economic consequences of lockdowns could have been mitigated by greater state support—and indeed the case was made by many on the left, probably in an attempt to appease their consciences, even though it was clear from the start that support would have been limited, given the dominant neoliberal orthodoxy—no amount of money could have ever compensated for the psycho-anthropological effects of months on end of enforced social distancing.

Many issues arise when considering this assault on the health of young people. Certainly, it's hard to look at this and pretend that the society of the pandemic was one in which children mattered in any way. Their future health was abandoned as they were encouraged to adopt sedentary lifestyles, adding to existing trends towards obesity and future ill health: indeed, as seen in the previous chapter, in March 2022 this was finally admitted by Chris Whitty, the UK's Chief Medical Officer, who acknowledged that there had been a significant worsening of childhood obesity which would lower future life expectancies and increase future cancer risk.[121] The mental health of children was savaged. Children's medical emergencies soared, but British society did not care—or certainly did not care enough to prioritise this above the government and social media lockdown police.

This socio-economic crisis for the young was apparent in all arenas. The consequences of this toxic cocktail of social warfare being waged on the poorer parts of British society was that it was poorer children who lost out the most in terms of education, with many who had worked hard to break through disadvantage finding that they had not been awarded the A-level grades they had hoped for and missing out on the universities of their choice. The haunting story of Keir Adeleke from Newham, east London, who was predicted one A* and two As for his 2021 A-levels and given teacher-assessed grades of BBC, stands as an indictment of a system which had enacted class warfare, wiping out the opportunities of disadvantaged children and ensuring that they would be far less likely to progress to advanced education and secure a better future.[122] Meanwhile, their peers in private schools were far less likely to have had their education interrupted, and more likely to have been predicted high grades by teachers concerned about the backlash from fee-paying parents if grades were assessed at a more realistic level.[123]

With the benefit of two years of evidence, the lockdown era destroyed many of the myths of British society. As the educational anthropologist Peter Sutoris noted, Britain was not a caring society:[124] it had destroyed the lives of millions of poor children and vulnerable women, and had enacted enormous cruelty on hundreds of thousands of elderly people confined to isolation and despair in care homes, unable to receive family visits in their declining years.[125] Neither was Britain able to claim to be a meritocratic society any more, given the assault on the educational potential of poor children, and the surge in home evictions which came alongside this.[126] Children were far behind in speech and understanding[127]—and yet at the same time they were controlled by a heartless authority, which still had the resources to send a police car round to the home of a 12-year-old girl in Manchester to make sure she was self-isolating when testing positive with Covid in July 2021.[128] By March 2022, two years into the pandemic, the future looked bleak given all the sacrifices that had been made: the biggest income drop since 1956, the highest tax burden since the 1940s, and a projected 9 per cent inflation, all of which would have to be paid by the younger people who had been assaulted by the public policies enacted during the pandemic.[129] And yet in spite of all this, social media warriors pilloried those who raised their heads above the parapet to question if these policies were the right way to handle Covid-19.

In sum, Britain—which here can stand as a case study for the wider world—had shown itself to be a cruel place, policed by the useful idiots of the neoliberal elites. And the impacts in the rest of the world showed that this pattern was a universal one.

***

In late 2021, media interest grew in a wave of new epidemics affecting young people around the world—from Afghanistan to Manchester. The WHO reported a raging measles epidemic in Afghanistan in November 2021.[130] Then, in April 2022, there were Hepatitis B outbreaks in young children reported in the UK, Spain, and the American state of Alabama.[131] The spread of monkeypox in May 2022 fanned the growing alarm.[132]

What had caused this alarming spike? As we saw in Chapter 6, the health of young populations had already been harmed through the freezing of standard vaccination programmes in many parts of the world. Adding to this, mistrust in the medical establishment caused by the response to Covid-19 and the coercion involved in the vaccine mandates had led to a serious fall in vaccination rates for MMR jabs in countries such as the UK.[133] Already in April 2021, an article in *Nature* was pointing to declining rates of diagnosis and vaccination for core diseases such as polio and measles in India, owing to the paralysis of healthcare services caused by the focus on Covid-19.[134]

In sum, the focus on a disease which overwhelmingly affected the elderly had caused the growth of serious medical conditions among the young. The young had been assaulted from all sides: politicians had decided to take a sledgehammer to their education, their economic futures, and their mental and physical health. It may take years fully to understand what this means for the future of human societies.

So why did politicians around the world continue in 2021 to promote severe restrictions of daily life, when the outcomes for socio-economic lives, mental and physical health, and the education of the adults of the future were so clearly devastating—and in spite of the fact that, as we have seen in this chapter, the evidence for this was enormous within just a few months, and had in fact been predicted? What were the factors that pushed this egregious decision—and why were the outcomes so poor?

To respond to the question of outcomes first, we can focus on the causes of educational breakdown. Politicians were too removed from the daily lives of citizens to understand how impossible remote learning might be. On the other hand, the October 2021 report from the Global Schools Forum found that one of the causes of sustained education loss in low-income countries was that when schools closed, teachers had to return to their home communities, which might be some distance away from their place of work—and the ongoing restrictions and impoverishment meant that it was very hard for them to return, meaning that they were effectively lost to the profession. In Nigeria, twenty-four of sixty-five surveyed schools reported losing between one and twenty teachers, while in Kenya the figure was twenty-nine out of sixty-four.[135] In wealthy countries, the loss of learning among deprived socio-economic groups was again the product of numerous factors: increased vulnerability, lack of adequate study space in confined and overcrowded conditions, and greater socio-economic anxiety and deprivation—all as predicted in the 19 March 2020 UNESCO report. Though much of the media attention focused on lack of computing hardware, the fact is that no one studies well under a table or on the stairs, which is what many children were faced with even in high-income countries.

What, then, were the core factors driving this sustained assault on young and old? On the one hand there was fear among those in decision-making positions for their health (Paul Dolan suggests this, as noted at the start of this chapter). On the other there was the intersection of media and politics, where media hysteria and hype meant politicians wanted to be seen to take decisive action—placing short-term political capital ahead of long-term futures. And then, as we saw in Part 1 of this book, there were powerful economic and political vested interests supporting lockdowns, including venture capitalists and tech entrepreneurs who saw the chance to push forward their vision of a future transhumanist society through the new dispensation, and pharmaceutical companies who prioritised the maximisation of profit over the well-being of the young in particular.

It was a toxic cocktail—so toxic that hundreds of millions of young and old lives were ruined. Meanwhile, a Reuters report from Manila in November 2021 described what all this had meant for one young girl:

> For the first time in her young life, two-year-old Nathania Ysobel Alesna was playing outside her house in the Philippine capital after 20 months of being kept at home by government coronavirus restrictions. [...] For many of the 40 million Filipinos under the age of 18, the pandemic has been a continuous lockdown.[136]

From an internationalist perspective, the inability to 'join the dots' and acknowledge that policy decisions in wealthy nations had had a decisive impact on those in low-income countries, with devastating consequences, was disturbing. Did healthcare practitioners and left-leaning critics think this was justified? Was this not an abuse of human rights? How could it be defended? It was hard to know, because so few of them spoke out, as democracy and freedom of speech became further 'casualties of the pandemic'.

9

THE ETHICS AND PRACTICE OF
AUTHORITARIAN CAPITALISM

It doesn't take an Einstein to figure out that the social, scientific, and economic transformations which we have outlined in this book had enormous political effects. The global assault on democracy was inevitable, once the decision had been made to roll out the most authoritarian measures in its modern history. And while, as we've seen, the scientific establishment was initially doubtful that China's virus suppression policies could be enacted in liberal democracies, what they apparently never stopped to consider in the rush to lockdowns and universal vaccination was what the political impacts of this might be. It's not clear whether democratic leaders were aware of these risks, either—or if they just ignored them, or maybe even if some of them saw them as an opportunity (not least for the associated kudos of being a 'wartime leader').

The consequences were immense. There was the massive increase in inequality, detailed in the previous chapters, in a context where before 2020 rising inequalities were already attributed by social scientists and liberal news organisations such as the *New York Times* as the cause of a growing and destabilising dissatisfaction with Western democratic politics.[1] There was a dramatic acceleration in pre-existing trends towards increasingly concentrated, oligarchic, and authoritarian capitalist modes of power. Then there was the radical exacerbation during the pandemic of existing trends of political polarisation, which had been part of this process of gathering democratic disenchantment. Most fundamentally of all, the two years of the pandemic saw the removal of rights hitherto seen as the bedrock of liberal democracy, such as freedom of movement, worship, and association, on the basis of a medical 'state of exception'. By the end of 2021, the liberal democratic model was effectively on life support, as Western governments had moved to implement a model of authoritarian capitalism.

To begin with, and as with our chronicle of the pandemic, it's worth reminding ourselves of some of the rights that were removed in the 'fight against coronavirus'. In most (formerly) liberal-democratic countries it became illegal at some point or another to attend funerals, get married, and have sex outside of marriage (civil or state-sanctioned) or cohabitation. Visits to elderly relatives in care homes and dying relatives in general were prohibited, and one heart-breaking video from the UK shows a desperate and highly articulate 104-year-old woman in a care home, pleading to be allowed to see her children and to 'make things like they used to be'.[2] Yet it was also periodically illegal even to meet up with elderly parents or grandparents who were still able to live in their own homes. In some places—Australia, Chile, Wales—it became illegal to travel more than a small distance from one's home, and freedom of movement was immeasurably curtailed by the new range of travel restrictions. Protests were also criminalised.[3] At the same time, ministers of state and police commissioners in the United Kingdom felt that it was their duty to encourage neighbours to inform on those they thought to be in breach of the rules, or to pronounce on whether grandparents could or could not hug their grandchildren.[4] Those seeking any form of spiritual solace from this emotional, social, and economic ruination were at times prohibited even from going to a place of worship.[5]

All of this was evidently in breach of international conventions on human rights safeguarding religious freedom, freedom of association, and freedom of movement. But in the remorseless war to upend value systems, human rights no longer mattered in the face of the fight against Covid-19—and the armies of global NGOs who had grown in previous decades fighting for such 'human rights' fell silent. Amnesty International, for instance, applauded the lockdown of poor countries such as Tunisia in March 2020, tweeting an image of workers locked down in one of the country's mask factories with the accompanying comment that 'stories like these from around the world keep us hopeful'.[6]

Of course, this was not the first time in history when informing on one's neighbour was given the status of a moral duty and obsessions with purity and lack of contamination dominated the public domain. Those with some knowledge of previous histories of state-sanctioned informants—the Stasi in East Germany, the 'familiars' of the Spanish and Portuguese Inquisitions—could not but see the parallels. Episodes of mass hysteria seem to come around in human affairs, just as they do in the extra-human world when lemmings leap off cliffs or wildebeest career through crocodile-filled creeks. In contrast to many creatures, however, hysterical outbursts in human societies can often be provoked by dominant institutions seeking to grab power, as was certainly the case in the era of the Inquisition.

As 2020 and 2021 passed, it appeared that what was taking place—alongside everything else—was a major reorientation in a large swathe of humanity's consciousness and ecosystem of relationships. This seems the only way to explain how citizens of liberal democracies were so willing to give up their freedoms to fight a disease from which, it quickly became clear, the vast majority of them were not in danger. Was freedom not one of the most cherished ideals of democratic societies? It turned out that the commitment to freedom had already become a simulacrum, which is to say that what seemed shocking was only possible because it had been developing for a long period of time. This transformation was not something that emerged from nowhere: as we suggested in the introduction, it grew out of decades of media and films enacting doomsday scenarios, of the distancing of people from their environment through remote technologies, and of the removal of so many people from the practice of production. Social (or better, antisocial) distancing was something that had been going on for a long time before it became a 'policy'.

Our view is that the deep-seated contradictions which were exposed in Western political ideologies in the era of SARS-CoV-2 emerged from a society which had come to hold fundamentally irreconcilable beliefs and values. One was the belief in the urgency of combatting ecological devastation, set against the reality of a society founded on mass consumption and the environmental degradation which went with it (which meant that usually the 'solution' to ecological pressures was marketed as a different form of consumption). Another was the 'free-market' structure which valued small and medium-sized entrepreneurs, set against the gathering power of a virtual world encouraging massive monopolies such as Amazon and Facebook. Then there was the growing influence of China's authoritarian capitalist structure, which was incompatible with any truly deep-held belief in freedom—but which did not stop any liberal consumers from piling up the products produced in Chinese factories with appalling labour conditions. And finally there was perhaps the most deep-rooted contradiction of all, between the belief that democratic capitalism offered general prosperity and the reality of the preceding two decades which had seen an enormous erosion of the privileges of the Western middle class.[7]

These contradictions had been created especially through this long-term process of social and world distancing. The Guyanese historian Walter Rodney once argued that European imperialism in Africa collapsed under the weight of its own contradictions.[8] Here we are forced to confront the possibility that a similar process might be underway, as the contradictions in global systems of thought and capital burst into the open. Having experienced the contradictions of democratic capitalism close up, and experienced its failings as living standards went into decline under neoliberalism, people were no longer as attached to this system of government as they once had been: they had already psychologically been prepared for the more authoritarian variant which appeared in 2020, whose emergence represented a radical continuity of processes that had begun long before.

Yet if on the one hand there had been a widespread psychological conditioning of the acceptance of the lockdown and vaccine surveillance model which arose in 2020 and 2021, it's also the case that governments were keen to impose these models. In this chapter, we consider how this happened. Our conclusion is that governments, too, had been conditioned into this structure because of the transformations of the previous decades. Much of this process then crystallised in the framework of the 'single scientific narrative' which was constructed at so many stages of the pandemic, as we've seen. History shows that whenever there is a single narrative of reality, an authoritarian model of propaganda and repression is required to impose it. Single narratives of truth are notoriously totalising, because reality, and our perception of it, is much more complex—and in the end, the totalising of truth is a uniform process, whatever angle it comes from.

In this chapter, we consider how the 'single narrative' was built, implemented, and enforced, and what the political consequences of this were. The framework required business, government, and media to come into alignment—an alignment which heralds the expansion of the authoritarian capitalist model, one which had been developing for several decades already to great success in China, the country in which reports of the new coronavirus had first emerged.

Constructing the single narrative through the media

As we saw in our chronicle of the pandemic, the Chinese response to SARS-CoV-2 conditioned much of the global response. That the 'single narrative' view of Covid-19 was so important to this model was made evident during 2022, when draconian lockdowns returned to major cities such as Shanghai, and the Chinese government made enormous attempts to censor the heavy criticism emerging on social media. It turned out that lockdowns hadn't completely suppressed Covid, and nor could they, but this did not matter to the Chinese government's Zero Covid vision of truth. The single narrative view of Covid certainly was incompatible with the freedoms which hitherto had been cherished by Western democracies—the latter had already made that pretty clear in the first two years of the pandemic, and it became even clearer in China in 2022.

To consider how the single narrative was framed in the media, we need to return briefly to the first months of the pandemic that we looked at in more detail in Part 1 of this book. As readers may recall, many scientists doubted that lockdowns would work in January 2020; as the *Guardian* reported on 23 January, 'there is also no guarantee that a lockdown will work to contain the virus. If it is indeed spreading fast and widely, then more and more cases are going to pop up all over the country regardless.'⁹

Indeed, this turned out to be a fairly accurate assessment of what eventually transpired, as we saw in our commentary on the medical effects of lockdowns.

Moreover, the novelty of the Chinese approach is underlined through the fact that, as we've seen, the November 2019 WHO report on pandemic mitigations—which, as its lead author Ben Cowling confirmed to us, considered the latest literatures—did not mention the word 'lockdown' once. Indeed, many of the policies which became standard issue in the two years to come were ruled out in that report, and in the scientific literatures which produced it: contact tracing, asymptomatic quarantine, and border closures.[10] These measures after all are perhaps those which are likely to have the most severe effects on the ordinary running of society, isolating many people who are not ill and preventing the movement of people and goods which is essential to modern life; they make a measured balance of epidemic risks against the social harms arising from aggressive suppression policies impossible to maintain.

It's worth noting here some of the many factors which may have led to the WHO's active promotion of this novel Chinese approach to respiratory viruses. In the first place, relations between WHO Director-General Ghebreyesus and Xi Jinping were already cordial before 2020. Ghebreyesus was the former Ethiopian Minister of Health under the authoritarian regime of the late Meles Zenawi and had previously been a senior figure in the Tigray People's Liberation Front, many senior members of which were also members of the Marxist–Leninist League of Tigray (MLLT), an organisation set up in the mould of Albania's Stalinist Cold War leader Enver Hoxha.[11] He had been appointed WHO Director-General with the support of Beijing.[12] In addition, China and Xi wished for a public health policy success after the criticisms of the handling of SARS in 2003. Thus, Chinese political imperatives on the one hand and

Chinese soft power on the other framed the initial response to the virus outbreak.

However, it's important to note that the initial response to all this in Western media was critical. In the first days after the Chinese government imposed the lockdown on Wuhan and other cities in Hubei province, the BBC published the diary of Guo Jing, a 29-year-old social worker and rights activist living in Wuhan. In this account, Jing described the growing isolation of the streets, the panic buying of essential goods (one man bought kilos of salt, because 'what if the lockdown lasted a whole year?'), and also something more sinister. 'Panic has driven a wedge between people', Guo Jing wrote. 'In many cities, people are required to wear a face mask in public. On the face of it, the measure is to control the pneumonia outbreak. But actually it could lead to abuse of power.'[13] At the time, in the wake of the violent pro-democracy protests in Hong Kong which had begun in March 2019 and gathered pace throughout the year, the abuse of state power in China was of concern to the Western media;[14] however, as SARS-CoV-2 unfolded and the policies of Western governments came to resemble those of China—and, indeed, in some cases all but outdid them in terms of scope and stringency—this concern vanished.

In this section, we consider the process through which the idea that the Chinese 'single narrative' was the right one was constructed by media and government. Some critics have pointed to Chinese investments in many news media organisations (such as the *Washington Post* and the *New York Times*).[15] Certainly, commercial factors and the size and significance of the Chinese market may have been a factor in the collective media decision to coalesce around this policy framework, for fear of antagonising Beijing. Moreover, as we'll discuss later on in this section, the previous two decades had seen the growing influence of China and the Chinese model of authoritarian capitalism. But other questions were also at work: as we'll see now, the information war in the age of the internet and of increasing political polarisation was key in the policy direction that followed. This in turn was something that itself grew from the expanding power of computing in the twenty-first century, as news media organisations coalesced around the single scientific narrative and began ruthlessly to police those who dissented from it.

To begin with, it's important to remind ourselves of some examples of what happened. As we saw in the chronicle of the pandemic in Part 1, during 2020 and 2021 esteemed figures such as a senior editor of the *BMJ* were removed from the internet if they diverted from accepted ideas—while those discussing theories such as the lab leak story, which turned out to have many factors in its favour, were also banned from Facebook and Twitter throughout the first year of the pandemic and dismissed as conspiracy theorists. At the same time, events which departed from the script of widescale public support for the Covid measures (such as the huge anti-lockdown protests in Berlin and London in 2020 and 2021, and against vaccine mandates worldwide in 2021) simply went unreported. The policing and silencing of dissent was reminiscent of wartime propaganda, and, given the number of political leaders who had likened the pandemic to a wartime situation, this isn't surprising; as we have also suggested here, the 'single scientific vision' version of history required a totalising vision of the truth, which was also inevitably going to lead down the path of propaganda.

A new global media framework called the Trusted News Initiative (TNI) was important in this process. This was established in 2019, led by the BBC, 'to protect audiences and users from disinformation, particularly around moments of jeopardy, such as elections', with the TNI partners consisting of the BBC, Facebook, Google/YouTube, Twitter, Microsoft, AFP, Reuters, the European Broadcasting Union, the *Financial Times,*

The Wall Street Journal, The Hindu, CBC/Radio-Canada, First Draft, and the Reuters Institute for the Study of Journalism.[16] Big Tech companies were heavily involved in TNI, and shared their thoughts through the initiative on how they could usefully combat social media disinformation.[17] As the pandemic moved centre stage, on 27 March 2020, on the heels of the launch of the WHO's global communications strategy discussed in Chapter 2, the BBC issued a press release surrounding a plan to tackle coronavirus misinformation which meant that 'partners will be able to alert each other to disinformation about Coronavirus so that content can be reviewed promptly by platforms, whilst publishers ensure they don't unwittingly republish disinformation'.[18] In time some of these partners (such as Reuters) then developed funded research projects which examined Covid disinformation,[19] while the Rockefeller Foundation announced a US$13.5 million grant to investigate health disinformation.[20]

How did this process of the coordinated implementation of a political and media strategy take shape? Central to this was not only a collective agreement among media and government partners on the 'correct' approach to the crisis, but also the censorship of alternatives. As 2022 proceeded, evidence as to the nature of this censorship began to emerge through lawsuits that were taken in the US by various figures who had been on the receiving end of it, including two of the GBD signatories, Jay Bhattacharya and Martin Kulldorff, and the former *New York Times* journalist Alex Berenson. These showed meetings between senior figures of the FDA and Twitter executives which led to the barring of some figures from the social media platform, and also the mooted existence of a hidden censorship framework in the US government, with the alleged identification of more than 80 federal officials across 11 federal agencies having secretly coordinated with social media companies to censor speech.[21]

Certainly, if Twitter, Facebook, the BBC, Microsoft, Reuters, and their peers all decide to push a certain framework and censor alternatives, that's going to become a pretty central aspect of the news environment. Some critics have seen a conspiracy, but again this is rather a publicly shaped coordination which no one is hiding, something which its actors clearly see as a good thing. More significant, in our view, is the political polarisation which had gathered through the previous years and the looming US presidential election which would take place in the November of the first year of the pandemic. As we saw earlier, political opinion around SARS-CoV-2 rapidly polarised, and with the TNI originally established to combat disinformation at elections (the BBC's landing page for the TNI is titled 'beyond fake news'),[22] it seems reasonable to deduce that the original targeting of disinformation around coronavirus was seen as an extension of that role—especially given the heavy criticism which had already been thrown at then-President Trump around his Covid response.

This intersection of Covid media policy and political polarisation was later spelt out by the director of the BBC's TNI programme, Jessica Cecil, who wrote: 'Disinformation online kills. That is one of the big lessons from Covid, where false cures and lies about vaccines have been rampant. It also corrodes democracy. The Capitol riots demonstrated that truth in the US.'[23] In the information age, the desire of government and major organisations and corporations to police information is an inevitable corollary of its importance. This is not a conspiratorial worldview, but simply a statement of facts widely available in the public domain: as we saw in Chapter 2, in February 2020, weeks before the pandemic was even declared, the World Health Organization deemed the situation an 'infodemic'. In this context, governments took measures such as the censorship of online content and the criminalisation of 'fake news', and infrastructures such as the TNI were already in place to enforce this policy. As we see here, major media organisations such as the BBC have directly connected elections and especially the US election with the TNI, and have then linked this to a coordinated policy to remove what is termed 'Covid disinformation'—which turned out to be anything that didn't chime with the official narrative—from the media and the internet. By the end of 2020, it emerged that intelligence services were collaborating with governments in pursuing this strategy of full-spectrum information control. Towards the end of that year, it was reported that Government Communications Headquarters, commonly known as GCHQ, one of Britain's intelligence agencies, was launching 'an offensive cyber-operation to tackle anti-vaccine propaganda'.[24] 'GCHQ has been told to take out antivaxers online and on social media. There are ways they have used to monitor and disrupt terrorist propaganda', the *Times* said, citing a source.[25] 'Now, the definition of terror is so broad,' said former CIA official Kevin Shipp, 'that any mention of Covid vaccines comes under their purview.'[26]

The Covid crisis thus emerges—alongside everything else— as a crisis of the age of information. As with the questions of inequality and Chinese soft power, this was a radical continuity of something that was already a trend in world societies prior to Covid-19. Alleged Russian collusion and propaganda in the 2016 US election[27] and Brexit campaigns[28] had already fuelled the war over information as a defining feature of twenty-first-century geopolitics. It was these concerns that led to the formation of the TNI, and to that coalition's expanded role during 2020 and 2021. As the crisis continued, Western governments moved further to develop concerted policies around access to information, with, for instance, the UK's Online Safety Bill[29] and President Biden's proposed Disinformation Board. Critics of Biden said that such a board was Orwellian,[30] while liberals accused the Biden government of folding under right-wing attacks—as the partisan divides simply grew too.[31]

Yet there was a deeper question here which went beyond political divides. This related to the issue of how compatible the age of information actually was with traditional views of liberal democracies based on rational-choice models of enlightened self-interest. These models, after all, assume an accurate flow of evidence on which to base reasoned decisions. Yet the response to Covid-19 demonstrated that the twenty-first-century imperative to control flows of information inevitably produces mechanisms of propaganda—and the problem is that, as we've also seen, what this means is that propaganda and disinformation burgeon on all sides. Indeed, inaccurate information was certainly widespread in media groups behind the TNI throughout the pandemic: plausible hypotheses about the origins of the virus were suppressed, eminent figures trying to bring some nuance to the discussion were censored, while 'fake news' about the vaccines halting the virus spread—contradicted by the medical officer of one of the main companies making the vaccines—circulated widely. Indeed, the Covid-19 crisis made it clear that states don't just censor information; they also actively engage in state information manipulation,[32] that is, the manipulation, fabrication, or cooptation of information for strategic purposes, of which we have provided ample evidence in this book. As one article in the *Journal of Human Rights* noted:

> Although many countries have justified censorship on the basis of the infodemic, this is not the only possible chronology. Rumors on social media may have arisen in response to perceived information vacuums or due to discrepancies between official figures and experiences on the ground. If this is true, states may have had other motives for censorship and information

manipulation, including as a pretext to silence critics and consolidate political power.[33]

In sum, a totalising narrative emerged on one side, just as a totalising narrative emerged on the other of a mass global conspiracy. As so often, reality was more complex, and the real casualty of all this was truth. There were those who had worked in some of these world-leading media organisations for many years who recognised the transformation in the news environment and were prepared to go public about it. In December 2021, a BBC employee wrote about the intolerance of a broad range of views and how this had shaped Covid reporting.[34] Two months earlier, in October 2021, Ole Skambraks, an employee of German public broadcaster ARD for twelve years, wrote an article which set out many concerns in detail:

> I can no longer remain silent. I can no longer silently watch what has been going on for a year and a half now within my organization, a public service broadcaster. Things like 'balance', 'social cohesion' and 'diversity' in reporting are principles embedded in the statutes and media state contracts. Today, the exact opposite is happening. There is no true discourse and exchange in which all parts of society can come together and find common ground [...] The same pattern is at work in the newsrooms. For the last one and a half years, I have no longer been working in the daily news business [...].[35]

Even more trenchant was Mark Sharman, who had served previously in the UK as Director of News at Sky for five years before becoming Director of Broadcasting at ITV. He said:

> It's created an environment which will lead to the biggest assault on freedom of speech and democracy I've known in my lifetime. [...] All the way through the pandemic only one side of the story was given. [...] Broadcasters picked up the torch that had

been created by these behavioural psychologists and created this fear. [...] This was a worldwide lockstep, and in parallel to media you had Big Tech, New Media, who were censoring everything. [...] There is a worldwide narrative, and the Big Tech and Media worldwide have followed it. Anybody who spoke out against it was censored.[36]

Here Sharman pointed to the intersection of media, tech, and policy which has been discussed above—alongside the way in which this worked in 'lockstep', as he put it, with one of the other key areas of this construction of the single narrative, which was behavioural psychology. For while control of major media platforms was important, the messaging was shaped—as Sharman indicated—substantially through the insights of behavioural psychologists and their role in applying 'nudges' to certain social behaviours. The way in which behavioural psychology was used to promote certain public responses during the pandemic was outlined by the British journalist Laura Dodsworth in her book *A State of Fear*, and was widely acknowledged to be an important element of how governments sought to shape public responses to Covid.[37] Indeed, the UK had long been one of the leaders in developing behavioural psychology as a tool of government, with the Cameron government developing a nudge unit in 2010,[38] and the export of this model to other countries becoming an aspect of UK soft power by 2018.[39]

The concept of the 'nudge' was developed by two American academics, Cass Sunstein and Richard Thaler, in their book of the same name.[40] It's a framework apt for the information age: by pushing certain avenues of information and choice menus, certain outcomes could be achieved by policymakers which they deemed desirable. Initially, in mid-March 2020, liberal media outlets such as the *Guardian* criticised the UK's response to the pandemic as being guided too much by 'nudge theory' and not enough by policy directives.[41] In time a combination of directives and nudges became the *modus operandi* of building the lockstep single narrative, and the well-known Scientific Pandemic Insights Group on Behaviour (SPI-B) became an important branch of UK SAGE, tasked with developing messaging which would ensure population compliance with the Covid measures.[42] However, some leading figures behind the 'nudge unit' in British government became uneasy about the uses to which the model had been put: Simon Ruda, who co-founded the UK government's behavioural insights unit, later wrote an article early in January 2022 in which he asked if nudge theory could survive the way it had been implemented in the pandemic.[43]

What emerges in this discussion is the confluence of pre-existing interests. Existing directions of travel in terms of political polarisation, the war for control over information, media power, and behavioural science combined to construct the single narrative version of the response to Covid. These were highly influential forces in society prior to SARS-CoV-2: combining their weight behind a unified vision created a vector of enormous power, something which is always dangerous in human societies and in human beings.

Some have pointed to financial interests as key in understanding this new propaganda framework. The Rockefeller Foundation has established an International Fund for Public Interest Media, set up in part to challenge disinformation.[44] And it's also true, for instance, that the Gates Foundation has become a major funder of large numbers of news organisations whose old finance models have been torn up by the internet age and the decline of advertising revenues. In late November 2021, an investigative report in *The Grayzone* showed that the Foundation had donated more than US$319 million to media outlets, ranging from the *Guardian*, the BBC, CNN, CNBC, and *The Atlantic* to *Le*

Monde, *El País*, and Al Jazeera.[45] The *Guardian* had received nearly US$13 million in total from the Foundation, including US$3.5 million in September 2020 to fund its coverage of global health.[46] Criticism of this influence is not limited to beyond the mainstream, and in an article in the *Columbia Journalism Review* of August 2020, Tim Schwab noted:

> Gates's generosity appears to have helped foster an increasingly friendly media environment for the world's most visible charity. Twenty years ago, journalists scrutinized Bill Gates's initial foray into philanthropy as a vehicle to enrich his software company, or a PR exercise to salvage his battered reputation following Microsoft's bruising antitrust battle with the Department of Justice. Today, the foundation is most often the subject of soft profiles and glowing editorials describing its good works. During the pandemic, news outlets have widely looked to Bill Gates as a public health expert on Covid—even though Gates has no medical training and is not a public official.[47]

Certainly this kind of influence—and the economic framework of the techno-media-pharma (TMP) complex discussed in the conclusion to this book[48]—can't be dismissed without rejecting the basis of most theories of economics. On the other hand, as we've also argued here, this new propaganda framework was perhaps the inevitable outcome of the information age—which itself emerged with the growing power of computing in world society in the twenty-first century. On this account, a re-reading of the events of 2020 and 2021 suggests that the power of computing and data has been central in the construction of the Covid consensus. What has taken place is a rapid acceleration in computer-driven trends towards digitisation, surveillance, and the polarisation of wealth and opinion which had already been reshaping human societies for at least three decades. During 2020 and 2021, a new ethical norm was constructed in which being a 'good citizen' required compliance with the data-driven projections and computing tools, such as digital bio-monitoring of vaccination status, that underpinned the unprecedented government interventions.

We have seen how the scientists who spearheaded the lockdown policies were computer modellers. These models were attractive to governments which were already strongly drawn to data-driven models of policy development. Allied to this initial policy decision was the way in which computing power very quickly enabled the tracking of the virus's impact in a way that had never before been possible. The imposition of the initial lockdown policies thus emerged from the privileging of these computer-simulated models and data tools over the experience of medical history in the treating of new epidemics: it was a new paradigm of power, within the framework of Thomas Kuhn's paradigms of scientific knowledge, as the historian Daniel Hadas has pointed out.[49]

A tale of two authoritarianisms

So if we want to understand the building of the single Covid narrative, many pieces of the jigsaw need to be put in place. Beyond the lockstep of global institutions which created a frightening new power, there was the surge of the information age and the desire to control information which followed. And beyond this, there was the role of outsourcing production of these digital devices, most often to China—and the consequent growing influence of the Chinese model of authoritarian capitalism on world societies. What we'll see in this section is how this framework grew out of a symbiotic relationship between this Chinese model and the Western neoliberal model—in which both offered authoritarian variants which had long suborned the liberal democratic model.

To begin with, the Chinese response to Covid-19 seemed like the logical one to Western consumers because it made real latent feelings and new approaches to human existence: the primacy of tech solutions and of information, and the silent admiration which the Chinese model of authoritarian capitalism had begun to awaken in Western consumers and politicians alike as the contradictions within their own system had been exposed over the course of previous years. In a world where autocratic management of ever more complex information systems had become a core part of government and business administration, the ruthlessness with which China controlled its population was something that struck a chord.

The reality was that in the two decades since the turn of the century, Western consumers had come to depend on Chinese products and the authoritarian capitalist structure which enabled their production. The UK and much of Europe relied on Chinese tourists and students to boost their capital flows. Through the need for Chinese capital and products, the coercive political structure which had made China so powerful was tacitly accepted. While democratic structures seemed increasingly chaotic as they veered from one pole to another (Obama followed by Trump), there was something that had the appearance of being very successful in what was coming out of China.

At the centre of this web of economic and cultural influence lay China's role in production chains for the Western consumer market, which also drove the growing power of computing noted above. Many leading Western brands manufactured their products in Chinese factories with conditions that would never have been permitted in a liberal democracy. Reports showed how Apple products were made by workers 6 hours from Shanghai on 60-hour working weeks, with inadequate protective equipment to shield them from the chemicals which were involved in the production process.[50] With supply chains touching much of

China, in November 2020 firms including Apple, Coca-Cola, and Nike lobbied against a new US Act of Congress prohibiting the import of goods produced by forced labour by Uyghur minorities in Western China.[51] The fact that this pressure against the Uyghur Forced Labor Prevention Act was supported by the US Chamber of Commerce shows how far Western corporations had come to rely on the forced labour which China's authoritarian capitalist mode of production provided.

Meanwhile, China's growing spending power had also begun to make inroads. Chinese international students became something like the financial bedrock of many Western academic institutions, especially in the United Kingdom, paying outsized fees, boosting the service sectors of economies through the sightseeing and consumption that formed key components of their study visits, and facilitating the construction contracts that followed as private companies developed new purpose-built luxury student flats.[52] With this growing dependence on Chinese capital, for many Western business leaders China became synonymous not with the reality of a repressive dictatorship but with the idea of a land of opportunity: for those with Chinese contacts, lucrative deals might always be in the offing, as became clear during the Covid-19 crisis in 2020 when those able to act as middlemen and set up PPE manufacturing centres in China made personal fortunes.[53]

Thus, as the 2010s unwound, China's influence began to exert clear changes in the Western political weather which went largely unremarked. What were once totemic issues for the Western left, such as the conditions in Tibet, were quietly side-lined. The requirements of Chinese students in Western universities came to be a consideration in course design, and even in choosing which technological tools were to be used (they had to be unblocked in China). Chinese firms began to build key elements of Western infrastructure, from power stations to telecommunications networks. Chinese consumer demand drove the opening of new businesses and buildings, all for a shared sense of growing prosperity among Western society's winners.

What had happened to Western societies was in fact the inverse of what had been promised at the start of the twenty-first century, when neoconservative ideologues of the George W. Bush presidency had argued that 'spreading democracy' in the Middle East was the surest way to spread human freedom—something which didn't work out when what countries like Iraq and Afghanistan got was not democracy but rather death, destruction, and the plundering of their resources. Indeed, far from 'exporting democracy', Western leaders, under the guise of the post-9/11 War on Terror, eroded democracy in their own countries as well, giving rise to increasingly powerful and ever-reaching state apparatuses. In this sense, if liberal democracies in the West came to depend on coexistence with China's authoritarianism it was also, and perhaps most importantly, due to authoritarian tendencies intrinsic to Western neoliberal capitalism itself.

Pierre Dardot and Christian Laval, for example, have argued that under neoliberalism crisis has become a 'method of government', where 'every natural disaster, every economic crisis, every military conflict and every terrorist attack is systematically exploited by neoliberal governments to radicalise and accelerate the transformation of economies, social systems and state apparatuses'.[54] As we've also seen, in her 2007 book *The Shock Doctrine*, Naomi Klein explored the idea of 'disaster capitalism'.[55] Her central thesis is that in moments of public fear and disorientation it is easier to re-engineer societies. Dramatic changes to the existing economic order, which would normally be politically impossible, are imposed in rapid-fire succession before the public has had time to understand what is happening. However, today perhaps it would be more apt to talk of 'crisis capitalism'—whereby Western capitalism is only able to function by creating a permanent state of emergency or exception through the exploitation (or engineering) of an endless stream of 'crises'.

This may help to explain why, for much of the past twenty years, the West seems to have been mired in a perennial state of 'crisis': the post-9/11 global terrorism crisis (and the disastrous wars that followed), the post-2008 financial-economic crisis (with particularly negative repercussions in Europe), the pandemic crisis, and now the military crisis in Ukraine—and all this against the background of a looming climate and ecological crisis.

In such a context, 'crisis' no longer represents a deviation from the norm; it is the norm, the default starting point for all politics. This of course raises a paradox. In her book *Anti-Crisis*, the anthropologist Janet Roitman notes that 'evoking crisis entails reference to a norm because it requires a comparative state for judgement: crisis compared to what?'[56] Its use today, however, implies an endless condition, where crisis has itself become the norm. Thus, as Roitman asks, 'can one speak of a state of enduring crisis? Is this not an oxymoron?'

This is largely a consequence of the crisis of the Western-led neoliberal regime itself: on a domestic level, neoliberalism's innate tendency towards ever-growing levels of capital concentration, and the Western elites' 40-year-long struggle to progressively insulate the dominant political-economic order from popular-democratic challenges, means that neoliberalism is no longer able to overcome its intrinsic stagnationary and polarising tendencies and to generate societal consensus or hegemony (in material or ideological terms). At the same time, internationally, Western hegemony is increasingly threatened by the rise of new regional powers—first and foremost China itself. This means that Western elites have been forced to rely on increasingly authoritarian, repressive, and militaristic measures—both domestically and abroad—in order to remain in power and stifle any challenges to their authority (think of the *gilets jaunes* in France, for example).

Hence the need for a more or less permanent state of crisis capable of justifying such measures.

So what are the main characteristics of this 'new normal' that had already been on the rise well before the pandemic? First and foremost, a generalised acceptance of the idea that we can no longer afford to organise our societies around a more or less stable set of rules, norms, and laws; the constant stream of new threats—terrorism, disease, war—means that we must be constantly ready to rapidly adapt to an ever-changing scenario of permanent instability. This, in turn, also means that we can no longer afford the heated public debates and complexities of parliamentary politics usually associated with Western liberal democracies—governments need to be able to enforce decisions with swiftness and efficiency.

It also means that any form of medium-term planning, any vision for the future—either on an individual or a collective level, the latter having been, historically, the main driver of social progress—is futile. Permanent crisis means being stuck in a perpetual present where all energies are focused on the fight against the 'enemy' of the moment: Islamic terrorism, 'financial instability', Covid—and now Russia. Moreover, reality is just too complex and unpredictable to hope to shape it according to any form of collective will. The consequences of this are devastating on an individual and psychological level as well, plunging people into a state of permanent existential precarity.

We didn't get to this point all of a sudden: it's been a slow, frog-in-boiling-water process, in which each crisis has been exploited to chisel away at our economic, social, democratic, and individual rights and liberties as well as, and perhaps most importantly, our concept of 'normality' by slowly shifting the Overton window of what is considered acceptable in public discourse and policy. In this sense, the pandemic should be understood as the endpoint of a decades-long process.

THE COVID CONSENSUS

Over the past two years we have witnessed in several countries—and largely accepted—the imposition of measures that would have been unthinkable up until that moment: the shutdown of entire economies, the mass quarantining (and subsequently the enforced vaccination) of hundreds of millions of healthy individuals, the closure of schools for an entire year (or 2 in some places), the shutting down of any meaningful form of public debate, the 'cancelling' of dissenting voices, and, of course, the exclusion from public life and subsequent demonisation and criminalisation of the unvaccinated—the new public enemy number one. These measures went hand in hand with more traditional 'emergency measures' that previous crises had already accustomed us to, such as the fast-tracking of laws, the crackdown on public demonstrations, and the procurement deals parcelled out to transnational corporations without proper tendering processes or legislative oversight, further strengthening existing capitalist oligopolies. In this sense, each new crisis builds upon the ground laid down by the previous one and prepares the ground for the next.

In light of the above, we should perhaps consider the troubling hypothesis that the Chinese and Western regimes, far from representing two opposites, may actually have come to embody two different types of authoritarianism, conflictual but symbiotic at the same time—as the strikingly convergent responses to the pandemic would seem to suggest. This is further reinforced by the fact that a consensus emerged almost immediately that the Chinese model had the answer to dealing with the coronavirus outbreak. From that time on, as we've seen, actors of the TNI media organisations and tech giants acted ruthlessly to promote this totalising vision of reality. Indeed, the pandemic dramatically accelerated the processes of monopolisation of information and hyper-concentration of wealth and corporate power—which of course go hand in hand—that have been underway for years.

The single narrative and the ethics of compliance

As we've already seen in this chapter, the process of constructing a single narrative around the Covid pandemic was already one with significant political consequences, because of the accumulation of power which went with it. Concentrations of power are likely to transform relations of representation and public voice. But while this required a large degree of coordination across media organisations and Big Tech—not something that happened in secret, as conspiracies do, but something that took place in the public sphere—the process of implementation was different. The implementation of the narrative, and its transformation into a normative consensus, required new ideological frameworks, and that's what we'll look at in this section of this chapter.

That something transformative was taking place is clearest, in fact, on the ideological level. Historians can look at the similarities to previous pandemics, and economists can compare the Covid economic crisis with previous economic shocks, but these comparisons can only take us so far in understanding Covid as an epochal event. We can look with disquiet at the idea of a 'new normal', only to find out that the same concept was being bandied about during the early years of the War on Terror following the 9/11 attacks in New York.[57] And we can devote our energies to considering the 'Covid crisis' only to recall that, as we saw in the previous section, neoliberal democracies have inhabited a world of crisis for many years already. What has changed is perhaps fundamentally a question of ethics, as mirrored in the political space.

What confirms this analysis is that a new ethical normativity developed during the Covid pandemic which superseded previous value systems, even those codes of values which to their adherents had hitherto been absolute. As we'll see shortly, ideas which had been all the rage among intellectuals were suddenly consigned in horror to the dustbin of the world, while religious leaders found that the precepts of their faith were not as important as the precepts of medical decrees—and vegans found that animal testing was not so bad after all. Something had happened which transformed the ideological terrain, and the moral tenets that go with it. These ideological and moral transformations are key to understanding the process of political implementation (which we'll look at in the last part of this chapter).

The emergence of a new moral framework does not start from nowhere. One of the lessons of the last two years is that it grows from shoots (or weeds, depending on your perspective) which have been setting down roots for some time without being really noticed. It's like the experience of seeing a nephew or niece in adolescence for the first time in a while, and finding out that they've suddenly shot up and are becoming an adult. In that way, these changes are also a product of time, which passes without our noticing much until the force of our aging looms large in the rear-view mirror.

The terrain for this new ethical normativity had been growing for a while, and we can begin by turning again to something that is the product of computing power—the surveillance society. The importance of computing capacity in managing the Covid-19 crisis was certainly understood very early by the WHO. In its 25 May 2020 press conference, Dr Michael Ryan—Executive Director of the WHO's Health Emergencies Programme—made it clear that computing technology was essential to its programme to monitor and suppress the disease. 'Right now', he said, 'countries in Europe, countries in North America, many other countries around the world in Southeast Asia have to continue to put in place the public health and social measures, the surveillance measures, the public health measures, the testing measures, and a comprehensive strategy to ensure that we continue on a downward trajectory.'

That is, surveillance—the contact tracing technology which had been ruled out in the WHO's own November 2019 report—was an essential part of the medical response. It's worth looking in detail at this report's mention of contact tracing, since it noted that there were 'a few ethical issues surrounding the implementation of contact tracing as an intervention. [...] There may be more ethical concerns when contact tracing is coupled with measures such as household quarantine'. Ethical concerns cited include the inefficient use of resources (including human resources) and questions of equity where the application of tracing requires an availability of resources and technologies. Moreover, the authors of the report also noted that evidence for the overall effectiveness of contact tracing was limited. This was confirmed by an early February 2021 study showing that in the UK it had achieved only a 2 to 5 per cent infection reduction.[58]

Nevertheless, political and security establishments moved quickly to get behind the new frameworks. Autocratic countries like China and Singapore were quick to adapt and extend existing digital surveillance technologies to monitor Covid-19, and democratic countries followed suit: in a matter of months, more than thirty-four countries enacted surveillance measures; twenty-two of them were liberal democracies.[59] The types of surveillance measures adopted in response to the pandemic included public surveillance of population movements under lockdown through closed-circuit television (CCTV), drones, mobile phone usage data, and biometric tracker bracelets.[60] But the most prominent form of surveillance has been the adoption of mobile applications that allow for Covid-19 tracking. In the UK, for example, by November 2020 the GCHQ monitoring arm of the British secret services had embedded a team in Downing Street, the *Daily Telegraph* reported. This team had been given access to phone data to track the public's movements during the second lockdown, sifting through the data to help to 'give Mr Johnson the most up-to-date information on the spread of the virus'. In several countries, the pandemic saw 'a rapid conversion of security technologies for use in the tracking, monitoring and mitigation of Covid-19', a study by the Danish Institute for International Studies found.[61] In the United States, for example, the Joint Analytic Real-time Virtual Information Sharing System, or JARVISS, developed to target criminal activity around army installations, has been used to track the spread of Covid-19 and monitor the impact of the virus on installation readiness, training, and recruiting. The process of ethical normalisation of practices of surveillance which had already been in place was gathering speed.

So why did governments press measures that were not proven to work, and why did citizens comply with them? As with the rise of a computer-driven scientific consensus and the question of economic inequalities, this was not a new process but a radical continuity of something that was already in train. The Edward Snowden affair had demonstrated that the American secret intelligence services already had access to all the data which citizens might exchange across internet and mobile phone networks, and that much of it was automatically monitored. Citizens in Western democracies effectively had already consented to this invasion of privacy through their growing use of these technologies. Thus the rapid adoption of test-and-trace technologies to monitor the spread of the virus—and then the vaccination status of citizens—was merely a step forward along a path that had already been cleared. Civil liberties groups such as Big Brother Watch protested when this data was shared with police, but it was only in countries with experiences of dictatorship in living memory such as Portugal that the public outcry was strong enough to make a difference—there, in late October 2020, the Prime Minister António Costa was forced to remove a law from parliament which he had tabled, by which the downloading of the test-and-trace app would have been mandatory.[62]

Once again, the Covid-19 crisis revealed the irreconcilable nature of many of the beliefs governing Western society in the early twenty-first century. The belief in freedom of choice in terms of sexuality, identity, and consumption was an ingrained part of many Western cultures; and yet underlying this belief was the reality of consent to constant mass surveillance by both governments and corporations through the use of social media platforms such as Facebook which had the power to constrain these freedoms at any time, as indeed the events of 2020 and 2021 demonstrated. How could these irreconcilable beliefs be maintained without in some way shifting the reference frame of normative ethical judgements, so that consent to surveillance became a moral choice designed to ensure the return to 'normal'— when the surveillance society had already been the norm for a number of years? Thus the political response to Covid-19 offered Western governments the opportunity to bring out into the open a moral transformation that had already occurred without the explicit consent of citizens; illogical in their own terms, within the terms of the previous arrangement of societies, and (as we've seen in this book) within the terms of previous medical and scientific practice, lockdown and vaccination policies offered a chance to realign the ethical and practical realities of governing structures, something without which political systems tend to implode.

This may explain in part why citizens did not see the Covid measures (and especially the surveillance which accompanied them) as such a major transformation: the previous years had conditioned a response which saw them as logical, even normal. Nevertheless, in spite of this clear continuity of surveillance practice, this was something which required a major realignment of consciously held ideas. That this characterised the Covid era—and the implementation of the ethics of the single Covid narrative—becomes clear when we consider the polemics surrounding the Italian philosopher Giorgio Agamben.

For two decades, Agamben had been feted as one of the world's most influential living philosophers. His concept of 'bare life' and its relation to 'sovereign power', developed in his work *Homo Sacer*, had been the subject of exhaustive critique, review, and endorsement by leading intellectual figures. His conceptualisation of the 'state of exception' during the War on Terror, as a way of understanding the exception as the new normal for neoliberal governance in the twenty-first century, had been the subject of exhaustive academic debate. Long reviews in journals such as the *London Review of Books*[63] and the *Los Angeles Review of Books*[64] were testament to the fact that he was seen as one of the Western world's iconic intellectuals.

Drawing on the famous pre-Second World War critic Walter Benjamin, and Michel Foucault's concept of biopower, Agamben's work was influential in critical race theory and other important left-wing intellectual schools of the 2010s. The French philosopher Michel Foucault (who had died in 1984) was another darling of the left, and many saw Agamben's development of Foucault's ideas as useful in explaining the discriminatory frameworks of the modern Western state. Political scientists such as Ayten Gündoğdu discussed how his ideas related to the contemporary rights-struggles of refugees without documentation.[65] The legal philosopher Arne de Boever considered Agamben's relevance to Marxist critiques.[66] Agamben was not just an iconic intellectual but an iconic intellectual of the left, as was Foucault. Yet by the middle of 2021, the *New York Times* was running an op-ed by Ross Douthat titled 'How Michel Foucault Lost the Left and Won the Right'.[67]

To understand how this turnaround took place, we need to have some understanding of what was at stake in the Covid era.

Why was Agamben's work seen as being of such relevance to the modern Western state in the first place? His fundamental argument in *Homo Sacer*—as his translator into English Adam Kotsko understands it—is that 'political power in Western societies is founded on the decision to include some people within the protections of the law and exclude others, stripping them of their human privileges and reducing them to a state he designates as "bare life". This is not a simple division between insiders and outsiders, as he conceives it. In this scheme, those who are reduced to bare life are not expelled from society, but included in it as a subhuman class that is excluded from the formal protections of the law but is nonetheless foundational to the social order.'[68]

So as the model of lockdowns moved to that of segregation by vaccination, it may not surprise some readers to discover that Agamben thought that his ideas might be relevant to the new dispensation. Beginning in late February 2020, Agamben published a series of articles on the crisis, which he later turned into a book.[69] Agamben saw this as the 'invention of an epidemic', the construction of a state of exception as the normative paradigm of government, and the militarisation of daily life.[70] In an interview in *Le Monde* published in late March 2020, he stated that 'modern politics is from top to bottom a sort of biopolitics', but that what was new in the Covid crisis was that 'health had become a juridical obligation to maintain at whatever cost'.[71] Then in early April 2020, he pronounced himself a sceptic of social distancing, which he said was not 'humanly or politically possible to live with'.[72]

It's interesting to note how in the early phase of the Covid crisis, these ideas did not draw the tempestuous ire that followed. Some students of his work wrote reasoned blogposts in which they critiqued some aspects of his interventions, but recognised that they were not surprising and in keeping with the philosophy that he had developed.[73] Kotsko, his English translator, prepared some of his blogs in English, while intervening over some of the comparisons that Agamben was making.[74] However, the atmosphere quickly changed, and a slew of vituperative denunciations followed from people who chucked decades of critical engagement into the trash can and ran as fast as possible so that they could be intellectually as well as socially distanced from this new pariah—these rats weren't just leaving the sinking ship, but were turning back to dance on its upturned hull before Agamben's oeuvre disappeared beneath the waves of history.

By late March 2020, calls were being made by Marxists such as Panagiotis Sotiris 'to rethink the very notion of biopower' (a revealing intervention, as it suggests an awareness that Agamben's redeployment of his ideas in the Covid age was not illogical; and indeed, subsequently Sotiris revised this position, inasmuch as he came out very firmly against the lockdown model).[75] The argument of many on the left was that political theory was now confronting scientific fact (in the nature of the virus) and material realities (in the nature of the eroding of the state's power to act in neoliberal societies). In sum, ideas and discourse took second place to science and the need to protect the vulnerable in society—something which, as we've seen in this book, is somewhat ironic given that what was proposed in fact massively increased vulnerability across the world. The fault line—and the basis of building the new ethical normativity which emerged—was Agamben's refusal to give primacy to materiality, as he stated: 'It is not my intention to enter into the scientific debate about the virus; my interests are the extremely serious ethical and political consequences which come from it.'[76]

It was Agamben's refusal to cede ethical normativity to scientists and their quantitative models which his critics could not stand. As we'll see shortly, this ground was after all being given up by the Pope, so why couldn't another Italian resident do the same? An important exemplar of this critique is the Californian professor Benjamin Bratton, who described how 'in this ongoing performance, Agamben explicitly rejects all pandemic-mitigation measures on behalf of an "embrace tradition, refuse modernity" conviction which denies the relevance of a biology that is real regardless of the words used to name it'. Beyond biology was the centrality of quantification, for Bratton: 'Agamben's pandemic outbursts are extreme but also exemplary of this wider failure. Philosophy and the Humanities failed the pandemic because they are bound too tightly to an untenable set of formulas, reflexively suspicious of purposeful quantification.' Philosophy and the humanities could only be relevant when recognising the primacy of 'the reality of our shared technical and biological circumstances'.[77]

In other words, the new ethical normativity which had emerged, above all others, was one grounded in the moral power of the mathematics which could enforce a biopower policed through the new datafication of the surveillance state. Bratton objected that a reckoning with Agamben's work was 'long overdue. His mode of biopolitical critique blithely ventures that science, data, observation and modeling are *intrinsically* and ultimately forms of domination and games of power relations.'[78] We think it's reasonable to argue that the evidence accumulated in this book suggests that Agamben is right, but as his approach refused the moral primacy of the mathematical modeller, it was one which provoked a moral outrage in those who had found it all too easy to adjust their value systems as needed.

Soon enough, Agamben grew a reputation as a conspiracy theorist and someone captured by the right, even though in his writings on Covid and the question of conspiracies he was clear: 'As Foucault showed before me, governments who operate through the security paradigm don't necessarily work by producing the state of exception, but by making use of it and directing it once it has emerged.'[79] Still, the clamour grew: Agamben's translator Kotsko wrote a piece in *Salon* trying to exculpate himself from having spent much of his career making Agamben available in English,[80] and Bratton's book on how philosophy failed the pandemic focused especially on the role of Agamben.[81] Most revealing of all was an essay by Sergei Prozorov, which argued that his 'problematic articulation should be abandoned for a theory that rather highlights the non-relation between sovereign power and bare life':[82] in other words, philosophers should abandon Agamben's attempt to see how political power over biological life works in practice—even though the past two years had demonstrated this in enormous detail—apparently largely because it was no longer reputationally expedient to proceed with it.

These transformations give the relationship to medical science a quasi-religious element (indeed, one of the chapters of Agamben's book is titled 'Medicine as Religion'). The decline of Western religion offered a need for a new moral normativity, one which was accepted even by figureheads of religious institutions. Both Pope Francis and the Archbishop of Canterbury Justin Welby described getting vaccinated against Covid as a moral duty,[83] and soon enough a Catholic parish in Nottingham refused to admit unvaccinated churchgoers.[84] In the case of Francis in particular, this is a curiosity, given that foetal cell lines were used in the testing of mRNA vaccines and in the production of the Johnson & Johnson vaccine:[85] the Pope's view apparently is now that abortion is wrong in all cases (even rape, incest, and terminal illness of the foetus),[86] but that the use of foetuses for the development of Covid vaccines is fine. Meanwhile the UK Vegan Society, while acknowledging the animal testing without which any vaccine is impossible, stated that it 'encourages vegans to look after their health and that of others in order to continue to be effective advocates for veganism and other animals'.[87]

Why then did religious leaders and animal rights activists make the ethical judgement that their core beliefs were of less value than the imperative to be vaccinated against Covid-19? In all cases, they referred to the obligation owed to others—clearly a core element of morality, and understandable. And this obligation derived, in fact, from the thread which has bound together so much of this book, which is the 'single narrative': there was no alternative to lockdowns followed by vaccination as a means to exit from what everyone could agree was a nightmare, and that full vaccination would produce herd immunity and the end of the pandemic. As we have seen in this book, however, this single narrative had many elements which had more to them than met the eye—and it was imposed by the propaganda framework which we looked at in the first part of this chapter, which had a key role to play in the ethical transformations which followed.

There is one rider which can place the foregoing in important relief. While Western intellectuals leapt to excoriate Agamben, those who lived in other world regions took a different approach. In their book *Covid and Custom in Rural South Africa*, Leslie Bank and Nelly Sharpley draw explicitly on Agamben's ideas, and describe the context of 'a greater state of exception in the rural areas [which] created a situation where Agamben's idea of the bare life—where mere survival was all that rural people expected after apartheid—became a naked life, stripped of dignity, spiritual security and the possibility of meaningful social reproduction'.[88] In other words, those inhabiting societies outside the West and China, in which the model of the surveillance society had not already become normativised, saw no contradiction between Agamben's theories and the worlds unleashed by the response to the Covid pandemic.

What all these examples show is the transformative ethics which the coronavirus pandemic crystallised in the West. The abandonment of Agamben by left-wing intellectuals was part and parcel of a process which saw the Pope and vegans accept that their beliefs in the primacy of life and not harming animals were secondary to the political framework and ethical normativity which had emerged. Such enormous moral transformations were essential in the compliance of the population with the extraordinary new pandemic measures of confinement, surveillance, and division according to biological status which followed: they were key in enacting the Covid authoritarianism which was one of the lasting political impacts of the response to Covid-19.

Implementing Covid authoritarianism

As these ethical and intellectual transformations took shape in the first months of 2020, some commentators began to look into the origins of slogans that had become household catchphrases in just a few months. A *New York Times* article noted that the concept of 'social distancing' first emerged in a 2006 paper commissioned by George W. Bush's administration in response to the SARS outbreak.[89] One of the report's authors, Dr Carter Mecher, a Department of Veterans Affairs physician, recalled in the piece that 'people could not believe that the strategy would be effective or even feasible'.[90] Yet by and by it was adopted by the US Centers for Disease Control, and a 2017 document commissioned by the Obama administration made this part of government policy for handling pandemics.[91] Even here, however, although the document used the phrase on forty-one occasions, it suggested that social distancing measures during the swine flu pandemic of 2009 had worked best 'in a few small, well-defined settings, including a summer camp and a cruise ship'.[92] It was a long way from here to the universal rollout of this concept in the new consensus of 2020.

This prompts the question of how this consensus emerged so quickly, and what was behind the inordinate speed of its spread—a meme that has proven every bit as powerful as the Covid-19 genome sequence. For a consensus is not a statement of objective fact; it is a statement of power which creates marginalisation, and a new consensus therefore creates a new pattern of marginalisation.* As we've seen in this book, many people were on the receiving end of this new pattern: those involved in economic activities which could not be done remotely, the working class, the poor, women, young people, and scientists and intellectuals of global repute who departed from the script. The question of how this consensus emerged—and how this marginalisation was legitimated—is therefore a crucial one.

In this chapter, we've now seen some of the political frameworks which promoted these outcomes. On the one hand, there was the agglomeration of tech and media influence to shape a single message or narrative, alongside punitive sanctions on those who had something else to say. On the other, there were the ideological and ethical transformations shaped by the new dispensation of power, to which people had already been unconsciously acclimatised through the transformations of previous years. These factors were driven by the new technologies of the twenty-first century, and the accumulations of power and capital which these had unleashed. The final piece in the jigsaw was the political mechanisms which enforced the consensus, and this is what we will look at in this section of the chapter.

As noted earlier in the book, one of the problems with allowing policies to be directed by scientists with no manifest understanding of social and political contexts was that they apparently failed to consider what the political consequences of medical authoritarianism might be. Some readers may recall Professor Neil Ferguson's comment at the outset of the pandemic that the difference between the UK and China in

---

* We are indebted to Angelo di Cintio for this observation.

lockdown response would be that the measures in the UK would be voluntary.[93] It would be interesting to know what the two women who were arrested for going on a socially distanced walk at a lake 5 miles from their home in Derbyshire—and told that the hot drinks they had brought with them were forbidden, as they were classed as a 'picnic'—during the winter 2021 lockdown would make of this 'voluntarism'.[94] As we've seen in this book, a voluntary approach turned out to be impossible, with policing of stay-at-home orders, restrictions on freedom of movement, and discrimination according to biological status (vaccination) baked into the pandemic response. It turned out that pandemic authoritarianism required political authoritarianism to implement it—and it was hardly surprising that at the end of this process, governments such as the British government legislated to try to retain these new powers, while the institutions which safeguarded democratic norms were ever weaker.[95]

This authoritarianism—or rather this amplification and acceleration of pre-existing authoritarian trends—was a key part of the Covid response in many world regions. Since the beginning of the pandemic, the Gothenburg-based V-Dem Institute has tracked violations of democratic standards in relation to Covid-19 measures.[96] In the first year alone, it found that thirty-two 'democracies' and fifty-five 'autocratic regimes' had violated international norms in their response to Covid-19.[97] Such violations included discrimination against minorities, violations of fundamental rights, excessive use of force, absence of a time limit for emergency measures, limitations on the legislature's ability to constrain the executive, official disinformation campaigns, and restrictions on media freedoms.

Several Amnesty International reports have focused, in particular, on the shocking increase in law enforcement violence and abuse throughout the world over the course of 2020 and 2021, under the guise of 'fighting the pandemic'. In a December

2020 report, it noted that during the first year of the pandemic, in at least sixty countries 'authorities have adopted punitive and coercive measures that have not only resulted in violations of a range of human rights but also divided societies and failed to tackle the health crisis'.[98] 'Time and again police forces have used excessive and unnecessary force in the enforcement of Covid-19 lockdowns and curfews, clamped down on peaceful protests and suppressed dissent', Amnesty claimed. The report documented the unlawful use of force, including lethal force, across regions to disperse crowds, conduct arrests, or punish those violating public health restrictions. In some countries, tens of thousands were arrested for pandemic-related infractions or placed in inhumane and unsanitary state-run quarantine centres. Several cases of abuse were reported across Europe, in Belgium, France, Greece, Italy, Spain, and other countries, in which 'law enforcement officials resorted to the unlawful use of force to impose lockdown measures on people who did not offer any resistance or constitute a significant threat'.

However, as is to be expected in contexts with low levels of public resources (and where as we've seen in this book people were plunged into economic misery and often had to try to get out in order to survive), the most rampant abuses of state power occurred in poorer countries, where '[i]n many places arrest and detention has been used as a first rather than last resort in response to non-compliance with public health measures often increasing the risk of contagion'.[99] In Kenya, at least seven people were killed and sixteen hospitalised as a result of police operations to enforce the curfew over the first 5 days it was in place.[100] In Nigeria, by May 2020, there had been reports of up to eighteen people killed by security forces during lockdown.[101] In South Africa, police fired rubber bullets at people 'loitering' on the streets on the first day of lockdown,[102] while by February 2021 Bheki Cele, Minister of Police, said that 411,309 people had been arrested for breaching lockdown rules in the country.[103] Zambia's police spokesperson explained the approach to people found on the streets during lockdown as: 'We hammer you, we hit you, then we do detention. If you escape, you are lucky.'[104] In El Salvador, a young man described how a police officer detained and beat him and shot him twice in the legs when he was caught going to buy food and fuel, allegedly in violation of a national quarantine.[105] In the Dominican Republic, police detained approximately 85,000 people between 20 March and 30 June 2020, allegedly for non-compliance with the curfew, and on several occasions people arrested for failing to wear masks were then rounded up without any physical distancing.[106] In Angola, seven men were arrested while going to buy food; on one occasion, a doctor was found dead in a police cell hours after being arrested for driving home from a shift at hospital without a mask, even though he had been alone in his car and driving with the windows closed.[107] In the Philippines, 100,486 people had been arrested for alleged violations related to lockdown and curfew orders by September 2020.[108]

These appalling examples (alongside the whole second part of this book, in truth) give the lie to the idea that the Covid response was compassionate. In Ghana, medical historian Dr Samuel Adu-Gyamfi described how the government response was being criticised for the concentration of power and authoritarianism which it required.[109] In Kenya, philosopher Reginald Oduor described how 'police came down hard' on people, and enforcement on public transport was 'really, really ruthless'.[110] In Mozambique, sociologist Pedrito Cambrão described how the stay-at-home orders created a parallel economy in which only those who could bribe the police were allowed out to try and make ends meet.[111] Meanwhile, in Chile, critics slammed the government's misuse of emergency powers. As Rocío Quintero of the International Commission of Jurists put it, '[t]he implementation of a state of exception in Chile inappropriately gave extremely overbroad powers to military officials who implemented sanitary measures for more than a year and a half. This was all done consistently with archaic constitutional provisions that do not set out satisfactory limits and restrictions on executive power during states of exception'— provisions which in fact dated from the time of General Augusto Pinochet's military dictatorship.[112]

Amnesty International noted how many of these actions actually contributed to the worsening of the pandemic:

> Far from containing the virus, decisions to arrest, detain, use force, and forcibly disperse assemblies have risked increasing contagion—for the law enforcement officials involved as well as those who are affected by police actions. Authorities across the world have forcibly evicted people from their home or detained them, all in the name of Covid-19 protection, even though such actions are likely to spread rather than contain the disease.[113]

Amnesty further noted how 'against the backdrop of fears of contagion, states have used the pandemic as a pretext to introduce laws and policies that violate international law and roll back human rights, including by disproportionately restricting the rights to freedom of peaceful assembly and freedom of expression'.[114] In the Philippines, for example, President Rodrigo Duterte gave orders to the police, military, and local officials to kill those who caused 'trouble' during the imposition of community quarantine.[115] State of emergency laws introduced in several countries further conferred unfettered powers on governments. Freedom of expression, as we have already noted, was severely curtailed. At least twenty-four countries passed laws or orders restricting or punishing the dissemination of false information, and in fifteen of these countries, the dissemination of false information became punishable with prison time. 'In many regions', Amnesty wrote, 'police forces have summoned for questioning or arrested journalists, bloggers, human rights defenders, political activists and social media users for merely expressing their views on Covid-19 measures or sharing information.'[116]

The organisation noted that this trend towards Covid authoritarianism continued throughout 2021, as at least sixty-seven countries 'instrumentalised the pandemic' to introduce new laws to restrict freedom of expression, association, or assembly.[117] As we moved into 2022, there was no signs of things getting any better. Chinese social media, for example, was awash with furious debate and critique of the draconian Zero Covid lockdowns of 2022, which the Chinese state censored in real time.[118]

An equally harrowing picture emerges in several Human Rights Watch (HRW) reports. One 2021 report documented how the Covid-19 pandemic 'spurred a cascade of human rights abuses', as 'many governments [...] used the pandemic as a pretext to grab power and roll back rights':[119]

> Some governments introduced restrictions on movement that were disproportionate to, or inappropriate for, the health threat. Governments instituted discriminatory policies, and authorities enforced measures in a discriminatory way and with excessive—and sometimes fatal—violence. [...] Governments have also used the pandemic to crack down on free speech and peaceful assembly. Military or police forces physically assaulted journalists, bloggers, and protesters, including some who criticized government responses to Covid-19.[120]

'During the pandemic, governments have used the public health emergency to grab power, abuse rights, and systematically neglect some minority populations',[121] said Tirana Hassan, Deputy Executive Director and Chief Programs Officer at HRW. Another HRW report noted how at least eighty-three governments worldwide had used the Covid-19 pandemic to justify violating the exercise of free speech and peaceful assembly:

> Authorities have attacked, detained, prosecuted, and in some cases killed critics, broken up peaceful protests, closed media outlets, and enacted vague laws criminalizing speech that they claim threatens public health. The victims include journalists, activists, healthcare workers, political opposition groups, and others who have criticized government responses to the coronavirus. In most cases, the security forces justified their excessive use of force by saying they were enforcing Covid-19 regulations.[122]

In many countries, including several Western democracies, governments invoked the pandemic to ban all street protests.[123] Most of these reports focus on the 'far too prominent role' of law enforcement in the management of the pandemic.[124] But an equally prominent and perhaps even more disturbing role was played by countries' military apparatuses. A study by the Danish Institute for International Studies (DIIS) documents how countries across the globe mobilised security forces to—allegedly—counter Covid-19.[125] This was often given a positive spin in the media coverage of this relationship. Several governments relied on their militaries and security forces for help in organising the provision of public health services, delivering food aid, constructing and running field hospitals, producing and distributing personal protective equipment, and conducting mass testing and vaccination campaigns, thereby blurring the line between the civilian and military domains in the provision of public services (in Italy, for example, a general was put in charge of the vaccination campaign).

However, in many countries armed forces also worked hand in hand with the police in enforcing lockdowns and social distancing. In France more than 100,000 military and police personnel enforced near-total lockdowns, with similar situations occurring across the world, including in India and Kenya. 'In states with more authoritarian systems, from China and the Philippines to several African countries, this securitisation and militarisation of the Covid-19 response has offered an opportunity to silence political dissent or violently push back against popular demonstrations', the authors of the DIIS report note.[126] On numerous occasions during the pandemic, governments deployed security forces disproportionately to police marginalised communities, which has increased the criminalisation of poverty and homelessness in a time of lockdown. This pattern has repeated itself in several low- and middle-income countries, including India, Nigeria, and Rwanda, during what has been dubbed a 'pandemic of repression'.[127]

Moreover, we have seen how military and intelligence services have played a role in the deployment of tracking technologies, as well as in the policing of the Covid narrative. Indeed, the dominating presence of military apparatuses in the pandemic response has led to calls for expanding the concept of what constitutes a national security threat and the mandating of security forces in response to such threats, particularly at the domestic level.[128] As the aforementioned Danish Institute for International Studies report notes:

> The post-pandemic effects of these developments are still uncertain, but the current militarisation of the Covid-19 response risks doing long-term harm to both public health and human rights, potentially solidifying authoritarian practices. The urgency of the situation has, broadly speaking, led to open-ended mandates, often without transition plans for military disengagement, without strong mechanisms of audit in place, and without accountability and democratic oversight. The protracted nature of the crisis might cement some of these new practices and could set a precedent for the future. The

danger is that governments might institutionalise some of the troublesome developments and that the effects will be felt long after the end of the pandemic.[129]

What, then, of the separation of powers which is supposed to be a key part of the balance of authority in a democracy, and which should have acted as a limiting power to this systemic over-reach? The courts—traditionally the best safeguard against political overreach—generally failed to counteract this concentration of authoritarian power. In the UK, the High Court threw out a case led by the entrepreneur Simon Dolan, and refused to hear a judicial review of the original lockdown order.[130] In Germany in April 2021, police raided the house of Christian Dettmar, a district court judge from Weimar, 18 days after Dettmar had issued a ruling that prohibited schools from imposing mask mandates, social distancing, and compulsory testing on children.[131] There were only a few outliers, such as Spain—where the Constitutional Court ruled in July 2021 that the pandemic lockdown had been unconstitutional,[132] stating that the Constitution had been violated by 'provisions ordering the population off the streets except for short shopping trips, unavoidable work commutes and other essential business'.[133] Another exception was Malawi, where in September 2020 the Constitutional Court passed a unanimous verdict that 'delivered an unequivocal condemnation of that country's Covid-19 lockdown regulations. [...] [T]he three judges found that the rules were unconstitutional as they were made in terms of a law that did not permit such rules to be made.'[134] But these are, in general, exceptions that prove the rule of judicial compliance with the march to the new political authoritarianism.

As all readers will know, the consequence was that several areas of daily life were suddenly placed under police control. Political enforcement of the new consensus required coercive measures. Movement was one of the most obvious, and vital: taking away the freedom of movement meant that harvests were lost in countries such as Angola, Ghana, and Portugal, reserves of food were used up, and prices had already begun to increase by the first months of 2021. But international travel restrictions also came with enormous impacts: over the previous decades a world had emerged in which many people lived dispersed lives, with family members dotted around the world. The world had been like this for many centuries, but the difference was that modern cosmopolitans were used to being able to see their families, and felt stranded without them.

The case of Australia is emblematic. Australia closed its borders in March 2020, and did not fully reopen them for almost two years. By September 2021, the pressure in the liberal media began to grow, as liberal globetrotters wanted a return to normal; an article in *The Atlantic* asked whether Australia was still a liberal democracy.[135] With internment camps established by the end of 2021 for contacts of people who had merely tested positive for Covid, this was certainly an extreme case.[136] The closure of borders in Australia led to 40,000 Australians being stranded for up to two years away from their families.[137] Western Australia closed its borders entirely to international and most inter-state travellers within Australia for two years, until March 2022.[138] Moreover, this was not just something that affected Australians; some foreign residents were also trapped in Australia for up to eighteen months before they could leave, as only tiny numbers of people were allowed on each flight, and formal permission had to be sought from the government to board a plane. As one report put it, some planes had no passengers at all, and others were only allowed between eleven and thirteen.[139]

It's worth mentioning that the closure of borders in general became an important part of virus suppression measures. During the first wave, the *Financial Times* claimed that Britain was an outlier for not having closed its borders fully.[140] Meanwhile, figures in lobby groups such as the UK's Independent SAGE wrote during the second wave in the winter of 2020–21 that tightening borders was crucial to suppress Covid-19. As Gabriel Scally wrote in the *Irish Times* on 30 January 2021, '[we] know that what works is to suppress the virus, keep it suppressed and act decisively to curb the possibility of importing new cases.'[141] The irony is that for years figures on the left—as Independent SAGE claimed to be—had been protesting against increasingly draconian border measures and the construction of 'fortress Britain/Europe/US'. But now closing borders was deemed progressive, even if it racialised inequalities, radicalised political authoritarianism, and was in fact contrary to previous public health advice as demonstrated by the November 2019 WHO report which recommended that border closures should not be implemented under any circumstances.

Alongside the policing of movement was the policing of people's bodies—which was of course connected to it. When the vaccine rollout began in 2021, freedom of movement was restored to those who consented to the new surveillance bioethics but not to those who did not. While many liberal commentators smeared those who had not been vaccinated as far-right conspiracy theorists, they conveniently passed over the fact that minorities represented a large proportion of those who had not been vaccinated against Covid-19.[142] In fact, the vaccine mandates in New York overwhelmingly targeted the city's African-American population.[143] The most extreme consequence of this racialisation of the restriction of movement was reported in New Zealand in June 2022, when a Māori family on the island of Nukunonu protested that they had been under house arrest for eleven months because they had chosen not to take the Covid vaccine. A letter from the island council in late 2021 stated, 'You will remain on house arrest with your wife [...] and your son

[...] for a further six months until you reconsider your decision. Your daughter [...] will also be on house arrest starting tonight at 10 pm.'[144]

In sum, policies of control increased across the board of global politics. What was driving this shift? Many potential explanations have been offered, and again we don't propose to come down on one side or the other as many of them may overlap. The desire for greater political control was seen by some on the left as a prerequisite for dealing with climate change, as the French philosopher Bruno Latour suggested.[145] Among libertarians, the framework of authority required by climate change and Covid was seen critically, as part of a move towards a 'socialist-controlled' society. And then again, the concentration of capital has been seen by some as guiding a desire for greater control over human beings, in order to protect the radical economic accumulation of elites in recent years.

Again, rather than focus on the why, we can focus on the what and the how. In this chapter, we've seen the narrative and ethical frameworks that were elaborated. In the West, core elements of the state were involved in this process. This goes beyond the 'nudge' units that we've already considered here, for there's no doubt that powerful political actors have been keen to push surveillance bioethics and its digital economy. An investigation by Jeremy Loffredo and Max Blumenthal for *The Grayzone* found that one of the major companies involved in promoting the vaccine passport technologies in the US was MITRE, a 'non-profit corporation led almost entirely by military-intelligence professionals and sustained by sizable contracts with the Department of Defense, FBI, and national security sector'.[146] Meanwhile in the UK, Paul Mason, one of the journalists who had heavily promoted the idea in left-wing media such as the *New Statesman* that the 'anti-vaxxers' were far-right conspiracy theorists,[147] was found by an investigation to be working in apparent coordination with a senior figure in the British security services.[148]

It is thus a matter of record that key elements of the military-intelligence state in both the UK and the US pushed the vaccine passports and the surveillance technologies which go with them. Did they do this because they had a clear view of the science of the new mRNA vaccines and of herd immunity, and understood the history of the concept—or because they wanted to use the crisis (as Giorgio Agamben suggested) to institutionalise the state of exception? We will leave readers of this book to look at the evidence that we have presented and to draw their own conclusions.

Of course, the answer to that question will also depend on how governments react as the threat of Covid inevitably recedes, with the virus becoming endemic, as some argue is already happening.[149] Will they roll back the 'emergency' measures introduced (allegedly) to fight the virus or will they cling on to their newly acquired powers? According to a UN report, there is a very real risk the measures in question 'may become normalized once the crisis has passed'.[150] Indeed, several authors have raised the question of mission creep in relation to many of the surveillance technologies rolled out during the pandemic—that is, the fact that 'governments will not be willing to abandon the new surveillance opportunities these apps offer and that personal data will be collected indefinitely and used for unanticipated ends'.[151] As Edward Snowden noted: 'When we see emergency measures passed, particularly today, they tend to be sticky. The emergency tends to be expanded.'[152] Activists across the globe have expressed fears that the Covid-19 pandemic may have ushered in a new era of normalised state surveillance. As scholars have noted:

In the United Kingdom, the government plans to retain the data it collects for up to 20 years and denies individuals an absolute

423

right to have their data deleted upon request. Rights groups have raised fears that the data may be used for other purposes, and have pointed out that the government has failed to conduct a legally mandated data protection impact assessment. There are precedents for these fears. For example, the US Patriot Act, passed in 2001 in response to the terrorist attacks of September 11, 2001, gave the government broad surveillance powers with limited oversight. It remains in place today, despite the lack of any indication there is an immediate threat of a foreign attack on US soil.[153]

How can we be sure that the wealth of data involved in the tracking and tracing of Covid won't be used—indeed, isn't already being used—for other purposes far removed from the original intentions behind the collection of the data? The problems are not limited to test-and-trace technologies. In May 2022, Human Rights Watch reported that 89 per cent of technologies used for remote learning harvested the learning, location, and personal data of students.[154] In several countries most of these apps, including Microsoft Teams, Zoom, and Minecraft Education, have remained in use even after Covid measures were lifted. Dhakshayini Sooriyakumaran, the Director of Tech Policy at Reset Australia, an organisation aimed at raising awareness about digital threats to democracy, said that during the pandemic, multiple data extraction technologies were launched under the guise of 'emergency measures'.[155] She added that these technologies do not come with sufficient data protection measures or well-defined purpose limitations. Therefore, they can be abused. As noted in Chapter 5, similar concerns have been raised in relation to vaccine passports:

> Having set these population-wide passport precedents, it is conceivable that they could be expanded in the near future to include other personal health data including genetic tests and

mental health records, which would create additional rights violations and discrimination based on biological status for employers, law enforcement, insurance companies, governments and tech companies. [...] Technology companies interested in biosurveillance using artificial intelligence and facial recognition technology have obtained large contracts to implement vaccine passports and now have a financial interest in maintaining and expanding them.[156]

It's a simple statement of fact that tech companies and international organisations such as the World Bank and World Economic Forum have long been promoting biometrics-based digital identity and health wallets—'digital passports' assigned to each citizen at birth and containing the person's demographic, biometric, and health data (and potentially any other type of data). To this end they have established initiatives and institutes such as ID2020 | Digital Identity Alliance,[157] the Commons Project,[158] and the Vaccination Credential Initiative (VCI).[159] It's also no secret that those same companies and institutions see vaccine passports as the precursors to digital IDs. As one tech analyst put it: 'By restricting and changing the shape of human interaction for over a year, the Covid-19 pandemic rapidly accelerated the digitalization of many services and, in doing so, reinvigorated efforts to establish a cross-contextual digital identity infrastructure.'[160] Another wrote that '[m]obile digital identity technology and infrastructure have been dramatically advanced by digital health passes, which provide the foundations of identity verification and linkage to credentials that can underpin mobile identity wallets.'[161]

Interestingly, Bill Gates, a long-time supporter of digital IDs, was already predicting as early as May 2020, only 7 weeks into the pandemic, that 'eventually we will have some digital certificates to show who has recovered or been tested recently or when we have a vaccine who has received it'.[162] Although, as we noted in Chapter 5, he has since distanced himself from vaccine passports for Covid-19, one may argue he certainly had a hand in making that earlier prediction come true. In mid-2021, the Gates Foundation funded, alongside the Rockefeller Foundation, a WHO paper providing 'implementation guidance' for proof of vaccination certifications across the world.[163] One may therefore also legitimately wonder whether the role of technology companies such as Microsoft, Oracle, Salesforce, and several other 'heavyweights' in launching the Vaccination Credential Initiative to develop digital immunisation authentication tools in early 2021 was motivated solely by public health concerns—after all, these technology providers certainly stand to gain from the institutionalisation of this kind of mechanism.[164]

Thales, one of the largest international defence contractors, called the digital vaccination passport a precursor to universal mobile-digital identity credentials, saying that 'Covid-19 health passports can push open the door to a digital ID revolution.'[165] Kristel Teyras, in charge of Thales's Digital Identity Services portfolio, wrote:

> Even as we start to return to a sense of normality, this digitalisation of services looks set to gather momentum. This is, in part, due to governments around the world asking their citizens to carry digital health passes to prove they are doubly vaccinated or have a negative test before they can access certain services.[166]

In an article on the company's website, Thales urged the company's government customers to 'regard the pandemic as an opportunity to create a platform for more ambitious digitalisation of their identity and health credentials.' And further:

> To facilitate the transition from short-term relief to ambitious redesign of public service delivery, the health pass can be extended into a wide-ranging and capable digital ID/health

wallet. Significantly, this provides a secure and intuitive smartphone-based location for an array of digital ID and health credentials.[167]

Another quote shows just how potentially endless the scope of these mobile IDs could be:

In health, forward-thinking ministries can digitalise not just vaccine certificates, but also general health and insurance credentials, as well as donor cards. Trusted online authentication also opens the door to efficient and user-friendly services such as ePrescriptions, and secure, user-controlled sharing of health attributes. Similarly, ministries responsible for travel credentials can use the wallet to facilitate the creation of digital companions for physical passports.[168]

As the German economist Norbert Häring writes: 'This would have the—entirely intended—side effect of turning Silicon Valley platform corporations into world passport authorities.'[169] Projects of this kind are already underway in countries such as India.[170] Meanwhile, in June 2021, the EU proposed a framework for a European Digital Identity, one of the largest digital identity projects ever.[171] As Thales notes approvingly:

The ambition is huge; both in terms of scale—as it applies to all EU member states—and also in the power it would grant to citizens throughout the bloc. For the first time, citizens would be able to use a European Digital Identity wallet, from their phone, that would give them access to services in any region across Europe.

The idea of a digital ID that 'gives you access to services' worries some people because it implies that your right to access the services in question could be 'switched off' at any moment. This is not some dystopian hypothetical scenario—this is exactly the fate that befell millions of people, in several countries, who were denied access to a whole range of public spaces and services on the basis of their unvaccinated status. A glimpse into what this may mean for the future was offered in June 2022, when a protest planned by hundreds of bank depositors in central China seeking access to their frozen funds was thwarted when authorities turned their health code apps red, several depositors told Reuters, making it impossible for them to travel.[172]

It's worth noting that the same organisations that are pushing biometric digital identity are also pushing to progressively eliminate cash.[173] It's easy to see how in a cashless society, where digital IDs are required to access most services, this would mean that banks and governments would have the ability to cancel noncompliant citizens. Again, this is not some hypothetical scenario: in February 2022, the Canadian government froze several bank accounts connected to truckers protesting the vaccine mandates in the country in order 'to pressure protesters to leave the city's streets'.[174]

This kind of threat was recognised by some of those involved in these projects. Elizabeth Renieris of the Notre Dame-IBM Tech Ethics Lab resigned from a technical advisory role on ID2020 citing 'risks to civil liberties' after the NGO teamed up with the Global Alliance for Vaccines and Immunization (GAVI) and with technology companies to design Covid vaccine passports backed up by experimental blockchain technology:

> The prospect of severely curtailing the fundamental rights and freedoms of individuals through ill-thought-out plans for 'immunity passports' or similar certificates, particularly ones that would leverage premature standards and a highly experimental and potentially rights-infringing technology like blockchain, is beyond dystopian.[175]

We think it's pretty clear that these kinds of concerns are connected to the 'social credit' debate. As Covid authoritarianism increased, some critics claimed that the rise of this model was because Western politicians were attracted to the model of 'social credit' which had emerged in China over previous years. By July 2021, some writers in the conservative press were claiming that without concerted action Britain would soon be adopting the social credit system.[176] In this account, the creeping influence of the Chinese model of authoritarian capitalism which we've described in this chapter was about to explode across the landscape of what had already become increasingly illiberal democracies. On the other hand, some publications ran pieces saying that the social credit system was not as draconian as critics said,[177] and that it had widespread support in China itself.[178]

So what was the social credit system? Writing in *Wired* before the pandemic, Kevin Hong described how the idea had been announced by the Chinese government in 2014 as an opt-in system that was managed regionally, with different regional criteria: in this model, major tech and social media outlets such as Alibaba and Tencent collected data on individual habits and churned this out into a score through an opaque algorithmic model.[179] Citizens received credit scores according to their observable behaviour, and a low score could bar them from routine activities such as travel and fast internet speeds.[180] Already by 2019, some journalists investigating charges of corruption were being prevented from travelling on trains or planes and taking out a loan.[181] With punitive sanctions including removal of pets, failed university applications, and career inertia, the system was certainly one which could fast-track social compliance in this model of authoritarian capitalism.[182]

Is there any evidence that this kind of 'nudge' is indeed the direction of travel for liberal democracies? The widespread rollout of vaccine passports could certainly be seen as a form of social credit, in which those without the appropriately sanctioned behaviour could not perform basic tasks and socialise with their peers, and were denied national and international freedom of movement. The connection of this technology to surveillance—with, as we've seen, the support of military intelligence—suggests a strong impulse in this direction. And on the other hand, as we've also seen in this chapter, and through the book as a whole, these interests of the state apparatus were also shared by the giant commercial interests who profiteered from Covid-19: the tech and pharmaceutical companies who made a killing, and for whom, of course, the vaccine passports were a key mode of protecting their profits (through the universality of the app on the tech side, and the way in which they fuelled vaccine take-up on the pharma side). As vaccine passports give way to even more pervasive digital IDs, the opportunities for profit can only multiply.[183] Ultimately, digital IDs remind us that it's pointless to look for a single overarching explanation for policies that emerge from a complex nexus of overlapping economic and political interests.

It's hard to overstate the political consequences of this. Authoritarianism was one side of what Ole Skambraks had observed as the media apparatus fomenting polarisation. This was polarisation on steroids, and made the 2010s seem like an era of polite debate. The accusation of fascism became almost universal, and it wasn't just liberal commentators who described their opponents as fascists: a powerful article by the former WHO Malaria Diagnostics Lead, David Bell, described what he called the 'emergence of neo-fascism in public health'.[184] With each side calling the other fascists, what was going on here?

Key features of the new political domain bring together much of what we've discussed in this chapter. On the one hand there's the uniting of commercial and political interests with oversight of a 'single narrative', and the attacking of anyone who diverges from it. On the other, there's the technical and ethical apparatus which legitimates new methods of surveillance and a new bioethics. And then there are the state frameworks which seek greater surveillance over the activities of citizens at a time of turmoil.

Meanwhile, in poorer countries with weaker state infrastructures, it was the imposition of a lockdown model which had the most significant impact in terms of entrenching authoritarian power. As we've seen, in all contexts authoritarian medical policies could only be imposed through authoritarian politics. Lacking the governmental infrastructure and media capture to develop nudge units and soft power techniques, in low-income countries authoritarian political power-grabs were always likely to result from the global demand that all nations should 'follow the science'.

What's the best way of describing this political earthquake? The American political scientist Joel Kotkin called it 'neo-feudalism',[185] and linked the new frameworks to Mussolini's conceptualisation of state and commercial power.[186] Mussolini had seen fascism as a vehicle in which political and commercial power were in harness together[187]—and that's certainly one way of interpreting the rise of Covid authoritarianism which we've set out in this chapter, and the devastating impacts which it has had on political economies around the world.

***

In this chapter we've considered a number of the political consequences of the 'single narrative' of the Covid-19 pandemic. As powerful Western democracies such as the UK move to institutionalise the power grab, it's hard not to conclude that the model of authoritarian capitalism is becoming embedded across the world. This transformation could only take place because of the united power of the members of the TNI, their policing of the new consensus, and the ethical framework which was created to buttress it. As we've seen, this was a framework which had in fact been building for a number of years, before it burst out into the open in 2020.

And yet precisely because of its totalising single narrative, the new consensus was riddled with contradictions which produced enormous cognitive dissonance. Many people will have felt that it was as if psychological warfare was being conducted against them by their own state. On the one hand, we were told that masks worked to stop infection and disease—and yet on the other that everyone had to wear them to protect others (who presumably, if masks worked, should have been protected). People would attend masked meetings with their colleagues, and then go to the cafeteria, take off their masks, and have lunch with them. In December 2021, people in Western countries were told that they had to take a third vaccine dose to protect themselves against Omicron—and yet at the same time, they were also being told that a global effort had to be made to secure just two doses of the vaccine for those in low-income countries who had not yet been vaccinated. Conservative politicians who had denounced their opponents for fiscal irresponsibility opened the floodgates to the biggest peacetime spending in democratic history. Left-wing thinkers who had denounced migration controls called for the closure of borders.

These chaotic and contradictory frameworks metastasised across society, which at the same time became more fragmentary and solitary than ever before. The question of isolation was closely related to the political framework, and was certainly manufactured by governments through their relentless use of propaganda during the onset of the crisis. Injunctions to 'stay at home, save lives' provided an ethical imperative to isolate yourself, as did the comments of senior government figures and their advisers that no one should hug their elderly relatives even when meetings did become allowed. Many of the slogans made swift inroads because they were borrowed from online jargon, with the wish that everyone 'stay safe' building from years of education on 'staying safe online'.[188] The propaganda that isolation and loneliness were morally necessary was rammed home by a media machine which suddenly began to commission new material such as the BBC's radio programme on the devastating damage caused by 'Aids denialism' in South Africa in the early 2000s.[189] Such propaganda and sloganising was fit for a context like Covid-19; according to the Nobel Prize-winning writer Elias Canetti, the word 'slogan' derives from the Celtic *sluagh-ghairm* ('the battle-cry of the dead').[190]

In her famous book *The Origins of Totalitarianism*, Hannah Arendt identified isolation and loneliness as the key building blocks of totalitarian societies. For Arendt, loneliness was 'the essence of totalitarian government'.[191] She saw totalitarian governments as only able to succeed once they had isolated people from one another as political actors, and then rendered private life impossible: 'Totalitarian government, like all tyrannies, certainly could not exist without destroying the public realm of life, that is, without destroying, by isolating men, their political capacities. But totalitarian domination as a form of government is not content with this isolation and destroys private life as well. It bases itself on loneliness, on the experience of not belonging to the world at all, which is the most radical and desperate experience.'[192]

Having fled Nazi Germany for America in the 1930s, Arendt also knew that isolation could often give rise to conspiracy theories. She knew that conspiracy theorists thrive in times of economic depression, and that sometimes those conspiracy theorists can give birth to a political movement such as Nazism—whose antisemitism was grounded in absurd fabrications such as *The Protocols of the Elders of Zion*. As a historian of conspiracy theories reminds us, these tend to arise when people feel marginalised and cut out from a new direction of power.[193] In such circumstances people cast around to grasp an explanation for this change of events, and find it in a conspiracy against them. In this way, the marginalised and discarded people of an economically depressed society come to identify with those who will banish the phantom—as happened in Germany in the 1930s in the wake of the Great Depression.

Given the framework of isolation, and of a totalising single narrative which was shot through with cognitive dissonance, it's hardly surprising that, as we've already noted, the response to Covid-19 has seen the rise of an almost bewildering variety of conspiracy theories. As this discussion suggests, this was only to be expected. We've already argued in this book, and have seen in this chapter, that there is no need for conspiracy theories to explain the political response to Covid-19. Much of this has been a coordination in plain sight rather than a hidden conspiracy. Meanwhile, the devastating impacts and people's acceptance of them were shaped by the pre-existing direction of economic power and technology and the way in which they directed certain outcomes once the new virus had been identified.

With so many crises flying about, and so many conflicting ideas as to cause and effect, we think it's important to return to what has happened, and also ask who has gained from this. Some things are clear: mechanisms of social control and coercion have increased, inequality has expanded enormously, and in that context China's exemplar of an authoritarian capitalism that neoliberalism had also been constructing for many years looms uncomfortably nearby. The winners have been massive corporations and their managers, government spooks, political autocrats and their cheerleaders, and authoritarian monopoly capitalism—and there's nothing much that's progressive about that as far as we can see.

CONCLUSION

We have examined a number of disturbing themes in this book. On the whole, our focus has been to try to explore what has happened, rather than why it has happened. Inevitably these aspects have at times overlapped, but the complexities are such that it is going to take more than just two researchers to resolve them.

Nevertheless, as we reach the end of this horror story, it's reasonable for readers to ask us to declare some kind of position as to the why as well as the what. It's our view that the framework of what we have called the single narrative is vital to understanding the past two years. This helps to understand the overturning of the preceding consensus, how a totalising and anti-scientific view of science and the truth was constructed, and what the consequences of this might be in the information age and in an era of the ascent of authoritarian capitalism.

As we have shown, the Covid policies represented an enormous and unprecedented scientific experiment. As the pandemic era becomes the era of Covid endemicity, we feel that it's the right moment to assess at least some of the results of the experiment. On the one hand, there is the question of the virus. As we have seen, many experts initially doubted the efficacy of lockdown models over the long term. Moreover, it was widely accepted by figures including Patrick Vallance and Neil Ferguson (and later Bill Gates) that a severe suppression of the virus in the first wave would lead to a more severe second wave, as indeed happened. The details matter, and 2020 and 2021 have given us important evidence so that we can understand why this is—and how attempts to crush the initial spread of a virus may lead to higher infectivity.

As we have seen during the Covid pandemic—and as was indeed predicted beforehand—once a virus has been established it will spread in any case. Key workers have to continue their jobs in warehouses, at supermarket checkouts, in waste disposal, and of course also in education and healthcare. They will inevitably interact with one another. The virus will spread. Meanwhile, the psychological and physical impact of living in isolation for eighteen months while being gnawed at by fear of the coming economic meltdown has a negative impact on well-being, with knock-on immunity consequences which may make people more susceptible to the spread of the virus as well as to other diseases. Apparently, all this is quite hard for people suddenly endowed with a newly enhanced sense of self-worth, working in comfortable offices with secure jobs staring at spreadsheets and mathematical models, to factor into their policy calculations.

Whatever we did, the virus just kept on spreading: this is a fair summary of what happened in 2020. Some countries, such as New Zealand, did manage to stop the virus from establishing itself by blocking anyone from coming into the country, regardless of the wider implications—a classic example of what we may call 'Covid nationalism'. The New Zealand model worked—for New Zealand. But it only worked for a time, and only with the hope of vaccines which in the end could not deliver the herd immunity that had been promised. It was also only possible because New Zealand is one of the most isolated places on Earth and could shut itself down before the virus arrived in a way not possible for most places. It was also only possible because New Zealand did not appear to care what the impact of its policies might be, if widely adopted, on poorer countries dependent on global trade. Moreover, it proved to be impossible to eliminate the virus, and New Zealand was eventually forced to abandon the goal of Zero Covid and in fact once it did so saw a rapid rise in excess deaths—in sum this failed policy could only ever have been achieved through complete global apartheid between richer and poorer countries, as indeed we saw in the past two years.

Once the virus was established, countries such as Nicaragua, Sweden, and Tanzania with soft restrictions did not have noticeably higher Covid and excess death rates than countries with severe restrictions such as Argentina, Belgium, Italy, Peru, and Spain. In fact, excess deaths in these countries were much lower than in their neighbours, as the long-term health impacts of the lockdowns began to reverse the short-term benefits that had accrued. Standard vaccination and maternity programmes were abandoned, and children's hospitals closed. Middle-income countries saw the dramatic rise of soup kitchens in poor areas as the ability to earn money vanished overnight. Children in poor regions were suddenly unable to access education, and the impact was so severe that on some estimates the follow-through in terms of lost skills will be felt for a century. Death rates in countries like Angola for malaria and dengue fever went through the roof as the state, plunged into an economic crisis more severe than anything since independence, withdrew services. Domestic abuse soared all over the world, while child marriage and trafficking increased. Meanwhile in cushioned Western countries, the savings of the rich grew as the poor found themselves falling into rent arrears and struggling to feed their families, and a generation of poor children found their life chances scarred so deeply that many educators wonder if they will ever recover. Schools closed everywhere, and in countries such as India and Uganda they took two years to re-open.

Then there were the impacts on civil and human rights. Elderly people were prevented from seeing their relatives. Peaceful protests became illegal in the second and third waves. In Spain, during the first wave children were seen as a lower priority than dogs: they were not allowed out under any circumstances, whereas dogs could be walked once per day. In Chile, the level of fear and the difficulty in some municipalities involved in getting police permission to go outside saw some people staying inside their apartments for seven months.

Meanwhile, as all this was happening, global inequalities were exploding. On one hand the technology giants and their owners made hundreds of billions of dollars (more on this in a moment). It was no coincidence that this also saw many small and middle-sized shops (and larger high street chains) going to the wall. In the Global South, the huge numbers of people who relied on informal work suddenly found themselves unable to earn a living. With the collapse in demand for resources, the world's poorest countries were forced to indebt themselves even further to large multinational institutions and lenders. The gulf between rich and poor widened as never before, both between countries and within them. The savings of the wealthier among the remote-working classes increased, and their lifestyles became more manageable—more sustainable, as they liked to say.

From the beginning, these responses could not be deemed progressive. They did not seek to reduce the inequality between rich and poor—a core aim of left-wing politics—and they targeted women, children, and the livelihoods and futures of so many people in poor countries. When vaccine passports appeared, they also targeted minorities who were less likely to be vaccinated. Meanwhile, the policies also did not protect poorer people in rich countries, since mortality rates from Covid were higher among these sectors of the population. In fact, what the lockdowns did was offer focused protection to the so-called laptop class. And yet the Western liberal left took a position that demanded more of the measures that were producing these very outcomes; all the same, over time, more voices from the left did criticise this position, while the two countries in the Western hemisphere with the least severe restrictions—Nicaragua and Sweden—had left-wing governments, and we think it's important to make this a matter of record.[1]

The reasons for this political framing are so complex that they will form the subject of debate for many years to come, but it's worth outlining just a few of the important themes that we have discussed here. These include the alienation from production in the West, and the associated rise of computing technologies which have produced a distancing from the world; the erosion of boundaries between public and private in business, work, society, and our personal lives; and the associated transformation in value systems which made the Covid response develop a remarkable normativity in Western society.

In fact, when we look at all of these, we'll find that there's one common thread: neoliberal economics and the politics that has enforced it over the past three decades (the outsourcing of production from Western countries and the inequalities and alienation this produced; the investment in computing technologies aggravating inequalities, surveillance, and the erosion of boundaries between the personal and the public; the revolving door between business and government). In that sense, the Covid policies were, as we saw in the last chapter, the logical conclusion of the neoliberal authoritarianism which has arisen in the twenty-first century. And that turn to authoritarian capitalism can lead to a variety of potential future outcomes which we need to consider before the end of this book.

***

On the one hand, as we have seen throughout the book, the pandemic—or better the political-economic and biomedical response to it—has led to a massive accumulation of capital by the world's billionaire class and in particular by a handful of mega-corporations, particularly in the Big Tech and Big Pharma sectors, at the expense of small and medium enterprises (SMEs) and the global working class.

A dystopian future is one potential path to emerge from the ashes of the pandemic—one in which not only are wealth and power more concentrated than ever in the hands of a small elite of individuals, but in which practically every sector of the economy is dominated by a handful of all-powerful mega-corporations. This radical continuity in existing trends of inequality shows that a rather different perspective emerges when we 'follow the politics' rather than 'following the science'. It turns out that those who have most profited from the pandemic response (tech moguls like Bill Gates and Mark Zuckerberg) are also those most likely to have supported that response and to have removed information from their portals which criticised it.

This is not a scenario in which governments disappear, but rather it is one that relies on increasingly powerful and authoritarian state apparatuses intervening to further the interests of big capital (*contra* small capital). It also follows the increasing dislocation of capital from human labour, resulting from decades of neoliberal restructuring and today exacerbated by the rise of digital and crypto currencies, the mechanisation of work, and the rise of what David Graeber called 'bullshit jobs'.[2]

However, there's a further element that makes this potential scenario even more disturbing, if possible, and that is the growing consolidation not only within but also between sectors. This becomes evident when we look at the investment funds that actually 'own' these corporations. BlackRock and Vanguard are the two largest asset management firms in the world, respectively

CONCLUSION

managing the mind-boggling sums of US$10 trillion[3] and US$8 trillion. That's 3.7 and 3 times more than the UK's annual GDP. These two funds are the top 'owners' of all the major Big Pharma (Pfizer, Johnson & Johnson, Merck), Big Tech (Facebook, Twitter), and Big Media (*New York Times*, Time Warner, Comcast, Disney, News Corp) corporations.

A 2017 paper in *The Conversation* claimed that BlackRock and Vanguard had ownership in some 1,600 American firms.[4] When you add in the then-third-largest global owner, State Street, their combined ownership encompassed nearly 90 per cent of all S&P 500 firms, with the three mega-funds being the largest shareholders in 40 per cent of all publicly listed firms in the United States. That number is likely to be even higher today. Even more worrying is the fact that '[d]espite having shareholdings of "only" 5–7 per cent, there is growing evidence that institutional investors such as BlackRock and Vanguard engage in active discussions with company management and boards with a view to influence companies' long-term strategies', as a recent paper shows.[5]

Worse, even, it would appear that these funds also coordinate among themselves. When analysing the voting behaviour of the two funds, researchers found that they coordinate it through centralised corporate governance departments.[6] This is hardly surprising if we consider that BlackRock and Vanguard are also each other's main institutional investors:[7] in other words, they 'own' each other. This means that we are effectively in the presence of a single super-entity that 'owns' and controls a huge chunk of the Western economy. While this was already the case before the pandemic, the response to the latter has accelerated this trend. More importantly, it has brought to the surface the way in which these funds, through their cross-sector corporate control, can 'harmonise' companies' behaviour to further their interests.

This is evident in the case of debate around pandemic strategies on social media, with rampant censorship exercised today by social media platforms against any voice, no matter how qualified, as we've discussed in this book—including the attempted cancelling of esteemed scientists. But this feature becomes even more worrying when we consider that the companies selling the vaccine, the media outlets shaping the mainstream vaccine narrative, and the social media platforms enforcing that narrative are, to a large degree, 'owned' and controlled by the same two funds: BlackRock and Vanguard, which, incidentally, are raking in billions from the vaccines.[8] This harmonisation among sectors (and between these sectors and governments) points to the rise in the West of a new ultra-powerful complex—what we have called the techno-media-pharma (TMP) complex. This is evident in increased interpenetration between these sectors. Take Google's growing investments in the health, pharmaceutical, and pandemic-prevention sectors, for example, or Amazon's investment in Covid-19 research.[9]

As we saw throughout the first part of this book, none of this would be possible without the active support of governments,[10] which use their financial power to create an enabling environment that rewards participants in the TMP complex. This is evident, for example, in the secrecy, overpricing, cronyism, and inefficiency that has characterised Covid procurement deals, as contracts for Covid tests, PPE, vaccines, and vaccine passport technologies have been parcelled out to transnational corporations without proper tendering processes or legislative oversight.

This is hardly surprising when we consider the extent to which these corporate giants have captured our political systems through the revolving door framework which has been a recurrent theme in this book. The US is a good case in point. Obama was very close to Eric Schmidt, CEO of Google,[11] who later became a close collaborator of the Pentagon in developing military applications of AI.[12] Today, Biden's economic policies are heavily influenced by the director of the National Economic Council, Brian Deese, a former BlackRock executive.[13] Biden also helped Robert Califf—senior advisory for Verily Life and Google Health, the biotech and healthcare subsidiaries of Google, and a huge Big Pharma stockholder—get confirmed as commissioner for the FDA.

This dystopian variant of the future would see this ultra-elite now in a position to shape every aspect of our lives. And as we've noted in this book, we are baffled by the fact that most on the left spent the past two years denouncing those who pointed out these inconvenient truths: that wealth is hyper-concentrated as never before, that this is as a result of the policy choices during the pandemic, and that these choices were unprecedented and have been supported by the TMP complex whose participants have enriched themselves enormously along the way, and censored any alternative point of view.

However, it's important also to grasp that the changes that Covid policies have ushered in have not been universal. As we've seen, the embedding of a new normativity in value systems and surveillance has been most pronounced in Western countries— and it's here that the liberal left has been one of the main advocates of this position. However, in other parts of the world the response has been quite different, and this is a more positive variant that it's also important to be aware of.

In Latin America, 2021 and 2022 saw the election and re-election of a series of internationalist left-wing governments— partly, as many observers recognised, because of the appalling war on the middle class and the poor that had been unleashed by Covid policies. The elections of Gabriel Boric in Chile, Ollanta Humala in Peru, and Gustavo Petro in Colombia, and the re-election of Daniel Ortega in Nicaragua and return to power of Lula da Silva in Brazil were all markers that a new coalition was beginning to form that was not prepared for a continuation of the same old markers of neoliberal extractive government. This was clear in the election of Petro in Colombia in June 2022, where his opponent Rodolfo Hernández ('Colombia's Trump') participated in parties sponsored by Pfizer,[14] and was supported by the global financial news sector in the shape of Bloomberg,[15] the *Financial Times*,[16] and the *Wall Street Journal*,[17] and yet was still defeated. It's in Latin America that these movements have won political power, but one might also cite as evidence of this shift the success in the June 2022 French legislative elections of the radical-left NUPES (New Popular Union) alliance led by Jean-Luc Mélenchon, who had slammed the French 'health pass' as 'absurd, unfair and authoritarian'.[18]

Meanwhile in Africa, resistance to the march of the dystopian variant of the future was also clear. This emerged in the rejection of the WHO's proposed reforms to international health regulations by African nations in May 2022,[19] and also in the fact that many African countries refused to march to the West's beat by supporting them in the conflict in Ukraine.[20] Lockdown colonialism and the neo-imperial framework of Covid policies meant that many leaders on the continent were unwilling to do the West's bidding any further.

Thus, while libertarians in the West simultaneously decried Covid policies and more global historical frameworks that included the Global South, it was in fact peoples of the Global South—primed through their own experiences of the authoritarian capitalism experienced under colonialism and neo-colonialism—who offered the greatest hope in the world of challenging and overturning the onset of a dystopian future.

***

Thus we can look at the future in either an optimistic or a pessimistic way. Historically, left movements offered a positive vision of a future which is more equal and democratic. However, in recent years this positive vision has been crowded out on the left by an almost unremittingly negative view of the future. As we've said, there are aspects of the changes that have occurred which can lead to a more positive view—but before we get to them, we need to consider some of the many things that have gone wrong since March 2020.

Computer modellers assumed that the Covid-19 virus would behave in the same way all over the world. This led to political and scientific pressure for a global rollout of lockdowns, which was disastrous in the Global South above all. The global medical establishment pushed a model of virus suppression developed in one of the most authoritarian states on Earth, without any grasp of the way in which social and political contexts can affect outcomes. They also assumed that there was no existing cross-immunity to the virus. And all these turned out to be false assumptions.

The wildly inaccurate projections of computer modellers were taken as sacrosanct because of our growing collective obsessions with data and computing. There was a fascination with the chance to study a pandemic, something that the global medical establishment had been preparing itself for ever since the redefinition of the meaning of the word in 2009. All this meant that no history lessons were taken from previous modelling projections in 2005 with avian flu and 2009 with swine flu, which in each case also saw overestimates by computer modellers of the mortality of the new virus.

In the beginning, leading scientists said that the government would have to balance the impact of the virus with the wider needs of society. However, over time many scientists and government leaders ceased to make any reference to such balance when making major policy decisions. Perhaps this was because no sustained attempt was made to take account of the nature of power—history shows that power is attractive to human beings, that it changes people, and that it is hard to give up, and yet those who had so swiftly been empowered were effectively given control over how and when they should relinquish that power.

Political leaders misunderstood (or pretended to misunderstand) the scientific method as one which led to objective truth. They did not understand (or at least appear to understand) that there are scientific disagreements, that it can take years to understand the impacts of policies, or that statistics themselves are not objective but subject to strong levels of interpretation in how they are measured and then assessed.

Data was presented by government and in the media without any context. The alarming rise in deaths (40,000, 60,000, 200,000) was presented without any sense of general mortality in the world: that nearly 60 million people die across the world every year; that 600 or 700 daily deaths in the UK sounds bad when presented by a government minister in sombre tones at a daily press conference, but on average around 1,600 people die every day in the country (and more like 2,000 in the winter).

With the exception of behavioural psychologists seeking to control outcomes, the social sciences were completely ignored in the development of major policy decisions. There was apparently no place at the key initial meetings for economists who could contextualise the likely social and health impacts of a depression, psychologists who could understand the mental health burden and its likely impact on physical health, educational experts who could project the social and learning outcomes for children of the long-term closure of schools, development economists who could discuss whether lockdowns really were viable strategies in informal economies, or historians of previous economic declines who might be able to give an overall perspective.

Political leaders and opinion formers in the West failed to grasp the interconnected worlds in which we live. The worst recession in

CONCLUSION

300 years brings terrible poverty to the world's rich countries, but starvation in the Global South because of the economic relations of dependence, exploitation, and resource extraction which have grown up over the past 500 years. Advocating lockdowns and the shutting down of borders in the West has the consequence of making children starve in Mozambique and further eroding their rights to profit from their own natural resources through enforced fire-sales of these assets to repay the new loans that have been taken out.

And finally, we can see how the idea that data and surveillance can save us has been revealed for the utopian worldview that it is. The Covid-19 crisis has revealed not only the miracle of science, but also its limitations. Technologies change, but as history shows, human beings and the power relations which govern their societies remain stubbornly enduring.

***

It's a pretty depressing list. What should have happened instead? Sticking to the existing scientific consensus and pandemic preparedness plans would have been a good start, alongside taking heed of the lessons from swine flu, avian flu, and the Ebola lockdowns in Sierra Leone and Liberia. For in March 2020, the lesson of the history of new influenza and coronavirus strains over the past twenty years was that initial projections are often overstated—and that lockdowns are counterproductive. It takes a few weeks at least for reliable data to come in.

All the same, it's true that—for many of the reasons outlined in this book in terms of propaganda and uncertain evidence, coming from China and elsewhere—the initial picture was unclear. Indeed, some scientists who became virulent lockdown opponents, such as Ari Joffe, Karol Sikora, and Mike Yeadon, supported the initial lockdown until late April.[21] During that time the data could have been analysed calmly, and in the meantime a plan developed to ensure proposals in line with existing knowledge, balancing the risks from the virus with the economic and health risks that would accrue from the paralysis of normal life for much longer than that. Yet as far as can be seen there was never any attempt to conduct this sort of comparative risk analysis on either national or global levels. Having looked at the evidence that we have presented, we leave it to readers to draw their own conclusions as to why this was.

Whatever the causes of all this, the results have been outlined in this book, and its subtitle: since March 2020 we have witnessed a global assault on democracy and the poor (and, we would add, on truth). If democratic norms and debate are to endure—and it's clear that for the time being they do, even if on life-support, as our capacity to research, write, and publish this book attests— this cannot continue. What must now be done, so that these mistakes are never repeated?

A more optimistic vision of the future, proper regulation of capital, and the reassertion of boundaries between public and private seem important starting points. But a full answer to this question is beyond the scope of *The Covid Consensus*. What we've tried to do here is outline what has happened, since that seems to us a prerequisite for making sure that it does not happen again. In the end, if we believe in freedom of thought, democratic discussion and decision-making, international justice, open government, and an end to the politics of crisis, we have to fight for them—individually and collectively, as best we can.

INDEX

INDEX

INDEX

INDEX

INDEX

453

INDEX

INDEX

emergency powers and, 419, 420, 424

War on Terror and, 395

Democratic Republic of the Congo, 268, 333

dengue fever, 269, 437

Denmark, 217, 218, 233, 238

DeSantis, Ronald, 235

Dettmar, Christian, 419

Deutsche Welle, 105

Devi, Asha, 327

Dhaka, Bangladesh, 324

Diamond Princess, 77, 117

disinformation, 73, 76, 160, 383–92, 412

Disinformation Board, US, 386

Dodsworth, Laura, 389

Dolan, Paul, 342, 373

Dolan, Simon, 419

domestic abuse, 22, 281, 286, 305–6, 312, 321, 322, 336, 437

domestic workers, 104, 304, 324

Dominican Republic, 414

Donaldson, Liam, 60–61, 96–7

Doshi, Peter, 62, 118, 171, 173, 193, 195

Douthat, Ross, 404

Draghi, Mario, 83, 189

Duterte, Rodrigo, 344, 415

Ebola, 15, 63–5, 84, 140, 216, 289, 339, 447

Ebright, Richard, 52

EcoHealth Alliance (EHA), 42–4, 48, 50

economics; economic impact, 2–3, 5, 6, 13–25, 105–7, 115, 178, 181, 225, 239, 286–340

agriculture/food production, *see* food

arts sector, 21

billionaires, 19, 283, 287–8, 311, 340, 440

concentration of capital, 169, 210, 270–71, 305, 312, 340, 438

debt, *see* debt

depression, 14, 261, 263, 288, 290, 293–340, 348, 350

distancing, 2–3, 440

furlough schemes, 283, 305, 307, 311, 312–13, 318, 321

health, relationship with, 13–14

household debts, 17, 324, 327, 350

inflation, 25, 282, 288, 299, 315, 316, 325, 331–2, 339

informal economy, *see* informal work

life expectancy and, 14, 263, 326, 338, 363, 370

lockdowns and, 103–4, 238–41, 256, 259, 261, 263, 268, 269, 286–340

national debts, 325, 331–5, 339

neoliberalism, 2, 165, 178, 220, 226, 241, 256, 309, 317, 370–71, 379

remote work, 2–3, 17, 20, 21, 59, 231, 307, 311, 316, 318, 438

small and medium enterprises (SMEs), 270, 287, 288, 315, 378, 440

INDEX

INDEX

INDEX

INDEX

461

INDEX

INDEX

INDEX

INDEX

INDEX

MERS (Middle East Respiratory Syndrome), 8
Metzl, Jamie, 44, 50
Mexico, 60, 61, 62, 75, 258, 283, 287, 312, 322, 362
MI6, 42
Miami, Florida, 88
Michie, Susan, 219
Michigan, United States, 57, 235, 254
Micronesia, 185
Microsoft, 18, 162, 383, 385, 391, 424, 426
middle classes, 4, 20, 184, 287, 289, 443
in Africa, 265, 289, 297
in India, 328
in Latin America, 242, 320–22
in Western countries, 308, 311, 379
Middleton, Sue, 170
migrant workers, 17, 102, 297, 303, 323
Milan, Italy, 72, 126, 134
militarisation, 51, 107, 160, 396, 405, 418
of lockdowns, 83, 93, 107, 413, 417, 418
war metaphors, 83, 93, 118
Minnesota, United States, 235
Miraflores, Lima, 360
Mitchell, David, 163
MITRE, 422
Mo Ibrahim Foundation, 331
modelling, 119, 211, 218, 232, 272, 274, 276, 294, 339, 392, 407, 445

Ferguson, 9, 12, 60–62, 91–8, 101, 211, 232
Sweden and, 238
Moderna, 18, 152–4, 163–8, 170–71, 173, 177, 191, 196, 202, 205–6
Modi, Narendra, 50, 101, 323
Moffatt, Jody, 251
molnupiravir, 177, 194
Montero, Llanos Ortíz, 63
Morens, David, 8
Morgan Stanley, 153, 163, 167
Morocco, 147, 185, 264
Mozambique, 100, 226, 265, 289, 414, 447
civil war (1977–92), 300, 301
deaths in, 264
education in, 361, 364
lockdowns in, 100, 102, 104, 268, 294, 296, 298, 414
vaccines in, 262
mRNA, 152, 153, 162, 170, 177, 193, 195, 202, 222, 408, 423
MSNBC, 162
Mucchielli, Laurent, 75, 94, 115, 135, 188
Mullis, Kary, 121
Munich, Germany, 72, 73, 234
musicians, 21, 103
Musk, Elon, 18, 305, 340

Nabarro, David, 96, 294
Nation, The, 177, 280
National Geographic, 46
National Health Service (NHS), 91, 256–7

INDEX

INDEX

INDEX

INDEX

INDEX

INDEX

INDEX

H1N1 pandemic (2009), 60
healthcare inequality in, 254–5, 261
herd immunity in, 89–90
hydroxychloroquine in, 144, 148
inequality in, 286, 313, 315, 317
libertarian right in, 283–4
lockdowns in, 83, 85–8, 93–4, 233, 235, 236, 254–6, 287, 313
mental health in, 352, 367
modelling in, 93–4, 101, 119
nationalism in, 151
obesity in, 255–6
Patriot Act (2001), 424
prisons in, 62–3
prophylactics in, 140–43
Public Readiness and Emergency Preparedness Act (2005), 175
revolving door framework in, 442–3
school shootings in, 368
single narrative in, 78, 86
social distancing in, 94, 111, 410
Trump administration (2017– 21), *see* Trump, Donald
vaccines in, 149, 152, 154, 163–5, 170, 171, 173–5, 179, 189–91, 195–6, 205, 209
vaccine mandates in, 184, 189, 422, 423
ventilator use in, 129

Wuhan lab leak theory and, 36, 42, 43, 44, 50, 52
University of Hong Kong, 303
University of Lagos, 330
University of Munich, 234
Uppsala University, 238
Uruguay, 275
Utah, United States, 287
Uttar Pradesh, India, 327
Uyghurs, 394

vaccines, 27, 47, 61, 115, 139, 148, 149–50, 151–78, 179–207
adverse effects, 169, 175, 192–5, 201–2
animal testing, 408
apartheid, 179, 222, 268, 432
booster campaigns, 181, 186, 191, 202, 204, 205–6, 211–12, 432
children and, 171, 182, 184, 202
clinical trials, 165–74, 190, 200–201, 209–10
conspiracy theories, 29, 73, 155, 157–8, 170–71, 175, 178, 194–5, 198, 386–7, 421, 422
development of, 47, 61–2, 91–2, 149–50, 151–78, 408
efficacy, 166, 167, 171, 194, 196, 212
foetal cell line testing, 408
Gates Foundation and, 155–60, 164, 165, 176–7, 182–3
healthcare inequality and, 204, 267, 268–9

475

INDEX

INDEX

INDEX

surveillance and, 400, 401

transmission, views on, 245, 359

vaccines and, 153–7, 159, 160, 161, 180, 197–200, 203–5, 210, 426

ventilators, views on, 129, 132

war metaphors, 83

Wuhan outbreak (2019–20), 31, 55, 57, 66

Wuhan lab leak theory, views on, 48–50, 51, 52

Worthington, Dani, 357

Wuhan, China, 31–3, 34–6, 42, 55, 66, 71, 82, 225, 236, 310

Wuhan Institute of Virology (WIV), 31, 35, 36–53, 110, 383

Wuhan Municipal Health Commission, 31

Xi Jinping, 55, 56, 67, 237, 381

Yates, Kit, 313, 338

Yeadon, Mike, 447

Year the World Went Mad, The (Woolhouse), 248

Yemen, 333

young people, 9, 20, 22, 23, 25, 89, 256, 260, 281, 285, 290, 318, 351–74

education, *see* education

employment, 295–6, 318, 321, 336, 357, 358

mental health, 215, 218, 318, 342, 352, 356, 367–9

long Covid and, 215

second wave, blame for, 358–9

vaccines and, 214

see also children

YouTube, 73

Zaire, 84

Zaks, Tal, 200

Zambezia University, 289

Zambia, 334, 335, 414

Zero Covid, 92, 236–7, 273–4, 276, 333, 337, 380, 416, 437

Zika, 269

Zimbabwe, 264, 331, 335

Zoom, 18, 47, 424

Zuckerberg, Mark, 440